William Angus Knight

Principal Shairp and his friends

William Angus Knight

Principal Shairp and his friends

ISBN/EAN: 9783744749138

Printed in Europe, USA, Canada, Australia, Japan

Cover: Foto ©Andreas Hilbeck / pixelio.de

More available books at **www.hansebooks.com**

PRINCIPAL SHAIRP

AND HIS FRIENDS

By WILLIAM KNIGHT

PROFESSOR OF MORAL PHILOSOPHY IN THE UNIVERSITY OF ST. ANDREWS

WITH PORTRAIT

LONDON

JOHN MURRAY, ALBEMARLE STREET

1888

PREFACE

THE distinctive feature in a memoir of Principal Shairp must be the study of his character. His outward life was uneventful, and its story is easily told; but to present an adequate picture of the man, in his manysidedness, is not easy; and it cannot be done by any of his friends, from a single point of view. He was something much rarer and finer, than either his writing, or his teaching—admirable as these were. He impressed himself with equal power on men of all classes, tendencies, and sympathies—on persons of the highest culture, and on poor students. There are not many such men at any time in the world.

Few of his contemporaries were as rich as he was in the friendship of good men,—in the loyal attachment of a large circle, moving in widely different spheres of thought and of action. Even from his boyhood he seems to have drawn towards him the esteem of the nobleminded; and, as life advanced, he instinctively won the admiration of all who were idealists at heart. In consequence of this, he has left his mark upon his time, in the most beneficent, although in the least showy manner. There have been men with greater powers of intellect, of learning, and of administrative power; but there has been none, in the academical history of Scotland, from whose personality a greater "virtue has gone forth," touching other lives to fruitful issues. In the pages which follow I have merely tried to build a memorial cairn, with the stones which have been sent to me, in reverent and affectionate memory, by those who owe to him some of the best influences of their lives.

Perhaps the most striking thing in these tributes to Shairp's memory, which have successively reached me from the most opposite quarters, is the unanimity with which they all express *gratitude for his friendship*—a friendship so strong, steadfast, and unselfish; and the picture of his life, now seen in retrospect under the light of these memories, is a very radiant one.

We naturally ask for an explanation of so remarkable a range of friendship, with men of the most opposite opinions, and whose tendencies were altogether divergent. Many causes contributed to it. It was not due merely (or even mainly) to the width of his own sympathies, but rather to his entering so heartily—and with so little thought of himself—into the subjects which most interested other people, just as they turned up. Naturally very sympathetic, he put himself at once, even with strangers, into the position of a listener—in self-detachment, and "a wise passiveness"—rather than assumed the *rôle* of an instructor. He never talked as if it were more important to be listened to than to listen; and, in consequence, there was nothing in him of the academic pedant, nothing either of the dictator or of the dominie.

In my own intercourse with him the most distinguishing feature of his character was its habitual unselfishness and real magnanimity. Few men have ever had a heart so much "at leisure from itself." He was never known to make an egotistical speech, or a self-complaisant reference to his own writings, or his own work. Still less was there a trace of what has been said to be a common infirmity of literary men, viz. jealousy of others. This was so entirely foreign to his nature that he could scarcely comprehend its existence. His appreciation, on the contrary, of the work that was being done by others—work which he knew he could not himself do—was a pervading feature of his character. Every one who knew him intimately must recall that wistful expression of countenance, calm, watchful, kindly receptive, accordant, but one in which *sympathy* was all dominant, with which he would so often listen to a narrative, or follow a train of thought, or take in the merits of a case put before him, either by a friend or by a stranger.

Throughout his whole career Principal Shairp had a very definite purpose in life, and many a noble ambition found its way to the front, and demanded realisation in practice; but it cannot be said that in the pursuit of any one of these, even the most engrossing of them, he "lived to himself." He certainly never sought preferment in the ordinary sense of the phrase. He accepted it, when it came; and he had from the first a large vista of laudable ambition, but all his work and achievement seemed to come naturally to him; and he entered into them without search, or restless struggle. Then—as will be seen in the story of his life—the way in which he accepted the defeat of several of his plans and ambitions was truly admirable. He simply passed on to the discharge of the next duty that lay before him, as if nothing had occurred to mar his equanimity for a moment.

He was often misunderstood by those who knew him slightly, and were themselves devoid of ideality; but this never disconcerted him. With such persons his manner may have had an occasional touch of austerity, out of keeping with his otherwise genial nature; but this was only when the unresponsiveness of others threw him inwards on himself for the time being. In consequence of this, we fiud him occasionally less honoured in his own country than beyond it. For all this he was a Scotsman, in the very core of his being; widened and mellowed it is true, by his Oxford training, and his subsequent residence in England; but conspicuous in his love for the traditions, the customs and the provincial features of his native land, and to the last more conservative than cosmopolitan.

Another very noticeable feature in Shairp's character was his courage in doing what he believed to be right, no matter what it cost his feelings—and these were unusually sensitive. If he had once made up his mind that a thing *ought* to be done—that it was a public or a private duty—nothing would turn him back from the discharge of the most painful part of it; and he was wholly indifferent to any misunderstanding that might follow. He came of a soldier race; and it was his strong sense of duty that gave him, on the one hand the courage that he showed, and on the other his superiority to criticism.

As will be seen from the following pages, his contributions to the Literature of his Country have been neither few nor small. Indeed their number and extent will be a surprise to many readers of this book; but in all the more important of them,—in his *Studies in Poetry and Philosophy*, in *The Poetic Interpretation of Nature*, in *Kilmahoe*, in *Burns*, in *Culture and Religion*, and in the *Aspects of Poetry*,—it is the moral element underlying the discussion, his treatment (direct or indirect) of the great laws of conduct, with their sanctions and their implicates, that distinguishes these books from the writings of other men on similar themes. In his treatment of all great perennial questions, as well as in everything else that he handled, Principal Shairp invariably struck an elevated note. He approached no subject from its conventional side, and discussed none in a commonplace manner. He thus contributed more than most writers of his time to raise the tone of literary work-manship.

It was well that his lifework was ultimately cast in Scotland, that he did not obtain the Oriel Fellowship, but returned, after his experience of Rugby, to a University in his native land, and afterwards to the Principalship of one of its Colleges. On more than one occasion he became a candidate for a Scottish chair of Ethics ; and many of his friends thought that such a chair would have been his most appropriate sphere.[1] It is true that into his lectures in the Humanity classroom he brought an unusually large amount of moral teaching : but, in a chair of Moral Philosophy itself, his scholarship, his knowledge of the history of opinion, his discernment of the bearing of Ethics on Religion, and the bright forceful intuitive way in which he invariably dealt with the problems of human nature, might have given him unique academic power. I do not think that he was a Speculative Philosopher by nature; and I have often heard him speak with a certain disfavour, if not of quasi-austerity, of "the metaphysicians." See, too, his letters to Mr. Shadworth Hodgson, pp. 244-252. Of a common friend, who was both poet and speculative philosopher, he used to say to me, "He has mistaken his calling; he is a poet, spoiled by metaphysics." He was himself not only a poet born, but he was a poetic idealist in all his views of life, and in all his conceptions of character. When a teacher of the classical languages at Rugby and St. Andrews, it was not in that direction that his powers chiefly lay, any

---

[1] So striking were the tributes he received on these occasions, from his many English friends, that I have given extracts from several of them. Perhaps the most interesting is the testimony of Matthew Arnold, who, in one of the last letters he wrote, spoke of the present Memoir as likely to give him an opportunity of saying something about "dear old Shairp . . . not only a most lovable man in the time when I knew him best, but also a very stimulating and inspiring one."

more than it afterwards lay in administrative work as Principal. It was as one whose soul was steeped in poetic feeling, one who had in his early boyhood received

> That first great gift, a vital soul,

or, to put it otherwise, by the help of other quotations from the poet to whom he owed so much, it was by the possession of " an intense and glowing mind "— the sure index of poetic endowment—that he could " see into the life of things," and was able to touch and to stimulate others. This poetic radiancy, blending with his high standard of action and endeavour, produced a sort of atmosphere, which seemed to move with him wherever he moved.

If we add to the unassumingness already noticed, and the poetic spirit now mentioned, his extreme conscientiousness whether in literary work or academic duty or the claims which society imposed on him, and his self-forgetfulness throughout it all, we have another explanation of his influence.

He was enriched at each stage of his career by getting the very best out of it, while his sympathies were widened by every new experience. Home life at Houstoun, school life in the Academy at Edinburgh, student days in the University of Glasgow, autumn holidays in Kintyre, undergraduate life at Oxford, the mastership at Rugby, visits to London, wanderings in the Highlands and in the Border Country, all matured him for his work at St. Andrews. But throughout these advancing stages he retained in a remarkable manner the heart of the child, unsophisticated, never sated or world-weary. There is no trace in the life of Principal Shairp as if he had lived through one set of experiences, and was done with them, and must push on to new interests and ambitions. To the end he returned to the old interests and the lowliest duties, feeling that they were not self-imposed, but that he was only the humble servitor of a higher Power.   Eight lines, written by him in February 1872, but never published, express perhaps better than anything else, the central purpose of his life—

. . . .

> So might I toiling morn to eve
>   Some purpose in my life fulfil,
> And ere I pass some work achieve,
>   To live and move when I am still.
>
> I ask not with that work combined
>   My name should down the ages move,
> But that my toil such end may find
>   As man may bless and God approve.

One naturally associates this with the *Ode to Duty* and the *Afterthought* to the Duddon.   To Principal Shairp, if to any in these modern days, " Duty " was " an unerring light," and " joy its own security."

What specially struck some of his younger or later friends—when they came to know him well—was the union in him of sympathies that are usually antagonistic, and of attainments seldom united.   For example, there is a point at which Poetry, Philosophy, and Religion meet. That point is not always a luminous · one ; and the links of connection between the spheres being numerous and subtle, they are never wholly visible to those who have not a practical acquaintance with all the three.   Now Principal Shairp was, throughout his whole career, a poet, a philosopher, and a religious man.   Possibly a writer, who had devoted his life to one of the three exclusively, might at the end have been greater than he was, in the special line selected ; but he would have been much less likely to discern the relations of the provinces, one toward another, than the man who—while less distinguished in· each—was accomplished in them all. ˙ By such a one the harmonies of knowledge, feeling, and action, of belief and practice, are intuitively discerned. They are seen as by a flash of inward light, and a "reconciliation" of their processes or results is quite unnecessary.

Another feature in Principal Shairp's character, equally important with his width of sympathy, was his reverence for the Past, and for everything that has come down to us consecrated by Time. No one could walk with him in any place where associations with antiquity clustered—an ancient battlefield, a ruined abbey, a castle of the Middle Age, a cathedral close, a Highland glen—with its ruined cottage-mounds, its hillsides where the Covenanters worshipped, or its burial-places where they sleep—without catching the contagion of his spirit, and feeling how vividly the whole pageantry of the past lived and moved again to him. His patriotic sympathies were most catholic, in the sense that they took in every genuine element of national life, and were therefore stirred equally by the Covenanter and by the Jacobite. In full accord with all that is best in Scottish life and character, he could also appreciate the broader stream of national life in the south, with which some Scotsmen have little sympathy. He was a wide-minded and a strong-souled man, loyal to the traditions of his ancestry and upbringing, yet with an eye quick to discern the defects of Scottish provincialism—whether in the student or the politician, in the literary or the religious man—and a hand ready to lay them bare. His dislike to Scottish roughness was not greater than his distaste to a mere mimicry of English ways, and the affectation of English habits by Scotsmen.

My aim in this book is that Principal Shairp should speak for himself, both to those who know his writings, and who knew the man and have been helped by him; that he should continue to speak a little longer, partly through his letters, partly through extracts from his private journals, and above all by the "reminiscences" of his friends now living. These, woven together by a few connecting threads, may serve to perpetuate the influence of his life. And little more can be done. The art of the mental and moral photographer is hard to learn.

As to his conversation, who can reproduce its indefinable charm? or give a picture of his expressive face in its changefulness—whether relaxed with humour, or roused to indignation, or touched with pity for some human sorrow, or thrilled by a vision of the beautiful, or bent in reverent worship? All his friends recall it; yet neither portrait, nor photograph, nor description can reproduce it. And as to his peculiarities of manner — those characteristic minor traits, in which so much lies hid — how often would he hesitate for the right word, descriptive of some subtle point of character or idea! and, when at last he got it (the happy phrase that summed up his conviction, and embodied it, so far as the medium of words can do so), how he would repeat, and re-repeat it, with incisive manner, and thrilling voice, and at times rememberable gesture; and how the tones of that voice often revealed a depth of conviction that the spoken word was powerless to disclose!

He was seen at his very best in the society of congenial friends; and, in a sympathetic group, his memory, his imagination, and his intellect were wonderfully quickened. His social powers were of a high order, and will long be cherished, not only in academic circles at St. Andrews, Oxford, and London, but at many a country house and in many a lowly home. He is missed in the old city by the sea, which he loved so well; in the cottages of the poor, as well as in the rooms of his colleagues; and not less at those delightful gatherings that have made Megginch and Linlathen places of happy memory to many of his contemporaries.

In addition to the books he has left behind him, Principal Shairp contributed memorial sketches of many of his friends to their respective "Lives," such as that of Arthur Hugh Clough, Norman Macleod, John Macintosh of Geddes, Thomas Erskine of Linlathen, M'Leod Campbell of Row, Bishop Cotton of Calcutta, and Bishop Patteson of Melanesia, Principal Forbes and Professor Ferrier of St. Andrews, and Dr. Park, of the same city, Archbishop Tait, etc. These, as *character-studies*, are extremely valuable, and as they are scattered in many volumes, I have made extracts from some of them in this book. It was my original intention to make them more copious, but the inexorable limits of Biography have prevented this. As these Studies, however, are amongst the finest of his writings—and reveal him in the capacity of moral analyst, as well as portray the friends whose characters he has delineated—it is to be hoped that they may yet be brought together in a volume by themselves.

It is a mistake in Biography only to publish the letters of the person whose life is being recorded, omitting those addressed to him by his friends. The latter often cast more light on the subject of a Memoir than his own epistles do ; and, as many letters passed between Dr. John Brown of Edinburgh and Principal Shairp, chiefly in reference to his poems and prose essays as they successively appeared, some of them are published in this volume. The Principal's letters to Dr. Clerk at Kilmalie, to Mr. Erskine of Linlathen, and, above all, to the home circle at Houstoun, are full of interest.

I have to express my sincere thanks to the numerous friends who have assisted me with their Reminiscences— above all to Mrs. Shairp, and her son—at whose request the work has been undertaken, and without whose assistance it could not have been carried out.

I have also to thank some of those who have sent contributions, for the generous way in which they have allowed me to divide their papers into sections—a process which, while necessary for the purposes of biography, destroys their literary completeness. Several having alluded to the career of their friend from his youth onwards, it was obviously impossible to print every paper, in the form in which it reached me, without repeating the same incidents over and over again.[1] In this connection my thanks are specially due to Professor Sellar, for the disinterested way in which he has acted in reference to his admirable paper on his friend. For the same reason my thanks are due to the Deans of Westminster and Salisbury, to Professor Veitch, and to Mr. Butler of Oriel College, Oxford.

The book has been called *Principal Shairp and his Friends*, both from the number of his friendships, from the many contemporaries whose characters he himself drew, and from the large number who have contributed to this memorial volume. Its underlying idea is a series of photographs of character, taken from many opposite points of view, by those who knew him best. It is true that a biography, which resolved itself into a series of obituary notices in praise of the departed, would not only become wearisome as it proceeded, but would have no special value to posterity. Perhaps, however, the variety to be found in these studies of character may give a distinctive feature to the book; and, although it may be true that we are becoming rather much of a memorial-writing age, and that our biographical literature is excessive, such tributes to a singularly pure and noble nature,—one who, as Mr. Poste writes (referring to their early Oxford days) "lived habitually in a higher level of thought and feeling than the rest of us," and was, as Matthew Arnold said only a few weeks ago, " that delightful self, which inspired such

---

[1] Where this has been partially done—as in the several accounts of the Highland walk and the visit to Clough at Drumnadrochit (see pp. 103-114)— it has been from some distinctive feature in the several accounts.

affection, and so well deserved to inspire it,"—may be fruitful of good to others.   *Longum iter est per præcepta, breve et
efficax per exempla.*

It may be as well to mention that the extracts from
papers which have appeared previously are printed in
smaller type, and that several of Shairp's poems are published in this Memoir for the first time.

CONTENTS

PAGE

PREFACE v

CHAPTER I

HOME AT HOUSTOUN 1

CHAPTER II

BOYHOOD : THE EDINBURGH ACADEMY . . . 7

CHAPTER III

GLASGOW UNIVERSITY 13

CHAPTER IV

OXFORD UNDERGRADUATE LIFE 31

CHAPTER V

REMINISCENCES OF OXFORD, AND OF OXFORD INFLUENCES AND
FRIENDS 49

CHAPTER VI

SUMMER HOLIDAYS IN WESTMORLAND AND SCOTLAND . . 63

CHAPTER VII

PAGE

MASTERSHIP AT RUGBY; AUTUMNS IN THE HIGHLANDS, AND
ELSEWHERE 98

CHAPTER VIII

MEMORIAL SKETCHES BY RUGBY FRIENDS AND PUPILS 130

CHAPTER IX

DOMESTIC LIFE AND INCIDENTS: YARROW . 168

CHAPTER X

FIRST HOME AT ST. ANDREWS, AND THE PROFESSORSHIP OF
LATIN 183

CHAPTER XI

LITERARY WORK AND FRIENDSHIPS: MR. ERSKINE AND
DR. JOHN BROWN . . . 205

CHAPTER XII

THE HIGHLANDS AND THE BORDERS . 253

CHAPTER XIII

THE PRINCIPALSHIP OF THE UNITED COLLEGE . 269

CHAPTER XIV

THE OXFORD CHAIR OF POETRY 330

· CHAPTER XV

PAGE

LATER YEARS AT ST. ANDREWS 356

CHAPTER XVI

THE RIVIERA : ORMSARY . 390

CHAPTER XVII

ESTIMATES IN MEMORIAM . . 408

APPENDIX I 427

APPENDIX II 437

APPENDIX III 443

CHAPTER I

JOHN CAMPBELL SHAIRP was born at Houstoun, Linlithgow-shire, on the 30th July 1819. He was the third son of Major Norman Shairp of Houstoun, and of Elizabeth Binning, daughter of John Campbell of Kildalloig, Argyleshire.

The property of Houstoun was acquired by the Shairps in the sixteenth century. The first of the family who held it was Sir John Shairp, through whom the cabinet and gloves, that once belonged to Mary Queen of Scots, and are now at Houstoun, came there.[1]

Shairp was a lineal descendant of Mary Scott, "The Flower of Yarrow." His great-grandmother, Anne Scott of Harden, who married Shairp of Houstoun, was the eldest daughter of John Scott of Harden, whose great-grandfather, Sir Gideon Scott of High Chester, was grandson of "The Flower of Yarrow."[2] She was a Scott of Dryhope, and her romantic wooing is referred to in Shairp's poem *Three Friends in Yarrow*, in the volume edited by Mr. Palgrave. His maternal ancestry had a great interest for Shairp; and an inheritance of goodness, reaching him from a distant

---

[1] It is probable that he was employed as an advocate for the Queen in one of the investigations into her conduct. When he bought Houstoun, in the year 1560, it was not a barony, but he purchased other neighbouring lands, and got the whole erected into a barony at a later date.

[2] His great-grandmother's only sister, Mary Lilias Scott, called the second "Flower of Yarrow," died at Edinburgh in 1790.

B

past, was probably an influential element in the moulding of his character.

His grandfather—still spoken of at Houstoun as "The Laird," and whose portrait, by Raeburn, hangs on the wall of the dining-room—married Miss M'Leod of M'Leod (whose portrait is also at Houstoun). A reference to the M'Leods will be found in Samuel Johnson's *Visit to the Hebrides*, when speaking of the charms and refinements of Dunvegan.

His father, Major Norman Shairp, was a characteristic example of the old Scottish laird of a past generation; a man of clear mind, strong sense, and spotless integrity of character; proud of his ancestry, and his patrimonial inheritance,—a keen fox-hunter, a strong conservative, a warm friend. During the eleven years in which he served in the Indian army he took part in thirteen pitched battles; and during the memorable campaigns of 1803-1806 he was with his regiment under canvas, exposed to all the trials of an Indian climate. He retired somewhat early from active service; but continued, for more than half a century, to lead the life of an honoured country gentleman,—the joy of all friends, and as good and true a man as could be found in Midlothian.

Major Shairp gave his sons the best education possible, but taught them that their future was in their own hands; and throughout his whole career—alike at Edinburgh, Glasgow, and Oxford, till his education was finished—his son John was generously treated, but without unnecessary luxury. In a letter to Dr. Clerk of Kilmalie, written after his father's death, Shairp said : "He has been spared to us beyond the allotted fourscore years, and yet when it came, his death could not have been more felt if he had been removed in middle manhood. He has taken with him so much of what was dearest in the past, that this old house is another place now."

Houstoun House—the home of his ancestors and of his own radiant childhood—is a picturesque relic of a past age ; and its associations with antique times, and a vanished type of Scottish manners, give it an interest of its own, apart from its being Shairp's birthplace. It is thus described in the poem *Kilmahoe*—

> An old white lofty-gabled Lowland home,
> Up to the sunshine, and the breezes all,
> For ages o'er the ancestral trees have clomb
>   Its stalwart chimneys tall.
>
> Far seen, far open on the south it gleams
>   To clear noons, like a white unfurlèd flag ;
> In rainy weather, dimmed with stains and scaurs,
>   Like a grey lichened crag.
>
> Far seen, wide gazing, the old mansion grey,
> Adown the long lime avenue, from its doors,
> Looks here to rich tilled lands, yonder away
>   To meditative moors.
>
> Hard by, hedge-sheltered garden, hiding woods,
> And morning fields, for childhood's summer play,
> Nor less responsive to more sober moods,
>   And life's autumnal day.[1]

He drew the picture of his mother, under the name of Moira, in the same poem ;[2] and he speaks of the two sisters, Moira and Marion (his mother and aunt), gazing in autumn from the deep window-nook at Houstoun,

> On the hairst moon, that from alcove of blue
> Silvered the garden, every bower and bield,
> Hedges of glistening holly, and dark yew ;
>   And up the household field
> Slanted the shadows of twin silver firs
> To white sheep couching on the moon-bathed sward,
> Till thought was lost in years that ne'er were theirs—
>   A far and fond regard.

Here it was, in the "stately pathetic old house" (as Dr. John Brown called it) that, in his earliest days, Nature laid her hand upon the growing boy, and "spake to him re-

---

[1] In Shairp's copy of *The Prelude*, which is pencil-marked in a very interesting way, the following words are underlined—

> Early died
> My honoured mother, she who was the heart
> And hinge of all our learnings and our love.

[2] See *Kilmahoe : a Highland Pastoral*, pp. 112, 113.

memberable things." In the quaint garden, with its recesses
and winding walks, shaded with large thick hedges of yew
(such as are now rarely to be seen), in the long avenue of
limes by which the house is approached from the east, or
out in the broad meadows to the south, he first saw that
"splendour in the grass" and "glory in the flower" from
which Wordsworth gathers one of the chief "intimations of
immortality."

His earliest education at Houstoun was carried on by a
tutor, Mr. Bell, a Dumfriesshire man, of whom in after years
he often spoke. Mr. Bell came to Houstoun in 1825; but
what chiefly educated Shairp was, first, the high-toned and
happy family life in the ancestral home, its gracious atmosphere; and next, the open-air country life of his childhood,
with the walks and rides, and country sports of his boyhood.
These—as in the case of the poet who afterwards influenced
him so much—were more influential than the formal lessons
of the schoolroom.

When eight years of age he was taken by his father on
his first visit to Kildalloig, his mother's home in Argyleshire, where his eldest uncle lived. At the same time he
visited Glen Saddell, also in Kintyre, and then rented by
a younger uncle. Kildalloig is the *Kilmahoe* of his
poems, and Glen Saddell is the *Glen Sallach* described in
his *Dream*. The early impressions of the coast of Kintyre
never faded from his mind; and this first visit awakened that
love of Highland scenery, of Scottish character, and Celtic
tradition, which lasted through life, and gave a special colour
to much of his subsequent work.

Few of his poems already published can be quoted
in this Memoir, but the *Dream of Glen Sallach* has a special
interest and an autobiographic value. It was the recollection of a boy of eight, for he never revisited Glen
Saddell.

> That summer glen is far away,
>   Who loved me then, their graves are green,
> But still that dell and distant day,
>   Lie bright in memory's softest sheen.

Are these still there, outspread in space,
   The grey-mossed trees, the mountain stream?
Or in some ante-natal place,
   That only cometh back in dream?

There first upon my soul was cast
   Dim reverence, blent with glorious thrills,
From out an old heroic past,
   Lapped in the older calm of hills.

Still after thirty summers loom
   On dreaming hours the lichened trees,
The ivied walls, the warrior's tomb,
   'Mid those old mountain sanctities.

How awed I stood! where once had kneeled
   The pilgrims by the holy well,
O'er which through centuries unrepealed
   Rome's consecration still doth dwell.

How crept among the broken piles!
   And clansmen's grave-stones moss-o'ergrown,
Where rests the Lord of all the Isles,
   With plaid and claymore graven in stone.

In deep of noon, mysterious dread
   Fell on me in that glimmering glen,
Till, as from haunted ground, I fled
   Back to the kindly homes of men.

Thanks to that glen! its scenery blends
   With childhood's most ideal hour,
When Highland hills I made my friends,
   First owned their beauty, felt their power.

Still, doubtless, o'er Kilbrannan Sound,
   As lovely lights from Arran gleam,
'Mid hills that gird Glen Sallach round,
   As happy children dream their dream.

The western sea, as deep of tone,
   Is murmuring 'gainst that caverned shore;
But, one whole generation gone,
   No more those haunts are ours, no more.

This *Dream* will recall to many readers a similar
experience in the life of Wordsworth; but without trác-
ing the parallel, it may be better to quote some stanzas
from an unpublished poem, which Shairp wrote between

1875 and 1880, and which he entitled *Retrospect, or Days
from out the Shadows.* He evidently meant to write in
verse a brief sketch of the more interesting points in his
own life. What survives is unfortunately very fragmentary.
In the first set of stanzas, entitled *Home,* he asks why
single looks, and scenes, or words, belonging to our childhood, cleave to the memory in our later years, when everything else around them has vanished? whether is it due
to "their own intrinsic might," or to "a diviner Presence
near us," awakening tenderness and awe, and giving us
"some reaching forward to the Infinite"? and he then
describes such a haunting memory of his childhood in the
garden at Houstoun, when his school-life first began.

A second time of similarly vivid experience in boyhood
was in Kintyre, which he describes in lines, which may be
taken as a sort of sequel to the *Dream of Glen Sallach*—

> The sunset on a wild West Highland shore
> Slow dying round a tawny sanded bay,
> The twilight waters shimmering before,
> The peaks of Arran gleaming far away,
> Send back their splendours, while the boatmen strong,
> With lazy oar-plash and low chaunted song,
> Drag the net shoreward, heavy with sea-prey.
>
> Then the large salmon, on the wet beach spread,
> Silver-sheened, quivered in the shadows dim,
> While the tall forester, with careless tread,
> Came bearing down the wild-cat, huge of limb,
> Slain in his cranny on the woody crags,
> And flung him full length on the shingly slag,
> The brindled beast, a portent strange and grim.
>
> Ah me! what awe on my young spirit fell,
> Entering the dark glen with its ancient wood,
> 'Neath which still trickled the clear Holy Well,
> And the old Abbey crumbled, time-subdued;
> How crept I 'mong the tombs, where moss-o'ergrown
> The Lord of Isles lies panoplied in stone
> Till I fled frighted from the weirdly dell.

CHAPTER II

IN October 1829, when ten years of age, Shairp became a pupil at the Edinburgh Academy. He and his brothers lived with their tutor in lodgings; and much good and solid work must have been done during the four years in which he remained at that school. With the exception of a few holidays at Christmas, six hours of each day, for five days of the week, were spent in school during nearly ten months of the year. Nearly as many hours each evening were devoted to the work of preparation for the classes next day. Writing to his father from Oxford in after years he said that, during these four years at the Edinburgh Academy, the basis of any scholarship he had was laid. He retained a real affection for the Academy to the very end of his life; and, as will be seen in a subsequent chapter, his interest in it was publicly expressed in a speech, at a dinner of old Academy pupils, in its jubilee year of 1875.

The occasional monotony of his school work was broken, and his life brightened, by holiday visits to Houstoun, which he reached from Edinburgh by coach or canal-boat. During one entire winter he remained at Houstoun, and was there tutored along with his brother Norman; but they returned to the Academy in the following year, leaving it finally in 1834, and spending the next winter in Edinburgh, where they took some private classes. It was during this winter of 1835 that Shairp first came under the influence of the poetry of Wordsworth.

To no one have I been more indebted, in the preparation of this Memoir, than to Professor Sellar of the University of Edinburgh; and his account of those early years, at the Academy and at Houstoun, I must detach from the rest of his paper, and insert it at this stage. I much regret that the continuity of Mr. Sellar's account of our common friend will suffer by its being broken up into sections, and inserted at different places; but this is a lesser evil than the inevitable repetition which would otherwise take place.

"I feel how difficult it is to convey to those who did not know him any adequate impression of the fresh and buoyant spring of life, which never failed our old friend and colleague during the forty years of my intimacy with him, of the frank natural enthusiasm, tempered but not abated as he grew older, with which he spoke on all subjects which interested him, of his affection for his friends, and, generally, of a nature singularly pure, genuine, and generous, and a character loyal, reverent, disinterested, and consistent, from his earliest youth till his latest years. I feel it also difficult to select, out of the long period during which I knew him, those recollections and impressions which might be thought most characteristic of him. I will try to recall my earlier impressions, and to give an account, drawn chiefly from what I have heard from himself, of the influences which formed him during the time of his education, and also of his work as Professor during those pleasant years when we were colleagues together at St. Andrews. I must leave you to select from these notes what may seem to you most suitable for the object which all his friends who take any part in this commemoration of him must have in view,—to give to those who did not know him some idea of a life, as true, beautiful, and, in its own sphere, as influential for good, as any ever known to us.

My memories of him go so far back as the year 1834, when he left the Edinburgh Academy. I cannot remember his appearance then, and as I was only in the second, while he was in the seventh class, it is very likely that I may never have spoken to him. But I remember in the prize-list of the year his name at the end of a poem in Latin hexameters, which I read long afterwards, and which showed, for one so young as he was at the time, good scholarship and good taste. I mention this because when I once spoke to him about it, he told me that the one part of his work which he liked at school was the writing of Latin verses, which, under our old rector, Archdeacon Williams, was, if not made so much of (to the exclusion of other subjects) as in the old English public schools, still sufficiently encouraged to give scope for the taste of those who had an aptitude for it.

Shairp had a just appreciation of the sound scholarly training and the fresh intellectual stimulus which we got from the teaching of our rector. Yet he did not speak with much enthusiasm about his school-days. He never at any time cared about school-games, which, though they did not then play so important a part in school-life as they do now, must always form a large ingredient in its pleasure, and are the chief bond of that companionship which men like to recall in after years. He cared still less for, in fact he always disliked and condemned, the strenuous competition which was the principal motive to work. He admitted the necessity of applying this motive, at least in the earlier stages of education, but he thought the desire of 'beating' somebody else neither a very elevated nor a Christian principle of action ; and he desired to see it give place as soon as possible to a sense of duty, and a sense of pleasure in the work done for its own sake.

The year of his boyhood which he liked most to dwell on was the year immediately preceding his last year at the Edinburgh Academy, when, for some reason or other, he was kept at home with a tutor. The love of his home was through all his life one of the strongest sentiments in his nature,—the sentiment by which more, I think, than by any other, the successive stages of his life were—as they were in him to a degree beyond what I have ever known in any other man—

Bound each to each by natural piety.

He always spoke of the influence of a happy home as among the most beneficent of the forces which mould character; and when in after days at Oxford he saw among his friends and contemporaries some who had evidently suffered much from the speculative perplexities which were then in the air, and by which he himself was for a time not absolutely unaffected, he seemed to attribute his own comparative immunity from them to this influence.

One pleasant reminiscence of that year was that he then had, if not his initiation into, yet his fullest enjoyment of the pleasures of 'hunting,' which was the one form of sport for which he thoroughly cared, and about which, though he had long practically given it up, he always spoke and wrote with enthusiasm. One of the most genuinely poetical and spirited of his poems, which I first heard him repeat with an account of the actual circumstances out of which it arose, in one of our rides together at Rugby, is *The Run*, published along with *Kilmahoe*, in the first edition of his poems. The pleasure which he felt in the sport, and to which he has given a singularly musical expression in that poem, was not the mere physical pleasure of hard riding, though he knew what that was, but the imaginative feeling of the poetry of the scenes through which it bore him, and the imaginative outlet which it gave to the chivalrous and adventurous spirit which he inherited, and which was conspicuous in his outward bearing.

The only other pastime into which he entered keenly, and of which also he discussed and celebrated the poetry, was 'curling,' the attraction of which to him was, partly, that it was an exclusively national game, but chiefly, I think, that it was associated with happy days at his old home in Linlithgowshire, in which some part of his winter holiday was passed every year of his life. If, therefore, his school-life, though it must have had its share in training his intellect, does not seem to have made any deep impression on his character, it was because its influence and any attraction which it might have had for him were overpowered by the strong and kindly influence and attraction of his home. Yet he was thoroughly loyal to his school, and I remember, as I sat beside him, how cordially he entered into the spirit of the jubilee celebration in 1875, over which his friend, the late Archbishop of Canterbury, presided, on the completion of the fiftieth year since the foundation of the school, when the older ones among us were reminded of the *actae non alio rege puertiae.*"

Mr. Sellar's paper will be continued in the next chapter. This one may be concluded by two additional fragments from the poem *Retrospect,* which have a distinct biographic interest.   The first was entitled "School Time," and the second "Bannockburn." The earliest effect upon Shairp of that great poet, whom he afterwards did so much to interpret, comes out in the former, as well as the happy influence of the home at Houstoun. The latter shows how his poetic imagination was stirred. in boyhood by his first visit to a famous historic field, and how the delight of a day of youthful sport, amid "the music of the baying pack," gave place to a still nobler enthusiasm, when "all the old chivalries came floating back," and mingled with the excitement of the present hour. To my mind the three stanzas on Bannockburn show Shairp at his very best, as a poet, not of Nature, but of historic incident,—a distant national event —famous but far past—being suggested and made to live before him, in the thrilling experience of the chase.

SCHOOL TIME

When in drear city pent, the heart forlorn
For green fields pined, and unpolluted skies,
The voice of Wordsworth soothingly inborne
Came to my boyhood with a glad surprise
As here and there some memorable line
Flashed on the soul a glimpse of the divine
Beauty that in the world undreamed-of lies.

Ah me! the joy some frosty afternoon
To leave the Town and wander westward home,
When the blue depth o'erhead with clouds was strewn

Like manes of flying coursers, white as foam!
Bright and more bright they in the sunset shone,
And yet another glory they put on
Illumined by the spirit undertone.

Wordsworth was singing in me—I aware
Of a new brightness in the full moon's look
As with her light she flooded the void air,
And one by one the stars their station took
Along the edges of the Pentland range:
O'er earth and sky I felt had come a change—
A glory that hath not this earth forsook.

BANNOCKBURN

Softly the West blew, and the May-morn shone,
When from an ancient beautiful abode
My father led me, all his field-gear on,
And o'er the plain of Bannockburn we rode
To meet the hounds, and the blithe hunter train,
Upon the moory hills beneath Dunblane,
And take the season's latest benison.

O that first look athwart the famous Field!
That vision of the Castled Rock sublime!
Through all my being how it glowed and thrilled
Pulsations of the unforgotten time:
Then, with the music of the baying pack,
All the old chivalries came floating back,
And mingled with the chevy and the chime.

And as the chase went crashing all day long
O'er Sheriff muir, and down through Kippen glen,
My heart, unweeting of the hunter throng,
Was busy with the Bruce and his brave men;
Then, at dayfall, the moon on our return,
Serene as on the eve of Bannockburn,
Looked from Demayet down with cloudless ken.

This will suggest to some the skating scene on Esthwaite,
when Wordsworth retired from the game in imitation of
the chase

The pack loud chiming, and the hunted hare,

to watch the winter sunset, or "to cut across the reflex of a
star" in one of the silent bays of the mere.

CHAPTER III

In the autumn of 1836 Shairp went to the University of Glasgow, where he spent three winter sessions, living with the Misses Macleod, sisters of the minister of St. Columba's Church, and aunts of his future friend, Norman Macleod. They lived not far from Norman's own home in Bath Street. During these years at the western University of Scotland he made several friendships of a deep and lasting character. There was Macleod himself, seven years his senior, the genial, brilliant, large-hearted man— most unworldly of ecclesiastics—whose force and directness of character, overflowing humour, strong Celtic sympathies, and rare devotion to duty, had special attraction for the younger student. There were John Macintosh of Geddes, afterwards Norman's brother-in-law, to whose Memoir Shairp contributed a most interesting sketch ; William Clerk, afterwards minister of Kilmalie, in the district of Lochiel ; Henry Douglas, afterwards his brother-in-law, and in later years bishop of Bombay, with several others.

The discussions that took place amongst this group of friends at Norman's house, or at his own, were perhaps more influential over Shairp's future life than those to which he listened within College walls. He doubtless owed much to the teaching of Sir Daniel Sandford, and to that of the late Professor Ramsay ; as well as to the knowledge of Formal Logic which he received from Professor Buchanan ; but it was at these delightful evening gatherings in Bath Street, when Coleridge, Wordsworth,

Sir Thomas Brown, and Jeremy Taylor were discussed, or at
the meetings of "The Peel Club," where the students met to
consider the politics of the hour, that the intellectual life of
this group of friends was mainly stirred.   Happy friendships
were formed during these Glasgow winters—a prelude to
those which awaited him at Oxford.   In both places the
set of men into whose society he was thrown was a
remarkable one.   They were drawn together by affinities
unusually deep; and when differences developed themselves
within the circle, each both received and gave an impulse
to the other, which was strong at the time, and the effect
of which continued through life.

In a letter to his sister, Miss B. Shairp, in November
1838, he wrote: "Ever since I came here the time has
been chiefly occupied in bustling about the election of a
Lord Rector for the University, and we succeeded in carrying Sir James Graham after much difficulty, at which you
may suppose there was a good deal of canvassing and
speechifying, in which I had my own share."

Professor Sellar writes thus of the time spent at the
University of Glasgow: "Of the years passed there he
used often to speak, and always with unmixed pleasure and
enthusiasm.   He quoted with sympathy a saying of one of
his friends of that time, when he met him in after years,
that 'he looked back on his Glasgow time as the romance of
his life.'   He had a very cordial feeling to all the Professors under whom he studied, and a grateful recognition
of the good he got from them.   He was especially distinguished in the Moral Philosophy Class, and I remember
hearing from the Professor of the subject, that his essays
were generally based on Coleridge, whose teaching was at
that time something quite new in our universities.   He
has told me that what made the most powerful impression
upon him among all the lectures that he listened to was the
inaugural lecture of Professor Lushington, in the opening
of the session 1838-39.   It was a lecture which not only
contained a most just and impressive survey and estimate
of Greek literature, but was surcharged with the new

thought and imaginative feeling pervading the remarkable Cambridge set to which he belonged, the names of most of whom are now well known to the world, and some of whom (and he certainly) looked on Coleridge then as their master, or at least as a teacher to whom they owed much. Shairp left the lecture, as he told me, repeating to himself the line—

> That strain I heard was of a higher mood ; [1]

and the impression thus produced was confirmed by his attendance on the private Greek Class. I can remember his quoting to me at Oxford happy translations of lines or half-lines of Sophocles, and pregnant bits of criticism from the lectures. He gained a prize at the end of the session for an essay on a comparison of the *Ajax* of Sophocles with the *Coriolanus* of Shakespeare, of which the Professor, who, though warm in his admiration of merit, was habitually temperate in the expression of praise, spoke in terms of more than common appreciation. The feeling with which they then regarded one another deepened in later life into one of affectionate friendship.

He had great enjoyment in his student-life, and was fortunate in the set of young men among whom he was thrown. During his time in Glasgow, Shairp was, for the only time in his life, a keen political partisan, and was, I think, one of the founders of the Peel Club, which had its origin in the election of Sir Robert Peel as Lord Rector, in the year 1836. He was consistent in after-life in adhering to the politics of his youth and early associations ; but he never again took an active part in, or cared much about the contests of parties.

To this time also he referred the beginning of his intellectual life, which, though expanded and modified by later influences, flowed consistently till the end in the channel which his spirit then struck out for it. Besides the impulse which he derived from the literary and philosophical classes,

---

[1] He frequently referred to this lecture in the last decade of his life, and always with the utmost enthusiasm.

he then first came under the influence of Wordsworth, which continued, I think, to be the master-influence of his intellectual life. It required an independent spirit, and a taste for poetry not learned from others or adopted from literary fashion, but αὐτοδιδακτόν, for a young Scotchman in those days to become an enthusiastic votary of a poet, who was then only known to the majority of his country-men by the satire of Byron, the parody in the *Rejected Addresses*, and the criticism of the *Edinburgh Review*. The influence of Scott he had felt from his childhood, and in one of the summers during his Glasgow college days, or in his early Oxford time, he met Lockhart in a country house, and had some conversation with him. He used often to recall his ' proud, sad face,' as of one for whom life had no more zest, since he had lost the companionship of the great man with whom he was so closely allied. With these two, Scott and Wordsworth, as he formed the earliest, so also he maintained the most constant of all his friendships in the world of letters.

At this time, too, he first felt the stirring within himself of the impulses and of something of the faculty of a poet. And the stirring of those impulses and of that faculty were then, as they were through all his subsequent life, intimately connected with what was the master-passion of his life, his love of Nature, especially as she revealed herself to him, in long and often lonely wanderings through the most picturesque scenes in the Highlands and the Border-country, or among the places which spoke to him of the more romantic memories of Scottish history. Till his physical strength began to fail in the last years of his life, he never missed passing some days or weeks in these wanderings; and there were few if any educated men who knew Scotland, highland and lowland, so well. He only once, I think, yielded to the almost universal passion or fashion of foreign travel, and though he got from his summer abroad a fair knowledge of German for working purposes, he seemed to regret a summer not passed in Scot-land as a summer wasted.

I was only on two occasions with him in his walks—once

in ascending Ben Cruachan in company with the late Dean
of Westminster, the present Master of Balliol, his friend
Poste of Oriel, and one or two others; and another time,
along with one other companion, in crossing the Minch
Moor to Innerleithen and back again to Yarrow, the outcome of which walk appeared soon after in one of the most
perfect of his lyrical poems, *The Bush aboon Traquair.*
One could not be with him on such occasions without per-
ceiving how deep and strong and natural was his enjoyment,
how eager and exact his observation of every sound and
sight that had attraction for him, and with what a
vigorous and elastic tread he went over the ground. I was
also struck by his resolute determination not to be satisfied
till he ascertained the exact spot which he came out to see.[1]
A chief source of interest in his poems to those who knew
him is that they are the faithful record—

Of what was passing in that brain and breast

(to apply to himself a line which he once quoted as applied by
some poet of the Lake country to Professor Wilson) in those
walks, into which he threw his whole heart and spirit.
Although he was entirely different from him in his social
temperament, though he had nothing of his exuberant
humour, and though he never could, even had he wished it,
have filled the same place in the eyes of his contemporaries,
which the older Professor did, and while his enthusiasm was
more subdued, and his imagination and taste were, I think,
chastened by a finer culture, yet he always seemed to me
in his youth to belong essentially to that one among
the various types, in which the *praefervidum ingenium* of
his countrymen manifests itself, of which Professor Wilson
was the most eminent representative.

After leaving Glasgow he passed a winter in Edinburgh,
before he was appointed to the Snell Exhibition to Balliol.
He attended, I think, some of the University classes, but
he spoke of that winter as an idle one, given up chiefly to

---

[1] Compare Lord Coleridge's reminiscences of his visit to Iona with Shairp
in 1878, given in a subsequent chapter.

C

amusement. It was probably, however, not wasted, and may have helped to give him that ease in social intercourse, of which young men, almost exclusively college-bred, often painfully feel the want. There was nothing in him at any time of the manner of a mere student or bookish man. He was perfectly at his ease with men of the most diverse tastes and pursuits—scholars, soldiers, or men of the world—people of every degree from that of a shepherd or a ploughman to that of those placed at the opposite end of the social scale."

The influence of the teaching which Shairp received at the University of Glasgow was lifelong. It was not exclusively classical. During these undergraduate years his mind awoke to the meaning of the perennial problems of philosophy, and the great questions of the ages. It is clear that his work in both the philosophical classes—that of Logic, and of Moral Philosophy—was thorough. In both he was adjudged the highest place in the list of class honours, by the votes of his fellow-students. His studies under Professors Lushington and Ramsay had deepened his appreciation of the literature of Greece and Rome, and had given him full insight into the best literary models of the past; while his attendance on the classes of Professors Buchanan and Fleming had at least opened his mind to the significance of Speculative Philosophy, and its bearing on conduct.

But it is easy to see that alongside of this academic training at the University, a far more powerful factor was at work, educating his mind, and moulding his character. His reading and reciting of the poets, his discussions on them with Norman Macleod and others, his own occasional efforts as a writer of verse, the combined influence of the Ballads of his Native Land, the Minstrelsy of the Border, the Lyrics of Wordsworth, and the Romances of Sir Walter Scott, and his contact with Nature itself when away from the University—these things touched him to the quick, and opened up the springs of imagination. It was by their influences, running parallel to the teaching of the University, that "the fountains of the great deep" were "broken up" within him, that imaginative insight awoke, and that the stream of poetry began to flow freely forth.

Perhaps the very strongest of these influences was that which came over him during every holiday, when his historical and imaginative sympathy led him to try—in the course of long wanderings on foot—to localise the allusions in the poems he most loved, and to identify spots that were familiar if not famous to a former race of men.[1]

In his nineteenth year, before returning to Glasgow for the winter, Shairp paid his first visit to the Braes of Yarrow ; and his record of the two autumnal days he spent there is perhaps the earliest specimen of his poetic work which we possess. It is in sixteen stanzas, and as they are of unequal merit, I select only six of them. He called it

A Remembrance of Two Days spent among the Braes of Yarrow, from the evening of Tuesday 25th till the forenoon of Thursday the 27th September, 1838.

> The night came down on the mountain brown,
>   The flakes fell fast and still ;
> But one lone gleam of sunset lay
>   On all the western hill.
> And I deemed it bade us gladsome hail
> To come and gaze on Yarrow Vale.

> .   .   .   .   .   .

> And Yarrow—Yarrow, as I stood
>   Beside thine ancient flood,
> My heart was proud that I was born
>   Of Scotland's ancient blood.
> For where, O where's the stream can marrow,
> The holms, the hopes, the hills of Yarrow ?

> Two days I wandered all alone,
>   Oft crooning some old rhyme,
> Some simple song that cadenced well,
>   With Yarrow's plaintive chime.
> Two nights the wakeful voice of Yarrow
> Sang by my rest till dawn of morrow.

---

[1] I may perhaps be allowed here to express a regret that Principal Shairp was unable to carry out an intention he once had of localising the allusions to place, throughout the poems of Wordsworth. Had he and Dr. Cradock done it jointly, it would have been a noble bit of work.

A forest this !—It giveth·back
No music to the breeze ;
Yet are there still upon the hill
Lone melancholy trees.
Each standing far off from the other,
As mourning for some long-lost brother.

Scott and Hogg are both referred to in the next stanza.

In Dryburgh, by his own dear Tweed,
One hath his dwelling narrow ;
One sleepeth sound on Ettrick side,
Deaf to the roar of Yarrow.
Ye may hear it in the twilight dim,
But that stream-voice is mute for him.

Come hither thou who ne'er hast known
The power of ancient sorrow,
Come all alone and find it here
Among the braes of Yarrow.
Here let thy soul drink deeply in
The power that sleeps this Vale within.

As casting light on Shairp's career at the University of Glasgow, and his subsequent years of friendship with John Macintosh and Norman Macleod, some portions of his estimates of these two men are quoted here.

In all Principal Shairp's writings there is nothing more interesting, or valuable, than his series of character-studies of the many friends he had, and to whose biographies he often contributed the most interesting sketch. As the aim of this biography is to illustrate the man in his manysidedness, a few extracts from these sketches—which are now scattered in nearly a dozen volumes—will be more acceptable than pages of commentary. The friends to whose lives he has contributed were John Macintosh of Geddes, Norman Macleod, Arthur Clough, Thomas Erskine of Linlathen, John M'Leod Campbell of Row, Bishop Cotton, Bishop Patteson, Principal Forbes, Dr. Park, Dr. John Brown, and Archbishop Tait. The reason why these sketches of his friends are so valuable to us is, that they at the same time reveal some things most characteristic of the writer—his views of life, his aspirations, his ambitions, and ideals— as nothing else does. The estimate of Macintosh is contained in a letter to his biographer, written from Rugby in 1856.

" RUGBY, 10th April 1856.

" MY DEAR NORMAN— . . . It was about the beginning of November 1837, I think, on his first coming to Glasgow College, that Macintosh and I met and became acquainted. Years before we had been at the Edinburgh Academy together, but as we were in different classes, we had not known each other to speak to. I knew him, however, by name and appearance ; seem now to see, as it had been but yesterday, the two brothers uniformly dressed in a suit of sky-blue from head to foot, sitting always together at the head of their class—the younger and smaller first, the elder next to him. Though it is fully twenty years since, his appearance is clearly before me, and the reputation that went with him not only for ability, but for character beyond his years. There was about him even then a calm collected air, as of one who had a purpose before him, and went straight to it, undisturbed by other aims. . . .

The time when he entered Glasgow College was, as you will remember, a stirring one in that University. Peel had been elected Lord Rector the year before. The Peel Club had been established to support his principles ; political feeling, which was then high among the students, added interest to life, and quickened the stir of thought. But it is not as a young politician that we think of him, as he then was, but rather as a chief favourite in that small circle of friends, of which your father's hearth was at that time the centre.

There were in all about ten or twelve of us, between the ages of sixteen and eighteen. Many of these had come from the Edinburgh Academy ; most were preparing for Oxford or Cambridge. We were then at the delightful time of life when the fresh heart of boyhood, first freed from restraint, leaps forward eagerly to the opening interests of manhood. Seldom do a band of friends live together on terms so happy, so intimate, so endearing, as those on which, evening after evening, we used to meet in that room in your father's house (known amongst us as the coffee-room), or in the lodgings of some one of our number. Many interests there met, and harmonised : poetry, philosophy, politics, or field sports, and other amusements.

.   .   .   .

He was not remarkable for any precocious activity, but rather for strict self-discipline and thoroughness of purpose, which made him, while earnestly seeking the highest things, never neglect the lowest duties.

.   .   .   .

I ought perhaps to add, that these high moral and religious qualities were at that time not unaccompanied by a certain shade of that austereness which some think characteristic of religious people in Scotland. But however this may be, all his companions felt the force of his goodness. Their great love for him as a friend was mingled with deep respect, I might almost say reverence, for his whole character.

. . . . .

After he had taken final leave of Cambridge, before returning to Scotland, he came to visit Oxford and some of his old Glasgow friends, who were undergraduates at Balliol College.

. . . . .

For several days we wandered together among the colleges and old gardens, and by the banks of the river ; and the antique air of the place seemed greatly to impress him.

. . . . .

The Oxford movement was then at its height ; and he took much interest in all he saw and heard regarding it. I can remember standing with him in the great square of Christ Church, to watch Pusey's spare, bowed-down, surpliced form, as he returned from prayer in the Cathedral. He was present also in St. Mary's on one of the last Sunday afternoons that Newman's voice was heard there, or elsewhere, as a minister of the English Church.

. . . . .

One change, and only one, seemed to have passed over him during our long separation. The tinge of severity which I was aware of formerly, had wholly disappeared. Without losing his singleness or strength of purpose, he had grown, I thought, more gentle, more serene, more deeply loving towards all men.

. . . . .

However widely a man differed in opinion or sentiment from himself, it seemed he did not care to dwell on the differences, but rather to open his mind fairly to take in whatever of good or true he had to teach. This open-mindedness, in one so earnest and fixed in his own mind, was very remarkable ; and the whole seemed so evenly-balanced, that while he was not only fair, but sympathetic towards all men, there appeared no symptom of that weakness and uncertainty of thought often visible in those whose sympathies are stronger than their heads.

. . . . .

Another time we met and whiled away part of a summer afternoon on the high pastures of Midhope, looking over the Firth of Forth. Then we made the burn our guide, and let it lead us from the open grass fields, down through its deep woody glen, past the antique house of Midhope, till it reaches the salt-sea water. Tennyson was among our other thoughts that day, and we chanted to each other that beautiful melody of his—

> Flow down, cold rivulet, to the sea,
> Thy tribute wave deliver.

We knew not then how truly that burden applied—

> No more by thee our steps shall be
> For ever and for ever.

But no shadow passed over that afternoon."[1]

.   .   .   .

In the reminiscences which Shairp contributed to the memoir of his friend Norman Macleod, we find more than in his sketch of Macintosh that bears upon the course of his own life at the University of Glasgow ; and they supplement, in an interesting way, the details given by Professor Sellar. He tells us that, when he went to the University—

"Norman was a young divinity student, ánd had nearly completed his course in Glasgow College.

To him his father committed the entire care of the three young men who lived in his house, and it was arranged that I, living with his aunts, should be added as a fourth charge. This I look back to as one of the happiest things that befell me during all my early life. Norman was then in the very hey-day of hope, energy, and young genius. There was not a fine quality which he afterwards displayed, which did not then make itself seen and felt by his friends ; and that youthfulness of spirit, which was to the last so delightful, had a peculiar charm then, when it was set off by all the personal attractions of two or three and twenty.

His training had not been merely the ordinary one of a lad from a Scotch Manse, who has attended classes in Glasgow and Edinburgh Universities. His broad and sympathetic spirit had a far richer background to draw upon. It was Morven and the Sound of Mull, the legends of Skye and Dunvegan, and the shore of Kintyre, that had dyed the first and inmost feelings of childhood with their deep colouring. Then as boyhood passed into manhood, came his sojourn among Yorkshire squires, his visit to Germany, and all the stimulating society of Weimar, on which still rested the spirit of the lately-departed Goethe. All these things, so unlike the commonplace experience of many, had added to his nature a variety and compass which seemed so wonderful compared with that of most young men around him. Child of Nature as he was, this variety of experience had stimulated and enlarged Nature in him, not overlaid it.

There were many bonds of sympathy between us to begin with. First, there was his purely Highland and Celtic blood and upbringing ; and I, both from my mother's and paternal grandmother's side, had Celtic blood. The shores of Argyleshire were common ground to us. The same places, and the same people—many of them were

---

[1] *Memorials of John Macintosh,* pp. 69-75.

familiar to his childhood and to mine. And he, and his father, and mother used to stimulate my love for that western land by endless stories, legends, histories, jests, allusions, brought from thence. It was to him, as to me, the region of poetry, of romance, adventure, mystery, gladness, and sadness infinite. Here was a great background of common interest, which made us feel as old friends at first sight. Indeed, I never remember the time when I felt the least a stranger to Norman. Secondly, besides this, I soon found that our likings for the poets were the same. Especially were we at one in our common devotion to one, to us the chief of poets.

I well remember those first evenings we used to spend together in Glasgow. I went to No. 9 Bath Street—oftener Norman would come over to my room to look after my studies. I was attending Professor Buchanan's class,—'Bob,' as we then irreverently called him, —and Norman came to see how I had taken my logic notes, and prepared my essay or other work for next day. After a short time spent in looking over the notes of lecture, or the essay, Norman would say, 'I see you understand all about it ; come, let's turn to Billy.' That was his familiar name for Wordsworth, the poet of his soul.

Before coming to Glasgow I had come upon Wordsworth, and in large measure taken him to heart. Norman had for some years done the same. Our sympathy in this became an immense bond of union. The admiration and study of Wordsworth were not then what they afterwards became—a part of the discipline of every educated man. Those who really cared for him in Scotland might, I believe, have then been counted by units. Not a professor in Glasgow University at that time ever alluded to him. Those, therefore, who read him in solitude, if they met another to whom they could open their mind on the subject, were bound to each other by a very inward chord of sympathy. I wish I could recall what we then felt as on those evenings we read or chanted the great lines we already knew, or shouted for joy at coming on some new passage which was a delightful surprise. Often as we walked out on winter nights to College for some meeting of the Peel Club, or other excitement, he would look up into the clear moonlight and repeat—

> The moon doth with delight
> Look round her when the heavens are bare ;
> Waters on a starry night
> Are beautiful and fair.

Numbers of the finest passages we had by heart, and would repeat to each other endlessly. I verily believe that Wordsworth did more for Norman, penetrated more deeply and vitally into him, purifying and elevating his thoughts and feelings at their fountainhead than any other voice of uninspired man, living or dead. Second only to Wordsworth, Coleridge was, of modern poets, our great favourite. Those poems of his, and special passages which have since become familiar to all, were then little known in Scotland, and had to us all the charm of a newly-discovered country. We began then, too, to have dealings with his philosophy, which we found much more to our mind than the authorities then in vogue in Glasgow College—the prosaic Reid and the long-winded Thomas Brown.

Long years afterwards, whenever I took up a Scotch newspaper, if my eye fell on a quotation from Wordsworth or Coleridge, 'Here's Norman,' I would say ; and on looking more carefully I would be sure to find that it was he—quoting in one of his speeches some of the favourite lines of Glasgow days. Norman was not much of a classical scholar ; Homer, Virgil, and the rest, were not much to him. But I often thought that if he had known them ever so well, in a scholarly way, they never would have done for him what Wordsworth did, would never have so entered into his secret being, and become a part of his very self. Besides Wordsworth and Coleridge, there were two other poets who were continually on his lips. Goethe was then much to him ; for he was bound up in all his recent Weimar reminiscences ; but I think that, as life went on, Goethe, with his artistic isolation, grew less and less to him. Shakespeare, on the other hand, was then, and always continued to be, an unfailing resource. Many of the characters he used to read and dilate upon with wonderfully realising power. Falstaff was especially dear to him. He read Falstaff's speeches, or rather, acted them, as I have never heard any other man do. He entered into the very heart of the character, and reproduced the fat old-man's humour to the very life.

These early sympathies, no doubt, made our friendship more rapid and deep. But it did not need any such bonds to make a young man take at once to Norman. To see him, hear him, converse with him, was enough. He was then overflowing with generous, ardent contagious impulse. Brimful of imagination, sympathy, buoyancy, humour, drollery, and affectionateness, I never knew any one who contained in himself so large and varied an armful of the humanities. Himself a very child of Nature, he touched Nature and human life at every point. There was nothing human that was without interest for him ; nothing great or noble to which his heart did not leap up instinctively. In those days, what Hazlitt says of Coleridge was true of him, ' He talked on for ever.' Since that day I have met and known intimately a good many men more or less remarkable and original. Some of them were stronger on this one side, some on that, than Norman; but not one of all contained in himself such a variety of gifts and qualities, such elasticity, such boundless fertility of pure nature, apart from all he got from books or culture.

On his intellectual side, imagination and humour were his strongest qualities, both of them working on a broad base of strong common-sense and knowledge of human nature. On the moral side, sympathy, intense sympathy, with all humanity was the most manifest, with a fine aspiration that hated the mean and the selfish, and

went out to whatever things were most worthy of a man's love. Deep
affectionateness to family and friends—affection that could not bear
coldness or stiff reserve, but longed to love and to be loved; and if
there was in it a touch of the old Highland clannishness, one did not
like it the less for that.

.   .   .   .

We all met in a common sitting-room. There, when College work
was over, sometimes before it was over, or even well begun, we would
gather round him, and with story, joke, song, readings from some
favourite author, or some recitation of poetry, he would make our hearts
leap up.
What evenings I have seen in that 'coffee-room'! Norman, in
the grey-blue duffle dressing-gown, in which he then studied, with
smoking-cap on his head, coming forth from his own reading-den to
refresh himself, and cheer us, by a brief bright quarter of an hour's
talk. He was the centre of that small circle, and whenever he appeared, even if there was dulness before, life and joy broke forth. At
the close of the first session—I speak of 1836-37—the party that
gathered in the coffee-room changed. MacConochie and Nairne went,
and did not return; William Clerk remained; and the vacant places
were at the beginning of next session, 1837-38, filled by Robert (now
Sir Robert) Dalyell of Binns; James Horne, and John Macintosh,
the youngest son of Macintosh of Geddes. There were also two
or three other students who boarded elsewhere, but who were often
admitted as visitors to the joyous gatherings in the coffee-room.

.   .   .   .

Before the close of the session of 1837-38 Norman was appointed
to the parish of Loudoun, in Ayrshire, and ordained as its minister.
When the close of our next and last session in Glasgow (1838-39)
arrived, he arranged that his old friends of the coffee-room should
go down and pay him a visit in his manse at Loudoun on the 1st
of May. The usual winding-up of College had taken place in the
morning, and by the afternoon a merry party were seated on the
top of the Ayrshire coach, making their way through the pleasant
country of Mearns, in Ayrshire, towards their friend's manse. That
party consisted of William Clerk, Robert Dalyell, Henry Douglas, and
myself. . . . It was a beautiful spring evening, and the green burn braes
as we wound along laughed on us with their galaxies of primroses.
You may imagine what a welcome we received when at evening we
reached the manse door. We stayed there three days, or four. The
weather was springlike and delightful. We wandered by the side of
the Irvine Water, and under the woods, all about Loudoun Castle, and
Norman was, as of old, the soul of the party. He recurred to his old
Glasgow stories, or told us new ones derived from his brief experience
of the Ayrshire people, in whom, and in their characters, he was
already deeply interested. All day we spent out of doors, and as we
lay, in that balmy weather, on the banks or under the shade of the

newly-budding trees, converse more hearty it would be impossible to conceive. And yet, there was beneath it an undertone of sadness; for we foreboded too surely what actually has been fulfilled, that it was our last meeting.

    .   .   .   .

On the last day of our wanderings Norman, who had hitherto kept up our spirits, and never allowed a word of sadness to mar the mirth, at last said suddenly, as we were reclining in one of the Loudoun Castle woods, 'Now, friends, this is the last time we shall all meet together; I know that well. Let us have a memorial of our meeting. Yonder are a number of primrose bushes. Each of you take up one root with his own hands; I will do the same; and we shall plant them at the manse in remembrance of this day.' So we each did, and carried home each his own primrose bush. When we reached the manse, Norman chose a place where we should plant them side by side. It was all simple and natural, yet a pathetic and memorable close of that delightful early time.

Early next morning we left the manse, and, I believe, not one of us ever returned. It was as Norman said. We went our several ways—one to Cambridge, two to Oxford; but never again did more than two of us foregather.[1]

Two things strike me especially in looking back on Norman as he then was. The first was his joyousness—the exuberance of his joy— joy combined with purity of heart. We had never known any one who took a serious view of life, and was really religious, who combined with it so much hearty hopefulness. He was happy in himself, and made all others happy with whom he had to do. At least they must have been very morose persons indeed who were insensible to the contagion of his gladness."

In all this picture of his friend, while Shairp had not a thought of himself, he gives us many a side-glance into his own character, and in some points he was unconsciously drawing his own portrait.

It is much to be regretted that so few of the many letters written by Shairp to Norman Macleod survive. Mrs. Macleod tells me they were most frequent before her husband went to Dalkeith, and during their residence there. Afterwards they were each too busy in their several paths to correspond much.

In one of them, an undated note from Houstoun, he writes of an intended visit, along with one of the subsequent " Balliol scholars," to Macleod's house :—

---

[1] *Memoir of Norman Macleod, D.D.*, vol. i. pp. 87-100.

" If nothing hinders, Prichard and I will be with you
on Tuesday morning to breakfast, by the route you mention.
' We'll make a day of happy hours,' not in steamer, please,
but among the nearest hills, or if you have any lonely
shores. Prichard is naturally a grave man, but a very
simple straightforward one too. None of the unnatural
hocus-pocus priestliness which you connect with Orielism.
At present, too, he has something to grieve him, and has
come north for change of scene. Therefore you must let
your spirits flow freely as of old, and give your fun free
play."

Writing again to Macleod of his Life of their common
friend, John Macintosh of Geddes : " . . . You have left
almost nothing to wish, unless it were that you had come
a little more forward, and made your own comment. But
this is a good fault. . . . If he had been here now, and
could have read that Life as the record of a stranger to
himself, it is just the kind of book he would have heartily
approved of. Well as I knew his goodness and loveableness,
these Journals and Letters have let me see far deeper into
his character, than perhaps even years of intercourse might
have done. What strength and singleness of will ! . . .
The last chapter sank deeper into me, reading it in the
silence of my room, than that day when you read it to us
in Glasgow. . . . As to reviewing it, I cannot. How could
I sit down to analyse *his* character, or to criticise it ? I wish
the book to be a treasured one for years to come, and were
I to read it through for reviewing, the freshness of it would
be gone."

Shairp's friendship with the whole of the Macleod family
was deep and unbroken ; and on the death of the old lady
of St. Columba's Manse—Norman's mother—he wrote thus
to her son-in-law and his college friend, Dr. Clerk of Kilmalie :

" I know that Mrs. Clerk and you will be feeling much
the departure of the dear old lady, though you knew that
her time was full come. She takes with her so much love,
and so many memories. A larger heart, and a finer, more

capacious mind, I never knew in woman; and then she had
with it the simplicity and single-mindedness, and deep
tenacity of affection, that belonged to an earlier time, and
seems much rarer now. You and I have often spoken of
her. How much of what was best in Norman he owed to
her noble nature. I trust that her descendants in the
second and third generations may be able to know what
she really was, and may live to be like her."

After Norman Macleod's death he wrote to Clerk—

". . . My happiest thoughts of him go back to Bath
Street, Loudoun, and Dalkeith. Then he was buoyancy and
strength and joy unbounded. You would get a whole night
of him from 9 P.M. till 2 or 3 A.M. in his study, when he
would let loose the whole man, and you did not feel then
that you were overtaxing him. It is a dreadful feature of
our modern over-centralised life that everywhere, and in all
professions, the foremost men are sacrificed rapidly to the
demand made on them by the world. . . ."

Of Macleod he also said, after he had made the acquaintance of the large and varied circle into which he was
introduced at Oxford : " I feel sometimes as if he were like
all my English friends rolled into one."

The following extract (the last) from the autobiographic
poem *Retrospect,* refers to the Glasgow College days :—

> . . . Can I forget the hour,
> In the dim city of the murky west,
> When first I passed beneath the antique Tower
> That crowned quaint College gables,—whither prest
> An eager throng of students, scarlet-gowned,
> And among these a gentle company found
> Of Scotland's youth, more lovely than the rest !
>
> And he was there—chief amid younger peers,
> Waiting the hour that soon should put to proof
> Those powers which Scotland owned in after years,[1]
> But then scarce known beyond his father's roof ;
> His lofty thought and aspiration strong
> In eloquence o'erflowing and in song,
> That kept dark city vapours far aloof.

---

[1] Macleod.

A voice that gathered, from the misty hills
And sounding shores of Morven, power intense
To pierce our listening souls with glorious thrills,
Blending the past with newer influence,
Till the whole world, past, present, and to be,
Before our sight dilated wondrously,
Lit by his shafts of natural eloquence.

Sometimes one listened there,[1] young soul serene
And gentle, through fair face and clear blue eye
Forth looking calmly on life's varied scene
Before him spread, with pure resolve and high,
Though blithe of heart, not many were his words,
But his low voice, more sweet than any bird's,
Beside me, day by day, made melody.

John Macintosh wrote thus to Shairp in February 1846 :
" I don't know how it is, but the Glasgow sessions do
certainly seem to be our Heroic Age, on which, like the
after-posts, we look back and linger with a pensive pleasure.
You are my Achilles of these days ; Douglas of course the
Patroclus ; Norman the ἄναξ ἀνδρῶν Agamemnon (but a
much finer fellow) ; and I perhaps, to outward appearance,
the pious Æneas. Do not wonder then that the sight of
you stirs up a thousand thoughts. I have been at Norman's
a night since, and so much did we harp on you and the
former sederunt, that it seemed like the ghost of the evening
you were there. I also saw the Dr. and Mrs. Macleod (πότνια
μήτηρ) very hastily at Glasgow. . . . I do believe it will
be a great relief to you to begin active work. I know
it has made me at times almost drunk with ardour and
pleasure, and has told most beneficially on my studies. I
attribute Norman's exuberance too to the same cause."

---

[1] Henry Douglas, afterwards Bishop of Bombay.

CHAPTER IV

IN April 1840 Shairp gained the Snell Exhibition from Glasgow University to Balliol College, Oxford, and matriculated in June of that year, his intention at first being to take orders in the Church of England.

Of his first visit to Oxford there is nothing particular to record. The long vacation of 1840 was partly spent in London, varied by a visit to the barracks at Ipswich, whither he sailed from London, giving a graphic account of the voyage in a letter to one of his sisters at Houstoun.

The letters he wrote from Oxford to the family circle at Houstoun show the gradual development of the poet and the philosopher, side by side with the scholar; and they further show how it was scarcely possible that he could come out, in the final schools, as a first in Classics. I hope that classical scholars may forgive my saying that he was doing even better than preparing for that most honourable close of undergraduate life. It was certainly so for him; and if he had worked so as to win a first, he might not have given to the world what he afterwards gave it.

These letters to Houstoun also show the strength and tenacity of his home affections, and how harmoniously his character developed during these years. The dignity with which he took the final award of the Examiners is instructive, and the letter to his father about it may be read in connection with a remark in Mr. Cotterill's paper of reminiscences, pp. 278-283.

Although not a remarkable letter-writer—amongst the

many who have been distinguished in this respect—the serenity and brightness of his nature, his good feeling, self-control, and inherent nobleness, came out in all his correspondence to a remarkable extent. I do not suppose he ever wrote a line which he had afterwards to regret. The entire absence of envy and of self-engrossedness, as well as of cynical criticism, or depreciation of others, is noteworthy. A serene, appreciative, sunny spirit is seen in every one of them. Here again I avail myself of Mr. Sellar's admirable memoranda:—

" It was in the year 1840 that he was appointed by the Glasgow Professors to a Snell Exhibition to Balliol, and he entered on residence, I think, in the October term. Balliol, though one of the three or four larger colleges, had by no means reached its present dimensions, nor had it the same cosmopolitan character that it has now; but under the judicious regime of Dr. Jenkyns it had gained the same rank that it holds now in University distinctions. The number of men in residence was about seventy or eighty, carefully selected by the Master from the best type of public schoolmen, most of them about that time from Eton, Rugby, Harrow, Shrewsbury, etc. The scholars were elected by competition open to all parts of the world, and among those who were contemporary, or nearly contemporary, with Shairp were the 'seven,' whom he has admirably characterised as they then were, in a poem which appeared some years ago[1] in *Macmillan's Magazine*, with the title 'Balliol Scholars.' The only survivors of the seven are now the Lord Chief-Justice of England and the Bishop of London;[2]

[1] In March 1873.

[2] Since these recollections were written, two of Shairp's oldest and best friends, who were both scholars of Balliol at that time, and have since been well known in the world, Theodore Walrond and Matthew Arnold, have passed away. To others, as well as to myself, among their surviving friends and contemporaries, this quick succession of losses must have recalled,—as much from the distinction of the men as from the bond of almost brotherly affection which united them together, at college and through all their later life,—the grand and pathetic lines in which Wordsworth mourns over the quick succession of losses among the best and greatest of his contemporaries—

How fast has brother followed brother
From sunshine to the sunless land.

but among them all the one of whom his contemporaries had the highest opinion and hopes, as a poet and thinker, was Clough ; and I think it was for him more than any of the others that Shairp then felt that idealising hero-worship, which generous young men, of imaginative susceptibility, feel for the genius of their contemporaries. He went one summer with him on a reading-party to Grasmere, and he often talked of its pleasant memories, especially of the delight and amusement which he and all of them had from seeing a great deal of Hartley Coleridge. He told me too of his having once, only once, after one of his long walks, seen Wordsworth standing at his garden-gate, and of how he had felt impelled to shake his hand, and to tell him how much he owed to him. But he shrank always from any kind of 'lion-hunting,' regarding it as rather a form of impudent self-assertion than a reverent tribute to greatness. The seven scholars of his poem were the immediate successors of others as gifted and remarkable, among whom were the late Lord Cardwell, Sir Stafford Northcote, Dean Stanley, and the present Master of the College, Professor Jowett, who was one of the younger Fellows when Shairp entered on residence, though the great personal and intellectual influence which, as Tutor and Master of the College, he has exercised over so many generations of pupils did not begin to assert itself till a year or two later. Among the immediate successors of these seven, with all of whom Shairp became intimate, were Archdeacon Palmer, T. Walrond, T. C. Sanders, F. T. Palgrave, the late Professor H. S. Smith, Sir A. Grant, and others.

There was no sharp distinction made between reading and non-reading men, but the whole College formed a very friendly society ; and one of the considerations which determined Shairp long afterwards to send his son to Oriel was, that it had not outgrown the size which admitted of a common family-kind of life among its members, of which he himself had felt the charm and benefit at Balliol. Into this society of young Englishmen the Scotch Exhibitioners from Glasgow were heartily welcomed. They brought some prestige with them, for members of their body had added distinction to the College before it had become famous ; and even now the names of Adam Smith, Sir William Hamilton, Lockhart, and the present Lord Justice-General of Scotland, are not unworthy to stand beside those of the most distinguished among former scholars. Yet I think the Exhibitioners who came after Shairp owed a good deal of their friendly reception to the place which he had secured for them by his personal popularity and his intellectual reputation. Among those who came immediately after him were his future brother-in-law, Henry Douglas, Sir Francis Sandford, and Patrick Cumin, Secretary to the Education Office. Shairp and all the rest of us felt both the pleasure, and the enlargement to our whole nature, of this intimate association with young Englishmen of culture, promise, and social vivacity; many of whom, in their turn, I am sure, felt the new zest given to the genial enlivenment and the varied intellectual life of the College by this Scottish leaven introduced among them.

In his first term his old love of hunting had a sharp struggle with his love of reading. I remember hearing, partly from himself and partly from some one else, that in the early days of his residence, before he had made many acquaintances, feeling depressed by the novelty of his position, he determined to cheer himself by a day's hunting. Some of the older members of the 'fast set' (as it was called) were out on the same day, and when they came back to Hall there was a general inquiry as to who the freshman was who had ridden so well and hard. He was immediately asked by one of them to his rooms, and as they were a manly and cheerful set of men, with whose life in the open air he had a fellow-feeling, if he had been of weaker character, or less confirmed intellectual pursuits, he might have drifted permanently into the set which was first opened to him. But another rumour soon got abroad about him which reached the older reading-men, who had been at first rather shy of him, owing to his fame in the hunting-field,— that there was a freshman in College who possessed a trans-

lation of Kant, and was believed to know all about it. I
have heard it said, though I cannot vouch for the accuracy
of the report, that the book was borrowed by the College
tutor, who, a few years later, did much to make the study
of philosophy more systematic in Oxford, and that the
reading of it was his first initiation into the subject.
Shairp soon formed his chief friendships among the
scholars and reading-men, and became himself one among
the latter.

The life of a reading-man was then somewhat different
from what it is now. The range of reading was more
limited, and examinations were fewer. There was, in fact,
for honour-men, only one examination of any importance—
that at the end of his three, or, in some cases, four years—to
which he looked forward from the beginning of his time.
This long postponement of their trial gave ample scope for
idleness in the first and second year, and many largely
availed themselves of their opportunities in that way. But
to those who read steadily it gave 'leisure to grow wise,'
to assimilate the thought and substance of their books, and
to read much of poetry and philosophy besides, for its own
sake, which had a no less important bearing on their mental
development. The accurate study of the form and language
of the books was not, as it is at present, sharply separated
from the sympathetic study of their substance and thought.
Scholarship was carried on, as I am inclined to think it
ought always to be, side by side with literature, philosophy,
and history, and not abruptly separated by an intermediate
examination. All of them formed part of the work of each
year. Shairp's chief difficulty was, I think, with his scholarship, especially (as it was with all the Scotchmen) with
composition, which was taught very thoroughly in English
schools at an age when the imitative faculty is most flex-
ible, and before the active powers of thought and of the
assimilation of knowledge are developed.

Good Latin composition was a *sine quâ non* for success
in every Oxford examination. The late Rector of Lincoln,
in one of the bitter criticisms which he has left on record

of the Oxford of his days, both unreformed and reformed, speaks somewhere of the College Tutor of the old school covering his intellectual nakedness with 'his rag of Latin prose.' Shairp, by dint of a good deal of uncongenial labour, did acquire this accomplishment, and I think he felt that he had got good by the discipline, though in his case it was somewhat against the grain. He had, however, real pleasure in getting up his books, especially his poets (among whom I think Æschylus was his favourite), and the Ethics of Aristotle. His previous reading made the philosophy—or 'science' as it used to be called, *a non lucendo*—interesting and familiar to him. The range of ethical study was not large. It comprised the *Rhetoric* and *Ethics* of Aristotle, Butler's *Sermons*, and the moral consciousness and experience of the individual student himself and of his private 'coach.' Yet this teaching, narrow as it looks, really called out the faculty and habit of ethical insight and criticism; and many men who were educated under it would in after life acknowledge that it was the most powerful influence in their intellectual development. Readers of his Life will remember how highly the use of the *Ethics*, as a text-book, was valued by Dr. Arnold. The range of history too was limited to Herodotus, Thucydides, the first decade of Livy, and occasionally the Annals or Histories of Tacitus. The works neither of Grote nor Mommsen had then appeared. The student had to work out historical problems a good deal for himself. Yet that the study of Herodotus and Thucydides, read and re-read by the light of Thirlwall and Arnold, and of Livy by the light of Niebuhr, was a good historical 'propædeutic' may be learned from the testimony of an historian who was trained by it, and whose time at Oxford was coincident with Shairp's—Professor Freeman.

But there were other more powerful intellectual forces acting on susceptible minds, then, than that of the regular studies of the place. By far the most searching and moving of these was that of Dr. Newman, then at the very zenith of his influence. No better account has ever been given of

that influence, no juster tribute has ever been paid to the
genius, sincerity, and by magical spell of him who wielded it,
than that given by Shairp in his essay on Keble.   He
never was in the least inclined to give assent to Dr. Newman's logical position, or to accept his theological doctrines ;
and he had a positive repugnance to the form which these
doctrines assumed in some of his adherents.   But he had
the sincerest admiration of the high, pure, unworldly type
of character realised by him, and by some of the older among
his followers and of those closest to him in personal sympathy.   The whole attitude of Dr. Newman, then and afterwards, touched his imagination ; and I remember long
afterwards his characterising him, in two lines of his friend
Matthew Arnold, as

> One of that small transfigured band
> Whom the world could not tame.

It was also during Shairp's time at Oxford that the influence of Dr. Arnold, beyond his own immediate sphere,
began to be felt.   This was partly a continuation of his
Rugby influence, transmitted through his pupils, some of the
best of whom were, and continued through all his life to be,
among Shairp's most intimate friends.   But it had been
brought more immediately to bear on Oxford by his recent
appointment to the Professorship of Modern History, and
the delivery of a course of lectures, probably the most eloquent, in the best sense of the word, ever listened to by an
Oxford audience : and the startling suddenness of his death,
though it entailed a great loss to English education, and a
still greater and permanent loss to English literature, added
to the impression produced by his teaching and personality ;
and this was still further deepened by the publication of his
Life a year or two later.   Though Shairp did not sympathise
with Dr. Arnold's political position either in Church or
State, yet I have often heard him express the strongest
personal and literary admiration for him ; and he, as well
as Dr. Newman, is to be included among those who helped
to form his intellectual and religious life.

But a larger wave of imaginative and emotional influence, which had begun elsewhere, and soon afterwards spread over the whole nation, then reached Oxford, and Shairp was one of the first to feel it—the influence of Carlyle. I remember his telling me how it reached him.

He had been tired by his morning's reading, depressed by the weather, which was too bad even for an Oxford 'constitutional,' and had gone, in a state of intellectual depression, into a bookseller's shop, had seen and immediately bought the four or five volumes of *Miscellanies*, which had just appeared, and carried them back to his rooms. The first essay on which he came was that on Edward Irving, which he read and re-read, walking about his room, feeling himself, as he said, possessed and carried away by a new passion, unlike to what he had ever experienced before. I can yet recall how he repeated with deep feeling, and that fine musical intonation which he gave to anything in verse or prose (as, for example, passages in Newman's *Sermons*) which deeply moved him, such sentences as ' His was the truest, bravest, brotherliest human heart mine ever came in contact with,' etc.; and that, ' He sleeps with his fathers in that loved birth-land. Mighty Babylon rages on by him henceforth unheeded for ever.'

This admiration, mingled with a kind of affectionate regard (though I don't remember that he had any personal acquaintance with him), continued through his life. But he had little sympathy with his later attitude to the world, and not much with some of the later developments of his literary style. All satire, even the greatest and most searching, was uncongenial to him; and that will partly explain his imperfect appreciation of one of the most powerful manifestations of Burns's manysided genius.

It was about this time too that the two volumes which first established Tennyson's right to rank among great English poets appeared. Shairp acknowledged the rising star, but this did not make him, as it did some of his younger associates, falter in his devotion to the older light, which was still shining. His taste in poetry had been early formed, and he was slow to admit even the two greatest among our living poets to an equal place in his heart with the older objects of his love. His love of poetry was rather deep and vivid than manysided. He was inclined to set his face against any new heresy of criticism—any

Vana superstitio, veterumque ignara deorum,

to which young Oxford then, as I fancy it still is, was prone. The worst of those heresies, which some adopted who should have known better, and which they probably outlived, was one, which if it had not its origin, at least found its strongest support in Carlyle,—a tendency to disparage Scott, not only as a poet but as a great creative genius. Against this heresy Shairp always indignantly protested, and I can remember the warmth with which he replied to some shallow but perhaps not altogether untrue criticism on some of his weaker places : ' I would as soon think of criticising my own father as Sir Walter.'

The first time I saw him was in the October term of 1842, the beginning of his third year of residence, when I was in Oxford for a few days as candidate for a-scholarship. I had heard much of him in Glasgow, where he left behind him a great personal and intellectual reputation. On arriving in Oxford I heard still more of him from the Snell Exhibitioners, who immediately preceded me and whom I had known in Glasgow. He had in the previous June added distinction to their body, and to his College, by gaining the Newdigate prize for an English poem on the subject of Charles XII., which was justly regarded as the poem of most original power which had appeared since Stanley's *Gipsies*. I have heard that it received some mark of recognition, in the way of letter or some other token, from old Bernadotte, who was then King of Sweden. It is one among very few prize-poems, indeed, that one can still read with pleasure and admiration. To those who knew him it has the interest of giving his own fresh impressions of Nature derived from those wanderings in spring, among

The dark woods and the silent hills

of his country, which had already begun. I can recall the
room in which I first saw him, and his appearance as he
stood on the hearthrug in front of the fire. He was a little
older than most undergraduates are, and he looked perhaps
a little older than he was—I mean more manly-looking and
more fully developed. He received me, as a newcomer
from Scotland and Glasgow, with that frank, kindly greeting
—'the smile in the eye as well as on the lip,' as in the
young shepherd in Theocritus—which was never absent in
our meetings after longer or shorter separation in later
years. I retain the impression rather of the high spirit and
animation, and of a kind of generous pride characteristic of
him, than of the milder, far-away contemplative look, which
became familiar to one in later years. Except that he
became bald and somewhat grey, he never seemed to change
much in other ways, during all the subsequent years that I
knew him ; and if he looked a little older than he was in
youth, he retained much of fresh youthfulness in his appearance, when he was nearly an old man. I remember being
present (then for the first time) at the annual dinner in which
the Scotchmen of the University celebrate, or used to celebrate, St. Andrew's Day, and that Shairp was the life and soul
of it, as he was on all similar occasions, speaking with that
happy mixture of serious enthusiasm and playful or banter-
ing allusion, which best befits convivial oratory.

When I came up as a freshman a few months later he
asked me to his rooms, and I felt pride and pleasure, in
the beginning of my career at Oxford, in any kindly notice
or encouragement from one who was himself so much of
a *vir laudatus.* But I did not become really intimate with
him till the Christmas vacation of 1845, when, for about a
fortnight, he, Walrond, and I, were the sole occupants of the
College ; he reading for a Fellowship, Walrond and I for our
degrees. He had taken his degree, I think, in the Easter
term of 1844, and like a large proportion of the men, about
that time, of most original gifts, and who have since gained
the greatest distinction in literature — including Clough,
M. Arnold, Mr. Froude, Mr. Freeman, M. Pattison, Sir A.

Grant and others—he was placed in the second class. We dined together daily and sat for two or three hours in one another's rooms in the evening; and as Walrond generally preferred tennis to a 'constitutional' in the afternoons, I was sometimes his only companion, as often afterwards, in the familiar round of walks in the country about Oxford. I can remember the pleasure and the profit with which I used then to hear him discuss speculative questions with serious and animated interest, or chant old ballads, and poems of Wordsworth, then unknown to me. I don't remember that he ever expressed much pleasure in the scenes through which our walks lay. The country about Oxford, as everywhere else, looks very different in January from what it looks in June, and the daily routine of constitutionalising is apt to deaden the sense of beauty. But that both his eye and heart did take in the characteristic charm of the place and its surrounding scenery, one could tell afterwards from the way in which he used to speak, of the truth, both real and ideal, with which M. Arnold has, in *The Scholar-Gipsy* and *Thyrsis*, made that charm live for all time in English literature. Yet his love of Nature, deep and passionate as it was, was in him intertwined with his affections. In later years he came to love Oxford next after Scotland, from the memory of happy study, and happier friendships formed there. And when he went back to it in those years, I think there were few among the habitual residents in the Colleges more sensible of its beauty.

The only Fellowship practically open to him then was the Oriel, for which, although sound scholarship was a requisite, the more special refinements of scholarship (such as Greek verse, etc.), which were necessary for the Balliol—the only other competition at that time open to Scotchmen—were not demanded. General intellectual promise and originality were looked for rather than either large or exact knowledge. Intellectual originality is a much better and more attractive thing than acquired knowledge or scholarship, if it could only be ascertained by as definite tests. Where there are two or three different kinds of original talent in the field, it becomes a matter of individual taste which should be preferred, and it is hardly possible that fortune should not have some share in deciding the issue. Shairp was unsuccessful in the competition; but it was known that some among the examiners, not the least qualified to estimate mental power, formed a very favourable opinion of his work.

It became necessary for him to decide on a profession. He never had any inclination, and probably not much aptitude, for the Bar. In many ways he would have made an admirable clergyman, and what he has written in his essay on Keble shows what attraction the beauty as well as the goodness which could be realised in the life of a country vicar had for him. But the English Church was not that in which he had been brought up; and with neither of the phases of opinion by which the men of most intellect and culture were then characterised—the new development of High Church doctrine, and the more advanced theology of the Broad Church—was he in perfect accord.

He went, I think, a certain length with the adherents of the Broad Church, and among his intimate friends were the men of most vivid imagination, and of the greatest speculative originality belonging to that school. Some of his other friends, with whom he may have talked more unreservedly on this subject than he was inclined to do with me, will probably say something about the grounds of his religious convictions, which continued henceforth very firm, and became the chief regulative power in his life. His nature was eminently conservative both in politics and religion, and his conservatism was based on feeling rather than on argument. He had more trust in what he had seen work for good on personal character, than he had expectation of good from novelties of opinion. Religion had never been presented to him in his childhood in a way to cloud his happiness, and it was associated with all that was dear to him in his home-life. I think it was to that simple belief, from which he had never gone far, that he returned. So far as he was influenced by doctrinal discussion, it was not to the writings of any English divines, but to the works of Dr. M'Leod Campbell and of his friend Mr. Erskine of Linlathen, that he seemed to feel his indebtedness. So far as my own relations with him were concerned, his religious convictions and his religious life seemed only to add greater seriousness, consistency, and hopefulness, to a character in all its human aspects noble and beautiful."

In his first long vacation, in the summer of 1840, Shairp, as already mentioned, went up from Oxford to London, intending to go on to Germany with two of his cousins, but on arriving in Town he found that they had gone. He thought he might proceed to the Continent after all by himself, but waited for orders from home before doing so, and meanwhile went down to Ipswich, whence, on the 8th June he wrote thus to his friend Henry Douglas—

" MY DEAR HENRY—Were I to give you a full, true, and particular account of all my sayings and doings since I left Scotland, I should have to write a book instead of a letter. I shall endeavour, however, to be brief though not ambiguous, comprehensive though not diffuse! I spent two days at Oxford, on one of which I passed my examination, which was somewhat more than I had anticipated. I slept at ' The Nigel,' but fed with my friends. None could be kinder than they were, especially Boyle.[1] . . . It is a queer place, quite unlike anything we have been accustomed to—I mean the colleges, their forms, etiquettes, etc. Ours is a very crack college, but one is scarcely prepared for the hauteur that many of the men, who consider themselves of the best style, assume. . . . When you come to Oxford I hope to act the same part by you that Boyle did by me. . . ."

A letter written to his sister from Balliol in November of the same year adds to Mr. Sellar's reminiscences, and gives Shairp's earliest estimate of Carlyle. From this letter

---

[1] Mr. John Boyle, son of Lord President Boyle, and stepbrother of the present Dean of Salisbury.

it will be seen that it had been a vision of his boyhood to become a gentleman sheep-farmer in Selkirkshire. : :

[Postmark, 1840.]

"BALLIOL COLLEGE, *18th November.*

"MY DEAREST BINNY—One's life here slips away so quietly, and with so few things to tell, especially to those who do not know the place and people, that it makes but a poor show in a letter. After preparing for lectures . . . I read a good deal, if I can find time, *in my own way and time.* My chief study just now is Carlyle's *Miscellanies,* which I have been extravagant enough to buy. These are a collection of all the papers he has written in the periodicals during these last ten years. There is one on Scott's life, very good and amusing, though not esteeming Scott highly enough, I think. . . . I have got hold of Pitscottie's *History of Scotland,* and am reading it. I shall bring down both these books with me when I come. . . . My sheep-farm vision in Selkirkshire has not yet left me, and I often turn to it in thought as to another Eden. It will be so much after my own heart, I think. Since I wrote last, I have never been on the river. I fear I am too lazy ever to make a boatman, besides I don't think any of us are *aquatic* animals. In the mornings after chapel, as I stand at my drawing-room table, I see the *pinks* flocking out to the 'meets' in all sorts of ways—go-carts, gigs, rover-hacks, etc.—and I cannot say it is always without a *secret pang.* The Christ Church and Trinity Fellows are those who most patronise the 'noble science,' being doubtless of opinion that at this 'seat of science' (as it is called) *this one* should by no means be left unstudied. Few Balliol men hunt, though some do, but I don't think we have any out-and-outers.

Some day soon, on St. Andrew's Day (whenever that may be), we are to have a Scotch dinner. I send you on the envelope a view of the boat-race, and Oxford spires in the distance. The handsome, self-satisfied youth on the right hand is a nobleman, or 'tuft,' as they are here called. That other on the left, perorating with uplifted arm, is a com-

moner.   There are several Eton fellows, freshmen, along
with me—nice enough men; and there is a man Byron, a
relation of the poet's, very handsome, a mixture of Johnny
Pringle and the Laird.   Tell Hetty this.   My society is
chiefly made up of those of recent standing, as by those who
have not known you before, nothing is in less esteem than
a 'freshman.'   But that is a fault that is always curing
itself.   How are ——?   Tell them I was 'speering' for
them.   The weather here is mirk, mirk (as the ballad says),
foggy and rainy—to-day making a feeble attempt to get up
some snow.   I suppose it is the same with you, and that
most of your day passes indoors now.—Yours ever affectionately,   J. C. SHAIRP."

Another letter from Oxford to his sister Grace may
follow the above—

[Postmark, 1841.]
                    "BALLIOL COLLEGE, *Wednesday, 2d June.*

"MY DEAR GRACE—. . . The Schools which I mentioned
in my last are over, and have told a tale, which has made
my hair stand on end.   Every one I know has been so wofully
disappointed.   Two of our scholars were in.   The Balliol
scholars are famous, Oxford over, for having been first classmen,
time out of mind, every one of them.   Of the two in this
time, one came out a second, the other a third; and one of
them has the reputation of being the best head Balliol has
had for years.   Poor Morton has only got a third; and this
is so little worth having, he might almost as well not have
gone into the schools.   This has made me quake, for he
was a better scholar far than I was when he left Glasgow,
and has read very steadily since he came here.   I am
almost shutting my books in despair.   If I wish to have
a chance of doing any good, I shall have to read seven hours
at least every day for the next two years and a half; and
such are the chances of war that, after all, it is very likely
to go for nothing.   I have been trying to put on the steam
of late more strongly than I did before.   This leaves me

little more to tell, for Herodotus and Aristotle are poor newsmongers. . . .

This is the time of the boat-races, which are considerable fun. All the colleges (not all, only nine, I think) have an eight oar in. They start in a long line, about fifty yards between each, at Iffley, a place a mile and a half down the river, and pull up to Oxford. When one boat 'bumps,' as it is called, the boat before it, it gets above that one. Therefore every one is trying all it can to catch the one ahead of it. The banks on each side are crowded, and then the bellowing of each college to its own boat is terrific. We are second lowest on the river, as our crew is nothing particular. Boyle pulls in it. . . .

[He describes 'Commemoration,' and the Duke of Wellington as Chancellor.] . . . I am in a very *sane* mood at present, as the Schools are beginning to throw their sobering shadow over me, even at this distance of time. But you need not expect from this that I will do anything in them. It is only feeling my deficiency in scholarship that makes me so alarmed, and in this I am sure to be floored. . . .—Your very affectionate brother, J. C. SHAIRP."

Again, in a letter from Portsmouth, August 1841, he refers to his friend Seymour's death, and to a sermon by Dr. (now Cardinal) Manning—

[Postmark, PORTSMOUTH, 22d *August* 1841.]

". . . We are all apt, after a very little time, to forget the dead. I hope I may not forget *him*. I have seldom, beyond my own family, met such loss as his, so true and steadfast. There was about him a purity which seemed quite unearthly. We, his remaining friends, are going to have a small monument raised to his memory in Balliol Chapel. . . .

On Sunday last (the Gunpowder Plot Day), Manning preached, and took occasion to speak strongly of Rome, as much as to say, 'Whatever others do, I have made up my mind not to go thither till she abjures her errors.' This has astonished and annoyed many of the strongest of the party, and they call him *Anglican.* Good-bye.—Your most affectionate brother,   J. C. SHAIRP."

The following undated letter was written to his eldest sister on the subject of Wordsworth's religion. It is a youthful letter, and possibly belongs to the year 1841, but it has an interest of its own :—

" What do I think of Wordsworth's religion ? A question easy to be asked, not so easy to be answered. You could not have asked me one that more interested me. The thing that people generally say is that he is *pantheistic.* Perhaps he is. You know how Carlyle answers the same charge made against Emerson : ' *Ists* and *isms* are rather becoming a weariness. Such a man does not readily rank himself under *isms.*' Now, without admitting this defence, there is no doubt that people mislead themselves by giving hard names to men and things, and then being alarmed by the name rather than the thing. There is, however, perhaps some little ground (I say it with great diffidence) for saying so of Wordsworth. If Pantheism means a forgetting the personality of God, a confusion between the Creator and creation, a thinking of God as ' a motive and a spirit that impels all thinking things, all objects of all thought, and rolls through all things,' rather than as the Father Almighty, there is something like this in many of his poems (see especially that one on *Tintern Abbey*). And yet it is the tendency more or less of all very imaginative minds, all at least who live in some strong belief of the Infinite and the Unseen, and who feel that what they see is but a veil to something deeper and truer underneath. It is the form that minds of naturally strong devotion take, when they try to represent to themselves God's infinity and omnipresence, and when they feel that all they see is divine. It is the tendency of minds of naturally high devotion, and is the highest form of the religion of Nature. But then Wordsworth had Revelation, and we cannot but wish he had brought in more

Christianity into his poems. The places where this is done most is his Ecclesiastical Sonnets. Still there is one thing never to be forgotten—that all Wordsworth's so-called Pantheism is unconscious. . . . There is a world of difference between a tendency unconsciously creeping in, and a belief consciously held and maintained. . . . One thing is striking. Almost all the best and most tender-hearted people I have ever known have loved Wordsworth. This shows how much more good there is in him than error. Few men's works, I believe, have ever gone deeper, and more impressed men's hearts. There is a large catholic charity in him—a charity not of word, but in deed and truth, such as I know not where else to find. The improvement he has made on the poetry of the age before him is his best defence. He teaches me to look on men, and all things, with a kind and loving heart, and with a deep faith in the goodness at the bottom of all things. He leads us far on the way, if he does not quite reach the haven of all Truth. No one ever yet read 'The Churchyard among the Mountains' with an understanding heart, and was not the better for it. Therefore read him, love him,   J. C. S."

CHAPTER V

MANY sketches of Shairp's undergraduate life at Oxford have reached me, from which I select only the most characteristic, although all are full of interest. Lord Coleridge's account of these years will be found in a subsequent chapter. The following is from Dr. Bradley, the present Dean of Westminster:—

"I feel most strongly the impossibility of reproducing, still more of adequately conveying to others, any faithful representation of one in many respects unlike any one else with whom I have lived in habitual intercourse. Shairp was of quite or nearly the same standing at the University as myself; but we were at different colleges, and only met occasionally in the rooms of common friends at Balliol. I have, however, a vivid recollection of the first time that I was in his company. It was in November 1840, when, as a freshman from Rugby, I was asked to join, after dining in my own college hall, a party—'a wine' in Oxford language—at A. H. Clough's. Clough was then living in lodgings, on the ground-floor of a small house, near Holywell Church, which I have often in later years pointed out to those who were interested in all connected with his memory. It was my first visit of the kind to one to whom I looked up even then with something more than ordinary schoolboy veneration; whose Rugby poems I knew largely by heart, and whose countenance, already familiar to me, though I had barely spoken to him,

E

still shines to me out of the distance as one of the most impressive, and, in a sense, of the most beautiful, that I have ever seen. I entered the room with a due feeling of youthful bashfulness. I can still recall the names and the very faces of some of the few guests whom I found there. Among them was a young scholar of Balliol, fresh from Eton as I was from Rugby, Seymour by name ; we sat, I remember, opposite each other, and were introduced by Clough, and I can still recall the impression made upon me by the striking and refined features and expressive face of one, who, a year before, had easily beaten a large field of candidates, myself included, and who looked, as I said to myself, fully worthy of his boyish reputation. He was the first of those who met that day to be taken ; his bright career was ended by an early death within a year or two of his coming to Oxford.[1] The other guests were Richard Congreve, Blackett of Merton, and I think I am right in saying Coleridge, the present Lord Chief-Justice, and one or two more. The conversation soon became general, and turned shortly to Wordsworth, and from him to S. T. Coleridge and the *Aids to Reflection.* By my side sat a somewhat large and strongly-built man, with a strong dash of Scottish accent, who seemed to me to be—it was a mere blunder of my own—but seemed to me to be considerably older than myself, and whom, indeed, I strangely fancied to be not an undergraduate but a visitor of Clough's. As the talk went on—not exactly in the direction to which I had thus far been accustomed at ordinary ' wines '— I remember my neighbour becoming extremely animated, and talking with such vehemence and gesticulation that my wine-glass was sent flying ; and I still can see him pausing for the moment, with perfect and unexpected grace, to apologise to me, and then plunging headlong into the now long-forgotten argument which he was maintaining against all comers. I was startled at hearing either that evening or the next morning that my neighbour was a Balliol man, a Scottish Exhibitioner from Glasgow University, scarcely older than

[1] See *Glen Desseray, etc.,* p. 216.

myself, and who, as I heard before the term was over, had already won a name, not only as full of enthusiasm and fire on his favourite subjects, but also in circles very different to that in which I had met him, as a hard rider. From that time, however, it was long before I met him again.   I had few acquaintances at Balliol during my first year, and at its close was non-resident, owing to a severe illness, for many months.   But after my return I met him from time to time in the rooms of Matthew Arnold, Theodore Walrond, and other friends.   I was much interested in his poem which gained the Newdigate in 1842 ; and I heard of him often, no more indeed as a riding-man, but as one greatly respected and liked in his own college, the writer of essays which won the special approval of the Master, and as one of the leaders of that energetic and able band of Scotsmen who have so often, I believe, in the history of Balliol acted, as they certainly did then, as links between the two societies of scholars and commoners.   We were both examined for our B.A. degrees at the same time, and some disappointment was felt by Shairp's friends at Balliol and elsewhere, among whom the opinion of his abilities and power of thought was exceedingly high, at his being placed in the second class.   It was accounted for, we always understood, by his deficiency of exact scholarship, and consequent inaccuracy of translation—especially of, if I rightly remember, the Greek and Latin poets, whose works were in those days included in the final examination. From after knowledge I can well believe that the laborious study of words and phrases, necessary to the mastery of so large a field of classical authors as was then exacted from candidates for honours, would have been exceedingly distasteful to him.   We met after this, as I said, from time to time, for we had many common friends.   I was always delighted to listen to his conversation, and we were, both of us, if I may so speak, prepared to be friends ourselves, if ever the opportunity should occur, without perhaps going much farther in our acquaintanceship than this."

The Dean of Westminster has referred to Shairp's competing

for and winning the Newdigate prize-poem in 1842. The subject was Charles XII., and as it was the earliest of his published verses, and is, as Mr. Sellar remarks, one of the few Newdigate poems that can be read with pleasure in after years, I give the synopsis, and a short extract from the poem itself.

CHARLES THE TWELFTH

A Prize Poem, recited in the Theatre, Oxford, 8th June 1842

SYNOPSIS

Charles in childhood—Charles after Pultowa—The contrast—The causes of the change—Scene in Pultowa—The evening after the battle described—Flight into Turkey—Sees the last remnants of his army taken by the Russians as he crosses the frontier stream—Feelings at this crisis—Heroic manner in which he afterwards bears his fall— Sustained by hopes of the future, and the remembrance of past glory— These remembrances described, including descent on Denmark, Narva, Passage of the Dwina—Field of Clissan on the morning of the battle, contrasted with its present aspect—The summit of his power—The Russian campaign—His overthrow as much the effect of the severe winter of 1705 as of the Czar's troops—His return to Sweden after long exile—Death before Frederickshall—Reflections.

The following is his description of the commanding form of Sweden's hero, as "the cloud-compeller of the rising storm":—

> So have I seen the cloud-rack fast and free
> Come thronging onward from the distant sea,
> Along the hilltops till the rising sheen
> Of morn had spread their parted roof between,
> And laughed away the masses dark and dull
> Into a radiance glad and beautiful.
>
> .   .   .   .   .   .
>
>   'Mid fallen potentates he stood
> Kingly, like Calpe, in his solitude,
> And earth lay hushed around him ; dark and vast
> His shadow fell, on many a nation cast ;
> It swept o'er humbled Denmark, eastward far
> It flung its terror o'er the haughty Czar :
> Behind him Poland low in ruins lay,
> Before him Austria crouching in dismay !
> And England, e'en thy chief of proudest fame
> Paused in the presence of a prouder name.

Again,

> Fair the awakening, fair the blush of bloom
> When springtime bursts on wintry months of gloom,
> And loud with song, and glad with sunlight thrills
> Far through the dark woods and the silent hills.
> Aye, fair the springtime, but who hath not seen
> More cloudless splendour, glory more serene
> Cast on the earth ? how brightly, briefly cast !
> When Autumn paused in love to look its last,
> Paused on the threshold of the western sky,
> Lingering at sunset as though loath to die ?

The most distinguished of Shairp's Oxford friends at this time was undoubtedly Arthur Hugh Clough, the poet who died with greater promise unfulfilled than any other Englishman since Keats. Clough was quite as interesting a man, as he was a poet; and Shairp's sketch of his friend, recorded in the brief Biography prefixed to the last edition of Clough's *Poems,* is one of the best of his many character-studies. I quote only one or two passages, that bear upon their common life and interests :—

"It was toward the end of 1840 that I first saw A. H. Clough. As a freshman I looked with respect, approaching to awe, on the senior scholar of whom I had heard so much, stepping out on Sunday mornings to read the first lesson in Balliol Chapel. How clearly I remember his massive figure, in scholar's surplice, standing before the brass eagle, and his deep feeling tones, as he read some chapter from the Hebrew prophets. At that time he was the eldest, and every way the first of a remarkable band of scholars. The younger undergraduates felt towards him a distant reverence, as a lofty and profound nature quite above themselves, whom they could not quite make out, but who was sure to be some day great. Profaner spirits, nearer his own standing, sometimes made a joke of his then exceeding silence and reserve, and of his unworldly ways. But as he was out of college rooms, and reading hard for his degree, we freshmen only heard of his reputation from a distance, and seldom came in contact with him.

It must have been early in 1841 that he first asked me to breakfast with him. He was then living in a small cottage, or cottage-like house, standing by itself, a little apart from Holywell. There he used to bathe every morning all the winter through, in the cold Holywell baths, and read hard all day. There were one or two other freshmen there at breakfast. If I remember right, none of the party were very talkative.

I have heard that about that time he wrote one day in fun an oracle, in the style of Herodotus, to his brother scholar, who was reading like himself for the Schools. The Greek I forget ; the translation he sent with it ran something like this—

> Whereas —— of Lancashire
> Shall in the Schools preside,
> And Wynter[1] to St. Mary's go,
> With the pokers by his side ;
> Two scholars there of Balliol,
> Who on double firsts had reckoned,
> Between them two shall with much ado
> Scarce get a double second.

This turned out only too true an oracle. Since the beginning of class-lists, the succession of firsts among the Balliol scholars was unbroken. And few Balliol scholars had equalled, none ever surpassed, Clough's reputation. I well remember going, towards the end of May or beginning of June, with one of the scholars of my own standing, to the school quadrangle to hear the class-list read out, and neither of our scholars appeared in the first class. We rushed to Balliol, and announced it to the younger Fellows who were standing at their open window. Many causes were assigned at this time for the failure—some in the examiners, some in Clough's then state of spirits ; but whatever the cause, I think the result for some years shook faith in firsts among Clough's contemporaries. It made a great impression upon others ; on himself I fancy it made but little. I never heard him afterwards allude to it as a thing of any consequence. He once told me he was sick of contentions for prizes and honours before he left Rugby. . . .

In the November of the same year he tried for a Balliol Fellowship, but was not successful. Tait,[2] however, was strong in his favour, and, I believe, some other of the Fellows. I remember one of them telling me at the time that a character of Saul which Clough wrote in that examination was, I think he said, the best, most original thing he had ever seen written in any examination. But Oriel had at that time a way of finding out original genius better than either Balliol or the Schools. In the spring of 1842 Arthur Hugh Clough was elected Fellow of Oriel, the last examination, I believe, in which Newman took part.

The announcement of that success I remember well. It was on the Friday morning of the Easter week of that year. The examination was finished on the Thursday evening. I had asked Clough and another friend, who was a candidate at the same time, to breakfast

---

[1] Head of St. John's College, and at that time Vice-Chancellor.

[2] Afterwards Archbishop of Canterbury, at that time Fellow and Tutor of Balliol College.

with me on the Friday morning, as their work was just over. Most
of the scholars of the College were staying up and came to breakfast
too. The party consisted of about a dozen. We had little notion that
anything about the examination would be known as soon, and were
all sitting quietly, having finished breakfast, but not yet risen from
the table. The door opened wide; entered a Fellow from another college,
and drawing himself up to his full height, he addressed the other
candidate : ' I am sorry to say you have *not* got it.' Then, 'Clough,
you have ; ' and stepping forward into the middle of the room, held
out his hand, with ' Allow me to congratulate you.' We were all so
little thinking of the Fellowship, and so taken aback by this formal
announcement, that it was some little time before we knew what it
was all about. The first thing that recalled my presence of mind was
seeing the delight on the face of Clough's younger brother who was
present." [1]

The long vacation of 1842 was spent by Shairp with
a reading-party in Wales, when he and Clough again
met.

" In the summer of 1842, while I was reading in a retired part of
Wales with two or three others, Clough, then wandering through the
Welsh mountains, one morning looked in on us. I took a walk with him,
and he at once led me up Moël Wyn, the highest mountain within reach.
Two things I remember that day—one, that he spoke a good deal (for
him) of Dr. Arnold, whose death had happened only a few weeks before ;
another, that a storm came down upon the mountain when we were
half-way up. In the midst of it we lay for some time close above a
small mountain tarn, and watched the storm-wind working on the face
of the lake, tearing and torturing the water into most fantastic, almost
ghostly shapes, the like of which I never saw. before or since. These
mountain sights, though he did not say much, he used to eye most
observantly." [2]

There are two pictures of undergraduate life at Oxford
written by Shairp, which give a better idea of the influences
under which he came at the University than any record by
his friends. The first is contained in his essay on Keble,
contributed to *The North British Review*, and afterwards published in his volume of *Essays*. The second is a paper written
at Rugby, describing the difference between undergraduate
life at the English and the Scottish Universities. The former
may be fitly preceded, however, by some of the reminiscences

[1] *Reminiscences of A. H. Clough*, pp. 19-23.   [2] *Ibid.*, p. 23.

which the present Dean of Salisbury has sent me,[1] and the latter will be found in the Appendix to this volume.

"In the year 1838 I first saw Shairp. He was then at Glasgow University, and was the intimate friend of some of my family. One of them was afterwards a fellow exhibitioner at Balliol, and the intimacy continued without a break until the close of Shairp's life. I was reading for the first time the *Lay of the Last Minstrel*, and I shall never forget the glow of enthusiasm with which Shairp read aloud the wonderful night-scene in Melrose Abbey. He spoke, too, on that occasion, of the beauty of some of the old Scottish Ballads, and I remember well how I saved pocket-money in order to become the possessor of a copy of Robert Chambers's *Ballads of Scotland*, and rejoiced to find in 'Kinmont Willie' and 'The Dowie Dens of Yarrow' the very stanzas that had struck me so much in his recitation. It was fortunate for me that whenever he came to my father's house he would ask what I had lately read, and many a useful hint have I had from him during the time when, under the leadership of Norman Macleod, he was making acquaintance for the first time with Wordsworth, Lamb, and Keats. . . .

What always struck me, young as I was, was his loyal devotion to his friends, and his desire to show the full weight of his intellectual obligation to them. During the next ten years of my life, Shairp was often a guest at my father's country-house in Ayrshire, and his visits were indeed to me golden days. I went to an English public school at the time when he was an undergraduate at Oxford, and as he knew some of those who had passed from Charterhouse to the University, he admitted me to great intimacy and told me much of the Oxford I was soon to see for myself. During one of these visits I remember well how, when in company with several others, we had

---

[1] Dean Boyle wrote a very appreciative notice *in memoriam* of Shairp in *The Guardian* of 30th September 1885. I use his valuable paper of reminiscences in the same way as Professor Sellar's, dividing it into sections. A sequel to the present extract will be given later on.

passed an afternoon amongst the woods of Auchans, and
suddenly came in sight of the Firth of Clyde, with the
peaks of Arran purpling across it in the afternoon sunshine,
—it was shortly after the publication of the two volumes
which fixed Lord Tennyson's place as a poet—Shairp repeated the well-known· lines 'Break, Break,' with indescribable fervour, and on the way home introduced us to
some of the more prominent poems, *Dora, The Lord of
Burleigh,* and *Locksley Hall,* by repeating snatches as he
could recall them.   He had at that time begun to know
Arthur Stanley and Clough well, and their names were
often on his lips.   But as my great interest at that time
centred in the sayings and doings of the Oxford school, I
listened with the deepest interest to his account of the
wonderful sermons at St. Mary's, and all that he had to tell
of Oakeley and Ward, at that time Fellows of Balliol.   I
remember well how I was struck with the fact, that although
he took great interest in Oxford, his old tastes and companions had still a vigorous hold upon him, and he used to
declare that he thought men who came up to Oxford from
Eton and Rugby could not appreciate it so fully as those who,
like himself, had gone through the Glasgow course.   He
contended that although men might be better scholars than
those who had sat under Ramsay and Lushington, they often
lacked a taste for the literary element of the classics.   He impressed on myself the need of diligent and accurate scholarship,
however, and owned his deficiencies in a way which ought
to have benefited me more.   Shortly before I went to
Oxford, I had read with intense interest Carlyle's *French
Revolution.*   Shairp thought that I was in danger of delivering myself entirely to the influence of the great Thomas.   He
was going to the station on foot, and he asked me to walk
with him there.   During the whole of the three-mile walk
he poured into my ear his conclusions as to Carlyle's teaching.   He talked much of Clough, and said that he believed
that Carlyle and Newman had contended, as it were, for possession of his mind, and so besought me not to read Carlyle
exclusively, but to devote all my energy to Roman

history, and especially to Arnold's three volumes. I can safely say that his advice was not thrown away. I am afraid that until this time I had thought with something like contempt of Wordsworth. But my reverence and feeling for Shairp was so great that I began to read Wordsworth for myself, and soon found that I had acquired a new pleasure in life. From Shairp, who had passed a considerable part of one long vacation at the Lakes, I heard so much of the charms of the region that I soon resolved to make acquaintance with it, and it was owing to Shairp's introduction to the singular man of genius, Hartley Coleridge, that I spent a whole Sunday afternoon with him, enjoying such a treat as Hartley in his better moments alone could give."

The account which Shairp gives, in his essay on Keble, of this great religious movement at Oxford, as he knew it, and was influenced by it—the movement of which Newman, with many notable men as coadjutors and allies, was the inspiration and the guide—is one of the best records we have of that remarkable phase in the religious life of England. In his poem, *Balliol Scholars : A Remembrance* he writes thus of the central influence of the time—

> The voice that weekly from St. Mary's spake,
> 　As from the unseen world oracular,
> Strong as another Wesley, to re-wake
> 　The sluggish heart of England, near and far,
> Voice so intense to win men, or repel,
> Piercing yet tender, on our spirits fell,
> 　Making them other, higher than they were.

The following are extracts from the essay on Keble—

" The movement when at its height extended its influence far beyond the circle of those who directly adopted its views. There was not, in Oxford at least, a reading-man who was not more or less indirectly influenced by it. Only the very idle or the very frivolous were strictly proof against it. On all others it impressed a sobriety of conduct and a seriousness not usually found among large bodies of young men. It raised the tone of average morality in Oxford to a level which perhaps it had never before reached. You may call it overwrought and too highly strung. Perhaps it was. It was better, however, for young men to be so than to be doubters or cynics.

If such was the general aspect of Oxford society at that time, where was the centre and soul from which so mighty a power emanated ? It lay, and had for some years lain, mainly in one man—a man in many ways the most remarkable that England has seen during this century, perhaps the most remarkable whom the English Church has produced in any century,—John Henry Newman.

The influence he had gained, apparently without setting himself to seek it, was something altogether unlike anything else in our time. A mysterious veneration had by degrees gathered round him, till now it was almost as though some Ambrose or Augustine of elder ages had reappeared. He himself tells how one day, when he was an undergraduate, a friend, with whom he was walking in the Oxford street, cried out eagerly, 'There's Keble !' and with what awe he looked at him ! A few years, and the same took place with regard to himself. In Oriel Lane, light-hearted undergraduates would drop their voices and whisper 'There's Newman !' when, head thrust forward, and gaze fixed as though on some vision seen only by himself, with swift noiseless step, he glided by. Awe fell on them for a moment, almost as if it had been some apparition that had passed. For his inner circle of friends, many of them younger men, he was said to have a quite romantic affection, which they returned with the most ardent devotion and the intensest faith in him. But to the outer world he was a mystery. What were the qualities that inspired these feelings ? There was, of course, learning and refinement, there was genius, not indeed of a philosopher, but of a subtle and original thinker, an unequalled edge of dialectic, and these all glorified by the imagination of a poet. Then there was the utter unworldliness, the setting at nought of all things which men most prize, the tamelessness of soul which was ready to essay the impossible. Men felt that here was—

> One of that small transfigured band
> Which the world cannot tame.

It was this mysteriousness which, beyond all his gifts of head and heart, so strangely fascinated and overawed,—that something about him which made it impossible to reckon his course and take his bearings,—that soul-hunger and quenchless yearning which nothing short of the Eternal could satisfy.

.   .   .   .

The look and bearing of the preacher were as of one who dwelt apart, who, though he knew his age well, did not live in it. From his seclusion of study, and abstinence, and prayer, from habitual dwelling in the unseen, he seemed to come forth that one day of the week to speak to others of the things he had seen and known.

.   .   .   .

The local, the temporary, and the modern, were ennobled by the presence of the catholic church belonging to all ages that pervaded the whole. His power showed itself chiefly in the new and unlooked-for

way in which he touched into life old truths, moral or spiritual, which
all Christians acknowledge, but most have ceased to feel.

.   .   .   .

As he spoke, how the old truth became new ! how it came home
with a meaning never felt before ! He laid his finger—how gently,
yet how powerfully !—on some inner place in the hearer's heart,
and told him things about himself he had never known till then.
Subtlest truths, which it would have taken philosophers pages of cir-
cumlocution and big words to state, were dropt out by the way in a
sentence or two of the most transparent Saxon. What delicacy of
style, yet what calm power ! how gentle, yet how strong ! how simple,
yet how suggestive ! how homely, yet how refined ! how penetrating,
yet how tender-hearted !

.   .   .   .

To call these sermons eloquent would be no word for them ; high
poems they rather were, as of an inspired singer, or the outpourings as
of a prophet, rapt yet self-possessed.   And the tone of voice in which
they were spoken, once you grew accustomed to it, sounded like a fine
strain of unearthly music.   Through the stillness of that high Gothic
building the words fell on the ear like the measured drippings of water
in some vast, dim cave.   After hearing these sermons you might come
away still not believing the tenets peculiar to the High Church system ;
but you would be harder than most men, if you did not feel more
than ever ashamed of coarseness, selfishness, worldliness, if you did not
feel the things of faith brought closer to the soul.

.   .   .   .

On these things, looking over an interval of five and twenty years,
how vividly comes back the remembrance of the aching blank, the
awful pause, which fell on Oxford when that voice had ceased, and we
knew that we should hear it no more.   It was as when, to one kneeling
by night in the silence of some vast cathedral, the great bell tolling
solemnly overhead has suddenly gone still.

.   .   .   .

Polemics by themselves are dreary work.   They do not touch the
springs of young hearts.   But he who, in the midst of any line of
thought, unlocks a fountain of genuine poetry, does more to harmonise
it, and win for it a way to men's affections, than he who writes a
hundred volumes, however able, of controversy." [1]

Though written several years afterwards, two letters referring to this article on Keble may here find an appropriate
place.   The first is from Cardinal Newman to the Publisher
and Editor of the *Review*, and the second from Dean Stanley
to Shairp himself :

[1] " Keble," in *Studies in Poetry and Philosophy*, pp. 244-257.

"THE ORATORY, BIRMINGHAM,
"*14th September* 1866.

"DEAR SIR—On my return from abroad I found on my table your letter and the September number of *The North British Review,* and I have read, I need scarcely tell you, with extreme interest, the article on Mr. Keble, to which you direct my attention.

I feel very grateful 'to a reviewer, as the writer of it, who describes with so much real sympathy and truth the characteristics of a religious movement, of which, naturally, I have such vivid recollections, and such affectionate though mournful remembrances.

And it is an extreme pleasure to read a critique on *The Christian Year* which speaks with such depth and exactness, both of the work itself, and of the character of its author.

As to what the writer says of me, I wish I deserved only half the praise he gives me; but still I cannot help being gratified at it, though I am not quite pleased with myself for being so.   Anyhow I can thank him for what is more than kind, though I do not feel it right to appropriate it.—I am, dear sir, very faithfully yours,

JOHN H. NEWMAN.

David Douglas, Esq."

"DEANERY, WESTMINSTER,
"19th *December* 1866.

"MY DEAR SHAIRP—Once more a few words to thank you for your Keble, which I had read before, but less attentively. Most deeply do I sympathise with most of it; fain would I with all of it.   Yet, as I read it, a melancholy feeling crosses me. 'How is the fine gold become dim!' Is it in me? or in them?   Is it that Keble and Newman have degenerated to the narrow partisanship of the modern High Church leaders, with their worldly polemics, and their bitter personalities? or that I have changed, and see only these, where once I saw the grace and beauty which you so well describe? Is it that I myself have become more narrow-minded? or

that there is something more supernatural in Cotton's un-
tiring desire to go about doing good, or in Church's calm
moderation, or in Temple's unwearying unhasting labour,
than in ———'s asceticism, or ———'s attacks on Colenso,
or ———'s eagerness for proselytes ?   Or was there nothing
of the earth, earthy, in Keble's repudiation of Arnold's friendship ? or Newman's attack on Hampden ? or was there
nothing of immortal birth in Arnold or in Robertson, in
Clough, or in the catholic spirits that I have known and
loved in other lands ?   These are sad thoughts, but I would
suggest one point in which you have done injustice to *The
Christian Year*, it seems to me.   Besides these four points,[1]
it has a real openness of mind for the whole large view of
the Church and world, quite unlike the later development
of the party, or unlike the earlier religious part.   It is what
I have omitted in the Preface to my second volume of
Lectures on the Jewish Church.   You have just glanced
at it, in speaking of 'the glorious sky,' etc.—Farewell, ever
yours truly,   A. P. STANLEY."

In connection with this letter, Shairp's appreciation of
The Christian Year should be mentioned.   He found intense
delight in it, and frequently perused it up to the very end
of his life.

---

[1] (1) "Religious feeling ;" (2) "Home feeling ;" (3) "Reserve ;" (4
"Descriptions of Nature," referred to in Shairp's essay on Keble.

CHAPTER VI

THE summer of 1843 was spent with a reading-party at Grasmere. In the party were Henry Douglas, and T. D. Harford Battersby, afterwards incumbent of St. John's, Keswick, and Canon of Carlisle. They lived in the farmhouse at Pavement End, close by Grasmere Lake. It belonged to the family of Greens, who are mentioned in the seventh book of *The Excursion*. Arthur Clough lived in a lodging hard by, to the west of Grasmere Church.

Three of Shairp's letters to the home circle at Houstoun give a vivid picture of these months at Grasmere :

[Postmark, *8th July* 1843.]

" AMBLESIDE, *Friday.*

" MY DEAR BINNY—As you are the only one of the family who has seen these places, you will be able to explain all the localities to the rest.

We reached this on Tuesday by mid-day, and immediately set out lodging-hunting. A lovely day, and as lovely a walk along Rydal Lake, past Wordsworth's. (By the bye, I hope it may not be with him as it was with Sir Robert Peel. You remember I used to say I never could admire him after I had seen him—especially seen him eat! So, though there is not much chance of our ever being admitted to see the Lion of the Lakes at feeding-time, yet when you see his little villa and his one-horse shay, and all that sort of thing, you begin to discover, ' Well, after all, he is only a man '.)

But to return — we walked on to Grasmere, about five miles hence, to see some lodgings we were told of. By chance we inquired of an old farmer standing at his gate, where the said lodgings were, and on getting into a crack with him, we found out that he had a large house, and few in it, so that he would not be loath to lodge us himself. This seemed promising, so we inspected the rooms; found he could give us five bedrooms and two sitting. We asked him what he would charge; and after retiring for a while, he and his wife returned, and offered to do everything for us for 30s. a week each (bed and board included). We snatched at the offer. The only obstacle in the way was that he had made an offer to some people at a distance, and we could not get a decisive answer till Thursday morning. Wednesday we employed in walking to Patterdale, at the head of Ullswater, ten miles hence, through the Pass of Kirkstone — very steep. We took a boat and pulled down the lake as far as Airey Force. You were there, if I remember right — a most sweet, delicate fall, is it not? Then, dined at Patterdale, and walked home the first part of our journey — thundering fearfully, and lightning whizzing immediately under our noses. Got home here very late, and I, for one, quite done. You know how bad a walker I am, and my condition at present is very bad.

Yesterday morning concluded the bargain, and to-day we enter on possession. I hope we are very fortunate. Grasmere is a most charming retirement. (By the bye, I am not *half* so fond of solitude, as I once fancied I was.) The farmer is well-to-do in the world, so I daresay will provide for our creature comforts well enough. The house is close by the lake, and we have a boat at our disposal. Douglas and Proby (an Irishman, but brought up in England) are here. Willock, who was with us in Wales, we met the first day we were here; and he has gone about with us ever since. He is on his way to Scotland. . . . Battersby joins us from town, I hope to-day or to-morrow, and Lawley from Yorkshire on the 11th. To-morrow I hope to fall

to, to the work, and I do hope these three months may be
of great use to me. . . .

It was bitter, bitter, leaving my rooms, and at the beginning of long vacation there is always one or more I am
sorry to say good-bye to. You know that Macintosh
visited me the last few days I was in Oxford. He is going
into the Scotch Free Church. I wish he had been at Oxford
these last two years, instead of Cambridge. Did I ever
mention Coleridge, one of our scholars? They have elected
him Fellow of Exeter. Certainly they have contrived to
pick up some of the pleasantest men going for their common
room. . . .—Your very affectionate brother,

J. C. SHAIRP."

[Postmark, *August* 1843.]

" GRASMERE, *Monday* 14.

" MY DEAR GRACE— . . . And now let me see what
I have been doing since I last wrote. Yes, on Saturday
week four of us set off for the top of the Langdale Pikes ;—
there are two of them—the 'two lusty twins' described
in the second book of *The Excursion* as making such many-
toned music. I had my Wordsworth with me. By reading
the description of the Solitary's dwelling, and having got
a few directions before, we made out the place exactly.
Nothing could be more perfect than the description. We
had scarcely got up when a storm came down upon us from
the higher hills. We soon bolted down, but such a soaking
I never got before. Marriott came on Tuesday afternoon.
Till that day the weather, for more than a fortnight, had
been very wretched. As a son of Coleridge's, who was
here, said, "He did not know whether it is true that 'the
king never dies,' but certainly the rain never ends." However, on Tuesday evening, it did end. On Wednesday
morning Douglas, Marriott, and I set off for Keswick. It
was

One of those heavenly days which cannot die.

We rowed down Derwent Water, or rather to the beginning
of Borrowdale. I am not sure whether I like this, or the

F

head of Ullswater best; this, perhaps—but then, the day !
it was such as you may live a lifetime without seeing
another like it. We walked up Borrowdale for six miles,
through the finest scenery I have seen in the Lakes.
Borrowdale runs up from Derwent Water to Wast Water,
twelve miles, and at its head are all the highest and wildest
hills in this country. I was very anxious to go and stay
all night near Wast Water, and go up Scawfell Pike, the
highest hill in England; but Marriott, who is not very
strong, did not like to stay out all night. So we turned
off to the side, after going half-way up Borrowdale, and
walked eight miles home, across the hills, without a path.
Just as we reached the highest part of our walk we stopped
on the hillside and saw the sun go down behind the multitude of mountains crowded before us. I do not remember
to have seen anything like this. It was beyond words.
I stayed a little after the others. Close opposite was the
hill with the fine name, so that I in very deed

> Lay and listened to the mountain flood,
> Murmuring from Glaramara's inmost caves.

Then, as we walked down Easdale, we had the full moon to
light up our way.

On Thursday Marriott, Lawley, and I walked over
to Patterdale by a short way through the hills. The
day was nearly as fine as the other. We rowed four
miles down the lake to Airey Force. On the way we
read the story about it out of the little Wordsworth Hetty
gave me; and, tell her, I gathered some flowers close by the
fall and put them in the book. After dining we returned,
not as we came, but over Helvellyn. On the top we saw
into Scotland, and the Mull of Galloway; and just below,
the hill where the man died thirty-six years ago, about
whom Scott and Wordsworth wrote each a poem; Scott's
much the best, I think.[1] I forgot, till after I had left it,
that once Scott, Wordsworth, and Sir Humphry Davy had
been there together. In one of his last poems Wordsworth,
speaking of Scott, mentions it—

[1] He altered this judgment afterwards.

Old Helvellyn's brow,
Where once together in his day of strength
We stood rejoicing, as if earth were free
From sorrow, like the sky above our heads.

But now for a catastrophe! The cold on the top seized Marriott, and then we drank largely of a well-head up there——the coldest I ever met with. M—— could scarcely walk; he lay down every yard and wanted to be left alone. Lawley and I of course would not allow this. So we forced him on, supporting him by each arm, and after much ado, and a great fright, by dint of a brandy bottle Lawley had, and by frequent rests, we got him down to a small public at the foot of the hill, Wythburn by name. There we got a conveyance for him, and brought him home quite exhausted. Next morning he was better, and left us. On Sunday Henry Douglas and I walked to Wythburn Church, a small humble one at the foot of Helvellyn, by the way-side. It was quite touching, the simplicity of it. How many people, do you think, were there? Three men, three women, and thirteen children, besides the parson. I never saw so small a church in Scotland. The clergyman had to act as his own clerk. It was almost a case of 'Dearly beloved Roger'—a clergyman whose whole congregation consisted of himself and clerk, and who would not begin the exhortation with 'Dearly beloved brethren.' . . . It is quite melancholy to think of these golden days being in the fells, and our being obliged to stick to in the house. [Speaks of his desire that the whole family should spend a summer there 'before we are all too old.'] . . . Don't think I am getting too sentimental. I am quite sane, I assure you. . . .—Your affectionate brother, J. C. SHAIRP."

To Miss E. B. SHAIRP.

[Postmark, 19th September 1843.]

"GRASMERE.

"MY DEAREST BINNY—This is Sunday, but I am not in church. I have sprained my ankle. It was leaping over

a hedge by the house I got it. . . . It keeps me from our
delicious walks when they are now not far from an end.
So I grudge it excessively. As I lie here on the bed, I can
see one outlying ridge of Fairfield, which forms one of the
sides of our valley, and I have been amusing myself all
morning with watching the comings and goings of the
lights upon it. Mrs. Green, our hostess, has been more
attentive and kind than I could have expected. I shall be
quite ashamed to leave without making her some present;
what do you advise? Do you think one of those fine plaid
or tartan shawls would be very expensive? If not, I should
like one sent. . . . It is quite a pleasure to live with
such people. John Green is one of the most respected
farmers in all this vale. In this country the valleys are
almost all originally held by what are called 'statesmen,'
something like Scotch Bonnet Lairds. There were very
few large estates, but almost every householder had a piece
of land in the valley, enough to grow hay for the sheep in
winter. Every one who has such a piece has a right to
turn out his sheep on the hills, which are called 'common.'
In many places this primitive state of things—this 'more
natural and righteous division of land,' as I have heard it
called—is more or less done away, but in Grasmere there
remain as many 'statesmen' as in most places. Our host
is one of these, only he and his fathers before him have, by
care and thrift, considerably increased their property. They
are very · well to do in the world, and are yet as unpre-
tending as the poorest. In the second part of 'The Churchyard among the Mountains' you will see about 'another
Margaret Green is come to Gold-rill side.' This was
a young sister of John Green; and he is one of the
'Seven lusty Brethren' mentioned there. 'Gold-rill side' is
the poetical name of our abode, which in plain prose is
'Pavement End!' . . . I fear I shall not be able to walk
for a week yet. The hills are changing colour now, but
this is about their finest time. Such weather as we have
been having—not a day anything else than lovely. We
have all become very well acquainted with this country,

though, had we had less reading, we should have had more
time to be out at all seasons, and know the hills at all
hours thoroughly, as they deserve to be known—no
time one goes out he sees something he has not
noticed before. Whenever I am out, I cannot help
thinking how you all would enjoy this country, for I think
you enter more truly into these things than most. The
way to enjoy them thoroughly is to live among them, not
to *tour*, though of course this last is better than nothing.
I often feel as if I could stay a day at each spot. . . .
Wordsworth, I suppose, is extensively devoured now that
Hetty has got it. Read the ode called *Intimations of
Immortality*. Don't mind if you do not quite make it all
out—only read it. It is one of the highest things which
human tongue ever uttered. To-day, from Mrs. Green,
I have been hearing the history of several of the characters
mentioned in 'The Churchyard.' The churchyard you
know is chiefly taken from *our* churchyard.

   .   .   .   .

    I have been lying on the grass by the house all after-
noon till the stars came out, and the owls were holloaing
from the hills. I have just this moment come in. It is
wonderful what enjoyment there is even in that, with such
an amphitheatre to gaze on. I do wish you all, or some
at least, were here for a time. Couldn't you come and
be with me the last week? They will all be gone except
me. I remain till the end, read for the next three weeks
uninterruptedly, and then hope to have a day or two for
rambling before going back to flat, ugly Oxford. A——
is quite right. It is a poor thing not to let loose one's
enjoyment on places worthy of it, because they are not
your own—a niggard, coward thing. Therefore be it far
from us. Lady Farquhar, Mr. Hamilton's widow, has been
living all summer, with an old lady, close by this. We do
not know them. The Poet is out of the county, in Hereford-
shire. I do not know whether he returns before we go. Proby
and Battersby went yesterday to spend the day at Hawes-
water, and return to-morrow. Lawley leaves us this week.

Most of the others, if not all, will be gone by the beginning
of October. Now write me a long letter. All blessed
thoughts be with you.—Your most affectionate brother,

J. C. SHAIRP."

The following letter, also written by Shairp at Grasmere, was to his friend, J. Billingsby Seymour, who was then
at Venice :—

"GRASMERE, 25th *September* 1843.

"MY DEAR SEYMOUR—It was delightful to see your
hand once more. All summer long I have been looking for
it, so you may guess how welcome your letter was when it
did arrive. Often at the beginning of last month I thought
of that Balliol band, collected under the shadow of the
Alps, for I had heard both from Fox and Constantine of
the expected gathering at Milan. I trust it did come to
pass. If I could but have looked in on you for *one* hour
only! You say you have had times, and high moments,
when you wished me by your side. It is no mere *tu
quoque* if I say the same. Yes, Seymour, I have passed
such a summer, in such a dear retreat! Do not laugh at
me when you compare Westmorland with Switzerland, for
I think there is here enough to satisfy the cravings of any
soul that truly loves Nature. Mine it certainly has satisfied.

It is so very delightful to settle down in a place and
see it and its neighbouring retirements in all moods and at
all hours. There is something unsatisfying, I always think,
in travelling for once only through a very beautiful or grand
country. There are so many spots, and single views, which
you could brood over for at least a day, that you cannot take
them in, you pass on unsatisfied. As it is—with all the
opportunities which evening after evening has given me—I
feel as if I had but touched the draught *summis labris*. There
is a something about these dales, when twilight has filled
them, and taken away all their outstanding lineaments, and
when the more distant hilltops are standing out against the
golden west, entranced as it were, and pondering, you would

almost think, on the mysteries that have been, or the mysteries yet to be, there is something then that I cannot get at—something that disturbs me with its depth of meaning. I know I am χωριστός as ever. I cannot explain myself, but it is something real which I hint at, and you may perhaps guess what I mean. But, to be sober, we have all, I think, been very happy, and I go from this country loving it with an exceeding love.

No one can know how true Wordsworth is till they have been here. He is, as it were, the true utterance of these hills —their very voice. I have seen him, but have not been introduced, though I should have liked it had it come easily and naturally. I did not make any exertions to be so. By the end of this week our party will have broken up, and be all gone save myself. I stay for a fortnight, and Clough remains with me for a week, to finish some work. You will be astonished, perhaps shocked, when I tell you my summer's work. I have read all my Sophocles, all my Æschylus, and hope to finish Thucydides for good—history and all. This, with a little Butler, makes good my summer's work. 'The Slows' are my bane, but I must be courageous and face what remains. My hopes are not high. If I could but secure a *second*, I should be happy; and if not, what then? Why, I don't think it will break my heart; for, to tell the truth, I fancy that I am getting marvellously indifferent to school reputation. You know I have always looked on it in no higher light than a mercantile speculation. It might advance my worldly interests, and this would be my chief pleasure in success. I do not mean to say that the συμφέρον is the only motive one has to work for. Every one has a duty for every day and every month, and ours, I suppose, is to work for the Schools; but viewed in the light which many regard it, and which the Oxford tone and system fosters, it is a very puny thing. I agree with you, life is larger than the Schools. They are not the end. There is 'an ampler ether, a diviner air.'

You have heard C. E. P.[1] speak of Hartley Cole-

---

[1] Constantine E. Prichard.

ridge, eldest son of the poet. We know him and have seen a good deal of him. You knew perhaps of his habits, which have been his bane. It is lamentable to see such genius so trampled under foot. His conversation— rather his discourse—is at times wonderful. I have heard him, when in the genial mood, roll forth his thoughts on poetry, philosophy, life, and all high things—thoughts such as you would in vain look for in any books, and which, if one would only remember them, are very precious. At other times inimitably comical and amusing, though of course you cannot always get him in either of these moods. He might do anything he liked in the way of literature, if he would but work, but instead of that he wanders about the country, and does nothing. He tells me that he is preparing some things for the press—whether they will ever see the light I should think very doubtful. By the bye, I wish you, when you write me, to give me what you think of Romanism as you have seen it in men's lives. Tell me this, for it is so much the fashion nowadays to praise it up at the expense of Protestantism one's old feelings are quite shocked.

Do you know, Seymour, I wish very much you would come home and take a degree without minding the Class Schools? I think it would take such a weight off your mind, and then, as to Fellowships, etc. etc., you need not be alarmed about that. Look at Coleridge; by the bye, what gain it was having him up another year; but you have, I doubt not, settled all about this with Constantine the Great. I have just heard that Newman has resigned St. Mary's.

Only fancy, next term I return, not to my dear old rooms, but to lodgings—Mason's—if you know where they are. I daresay I shall have some dreary enough days in them before all is over, which would I had you with me to relieve! All our party go the end of this week. I remain and read a week, and then have, I hope, a few days to ramble about among the more solitary of these hills which I have not yet seen. I do hope this is not my last sojourn here.

Since I wrote the beginning of this letter last night Hartley Coleridge has been here, and I heard him talk alone for a quarter of an hour about Shakespeare. It was worth all the commentaries and essays on him I ever saw, but it is always somewhat painful to hear him. *Punch* says in his latest intelligence from Oxford, ' The thermometer has taken a very high degree ! ' Write to me soon to Oxford, and tell me all about yourself. I don't at all hail the beginning of term except for seeing one's friends again, from whom I hope to hear all about you. Their society and news of you will tend to console me for exchanging this pleasant land for ugly Oxford. I must not cross this, or you will not be able to read it. Excuse me for having been more egotistical than usual, and believe me, ever your affectionate friend,   J. C. SHAIRP."

As Seymour was one of the " Balliol Scholars " commemorated in Shairp's poem, an extract from a letter written to Shairp by Constantine Prichard, another of these scholars, and an intimate mutual friend, after Seymour's death, may here be given—

"Who, like him, could rejoice when we were glad, and be sorry with our sorrow, and feel with and for us in whatever we were engaged ? . . . How remarkable in him that perception of all laughable things in persons, manners, and characters, without being joined to the slightest disposition to sarcasm, was it not ? What a pleasantness there is about his memory. It is only less gladdening than his presence used to be. I am thankful to say that I can think of him more cheerfully now, and do not need, as at first, to forget him, in order to be cheerful. . . . How consoling it is to think of Seymour's purity and virtue, and yet how almost more consoling to think of his *reverence !* "·

To these letters may be added another section of Shairp's reminiscences of Clough, who was one of the Grasmere reading-party—

"Early in the autumn of 1843 Clough came to Grasmere to read with a Balliol reading-party, of which I was one. He was with us about six weeks, I think, staying till towards the end of September. This was his earliest long vacation party; all things on a smaller scale than his later ones by Loch Ness or on Deeside, but still very pleasant. He lived in a small lodging immediately to the west of Grasmere church; we in a farmhouse on the lake. During these weeks I read the Greek tragedians with him, and did Latin prose. His manner of translating, especially the Greek choruses, was quite peculiar; a quaint archaic style of language, keeping rigidly to the Greek order of the words, and so bringing out their expression better, more forcibly and poetically, than any other translations I had heard. When work was done we used to walk in the afternoon with him all over that delightful country. His 'eye to country' was wonderful. He knew the whole lie of the different dales relatively to each other; every tarn, beck, and bend in them.

He used, if I remember right, to draw pen-and-ink maps, showing us the whole lineaments of the district. Without any obtrusive enthusiasm, but in his own quiet manly way, he seemed as if he never could get too much of it—never walk too far or too often over it. Bathing, too, formed one of his daily occupations, up in a retired pool of the stream that afterwards becomes the Rotha, as it comes out of Easdale. One walk, our longest, was on a Saturday, up Easdale, over the Raise by Greenup, Borrowdale, Honister Crag, under the starlight to Buttermere. In the small inn there we stayed all Sunday. Early on Monday morning we walked, by two mountain passes, to a farm at the head of Wast Water to breakfast. On the way we crossed Ennerdale, and up the pass, close under the nearly perpendicular precipices of the Pillar—a tall mountain, which is the scene of Wordsworth's pastoral of *The Brothers.* From the head of Wast Water, up past the great gorge of the Mickledore, to the top of Scawfell, then down past the east side of Bowfell towards Langdale Pikes, and so home to Grasmere. As we passed under Bowfell, a beautiful autumn afternoon, we lay a long time by the side of the lovely Angle Tarn. The sun, just before he sunk beside Bowfell, was showering down his light, which dimpled the smooth face of the tarn like heavy drops of sun-rain. Every now and then a slight breeze would come and scatter the rays broadcast over the little loch, as if some unseen hand was sowing it with golden grain. It was as memorable an appearance as that different one we had seen a year ago on Möel Wyn. These things, though Clough observed closely and took pleasure in, he did not speak often about, much less indulge in raptures.

Some of our party were very good hillmen. One day five or six in all set out on a race from our door by Grasmere Lake to the top of Fairfield. He was the second to reach the summit. His action up hill was peculiar; he used to lay himself forward almost horizontally towards the slope, and take very long strides which carried him quickly over the ground. Few men so stout as he then was could have matched him up a mountain.

Shortly after this time, at Oxford, somewhere that is between 1843 and 1845, I remember to have heard him speak, at a small debating society called the Decade, in which were discussed often graver subjects, and in a less popular way, than in the Union. Having been an unfrequent attender, I heard him only twice. But both times, what he said, and the way he said it, were so marked and weighty as to have stuck to memory when almost everything else then spoken has been forgotten. The first time was in Oriel Common-room; the subject proposed : ' That Tennyson was a greater poet than Wordsworth.' This was one of the earliest expressions of that popularity— since become nearly universal—which I remember. Clough spoke against the proposition, and stood up for Wordsworth's greatness with singular wisdom and moderation. He granted fully that Wordsworth was often prosy, that whole pages of *The Excursion* had better have been written in prose ; but still, when he was at his best, he was much better than any other modern English poet—saying his best things without knowing they were so good, and then drawling on in prosaic tediousness, without being aware where the inspiration failed and the prose began. In this kind of unconsciousness, I think he said, lay much of his power. One of the only other times I heard him speak was, about the same time, when a meeting of the Decade was held in Balliol Common-room. The subject of debate was : ' That the character of a gentleman was, in the present day, made too much of.' To understand the drift of this would require one to know how highly pleasant manners and a good exterior are rated in Oxford at all times, and to understand something of the peculiar mental atmosphere of Oxford at that time. Clough spoke neither for nor against the proposition ; but for an hour and a half—well on two hours—he went into the origin of the ideal, historically tracing from mediæval times how much was implied originally in the notion of a ' gentle knight '—truthfulness, consideration for others (even self-sacrifice), courtesy, and the power of giving outward expression to these moral qualities. From this high standard he traced the deterioration into the modern Brummagem pattern which gets the name. These true gentlemen of old time had invented for themselves a whole economy of manners, which gave true expression to what was really in them, to the ideal in which they lived. These manners, true in them, became false when adopted traditionally, and copied from without by modern men placed in quite different circumstances, and living different lives. When the same qualities are in the hearts of men now, as truly as in the best of old time, they will fashion for themselves a new expression, a new economy of manners suitable to their place and time. But many men now, wholly devoid of the inward reality, yet catching at the reputation of it, adopt these old traditional ways of speaking and of bearing themselves, though they express nothing that is really in them.

One expression I remember he used to illustrate the truth that where the true gentle spirit exists it will express itself in its own rather than in the traditional way. 'I have known pleasant men and women in the humblest places, in whom dwelt these faculties as truly as they ever did in the best of lords and ladies, and who were very poets of courtesy.'

His manner of speaking was very characteristic, slow, and deliberate, never attempting rhetorical flow, stopping at times to think the right thing, or to feel for the exactly fitting word, but with a depth of suggestiveness, a hold of reality, a poetry of thought, not found combined in any other Oxonian of our time."

Six years afterwards Shairp returned to Grasmere, and there he wrote the following lines :—

> Since our long summer in yon blissful nook,
> Six years, not changeless, intervene ;
> Those friends all scattered, I return and look
> Down on this peace serene.

> O happy vision ! depth of spirit-balm !
> For hearts that have too deeply yearned,
> This still lake holding his majestic calm
> 'Mid his green hills inurned.

> There dwell, repeated the clear depths among,
> Hills more aerial, skies of fairyer cloud,
> Hard by, yon homestead, where the summer long
> Our laughters once were loud.

> Still gleam the birch-trees down that pass as fair,
> Nor less melodious breaks
> The Rotha murmuring down his rocky lair,
> Between his sister lakes.

In his article on Wordsworth, in the *Studies in Poetry and Philosophy*, he thus refers to his visit to the Lakes, in 1849—

"As late as the autumn of 1849, as a stranger came down the road from the back of Rydal Mount, he met Wordsworth walking slowly back towards his home from the highway, to which he had just conducted some visitors. His head leant to one side, and in his hand he carried a branch with withered leaves. He who passed him happened to have on a plaid, wrapt round him in Scottish shepherds' fashion. This attracted his notice, and as the stranger looked round, thinking it might be the last sight he should ever have of him, the poet had turned round, and was looking back too.   There was one long look, but no word, and both passed on.

> Matthew is in his grave, yet now,
> Methinks, I see him stand,
> As at that moment, with a bough
> Of wilding in his hand. " [1]

Returning to Oxford, in the late autumn, for his last term, Shairp gives an account—in a letter to his father— of a meeting with Lockhart, the biographer of Walter Scott, and of his own thoughts of a curacy, and his chance of a Fellowship at All Souls'.

[Postmark, 17th December 1843.]

" BALLIOL, Sunday.

[Speaks first of the purchase of a horse at Oxford, and of his paying a visit to Hastings for a week.]   " The other day I met Lockhart, the author of Scott's Life, at dinner at the Master's.   He is an old Balliol man, a Scotch Exhibitioner, and had come up to enter his eldest son, Walter Scott, at Balliol.   The son seemed a nice fellow, and struck me as having a great look of the pictures you see of Scott, but perhaps this might be fancy.   Lockhart himself is a very gentlemanly-mannered man, and amusing in his talk ; but he seems to be a good deal broken down, and his spirits to be chastened from what they must once have been.   He has the remains of very good looks.

I wish to speak to you of another thing about myself. If I could manage to get into any college here, as Fellow after my degree, I think it would suit both my likings and my interests better than going down immediately into the country as a curate.   Besides, a man may make more of himself by remaining and improving himself here for a few years, than he can possibly do by being a solitary curate, left alone in some remote country corner, without anything to improve him but himself.   Therefore, liking, interest, improvement being all one way, I think it would be desir-

[1] *Studies in Poetry and Philosophy*, p. 94.

able if it could be effected. But then I am a Scotchman.
Balliol and Oriel are the only places left except one.
These two would suit me best, as they are in themselves
a livelihood; but then at Balliol my chance is *nothing, zero.*
They require so much scholarship. At Oriel it is the
faintest in the world; nothing, in fact, to build and hope
upon, as far as I can judge.

There is another place — All Souls'. It is difficult
fully to explain the nature of the Fellowships there. I tried
to do so to Tom, if he remembers. They have generally
been given wholly by interest. The qualifications have not
been so much *learning*, as gentlemanly manners, being well-
connected, and being a pleasant fellow.

The great interest they have generally required, added
to the fact that they are not worth more than my Exhibition, and that I cannot hold both together, made me never
think of All Souls'. But one of our tutors, who takes an
interest in me, has been at me several times lately to get
me to stand. He says they are beginning to look a little
more to public opinion than they did. They are beginning
to be more shy than they used to be of men who, while
undergraduates, have been what is called 'fast' here; and
they pay a little more attention than formerly to the class-
list. I believe they would not refuse a first class man,
however small was his interest, if he were in other respects
unobjectionable; and a *second* would have some weight
with them. When the tutor spoke to me, I told him that
I was afraid it would not do for me, as, after my degree, I
must look to my *temporalities.* He said that, even in a
pecuniary point of view, he thought it would be better than
the Exhibition, as it went on increasing, and might lead to
something else, which the Exhibition does not do. If I am
to stand, I know that my interest with the Fellows would
be less than that of most who stand, so that I would have
to trust to my character, and to how the *Schools* turn out
for me. At present I scarcely know any of the Fellows;
but, through some of my friends here, I could get at two
or three of them pretty strongly. But there are *thirty* in

all. . . . There are four vacancies in November next.   On
the whole I do not know what to think.   Jowett, the tutor
who is my adviser, says that between the Fellowship and a
curacy which I could get, I could keep myself; but I am
not sure.   I wish you would give me your advice.   I cannot explain it to you more fully in a letter.   If I do stand,
it must be declared soon.   My standing there would not
prevent my standing elsewhere, if I had any chance; but
Jowett tells me he thinks I have a better chance there than
elsewhere.

A Fellow of All Souls' in the eyes of the world is
excellent, and men of the highest family in England are
proud to belong to it; but this is nothing.   It is not the
opinion of the world we must live by, in *any* sense.   I have
not in the least set my heart upon it, and whatever way
you decide, I shall not be disappointed. . . .

I am now out of lodgings, and back into College for
the vacation.   It costs me less.   There are only four in all
up.   One of them is Proby, who hunted with Tom and me
the day from Tiddington, and whom I think he liked.
There is nothing I look back to with more entire satisfaction than Tom's visit. . . . —Your most affectionate son,

J. C. SHAIRP."

In the spring of 1844, he was at Houstoun, and the
following is an entry in his Journal of that year:—

"HOUSTOUN, *Saturday*, 9*th May*,
" GREEN ROOM, 10.45 A.M.

" Here in the middle of this lovely season I would note
down a few things as they pass. . . . On Thursday I rose
early and left this by eight o'clock to ride to Winchburgh
to take the train to town.   It is long since I have felt so
happy.   There was a light, playful breeze from the west,
morning sunshine beautified by clouds, and all earth rejoicing.   As I rode along the road by Green Dykes I could
have shouted for glee.   The hills looked so delicately veiled
with tender light; and all the vale between, shadowy and

glorious, under the mingled clouds and sunshine. Then the brairds of virgin green were springing newly in every field, and the larks were busy overhead. . . . All along the roadside I saw the braird springing so freshly, with that '*purpureal*' bloom upon it; and the haughs near Carlowrie were 'made blithe by plough and harrow,' at work in the fallow, or preparing for green crop. Near the viaduct, both going and coming, I saw a swallow—the first of the year for me. On Wednesday afternoon (6th May) I heard the first cuckoo. He was among the row of beeches on the meet of the Cannonland Park. . . . Surely the morning is their favoured time. There is such a depth and fulness of light and shadow on them, with an underground of delicate gleaming light, pervading their whole range. Those dear hills. I could not help thinking how much more cheering and beautiful this is *to me* than any part of England I have seen—so free, such scope for the spirit's play. It is interesting to watch the trees in the bursting of the bud ($\kappa\acute{a}\lambda\upsilon\kappa\sigma\varsigma$ $\acute{\epsilon}\nu$ $\lambda\sigma\chi\epsilon\acute{\upsilon}\mu\alpha\sigma\iota$). Many of the planes have nearly completed their foliage, though the leaf is not yet full; while the fourth, fifth, and sixth, beginning from the east, have scarcely shown any green yet. The willow in the garden is out, but not full-leafed. The three chestnuts in the garden park are full. The larch everywhere out at the loveliest; and the birches in the wood are past their first virgin look. The thorns are quite green. But the oaks and ashes rise quite dark yet, not a leaf in them. Scarce any beeches are out, though that scraggy one in the middle of Kid's park has burst, and this morning was rejoicing in the sun. 'The limes' are opening, but scarce show green. My tenement for sleeping and reading is the green room with its cheerful outlook."

I may be pardoned if I ask the reader, who appreciates this extract, to compare it with what is already published of the Journal of Dorothy Wordsworth, and with what will shortly be published in the first volume of her brother's Life.

Shairp returned to Oxford in the early summer of 1844,

and in the final Schools obtained a second. He wrote thus of the result to his sister at Houstoun—

"I have got a second. I never calculated on more, though it was just possible. I feel quite happy."

Again, to his father,

[Postmark, 24*th May* 1844.]

"OXFORD, *Thursday.*

"I am glad you are satisfied, though I can assure you that I am *not*. All along, you will remember, I said a second was my place; and in saying I am not satisfied now I do belie my former words; for when I took all things into consideration, I saw that, putting hopes and sanguineness aside, it would not be prudent or safe to build on the chance of more. Still I was told that I had *a chance of a First*, and for this last year I have been working on that chance; for I suppose I could have got all I have got, with a good deal less trouble. If you have seen the list, you will see that there is a small first class and a larger second. I have been told by one of the Examiners that I was one of *three* who were the best in the second class; and I have heard further (though not from the Examiner) that there was a doubt among the four Examiners at one time whether they should make the list four or seven. Had they made it the latter number I should have been there. One cannot always trust these rumours, though I daresay there is something in this.

However, I cannot wonder at the result, for I was always shaky in my scholarship. I have done a good deal towards it since I came up here, but not enough. Being naturally inaccurate, these long *gaps* in my classical reading were bad for me. In fact, I think now that the four years I was at the Academy were the only ones I ever really learned much in this way. I was as good a scholar at fourteen, when I left the Academy, as when I came up here. Had the scholarship been up to the mark, I believe I knew enough history, and quite enough philosophy, for

G

the Schools. However, there is no use running on with
'ifs.' I should have liked a first, in a *mercantile* point of
view. By a second I feel neither lowered nor raised, but *just
exactly where I was.* What you say about settling my
plans before coming down is just what I proposed doing
before hearing from you. This last term consists of eight
weeks, and as I put on my bachelor's gown on Saturday
(which cost me £12 by the bye), I had better keep my
term for Master's degree now. It is as well to do it
immediately, and besides I shall have time for arranging
things.

The fearful question, 'What next?' (which has long
been haunting me), the evil of the Schools being withdrawn, has now come to stare me in the face, and must be
answered.

Two plans are open: one, to take orders as soon as I
decently can, and go down somewhere to the country as a
curate ; another, to try for a Fellowship. As to the former,
I must say I do not much like the thought of it. . . . As to
Fellowships, they are easier talked of than got. All Souls'
I have quite ceased to think of. It and I are both too
poor to come together. Oriel then is my only chance.
Now firsts or seconds are all the same here. They try you
for themselves, and judge for themselves. Therefore, as far
as reputation goes, my class can do me no harm here. But
the same thing that told against me in the Schools will
do so at Oriel. They require a fair amount of scholarship,
more, than at present I have to give. The query comes
to be, whether by working at scholarship till next Easter
I would have a chance of so far improving in this, as to
make it prudent to look forward to trying ? Scholarship is
a thing that boys can get up better than men. You get
past the age for it. Nevertheless I feel quite ready to begin,
and set to, if I have any chance of making it pay.

I sometimes *grieve* that I have not worked at it before,
as here in all places it is necessary, and the want of it pre-
vents any other reading telling as it would do. However,
at Oriel the philosophy I have read in Scotland would be

of more use than in the Schools, though without the other
it would be of little use. At present I am consulting with
those here I can best depend on, whether, *on the whole,* Oriel
is the best thing I can think of, or whether it would be
advisable to give up the thought. If I do think of trying
I must not be idle this summer. If I do try I must see
what I can do for my own maintenance between October
and Easter. These, and other things, I shall plan as well
as I can, and let you know all I hear, in order to have
your advice and approval. I am very sorry I shall not be
able to go down to Hastings, till after term is over, as by
losing one day now I shall lose a term. Good-bye! I shall
hope to have come to something definite before long. In the
meantime, if anything of my present suggestions does not appear right to you, I hope you will let me know. I fully agree
with your feelings about not trusting to interest. If possible,
I should like to steer quite clear of it. I have seen so little
good come of it. . . . I look forward much to being home
once more.—Your most affectionate son,   J. C. S."

In the autumn of 1844 he paid another of his delightful visits to Houstoun. In October of that year, we
find Norman Macleod writing from Dalkeith to John Macintosh, at Geddes, thus—

". . . Well, I had such a day and night with Shairp.
I went to Houstoun. We talked—and you know my powers
in that part of wordy drizzle—we talked the moon down.
We talked through the garden, and along the road, and up
the avenue, and up the stair, and in the drawing-room, and
during music, and during dinner, and during night, and,
I believe, during sleep; certainly during all next morning, and even when one hundred yards asunder—he being
on the canal-bank, and I in the canal-boat. What a
dear, noble soul Shairp is! I do love him. Would that
our Church had a few like him. We want broad-minded
meditative men. We want guides, we want reality, we
want souls who will do and act before God; who would
have that disposition in building up the spiritual church,

which the reverential Middle Age masons had, when elaborately carving some graven imagery or quaint device, unseen by man's eye, on the fretted roof of a cathedral, they worked in God's house and before God."[1]

From Houstoun Shairp proceeded with his father to Berwickshire; thence he went alone from Kelso to Flodden Field, and on to Newcastle, whence he took train to Rugby, on a visit to the new head-master, Dr. Tait, Arnold's successor in the school. The following is his account of the ride through Berwickshire, and the visit to Flodden, in a letter to his sister Grace :—

"RUGBY, *Thursday,* 17*th October.*

" MY DEAR GRACE— . . . Here I am, safely harboured in the house of the head master of Rugby. By the time this reaches you my father will have returned. . . . Even dreary Berwickshire looked half interesting. As we neared Kelso, father *illustrated* all the country by stories of *runs* and rides, etc., long ago. When we got past Mellerstain, to the top of the hill between it and Stitchell, he made me look back on it (Mellerstain) with its wooded background of hill gradually rising behind it. I had no notion there was any such view of it. There it was—quite an *ocean* of unbroken wood and immense trees, each tree looking like a little wave when the sea is gently ruffled; and then they were all touched by the hues of autumn. Father and I parted at Kelso; thence I pursued my journey alone. Though this road is much more level than the Jedburgh one, I was glad I came. When I passed over Flodden Field I could not help chiming to myself

> Green Flodden, on thy blood-stained head
> Descend no rain nor vernal dew.

There it is, a glorious battlefield if ever there was one. On the right (*i.e.* to the west as you go south) rises a height as high as Dechmond Hill. On this the Scotch were drawn up. This is Flodden Hill. Three miles to the east

[1] *Life of Norman Macleod,* vol. i. p. 219.

stands Ford Castle upon the Till. These are the two
prominent features. Flodden Hill looks down towards
Ford, and Ford looks defiance back on Flodden. All between is plain. The English advanced from Ford. The
Scots were too impatient to meet their attack, and rushed
down to meet them in the plain. Where the road passes
over was the very thickest of the onslaught. On that spot,
and for miles round, lie ' The Flowers of the Forest '—

> The prime of our land are a' cauld i' the clay.

Two miles to the south Garvan Bell and something ——
Thor, the most eastern peaks of Cheviot, look down on the
Field. Flodden itself is now all cultivated, and divided into
fields. We wound along the eastern base of the Cheviots.
They look very interesting. I should like to have a wander
among them some day. I dined at the 'Tankerville Arms,'
near Wooler, got to Newcastle about 8.30. . . . Left by
rail at 10.45, and after a frosty night reached Rugby at
9.30 A.M.; got to bed, and at 1.30 came to Dr. Tait's in
time for luncheon; then had a short drive with him and
Mrs. Tait, and a married sister of his, who is here. For
half the week he had only one hour in the day to himself
for exercise. The other three days are half-holidays, and
then he is done teaching by 12, but has lots to do besides.
Certainly this is a place of 'unhasting, unresting diligence,'
as Arnold's Life calls it. Nothing but good hard work
going, such as only one man out of ten could stand. But
then, to a man who is able and active, there are few other
places where he could find himself so thoroughly useful.
Everything goes on like clockwork. Every moment of the day
seems precious. Tait is very kind, and his wife seems a very
nice person. Yesterday when I arrived I found a note from
Marriott's sister, saying he could not receive me, owing to
another attack of illness. To-day at one I am going to
walk over to Cottesbach with J. Douglas to ask for him.
To-morrow I hope to go to Oxford, where I shall be very
glad to see Henry Douglas again. Tell A—— and B——,
if they can get hold of the *Quarterly,* to read in it an article

on Stanley's *Life of Arnold.* It is by Lake, an old Fellow and Tutor of Balliol, and an old pupil and favourite of Arnold's. I hope Tom is shooting often this fine weather. Tell me how much he gets, and where he goes; and send a regular bulletin of Pincher's health.—Your affectionate brother,   J. C. SHAIRP."

Returning to Oxford from Rugby, he was busy for some time in preparing for a competitive examination for one of the Fellowships at Oriel College.

The following letters to his father and sister show his feelings about this Fellowship, both before and after the examination. The dignified way in which he announced the result and the magnanimity displayed in the letter of 9th April 1845, are noteworthy:—

[Postmark, 18*th March* 1845.]

"OXFORD, *Sunday.*

" MY DEAREST FATHER—There are just five days for me to work, and then comes the trial. I have tried to work steadily. The candidates are several of them very *tough* and hard to beat—Park, Arnold, Moberly. You will see *one* of them at least, if not *more*, chosen. There may be others whom I know not of. . . . It is snowing now. It cannot blow more drearily over Shotts Moor than it does here. Almost all the men have gone down."

[Postmark, 21*st March*.]

". . . I do not think there is any bread for my mouth here. There is some difficulty about my standing at Oriel. I had an interview with the Provost, and he told me they were only allowed to have a certain number born out of England; and he was not sure but they had that number among their present Fellows. However, he is to have the statutes examined by a lawyer, and let me know. . . . Don't be troubled about this hitch, for I am not."

[Postmark, 9th April 1845.]

"OXFORD, *Friday.*

"MY DEAR FATHER—Well, I have *not got it.* If I could think that all you at home would not be very much disappointed, I would easily make up my mind to it. The thing that makes me chiefly sorry to have failed is that, of course, I must soon leave Oxford, where I should have liked well to have stayed a little longer. I do not think there will soon be another Fellowship open to me; and, though there was, I do not wish to stand again. The two who got in, out of the ten who stood, are Arnold of our College, and Coleridge, a brother of a friend of mine. It is rather singular these two names coming together. Their fathers were such friends. We had four hard days, working from ten to five without stop. Two days we were taken in among all the Fellows, and had to construe Greek and Latin we had never seen before. . . . —Your most affectionate son,

J. C. SHAIRP.

Many thanks for the description of the Run.—J. C. S."

The autumn of 1845 was spent—as the autumns usually were—in the North, and here the concluding portion of Shairp's reminiscences of Clough finds its natural place :

"It must have been in autumn of 1845 that Clough and I first met in Scotland. One visit there to Walrond's family at Calder Park I especially remember. On a fine morning, early in September, we started from Calder Park to drive to the Falls of Clyde. We were to spend the day at Milton Lockhart, and go on to Lanark in the evening. Besides Walrond and Clough, there were T. Arnold, E. Arnold, and myself. It was one of the loveliest September mornings that ever shone, and the drive lay through one of the most lovely regions in south Scotland, known as 'the Trough of Clyde.' The sky was bright blue, fleeced with whitest clouds. From Hamilton to Milton Lockhart, about ten miles, the road keeps down in the hollow of the trough, near the water, the banks covered with orchards, full of heavy-laden apple and other fruit trees, bending down till they touched the yellow corn that grew among them. There is a succession of fine country houses, with lawns that slope towards lime-trees that bend down over the river. It was the first time any of us but Walrond had been that way ; and in such a drive, under such a sky, you may believe we were happy enough. We reached Milton Lockhart, a beautiful place, built on a high grassy headland, beneath and round which winds the Clyde. Sir Walter Scott, I believe, chose the site, and none could be more beautifully chosen. It looks both ways up and down the lovely vale.

As we drove up, near ten o'clock, we found the late Mr. J. G. Lockhart (Scott's biographer) walking on the green terrace that looks over the river. The laird himself being from home, his brother was our host. Soon after we arrived, his daughter, then very young, afterwards Mrs. Hope Scott, came out on the terrace to say that breakfast was ready. After breakfast she sang, with great spirit and sweetness, several of her grandfather's songs, copied into her mother's books by herself, when they were still newly composed. After listening to these for some time, her brother, Walter Scott Lockhart, then a youth of nineteen or so, and with a great likeness to the portraits of Sir Walter Scott when a young man, was our guide to an old castle, situated on a bank of one of the small glens that came down to the Clyde from the west. It was the original of Scott's Tillietudlem in *Old Mortality*. A beautiful walk thither ; the castle large, roofless, and green with herbage and leafage. We stayed some time, roaming over the green deserted place, then returned to a lunch, which was our dinner ; more songs, and then drove off late in the afternoon to the Falls of the Clyde and Lanark for the night. It was a pleasant day. Clough enjoyed it much in his own quiet way—quietly, yet so humanly interested in all he met. Many a joke he used to make about that day afterwards. Not he only, but all our entertainers of that day, Mr. J. G. Lockhart, his son and daughter, are now gone."

The Rev. Mr. Robertson of Whittinghame says, that in those conversations at St. Andrews in later years, which went back to his Oxford friends, " the name that most affected him was Clough's. He used never to speak of him without special reverence."

Amongst Principal Shairp's papers was found an elegiac poem on his friend, which he had evidently meant either to recast, or not to publish. It is fragmentary, and it is therefore inexpedient to print the whole of it as it now stands. It is too *intime* for that, and the appreciative must read between the lines of the following stanzas, which are significant, and very characteristic. The whole poem is perhaps too analytical and subjective to show the writer at his best ;[1]

[1] Compare Professor Palgrave's remarks in his Preface to Shairp's Poem, *Glen Desseray, etc.*

but it enters, with great truth and intensity of feeling, into the struggles through which Clough passed,—especially in the stanzas omitted—when his faith was "from its old centre hurled."

No Thyrsis thou, for old Idyllic lays,
    But a broad-browed, deep-souled, much suffering man,
Within whose veins, thrilled by these latter days,
    The ruddy lifeblood ran.

Warm throbbing from a heart as hero's brave,
    Yet sensitive and tender as a child's ;
Stirred with all human passion glad or grave,
    By shores and mountain wilds.

A poet wanderer, loving lone to go
    Where long Glenmaly roars with all her pines ;
Or where Ben Nevis, touched with early snow,
    Huge o'er his Brethren shines.

Lochaber, Moidart, Morar, stern delight
    From these he drank, his soul new power received ;
Stood wrapt, where the Atlantic's swinging might
    O'er Ardnamurchan heaved.

Ah ! had he walked aloof in that cool air,
    Braced all his boyhood time, till heart and brain
Were fully tempered, and annealed to bear
    Life at its tensest strain.

Too soon, too soon, the place of early trust
    Constrained to leave, down Thought's strong current whirled,
And face to face alone too rudely thrust
    With problem of the world.

And Voices then the loudest England knew.
    In his distracted ear were thundering. Some
"Push boldly forward " ; some—"lo ! here the haven true,
    Here rest, or be undone."

From these he turned ; o'ermastered by the stress
    Of yearning for the myriads of his kind,
Who, buried in the city's wilderness,
    Unknown, uncared for, pined.

Their privilege—toil, ignorance, disease,
    To live unhappy and untended die—
While brother men in gilded pageantries
    Of pomp and wealth went by.

And of the poor no knowledge had, nor care,
  Nor once stooped from their heights to hear what groans
The sufferers heaved, no more than if they were
  Beasts, or insensate stones.

.   .   .   .   .

While they who taught, mid strife of tongues profane,
  Hurled holy names for wrangle and dispute,
But drew therefrom no balm to heal the bane
  That gnawed life's inmost root.

These things he saw, and felt, as few can feel,
  Nor wotting God's long patience with His world,
Too deeply questioned, till faith 'gan to reel,
  From its old centre hurled.

Soul-sick, he cried, " how long"! " O heaven, how long,
  Shall rich men surfeit—the poor die for need ?"
Still unabashed the kingdom stands of wrong.
  Is then Christ risen indeed ?

.   .   .   .

Ah, when that Day ! we know not where or how,
  Of restitution on the world shall break,
O friend, shall any gladder soul than thou
  From the long sleep awake ?

To find thy dark misgivings all at rest,
  All thy deep yearnings at the fountain stilled,
To see what sage and prophet dimly guessed,
  Beyond all hope fulfilled.

Meantime, in peace repose those fevered brows,
  Where Arno's waters round fair Florence lave,
And shadows, flung from the grey olive boughs,
  Chequer thy quiet grave.

Returning to Oxford, after this summer in the North, Shairp made some new friends. In the Michaelmas term of 1845, Coleridge Patteson, afterwards missionary-bishop of Melanesia, came up from Eton to reside at Balliol. He had the same experience of failure that Shairp had recently had, though his was only the competition for an entrance scholarship at Balliol; he, and Hornby, the future head-master of Eton, were bracketed fifth. Patteson soon made friends with the best men in Balliol—Palmer, Riddell, etc.—and Shairp wrote thus of him—

"Patteson, as he was at Oxford, comes back to me, as the representative of the very best kind of Etonian, with much good that he had got from Eton, and with something better, not to be got at Eton, or any other school. He had those pleasant manners, and that perfect ease in dealing with men, and with the world, which are the inheritance of Eton, without the least tincture of worldliness. I remember well the look he then had, his countenance massive for one so young, with good sense and good feeling—in fact, full of character. For it was character more than special abilities that marked him out from others, and made him wherever he was—whether in cricket, in which he excelled, or in graver things—a centre round which others gathered. The impression he left on me was of quiet, gentle strength, and entire purity, a heart that loved all things true, and honest, and pure, and that could always be found on the side of these. We did not know, probably he did not know himself, the fire of devotion that lay within him, but that was soon to kindle and make him what he afterwards became."[1]

A letter from Bishop Patteson to Shairp, on his *Essays*, —the last the Bishop wrote—will be found in a subsequent chapter.

A few extracts from one of his note-books, written during the years 1843-46, will show, better than any letters or commentary can do it, the direction which Shairp's thoughts were now taking, both towards Poetry and Philosophy. They show how his Oxford training bore fruit, and confirmed the original bent of his mind, toward those subjects in which he afterwards did his best literary work.

The first is dated

"*Thursday Eve*, 28th *November* 1844.

"Whenever we come face to face with truth then poetry begins. To see any truth clearly with our own eyes, to make it our own, inwardly awakens a feeling akin to the

[1] *Life of John Coleridge Patteson*, vol. i. p. 36.

poetic one. Whoever, whether by reading or by his own thinking, has had a truth flashed suddenly upon him, must have
felt this. The keen feeling, the εὔρηκα ẅhich follows
on such clear seeing of a truth—when we see it for ourselves, not HEAR it only, when all darkening media are
swept away, and the bare truth and the bare soul stand
fronting each other—this keen feeling is poetical; its
utterances would be poetry. What does this point to? It
is a fact of consciousness. How is it connected with the
true nature of poetry?"

From its relation to the foregoing entry, a few sentences
written at a much later date (twenty-one years afterwards),
may follow it, rather than be reserved for a subsequent
chapter:—

"St. Andrews, 1st *April* 1865.

"Poetry can never cease, while the outward world, with
all its movements, continues fresh and strong, and the
human spirit is alive to receive it. The meeting of these
two must strike out from age to age some new music.
Neither of them are fixed and dead, but both are living
entities, and the vibration which one gives out to the stroke
of the other is always poetry. Neither is there any fear
that it should prove the continual recurrence of the same
note. The two forms are not fixed and stereotyped in their
relations to each other, but these two change from age to
age. Nay, the vibration called forth is not the same in
any two human spirits in the same age. Not even is it
the same, from year to year and day to day, in any one
spirit. I have just come in from a walk in the twilight
along the scores. After a charming spring day there was
an intensely blue evening sky, and in it the young moon,
not yet half full, and the evening star larger than usual,
and with the same serene angel light, and a few other stars
coming in a moment from the infinite, made me feel as I
never felt before. How young, and how infinitely various
in its influences, felt the sky, and the sea, and the earth
to-night! To me, there was something in them to-night, not
felt before; and there will be something new, something I

have never felt in them, to countless souls of men, ages after
I am gone."

Returning to the Oxford Journal—

"*3d July* 1845.

"All earnest thought has been labouring towards one
common end, viz. to find some utterance, if possible, in the
conscious understanding, for the truth which lies unuttered
in the silent and unconscious region of the soul. For even
if our own thoughts are ever so relative, if, by the necessity
of the case, as soon as anything is moulded into a distinct
conception it has ceased to be absolute, and become relative
truth, still there is an equal necessity that we should think
of *an absolute* as existing somewhere. It may be external
to us or it may be within us—somewhere it must be.
Else our thoughts are a contradiction. For instance, the
conception of right, unless it has some existence independent
of all our thoughts about it, is an absurdity. If nothing
else that we think of does so, certainly our moral consciousness refers us to some absolute truth, independent of ourselves. Apart from this moral consciousness I doubt
whether anything else would help us towards the knowledge
of God. For it might be demonstrated by the most incon-
testible logic that there must be a first cause, that this
order of things proves an Orderer. Yet even if these
did necessarily prove a Personal God in our conceptions of
things (which is at least doubtful), still there arises the
feeling from within, all this is very true of our conceptions,
but then there is the boundless, mysterious Universe. Our
conceptions are no measure of this, we cannot argue from
things as they seem to us to the absolute nature of things
in themselves.

But conscience points to absolute truth with a directness
which nothing else does. The command—the 'Thou shalt'
with which it speaks—sends us at once out of ourselves.
That which is behind it, and in virtue of which it speaks,
must be the *truth* of the universe. Even though in itself
phenomenal, it is a phenomenon which comes straight from

the absolute. It is the golden thread which links man's being with the harmony of things—the absolute in man. Still it seems doubtful whether even from this ground man could ever rise up to know God. . . . That which is behind it is unutterable—such as no language, no thought can compass. Or if forced to speak and give it a distinct form, would one not in all probability fall back on 'pantheism,' or a dreary 'destiny,' or an 'unalterable nature of things,' in the yoke of which it was fast bound. I doubt whether conscience unenlightened could ever arrive at the Divine Personality and Will. A rule of life it is without being a guide to true knowledge. Hence Aristotle wrote a book of morals (wonderfully perfect) without even directly alluding to God's Being or the existence of conscience. It told him what was right, without saying anything about itself, much less about him whom it represents. Plato's knowledge of God (*Theaet.* chap. xxv.) is wonderful, yet was it not the remnant of a tradition, caught up and purified by his pure soul, or perhaps a direct inward inspiration ? . . .

It seems as if the whole ancient world, when rightly understood, uttered one cry, 'Shew us the Father.' This inability to find out God was a veil spread over the face of all nations. Man was not able to retain the knowledge of God ; so God lowered himself to meet the needs of man. Here is one great end of the Incarnation. Besides all the manifold other benefits of it we are no longer left in uncertainty as to God's nature. No longer fall back in despair from an inability to grasp his infinity. He has become finite (if we may say so), so that the least gifted mind, if it loves truth and goodness, may grasp the nature of God, for that nature is revealed to us in Christ."

Again—

"*Mythology and Natural Religion.*

"*2d March* 1846.

" It is probable that the earlier mythologies had a moral meaning, and sprung from a real base of inward truth.

Myths were the shape which the truths of man's moral being took, when projected outward, and mingled with the facts of a nation's origin and early history.   In time the myths got detached from this their moral ground, ceased to be the ex-' pressions of man's inward convictions, and so grew meaningless and false.   Here we see a process of truth passing outward, till it ceases to be true.

In religion we find just the opposite tendency.   The facts of religion are always tending to realise themselves inwardly, and become living ideas.   Accordingly, in time men begin to separate the inward from the outward, to analyse all that part of Christianity which has ceased to be *mere* fact, and has become at once fact and idea, and to call it Natural Religion, as if man could have got at these truths for himself.   Then comes another process.   Having organised into a system all of Christianity that has got a moral meaning, they call it Natural Religion, and begin to make an opposition between it, and that part of Christianity which has never yet passed inward—between man's moral convictions which have been first called out and purified by Christianity, and the Christianity that has so purified them.   And then comes the problem of reconciling these two.   Having first chosen to make the chasm, we next set ourselves to the task of bridging over it.

What seems to favour this view of things is that the so-called Natural Religion has never yet been found extant as a fact, but where Christianity has gone before.   Mythology is the fact; you nowhere find Natural Religion."

Again—

" *Systems of Philosophy.*

" *September* 1846.

" What end have the innumerable Systems served?   Age after age has produced its system, or its rival systems, and the next age has swept these away, and replaced them with ones of its own.   Have they then been all false and useless, mere cobwebs?   No, say some.   They have in their day served as scaffolding for other work—for men's thoughts on theology, history—for men's practice. . . . Having done this, they have done their work, and disappeared. This is hardly satisfactory. It does not seem reasonable to think that the greatest intellects of each age should have toiled for so little. . . .

Eclecticism would say that there are certain true points in every system; seize these, reject the others, and put these true points together, and you will have the truth. . . .

There is still another view, and it is this: Each philosophy has a truth in it, not a truth in its peculiar doctrines, but a truth relative to its age. Therefore the truth of each philosophy lay *where its founder least dreamt.* They retired from the world, sought to shake themselves free from all the influences of their time, and to think out something concerning the absolute nature of things, wholly irrespective of their own particular age, which would hold true for all ages and all men. But this thought, to get into a region where their time had no influence, was a delusion. Each thinker, however little he dreamt it, is and must be influenced by all the thinkers who have thought before him, by all the circumstances that have gone before him, and are now around him. No man can get out of these. Therefore the true philosophy will no longer strive to rear itself independently of all previous philosophies. Men are beginning to distrust the possibility of getting at one absolute philosophy. These are signs of the coming of a new method. Each of the past philosophies seems to be one movement or step in the great order of thought. This order has gone on, and evolved itself while men were overthrowing each other's systems, and this overthrowing of systems is part of the order. Each age had some particular quality or qualities of mind, of which philosophy is the exponent. The philosophy is the age systematised and put into its intellectual·shape. Therefore a searching criticism of all past philosophies is the new method, and this will evolve the particular qualities of mind which each philosophy has uttered, and will (it may be) ascertain and fix the whole order of thought, which comprehend these qualities of mind as its portion.

But is not this new method of ascertaining the moment of thought, and so getting a true philosophy, itself a product of its age, one of the moments ? Will not the next age number their method too with the things which have been, and assign it a truth *only* relatively to its own age ?"

H

CHAPTER VII

In the autumn of 1846—when twenty-seven years of age
—Shairp received an invitation from his friend and former
tutor at Balliol, Dr. Tait, then head-master at Rugby, to
work along with him in that school. He accepted it, and
there he spent the next eleven years of his life. He had,
for friends and colleagues in the school, A. Benson, now
Archbishop of Canterbury; G. G. Bradley, the present Dean
of Westminster; Bonamy Price, the late Professor of Political
Economy at Oxford; Theodore Walrond, afterwards Secretary
to the Civil Service Commission, and in later years himself
a Commissioner; Dr. Goulburn, now Dean of Norwich, and
others; and amongst his pupils were Dr. Jex-Blake, the late
head-master; Sir Horace Davey, Vernon and Godfrey Lushington, Mr. Edward Scott, Henry and James Rhoades, Mr.
Kitchener of Newcastle, Mr. Thomson, keeper of the MSS. in
the British Museum, etc. Memorial sketches by some of
these friends and pupils will be found in Chapter VIII.

It was a time of eager interest to him in many ways;
but, while he enjoyed the work, the schoolmaster's was not
his special vocation. Besides, his strong Scottish sympathy
led him to prefer a sphere of labour in his native land;
and during his residence at Rugby his national enthusiasm
deepened. It comes out in characteristic fashion in the following passage in an undated letter to a friend in Edinburgh. He
was urging his friend to keep his eye on *The North British
Review*, "if any opportunity offers of getting it into your hands.

There is one purpose which it might serve. Without wishing it to take up ' the Scottish grievance,' it might help to strengthen whatever is best in Scottish National Life. In a wise and temperate way it might advocate Scottish interests even more than it has done. They much require some wise advocacy, both in Religion and Politics. Anglicised Scotchmen are generally poor creatures; and an Anglicised Scotland will be a contemptible country."

When Theodore Walrond gave up his mastership in 1857, Shairp succeeded to his boarding-house at Rugby, and Walrond remained to the last one of his closest friends.

Returning to Mr. Sellar's account of this period of Shairp's life, we find it thus described—

" His difficulties as to a profession were settled by his receiving an invitation from Dr. Tait—then head-master of Rugby, who had been senior tutor of Balliol when Shairp entered, and as having himself been a Snell Exhibitioner, and probably also a family friend, had from the first taken a great interest in him—to accept a mastership in the school. Of his work in the school, and of his personal influence on his pupils, you will no doubt hear from some of his surviving colleagues, and from some younger men, who received from him their first literary and intellectual impulse. I saw a good deal of him in those days, and was often at Rugby—once for several weeks at a time—sometimes as his guest, and sometimes as the guest of his friend and colleague, Walrond. The routine of work, while making him less desultory, did not seem to me to quench to any degree the ardour of his enthusiasm either for poetry or speculative discussion. He was then, as he always continued to be, an animated and excellent talker, and I can remember some of his encounters with one who only the other day was still a vigorous veteran of controversy, Mr. Bonamy Price,—one in particular, at the house of the latter, on some point of doctrinal theology, which almost assumed the proportions of an old disputation. Shairp took the first innings—and a long and admirable innings he played. The match, however, was drawn ; for Shairp and óne or two of those present had fallen asleep long before his keen and clear-headed opponent had made up his score. He had great pleasure in his intercourse with his more advanced pupils ; but he probably grew a little weary of the drudgery of teaching boys in one of the lower forms. He got fully to appreciate the good of the English public school system—the friendships which were formed by it ; the manliness of character, the spirit of honour, and the frankness of manner conspicuous in the better type of public school men. He thought, however, that it had a tendency to dwarf originality. It is true that a public school prepares men to live in and act upon the world, rather than to live apart from it and to act upon it from a distance as Wordsworth or Carlyle did. . . . But Shairp would have admitted, I think, that for one genius lost by the training of a public school, a hundred clever lads were improved by having the conceit or eccentricity thereby knocked out of them. It was his appreciation of its good influence on character and manners that made him anxious to realise, and for a time successful in realising, something of the same influence in the College Hall of St. Andrews."

Shairp's own account of his early life at Rugby is contained in letters to the Houstoun circle. To his sister he wrote thus, a month after his arrival—

[Postmark, 2d *November* 1846.]

"RUGBY.

" MY DEAR BINNY—This is Sunday evening. . . . This week has been a tolerably busy one, but not more so than I shall have usually. Wednesday and Friday are fagging enough. On these days I am employed from ten to twelve hours. The work in the school with my ' Form ' I like best. Besides the Latin and Greek I teach them (which is of the most ele-

mentary kind), I have History; and once a week I read French
with them. Besides my Form, I have nearly thirty private
pupils, who come to me three times a week, a little more
advanced. What bothers me most is about 160 'copies,' one
way or another, which I have to look over, and most of them
to correct every week. . . . I have dined out once or twice.
You may have heard mention of a Mr. Price. He is second
master, was here all the time with Arnold, and is certainly
a remarkable man, as his wife is a woman. They are a
sort of king and queen of Rugby. He is a great politician
(Liberal of course), and a great discourser on all subjects,
floods of talk, and indomitable energy. The same applies to his wife, with the addition that she has been,
and is, a very handsome woman. She is a cousin
of Macaulay's. The man and wife keep the whole district a-stirring. They both ride, and scour the country at
full gallop—altogether a 'remarkable pair,' one might say.
. . . I have had two or three pleasant rides. Bradley is my
mainstay for companionship, as most of the others are
married. He is about my own age, and of the same college
standing; and many of the people in Oxford we know in
common, and he is a very good master and amiable fellow.
. . . All the people here are Liberals. A Tory or Conservative does not exist; but then they differ each in the
kind, degree, and form of his Liberality. . . . Good-night,
and joy be wi' you a.'—Your very affectionate brother,

J. C. SHAIRP."

His chief amusement at Rugby, as in earlier days at
Houstoun, was that of hunting, a luxury in which, however,
he seldom indulged. He had no special relish for any
other kind of field sport. He has described the delights of
hunting and of curling in two remarkable lyrics; but he
became increasingly indifferent both to shooting and fishing.
The only sport which he told me he regretted in later years
he had not become proficient in when young, was golf. Living
so long in St. Andrews—where he had the best opportunity
of seeing the effect of this noble game on mind, body and

character, and of practising the art—he used to confess that he had missed something by not having learned it.   His appreciation of the hunting-field, however, led him to write the following lyric, which is perhaps the finest poem on hunting in the English language.   It is certainly superior to anything that Somerville, or Cowper, or Kingsley have given us, and it will recall his former poem on Bannockburn :—

THE RUN

Hark hollo ! brave hearts !
　'Twas the hounds I heard ;
With the sound of their going
　All the land is stirred.
They have made every peasant
　From work stand still,
With gazers they've crowned
　Every crag and hill.

And the ploughman cried loud,
　By my team I stood,
And heard them crashing
　Yon old fir-wood.
Down yon ash-tree river-banks,
　Where the sunbeams slant and fall,
Flashed the dappled hounds,
　Making the dens musical.
For sweeter they be,
　Than any chime of bells,
The melodies that linger
　All year in yon dells,
Till the hounds come by and awake them.

And the pedlar answered,
　From beneath his load,
At noon they went streaming
　Right o'er my road
From the farmsteads the lasses
　Rushed out to see
How they skimmed like swallows,
　Over plough and lea.
As they went to the hills
　What a head they bare !
Like snow-drift scudding
　On the stormy air,
And few were the steeds could o'ertake them.

Forward waved the shepherd,
    They are west away,
On the moorlands startling
    The plover grey.
Ever on as they sped,
    More mute they grew,
And the riders waxed fewer,
    And yet more few,
Till only one hunter attended.

And the widow, as she sat
    On her lone cottage floor,
Heard their cry thro' the dark
    On the midnight moor ;
And at morn came the worn hounds
    Home, one by one,
And the huntsmen knew
    That the chase was done,
Never knew how nor where it ended.

During the autumn of 1847 Shairp took an excursion
on foot, with some friends from Houstoun, to the central and
north-western Highlands of Scotland. They went by Rannoch
and Loch Ericht to Dalwhinnie ; thence northwards by Corryarrick to Fort Augustus ; and on to Drumnadrochit, on Loch
Ness. So far as the party of friends was concerned, this was
the most interesting of his many Highland excursions on foot ;
and the separate records of it by several of the friends are sufficiently graphic, and supplementary each to each, to warrant
their publication, along with Shairp's own letters to Houstoun.

From Drumnadrochit he wrote to his sister—

                     " DRUMNADROCHIT, *Sunday.*

"We reached this last night, or rather this morning, at
three o'clock. . . . On Thursday we split, four to the east
end of Loch Rannoch for the night, the other two (to wit,
Tom Arnold and I) to the west end. Next day the four
went along Loch Garry to Dalwhinnie, we two up Loch
Erichtside, a long lonely loch, winding under Ben Alder,
—quite a grand solitude. We passed only two houses all
the day, and these two mere bothies of Lord Abercorn's

foresters. Loch Ericht is the southern boundary of his forest. At one of these, about six miles from the loch head, we slept, after a long but very interesting walk. It is a most unvisited region. The tourists never touch it; even men who had lived all their lives on Rannochside knew little of it. On Ben Alder side we saw the cave where Charlie lay hid for the last three weeks, with Lochiel and Cluny Macpherson, just before he left Scotland for good. Nothing interests me more than these haunts of Charlie's. Clough says that it is only a few young ladies and boys and old women who care about the Prince himself; and the rest infer that I, not being either of the first two, must be one of the third. Yesterday was a long and grand day for four of us. A car from Dalwhinnie to Garvemore, near Speyhead; then on foot, over Corryarrick. From its ridge a view of every mountain-head from Moray Firth to the Peaks of Skye—nothing I ever saw like it. We may live for years ere we see such another. From Fort Augustus we started about half-past nine, and reached this about half-past two in the morning. We go for Skye to-morrow, and are at Fort William we hope by Saturday, and at Houstoun probably by Tuesday. . . ."

With this may be compared the lines he contributed to *Good Words*, in August 1874, called *The Wilderness*—also named by himself *Loch Erichtside*—where he writes of the

> . . . Desert dun
> That heaves and rolls endlessly north away
> By Corryarrick and the springs of Spey,
> The grand old country of the Chattan clan.[1]

Mr. Thomas Arnold gives a vivid account of this excursion.

"2 BRADMORE ROAD,
"OXFORD, 5th *September* 1887.

"I remember that walk by Loch Erichtside very well. We were a pretty large party—I daresay it was six when we set out from Calder Park, the Walrond's place near Glasgow; those composing it were Shairp, Theodore Wal-

---

[1] See *Glen Desseray, and other Poems*, p. 140.

rond, two cousins of Shairp's, the Scotts (one of them is now Archdeacon of Dublin and Wicklow, and lives at Bray), myself, and I *think* Lloyd, son of a former bishop of Oxford; but of this I am not quite certain. We all kept together as far as Loch Rannoch, heavy rain having made us wet through, in crossing the fell from Lochearnhead. I think we slept at a little inn somewhere upon Loch Rannoch, but I have no recollection of the house. Next day some one made out that there was a path along the western shore of Loch Ericht, by which one could go to Dalwhinnie inn. Shairp and I liked the idea of this; the others did not—I forget why; however it was arranged that they should go the longer way, by Kinloch Rannoch, I suppose, and Dalnacardoch, and meet us at Dalwhinnie that same evening. Shairp and I started. We found it rough and tedious walking through the heather for the first five miles or more, till we reached the foot of Loch Ericht. Then we got upon a well-marked path, but with bends and ups and downs innumerable; and though we made what haste we could, we saw that nightfall would come on before we could reach Dalwhinnie. The shores of the lake left upon us the impression of a solitude more utter than we should have thought possible within 100 miles of Glasgow. It was Lord Abercorn's deer forest, we had heard; not a sheep nor a steer was to be seen; nor a human habitation, except the one which I am going to speak of. Yet there were many spots, we thought, in which humble human lives might have been led; particularly I remember a lonely strath coming down to the loch on the east side, near its head, which an Australian settler would have deemed positively inviting. But its green bottom and pleasant slopes were silent and tenantless like the rest. About two-thirds of the way along the loch, a place was marked on the map ' Toper-na-fuosich.' I think they told us at Loch Rannoch that this was a forester's hut. By the time we reached it, the sun had set. I remember we saw, just before coming there, on a little ridge on our left, several noble-looking red deer, outlined against the lingering light in the west. The forester and his wife, though our appearance was *most* unexpected, treated us with much hospitality, and let us sleep in the hut. Next morning we went on, and rejoined the rest of the party at Dalwhinnie. . . .

Clough, to whom we told our story, and who was then writing his 'Long Vacation Pastoral' at Drumnadrochit, chose *The Bothie of Toper-na-fuosich* for its principal title. This was in the first edition, afterwards he wrote to me that he had been told the word had some unseemly meaning in Gaelic, and that he had altered it to *Tober-na-Vuolich*.

I always had a strong affection for my dear old friend, the purity of whose character, when we were all young men together, impressed me with great respect, and made me wish to imitate him. But I know not that I could say anything about him that some other friend has not better said. I have often thought with wonder of his comparatively early death, remembering the healthy temperance of his life, and that he was not overworked, nor weighed down by household cares or family afflictions. Herodotus, indeed, tells us that to die early is a mark of the favour of the gods—which may be very true—but it may also be sometimes a sign that a man has run his mortal course—has come to the end of his tether; that in this world his Maker and Master has no more work for him to do, though much service may be reserved for him *là haut*. I shall await anxiously the appearance of your Memoir, for it will bring the friend whom I can never forget, in many ways more vividly before my mind."

The following is part of Mr. Edward Scott's reminiscences of the same tour:—

" In the summer vacation of 1847 he asked my brother, Archdeacon Scott, and myself to be his companions during a tour in the Highlands. We spent a few days with him at Houstoun, and saw Edinburgh. I remember his meeting us on the platform of Winchburgh station with a check shepherd's plaid across his shoulder, and a huge shepherd's

crook in his hand. This crook was his Pilgerstab during
our wanderings. He had dipped it under the waters of
every noted stream he had passed, carrying it in his hand,
especially Yarrow. It was a sacred stick.

How racy he was ! how he pointed out customs and manners and phrases that were native to the locality and strange
to us ! And yet with a sly humour at times, as when, on
being asked whether there was an evening service at Uphall
Church, he explained that the congregation, and probably
the minister too, found it answer to take the two services
in direct succession, one after another ! a Scotchman, I felt,
yet with a difference that made his companionship the richer.

On our visit to Edinburgh we spent a night at Dalkeith, in the house of his friend, Dr. Norman Macleod. My
brother has added some reminiscences of the evening. I
remember well the pipe, and the roll of his stories; his
pride also in ' Deutschland,' his second mother; and Shairp's
delighted pride in him. One story he told of a Frenchman who had been to the Jardin des Plantes, and was
very much struck with the greatness of Cuvier; ending
his remarks by saying that ' if Moses had known Cuvier
was to come after him, he would not have written that
book of his.' He also took us under his wing to stay
a night under the roof of a friend of whom I had often
heard him talk, and whose singing he admired greatly—
Mrs. Murray Gartshore of Kirkintilloch.[1] Mrs. Gartshore
stood before the instrument—she never sat while she

[1] Mrs. Murray Gartshore was the daughter of Sir Howard and Lady
Douglas. She married the late John Murray of Gartshore and Raveletone,
and died at Lymington in 1857. Her friendship was a great interest to
Shairp. He often spoke of her and her wonderful singing. After the visit,
to which Mr. Scott refers in 1847, he wrote—

> Whether thy song hath a wanderer been
>   Through green fields echoing childhood's laughter,
> Or overtakes i' the far Unseen
>   Thoughts of the still Hereafter,
>
> I cannot deem it of the things
>   That perish with their brief to-day,
> It stirs perchance some fountain-springs
>   To murmur in our hearts alway.

played—and sang. I had heard some of her songs at
Houstoun, where they were favourites. But her singing of
them justified all Shairp had told me of them. One was
called 'River, River.' Another was the wail of a mad girl,
with a refrain, 'Ho ro Mhairi Dhubh turn ye to me'—if I
may be forgiven for perhaps mangling a language which I
do not know.

From Kirkintilloch we were to drive to the Broomie-
law and catch the Loch Lomond steamer. Alas! we arrived
late. The other members of the party—Mr. Theodore
Walrond, then a master at Rugby; Mr. Thomas Arnold,
then in the Foreign Office, and on the eve of his journey to
the Antipodes; and Mr. Charles Lloyd, who had been a
master at Westminster, and was then a student of Christ
Church, and an enthusiastic lover of Scotland, where he
spent much of his vacations at Loch Ard—had started from
Mr. Walrond's house at Calder Park. They had been more
punctual than we, and had gone on. What was to be done?˙
It was resolved to take the train to Greenock, and catch
the steamer to Arrochar. Possibly we might overtake
our companions at Inversnaid or the Trosachs. But fate
was against us. At the entrance of Loch Long some part
of the machinery gave way, and we returned hastily to
Greenock, thinking ourselves lucky to escape with no worse
mishap.

The only plan then remaining was to cross to Dum-
barton and follow on the steps of our more punctual friends.
Accordingly we walked to Balloch, and took the steamer
for Inversnaid. Shairp was full of the *Highland Girl*
and the poem *Stepping Westward*. I believe we slept at
Inversnaid, if not at the Trosachs. The idea was to cross
the Braes of Balquhidder, and so strike in on the probable
route of our companions at Lochearnhead. But fate again
was unpropitious. We missed our way, and after crossing
the shoulder of Ben Ledi, came down on the Callander road
below Strathyre, and had a memorable meeting with our
three friends, who were on the road northwards. How I
remember Walrond's laugh as he recognised the shepherd's

plaid, and shepherd's crook, and the would-be tourists, who had begun by missing their steamer!

Whatever they thought of our unpracticality, they would not hear of going on without us and letting us overtake them next day. We had had enough of it climbing the slopes of Ben Ledi, and were glad enough to make our way to Callander, where we slept. Next day we walked by the coach road, past Loch Lubnaig (where Wordsworth's 'Daffodils' were not forgotten), to Lochearnhead and Killin. In the morning we took the road over the side of Ben Lawers, and across Glen Lyon. The weather broke before we reached Loch Rannoch, where we separated— Shairp and Arnold going westward with the intention of tracking one of Prince Charles's haunts on Ben Alder, and so passing along Loch Erichtside to join the rest of the party at Dalwhinnie.

Throughout these wanderings Shairp had been keenly interested in anything that bore on the '45. We were bound for Skye, possibly for Glenfinnan—all was open to us,—and any road that led us on to the Prince's tracks would be a welcome one to the head of our party.

At Dalwhinnie we again separated. . . . The rest went on foot by Corryarrick and Fort Augustus. We arranged to meet at Drumnadrochit, not far from Meal-fourvonie, where Clough had a reading-party. Fortunately for myself, I was one of those who crossed Corryarrick. It was one of those heavenly days (as I think Shairp said of it either then or afterwards) that cannot die. As we reached the summit of the Pass the July sun was setting behind the ranges of the Inverness and Ross-shire mountains. In the west, serrated like the teeth of a saw, lay the Coolin Hills, our farthest aim. In the rifts of the mountains lay some gleaming lakes : 'the eyes of solitude' he called them. I have seen distant ranges again and again, from far greater heights in Switzerland, but no view has stamped itself so deeply on my memory. I see it now, and have always been able to recall it, and I know it impressed him at least as powerfully. There was a poetry about it which

I have not elsewhere felt so consciously. Part of its charm may have been due to its novelty, but I think it was almost wholly drawn from the companionship in which I saw it.

By the time we reached Fort Augustus it was late; so we took a carriage, and drove along the shore of the loch to Drumnadrochit. No precise appointment had been made as to the date of our arrival. We were to appear when we could. As it was, we turned up in the small hours of the morning, and did not even know which was the inn. I remember, in the twilight, Arnold climbed in by an open window, and returned with a book which proved to be Consuelo. Assuredly a book from Oxford. Meanwhile Walrond, always practical, had gone upstairs and invaded a bedroom. The occupant started and remonstrated, but Walrond nevertheless had secured his prize, and returned triumphant with a sock on which was marked the name Scott. This was taken as an indication that my brother and Lloyd had arrived, although, as a matter of fact, the garment belonged to another person of the same name, a Christ Church man, who belonged to the reading-party. Putting together these sufficient tokens, we felt justified in rousing the household, and accepting what beds we could get. We stayed three days. It was a visit not to be forgotten, because the poem of *The Bothie* may have been already in contemplation. It was written, if I am correct, in the following summer. Certainly Drumnadrochit formed the background in several marked particulars. 'The grave man nicknamed Adam'; 'the kilted Hobbes'; 'Arthur, the glory of headers'—all rise before my mind in the persons of Clough himself, Ward Hunt, and Walrond; while 'Philip' recalls to me traits both of Shairp and Tom Arnold, while there are elements in him that belong to neither. The romance, and the ladies that give rise to it, are, I suppose, imaginary; there were no visible traces of any such. At the time, Arnold was to go shortly to Van Diemen's Land. The original name of the poem, which has been altered since, was derived from a lonely shieling on Loch Ericht where Shairp and Arnold had sheltered themselves, either for a while or for a night, in their tiring walk along the loch side. I may add that one trifling incident in the poem was a very free rendering—say rather a travestie— of what had occurred as we crossed Loch Ness, with Clough as our companion, to see the Falls of Foyers. A simple and pretty Highland girl had taken an oar in the boat. Shairp, as I remember, noticed her and asked, with a chivalry that never deserted him, whether she often took her brother's place. I can almost hear him, and see him, now. I need not say the situation was not lost upon Walrond, who often chaffed him during our walk, upon the girl he had left behind him at Invermoriston.

There were other members of Clough's party *qui carent vate sacro.* Amongst them was Lawrence, the author of *Guy Livingstone,* who cannot have been a spirit congenial to the 'grave man Adam.' Another was Blackett, a friend of Congreve's."

The recollections which follow are by the Rev. J. George Scott, Archdeacon of Dublin, written after he had read over the previous paper of reminiscences by his brother:—

" My brother has asked me to read his notes, and add any incidents which might fill up the picture of Shairp's Rugby days." [He gives a detailed account of the pedestrian tour to Drumnadrochit, from which I extract the following.] " Shairp had a volume of Fichte in his pocket on our journey. He was making his first study of Fichte's system, and on entering the house of Mrs. Murray Gartshore, he put the Fichte on the hall table. After luncheon he could not find it ; and when he came in before the evening meal he found that our hostess had seen the volume, and had managed to devour a large portion of it during our afternoon walk. The eagerness of Shairp's conversation with her on the metaphysical problems suggested remains on my memory ; the enthusiasm of Shairp, and the rapid acquisitive power of Mrs. Murray Gartshore's mind, equally arresting my attention and my wonder.

The subject was one into which at my age I was imperfectly fitted to enter. But it gave me the first glimpse of a characteristic, which afterwards seemed to me so marked in Shairp, viz. an interest in the whole range of human thought, a sympathy with the efforts of men searching in different directions, along with a firm faith and hope by which his soul held anchor, convinced that there were truths for which room must be found in any speculations, whatever ideas formerly associated with these might be set aside.

In 1849, or 1850, I was with a reading-party at John Green's house at Grasmere—the same house in which Shairp had been on that party in his Oxford days with Walrond and Proby and some others, to which my brother has alluded. One day, to my great surprise, Shairp came to seek me out there. He was on his way in a covered carriage to see A. H. Clough in Borrowdale, and he asked me to accompany him in his drive. The weather was very bad, and we drove all the way, and found Clough with two or three pupils at ' The Grange ' in Borrowdale. He persuaded us to stay for the night; though unprepared, Shairp dismissed the carriage, and we strolled about in the afternoon, for the sky had cleared, and arranged to walk over the Styhead Pass in the morning. While we were in Borrowdale I had not much conversation with Shairp, for I knew that he had come for a long talk with Clough, and I did not interrupt them, but chatted to the rest of the party. But in the morning we all set out together to walk to the head of the Pass. The river was very full after the rain, but when we came opposite to the Yew-trees, ' the fraternal four of Borrowdale,' Shairp could not be restrained from wading the stream ; and after he had stood for a few minutes under the trees, he came out, and shouted to me to cross over to him, and there he rolled out these majestic lines. I can think I hear him again, as he stood there (it was too wet to lie), and threw himself into the melody of the closing verses—

> To lie and listen to the mountain flood
> Murmuring from Glaramara's inmost caves.

At the head of the Pass, Clough sadly bade him farewell. They returned to 'The Grange,' and Shairp and I walked on down Langdale, and up to the top of the Pass of Lough-rigg, where he told me how, on the last day of his former sojourn with the party in Grasmere, he had walked down from Loughrigg to Rydal Water, as he was about to do again, repeating over and over to himself—

> Flow down, cold rivulet, to the sea,
> Thy tribute wave deliver ;
> No more by thee my steps shall be
> For ever and for ever."

Shairp's own account is as follows:—

"In the summer of 1847 Clough had a reading-party at Drumna-drochit, Glen Urquhart, about two miles north from Loch Ness, where, about the beginning of August, I, along with T. Arnold and Walrond, paid him a visit. Some of the incidents and characters in *The Bothie* were taken from that reading-party, though its main scenes and incidents lay in Braemar. One anecdote I specially remember connected with that visit. On our way to Drumnadrochit, T. Arnold and I had made a solitary walk together from the west end of Loch Rannoch, up by Loch·Ericht, one of the wildest, most unfrequented lochs in the Highlands. All day we saw only one house, till late at night we reached another on the side of the loch, about six miles from Dalwhinnie. It was one of the loveliest, most primitive places I ever saw even in the most out-of-the-way parts of the Highlands. We told Clough of it, and when his reading-party was over, later in the autumn, he went on our track. He spent a night at the inn at the west end of Loch Rannoch called Tighnaline, where he met with some of the incidents which appeared in *The Bothie.* He also visited the house by the side of Loch Ericht, a small heather-thatched hut, occupied by one of the foresters of the Ben Alder forest. He found one of the children lying sick of a fever, the father, I think, from home, and the mother without any medicines or other aid for her child. He immediately set off, and walked to Fort William, about two days' journey from the place, but the nearest where medicines and other supplies were to be had. These he got at Fort William, and returned on his two days' journey, and left them with the mother. He had four days' walk, over a rough country, to bring medicines to this little child, and the people did not even know his name. On these occasions in Scotland he told me that he used to tell the people he was a ' Teacher,' and they were at once at ease with him then. I doubt whether he mentioned this to any one but myself, and to me it only came out casually. . . . In this year he visited the West High-

I

lands, and went through 'Lochaber, anon in Locheil, in Knoydart, Moydart, Morrer, Ardgower, and Ardnamurchan.' In the first edition this line was—'Knoydart, Moydart, Morer, Croydart, and Ardnamurchan.' But he discovered afterwards that Croydart was only the way that the Gael pronounce what is spelled Knoydart. During this wander he saw all the country about Ben Nevis westward to the Atlantic—

Where the great peaks look broad over Skye to the westermost islands.

He walked 'where pines are grand in Glen Mally,' and saw all the country which, in a few lines here and there, he has pictured so powerfully in *The Bothie*. The expression about Ben Nevis, with the morning sprinkling of snow on his shoulders, is absolutely true to reality.

In this expedition he came to Glenfinnan, at the head of Loch Shiel, the place where Prince Charles met the Highland clans, and unfurled his standard. Here there used to stand a nice quiet little-frequented inn, where one could live for weeks undisturbed. But at the time when Clough reached it a great gathering was being held there. The Queen had gone to Loch Laggan, and the ships that escorted her to Fort William were lying at the head of Loch Linnhe. M'Donald of Glenaladale had invited all the officers of these ships to have a day's deer-stalking on his property of Glenaladale, down the side of Loch Shiel, and to have a ball at the Glenfinnan Inn after their day's sport. Clough came in for the ball. It was a strange gathering,—the English sailors, officers, a few Highland lairds, Highland farmers and shepherds, with their wives and daughters, were all met together at the ball. Clough and one of his reading-party were invited to join the dance, and they danced Highland reels, and went through all the festivities like natives. The uproar was immense, and the ludicrous scenes not few. He often used to speak of it afterwards as one of the motliest, drollest gatherings he had ever fallen in with.

Often afterwards he used to speak of his Scotch adventures with great heartiness. There was much in the ways of life he saw there that suited the simplicity of his nature. Even when Englishmen would laugh at the baldness of our Presbyterian services, he would defend them as better than English ritualism and formality."

Returning to Rugby, after this delightful visit to the North, the routine of school work and duty was not broken by any remarkable event, till the long vacation of the following year.

A letter to his sister Grace, in the late autumn of 1847, tells of his intention to spend some part of his next holiday in Germany, and of a visit to Combe Abbey.

[Postmark, 1*st November* 1847.]

"RUGBY, *Sunday night.*

"MY DEAR GRACE—You heard of my being at Oxford. The evening I arrived Walrond had a very pleasant party at dinner for me—Clough, Matthew Arnold, Riddell, Sellar, and one or two more. After that came a meeting of the Decade, at which I had to open. Jowett got me a room in college. Balliol looked more inviting than ever. There seem a very nice set of men there now, some very clever ones, with life and health stirring and strong within them. I more than half wished that I were just going up, as this time seven years, especially if I had been as well prepared for it as many who go from this. No doubt the undergraduate time is the most interesting, but even when that is over, Balliol is a very interesting workshop to those who have work there. I know no other so much so. My time was too short. . . .

I am thinking of spending the first part of the Christmas vacation in Germany, if there be no reasonable let or hindrance. You know I feel the want of German very much in several ways. In fact it cripples me on all hands. Jowett thinks of going to Bonn, for a month or five weeks during the Christmas vacation, and has asked me to go. It seems a good opportunity, as he knows German well, and in other ways would be an admirable companion. I always liked him, and he teaches you much. Besides he would put me on the right way of mastering German; and in five weeks I might break the neck of the difficulty.

During the whole holiday (Friday week) I gave Edward Scott my mare, and rode Arnold's. We went to Combe Abbey; about nine miles from this—Lord Craven's,—an old abbey; the cloisters now form part of the house. Even I could not help feeling there was something unhallowed in turning to 'uses base,' what *might* have served so much higher an end. But in England and Scotland the Reformation, if it brought much good, was also a scramble for selfishness. The church lands might have been turned to much better

and more national purposes than that of fattening certain
nobles or lairds. There are many fine pictures there of
Charles I.'s family and people. Vandyke's seem to abound
in this country. . . . —Your very affectionate brother,

J. C. S."

Another winter of uniform and strenuous work at Rugby,
with the usual Christmas and Easter holidays, made up the
record of that season, 1847-48 ; and in the autumn of 1848,
Shairp paid a visit to his friends the Scotts, at Delgany,
County Wicklow, some seventeen miles from Dublin.

Of this visit to Ireland, Archdeacon Scott writes : " I
remember his thorough enjoyment of our varied scenery, his
amusement at the humours of the country people, and
especially at my brother John's way of turning off everything with a good-natured joke, his enjoyment of the free
hospitality at Glendalough, where it happened that there
were only children to welcome us—the master being absent—
and his remark that small as the County Wicklow is, it
contained every element of variety in natural scenery, and
that he could understand our not feeling that we needed to
look for pleasure beyond our own resources."

In another letter Mr. Scott writes : " He was markedly
struck by, and often spoke of, the brilliant colouring of the
Irish hills. As he drove from Kingston to Delgany, some
nine miles, he passed the Little Sugarloaf, and often has
he recurred to the vivid impression he then received. The
heather, gorse, and bracken were all at their brightest, and
the line of demarcation between them was marvellously
sharp. It looked almost as if a streak of colour had been
drawn by the brush."

The following are extracts from the Journal written by
Shairp during this visit to Ireland :—

" DELGANY, IRELAND.

" *Friday,* 14*th July* 1848.—Rose before 5 A.M. to have
my first look of Ireland from the sea. A calm cloudy

morning. . . . Looked for some time at the washing waves;
went in a boat to Bray Point, and clambered up to the top of
Bray Head. Thence the view lovely seaward, far as the hills of
Wales—one dimly yet certainly seen; northward by Howth,
Lambay, far as the Mourne Mountains (Slieve Donard).

Thence descended to the beach a little north of Grey
Stones, and bathed just as the sun got behind the hill. . . .
We came home quietly through the fields; had tea near
nine; and then a lovely full moon looking in calmly on
the glen from the farther side—the night-scented stock
filling the air—a calm and soothing time.

Tuesday, 18*th July.* — Breakfast by 8.30. Off by 10
to the seven churches through Annamoe. Saw them all
seven in the following order: (1) The Church of the Holy
Trinity; and then (2) beyond St. Kevin's Bed on a small
landing-place off the west side of the lake. No lonelier place
ever chosen for a church—nothing but the foundations
seen. (3) The one below the waterfall called ——, where
are buried the O'Tooles, the old Irish kings—crosses many
on all sides strewn about; this, overgrown with natural
wood and graves of a thousand years ago, I think the most
interesting of all. (4) Then the one called St. Kevin's
Kitchen with its Tower; (5) Then the Cathedral in the
middle of the burying-ground with its large cross in the
centre; the Round Tower in a corner of the burying-ground.
(6) The Church of our Lady and the great gateway and
arch entering on the burying-ground. Last of all (7) apart,
the Priory of St. Saviour's, in a plantation by itself, apparently with Norman pillars and devices, and not so ancient
as the others. I never saw anything like these before.
They give you a notion of Christianity as it existed in the
loneliest and most savage places, before almost the dawn of
civilisation of any kind. Thence over the hills to Drum-
goff, the inn of Glenmalure—a waterfall at the head of the
glen, about three or more miles above the inn, and the whole
glen strewn from head to foot with rocks—most desolate; as
much so as Glencroe. Soon left desolation behind, and got
into the Vale of Ovoca, down which we drove for seven or

eight miles to the Wooden Bridge at the lower meeting of the waters—for there are two. A lovely vale. I know none lovelier.

19th July.—Started after breakfast from the Wooden Bridge down the Vale of Ovoca to Arklow-by-the-Sea. All the vale most lovely, with high stately banks of noblest young wood. I never saw so perfect a *vale*. The wood has something peculiar about it, or rather the high sweeping curtain-like banks on which the wood grows. Lunched at the Ovoca Inn, near which the first or highest meeting of the waters—where the Avonmore from Annamoe and the seven-church stream meet with the Avonbeg from Glen-malure. The lower meeting of the waters is at Wooden Bridge, where the Avonmore River meets with the united stream of Avonmore and Avonbeg.

The variety and rapid change between undulating hill and glen, and loch and vale and sea, is what most strikes me here. They lie all so close together, and you pass so naturally and enjoyably from one to the other.

20th July.—From the Tent (at Delgany) we watched the cloud-shadows leave the land, and go scudding seaward as I had never observed before.

21st July.—A lovely forenoon through the Down Glen, Sir G. Hodson's place, Kilmacalogue, to the Glen of the Dayle; most enjoyable glen scenery. Sat watching the stream for some time with its gentle, crisp, and many delicate lines, as it flowed fully yet gently between the stones. Got up as far as the great gateway of Rock, where the stream comes through.

26th July.—We all went down to the sea. Aug. and Robert rowed us out for about half an hour, then got on shore and lay on the shingly beach to the north of Grey Stones. E—— read his Sheridan. I read to George Shelley's *Ode to the West Wind,* ' Away, the moor is dark,' etc. Returned home about 7.30. After tea E—— fell to reading aloud to John *Mariana in the Moated Grange,* and *Mariana in the South.* I listened; they two preferred the former, especially the burden.

27th July.—All day I have felt the farewell feeling like an undertone thrilling every thought and word. I wish there were only another fortnight. May our friendship never fail, but be hallowed for ever."

The visit to Germany—referred to in the letter to his sister in November 1847—was postponed till the summer vacation of 1849, when Shairp accompanied Mr. Poste to Dresden. At Dresden they were joined by his colleague at Rugby, Mr. Cotton (afterwards Bishop of Calcutta), and his wife, and together they visited Prague.

The estimate of Cotton, which Shairp contributed to his *Memoir*, has much that bears upon their common life at Rugby, and their visit to Prague, etc. The whole is best told in his own words—

"There are few things that I look back to with such pure satisfaction as the privilege of knowing intimately the late G. E. L. Cotton. In trying, however, to recall those years of familiar intercourse with him I find it hard to do so. The throng and pressure of that busy time have so jostled the incidents and blurred their outlines. It is only the total impression for the most part that remains.

Towards the close of 1846, by the kindness of the present Bishop of London, I went, after leaving Oxford, to Rugby, to undertake one of the masterships there. During the few first days, while I stayed as guest at the schoolhouse, Dr. Tait told me a good deal of the new life and work that lay before me, and spoke of the colleagues I should meet with.

I can distinctly recall the way in which he spoke of Cotton, as one whom it might do any one good to know, whose whole life and work were a great example. Dr. Tait had at that time been a little more than four years head-master, and I could see that he had formed for Cotton a peculiar admiration and affection.

I cannot quite recall the first impression Cotton made on me, only I think it was of one who stood calm and self-possessed in the midst of a great whirl of work and many more excitable persons.

In general he received strangers quietly, and it was not at first that they were most taken by him. In due time, by our mutual friend Bradley, we drew to each other, and began to have walks together on half-holidays and Saturdays. Having lately left Oxford, I was full of views and thoughts which were then seething there below the surface. In these Cotton was much interested, with firm intelligent desire to know what way the currents were set in the University, and from kindly sympathy with young men and whatever engaged their thoughts. In these conversations two things in him soon struck me : first, the large tolerance, and perfect fair-mindedness, with which he tried to understand and judge ways of thinking that were different from his own ; and secondly, his stability. While opening his mind to new views he was not carried away by them. He held fast without effort by his old fixed moorings—those truths, few and simple, which were the roots of his being.

During these early years of our intercourse I remember a characteristic point of his mingled humour and practical downrightness. Mr. Mill's *Political Economy* had just been published, and several of the masters agreed to read it, and discuss it together afterwards, chapter by chapter. Cotton was one of these. In one walk the early chapter on Productive and Unproductive Consumption formed topics for discussion. The truth was brought out very clearly, that all that was spent in recreation, banquets, etc., beyond what goes to invigorate body and mind for fresh productive labour, is so far wasted, and a loss to the community. With most persons it would have stopped there. Cotton, partly from love of a joke, partly from his earnest practical turn, began to press this truth home. Banquets among the masters had at that time, in some quarters, grown to rather large dimensions. He urged that all banquets should straightway be curtailed within the limits prescribed by political economy. This proposal to square practice by speculation caused much discussion and amusement, and gave rise to one humorous incident.

. . . .

Our intimacy, once began, was ripened into friendship by some time spent together abroad in the summer of 1849. We met at Dresden, where Cotton and Mrs. Cotton were staying, two of his sixth form pupils accompanying them.

Together we all travelled to Prague, spent some days there, and returned to Dresden.

It would be impossible to find a more delightful travelling companion than Cotton was. His entire unselfishness, his perfect temper—placid, even, and always interested—the continued play of his quiet peculiar humour on all the little incidents and traits of character we met with, his unwearied love of things and places historic, the thoroughness, the kindliness that pervaded all he said and did, made his society at once calming, strengthening, and exhilarating.

Prague, I remember, greatly charmed him. He was struck by the Eastern look it had, which was something new to all of us. There was the palace and church of the Hradschin, with its tombs of the Bohemian kings nine centuries old ; the bridge with its crucifix and ever-burning lamps, supported by a fine laid on the Jews; the mouldy synagogue, one of the earliest in Europe ; while in the shattered windows and battered walls of the houses were freshly seen the marks which Winditzgratz and his Austrians made on the town during last year's revolution. It was the enlargement it gave to his historic sympathies that formed to him the greatest charm of travel. One occurrence at Prague greatly amused Cotton. On the first evening after our arrival we were invited to a party, which turned out to be made up of German-hating Czechs, the name of Sclavonic inhabitants of Bohemia. We had never till that day exactly known of the existence of this small race of Sclaves. But that evening we found ourselves sitting with a number of fierce, patriotic Czechs, toasting in German wine, 'Auf die Bruderschaft der Czech und der Engländer.'

While Cotton was at Rugby, each summer vacation—sometimes the Christmas ones too—was laid out methodically, not merely for ease and pleasure, but to combine needed relaxation with some increased enlargement of his knowledge of men and of places famed in history.

In the summer of 1850, while Cotton and Mrs. Cotton were in Germany, he had a severe attack of rheumatic fever, which prevented him from returning at the usual time to his school duties. As I had then no boarding-house of my own, Cotton wrote asking me to undertake the charge of his for a time. After some weeks he was so far recovered as to return to Rugby, still quite unfit for work. He and Mrs. Cotton returned for a week or two, and lived in their own home as guests—the name and character he insisted on assuming. After a short stay he left again for the rest of the half year; but I still vividly remember with what consideration and good feeling he carried the whole thing through, so that he converted what might have been an embarrassing situation into a most pleasant and friendly visit. During the weeks I took this charge I had an opportunity of discovering, what I had always heard of, the excellence of Cotton's work as head of a boarding-house. It was a house in all things well ordered, filled with a prevailing spirit of quiet industry and cheerful duty-doing.

.   .   .   .

It was early in 1852 that he accepted the headship of Marlborough. His going from Rugby was the greatest loss it could sustain. But he felt that his work there was done, and that he could put forth fresh energy, in a place which he could mould to his own mind. That summer, just before he went to Marlborough, he came down to Scotland and visited at my father's home.

.   .   .   .

When we left my father's house he made me lead him through the vales of Tweed and Yarrow. Dryburgh Abbey we visited in the beauty of a summer morning, then Melrose and Abbotsford. In the afternoon I took him up Tweed, through the beautiful woods of Yare, to the ridge of the hill behind it. There, pausing and looking westward, we saw beneath us the whole course of the Yarrow, as it winds from the lochs down through the green interlapping hills. The westering sun was streaming down the 'bonny braes.' Two nights we stayed by still St. Mary's Lake, and all day we wandered among the hopes and side-glens that come into Yarrow—the Douglas Burn, Kirkhope, by Dryhope Tower, and the rest—while I told him the traditions and ballads that still haunt the spots, and make more than half their charm. We then walked down Moffatdale, and parted at Moffat. Sometimes during this short tour, as we wandered among the green hills, Cotton would begin to discuss some difficult question of education or scholastic management. The enterprise of remodelling Marlborough, now close before him, was evidently much on his mind. After one or two conversations I bargained that these topics should be left till we had reached our inn at night. Savouring as they did of the work-day world, they seemed alien to the dreamy stillness of those green pastoral uplands. To this he readily agreed. In a letter which I received from him soon after we parted, he told me that his enjoyment in this short tour had been only second to what he had felt in seeing the two or three great-world sights of his life."[1]

. . . .

. Mrs. Cotton has sent me an undated letter of Shairp's to her husband from Houstoun, which evidently belongs to the year 1850, and from which I extract the following :—

"19*th January.*—My days have been, most of them, spent in *curling*, a game on the ice peculiar to Scotland. During these three weeks past I have thought nothing of the late contest, and very little of future prospects. Time and oblivion are better healers I find than one's own conscious efforts. Being always averse to pushing and promotion-hunting, I do not intend to do it now, further than I should probably have done if there had been no change in the head-master. If I see Temple I shall tell him that I do not wish to spend all my best years at Rugby. Further than this, I shall do nothing. . . . I rather enjoy this snowstorm, the greatest they say since 1838. . . . οἱ νεόγαμοι will have full time to indoctrinate their brides these snowy days. If my 'Greek Kalends' ever come, may they fall in summertide !"

The above was written during the Christmas holidays of 1849-50, which were spent as usual in Scotland. During this time Shairp kept a Journal of his daily life, and several extracts from it will reveal another side of his character. There is a curious resemblance between the points noted in almost all of his Journals, and the way in which Dorothy

---

[1] *Memoir of George Edward Lynch Cotton, D.D., Bishop of Calcutta*, pp. 18-29.

Wordsworth chronicled the events of the day and the hour in her numerous Diaries. The resemblance is not only in the direct pictures, and simple graphic touches, in recording even the weather changes, and anything unusual in the face of Nature, but also in the minute interest shown in things that to others would be too [trivial to note. In both cases these familiar jottings are redeemed from commonplace by the way in which they are handled.

" *Houstoun*, 19*th December* 1849.—Once more at home, and find all calm and quiet as it has so long been. Let me use this well and thankfully while it lasts, that so using it we may all gain that true inward life which will sustain us when this life of our earthly homes is no more allowed us.

On Thursday last (13th December), at Rugby, there was a deeply interesting day to me. I never felt before so strongly the interest of my work there. It was the spirit as opposed to the letter, and mechanism, which so often burdens me ; a day of advice and encouragement (a re-buke to one), and of leavetaking, and of words spoken for the journey of life. After second lesson I had a long and most delightful talk with Horace Davey. First I looked over his Philology Paper, which he had done for the Exam., and told him what I could about it ; then spoke to him of his being in the sixth next year. Before this I advised him to read some of Cicero's *Letters to Atticus*, Book XIV., during vacation, but by no means to burden him-self with work, but to refresh ·body and mind. I had ad-vised him to read the poetry he liked, and then followed the Wordsworth and the *Christian Year* with his name on them. He seemed calmly delighted and went his way. All this first half-year my affection for him has been growing. My intercourse since ever he came to Rugby has been un-brokenly delightful, and this last half-year I have seen over and above his clear keen spirit. If life and health are given him, my hope for him is high.

Houstoun, Sunday Evening, 23*d December.* — In the afternoon read Isaiah xxxii., also Keble's most beautiful

hymn for the first Sunday in Advent (to-day). Then the
fifth of Newman's *Discourses*, a most striking setting-forth
of the general worldliness of society, as seen in the worship
everywhere of the two great idols, wealth and notoriety; and,
contrasted with these (the world's standard of things), the
Christian's standard, saintliness. All that he applies only
to the Catholic would seem to hold of the real Christian,
whatever his church.

Christmas Day, 25th December 1849.— . . . Read to
B—— a part of Newman's Sixth Sermon, and then
finished it by myself. It is on every man being born for
a purpose—to do some work—not to live by his will but
by God's. All but some isolated Roman sentences seemed
true, so deeply true. It is perplexing to read these, and
find so much which seems as true as any human words can
be, intermixed with other things held by him as equally
true, which, to one bred as I have been, it is impossible to
believe. One is led to ask whether, between what seems
true and what untrue, there is some secret necessary link
which I do not perceive.

Houstoun, Sunday, 30th December. — T—— and I
walked over to Ecclesmachan. J. Smith preached a very
feeling sermon on Psalm ciii. 14-19. It was full of
touching thoughts and allusions to the fleetingness of our
life here, and the need of a resting-place in God. After
church I went and had a long talk with him. Came away
about 3.30. The sun was down—a calm evening; golden-
orange glow in the west, · smallest white fleecy clouds
overhead, like the ripple on a calm sea. A quiet hour as
I walked homeward. . . . Many things haunt me, in the
calmness and unbroken flow of my life here. I often wonder
whether or not it would be better to give up some of the
pleasures—hunting for instance; not that I think it wrong,
but I have scruples about it. Perhaps it breaks in on any
dawnings of spirituality; on the other hand it is freshening,
exhilarating, strengthening for body and mind. And it
does not do to encourage morbid or womanly feelings, nor
to begin a life of self-denial from which one may after-

wards recede. Better to be slow in beginning than too
quick and rash. Still let me try to be honest.

Cathlaw,[1] *Wednesday, 9th January.*— Read after breakfast some of Bushnell, also a page of German (Goethe's *Italian
Journeys*). About 2 went out to meet T—— and C——,
who had been looking at Charles and the Torphichen curlers.
We two walked up by the Silver Mines, and looked at the
strata in the lime quarry immediately north of the Knock
Hill. Then by the Mount E—— cottages, and down
alongside of the South Silver Mines or quarry—a surface
layer of 8 or 10 feet of black blaze ; then the limestone
strata over some whinny, mossy ground ; traced the ' tods '
among the snow. Went into a weaver's cottage on the
west side of the hill, then across the fields to where the
Torphicheners were curling, chill and dark the air, still
freezing keenly. Then over the Torphichen Hills to the
north side of Torphichen village to have a look at the old
Preceptory, very fine with the hills as a background.

Calder Park,[2] 10*th January.*—Got to Calder Park just
in time for dinner. Sir Henry Stuart there. A pleasant
evening.

Lochwinnoch Day, Friday, 11*th January.*—Still cloudy,
with bitter wind from south-east. About 11.30 Walrond
and I started for Glasgow. At 1.30 we set off by train for
Lochwinnoch, and reached rather before 2.30. There was
a grand sight. About 150 rinks from all parts of the
country — Perthshire, Stirlingshire, the three Lothians,
Lanarkshire, Renfrewshire, Ayrshire,—perhaps Peeblesshire
and Dumfriesshire,—assembled, besides crowds of spectators.
There were three rinks of ' Upha' chaps.' My father did not
go, from his influenza. Two of the rinks won ; the 3d
E. Glens was beat by Kilmarnocks only by three shots.
Altogether a cheering and most national game.

Houstoun, Monday, 21.—Our last day's curling. In
bed in the morning I put together five verses of a bonspiel
song.

---

[1] A place rented by his brother-in-law, Captain Leckie.
[2] The home of Theodore Walrond's father's family.

Tuesday, 22d January.— I went to Dalkeith. As I passed along in the train there was a still solemn sunset behind the eastern peaks of the Pentland Hills—dark ribs of heavy cloud, interlined with deep streaks of crimson and orange. A still solemn background to this bustling moving world. This was over Penicuik, W. Clerk's home. Somehow the stillness and solemnity of it made me think much of him—going too, as I was, to Norman's manse. Met Norman, and went home. A calm, quiet evening, with much grave talk; strengthening and elevating. We sat till 1 A.M.

Saturday, 26th January.—My father and C—— returned from the funeral at Wallhouse. Less than a week ago Mrs. Gillon was alive. Not very well this day last week, but better on Sunday last, and in great spirits on the Sunday evening. And at this moment the moon is shining on her grave in Torphichen churchyard. It is a clear blue night—frosty—the full moon a little west of the zenith. A few of the greater stars out—Orion, the Pleiads, and Sirius (I think); the ground thinly covered with snow. And she lies there. Many a Sunday in going out and in to church she passed the place."

This is the Bonspiel Song mentioned in the Journal, which was written after the Lochwinnoch curling match—

THE BONSPIEL

Cauld and snell is the weather, ye curlers ! come gather.
Scotland summons her best frae the Tweed to the Tay,
It's the North o' the Clyde 'gainst the Southern side,
And Lochwinnoch the tryst for the bonspiel to-day.

Ilk parish they've summoned, baith landward and borough,
Far and near troop the lads wi' the stanes and the broom,
The ploughs o' the Loudons stand stiff i' the furrow,
And the weavers o' Beith for the loch leave the loom.

The braw shepherd lads, they are there in their plaids,
Their hirsels they've left on the Tweedside their lane,

Grey carles frae the moorlands, wi' gleg e'e and sure hands,
Braid bannet o' blue, and the big channel stane.

And the Loudons three, they forgather in glee
Wi' tounsfolk frae Ayr, and wi' farmers on Doon,
Out over the Forth come the lads frae the north,
Frae the far Athole braes and the palace o' Scone.

Auld Reekie's top sawyers, the lang-headed lawyers,
And crouse Glasgow merchants are loud i' the play,
There are lairds frae the east, there are lords frae the wast,
For the peer and the ploughman are marrows to-day.

See the rinks are a' marshalled, how cheer'ly they mingle !
Blithe callants, stout chiels, and auld grey-headed men,
And the roar o' their stanes gars the snowy heights tingle,
As they ne'er did before, and may never again.

Some lie at hog-score, some owre a' ice roar,
" Here's the tee," " there's the winner," " chap and lift him twa yards,"
" Lay a guard," " fill the port," " and now there's nocht for 't,
But a canny inwick, or a rub at the guards."

Gloamin' comes, we maun pairt, but fair fa' ilk kind heart !
Wi' the auld Scottish bluid beating warm in his veins.
Curlers ! aye we've been leal to our countrie's weal,
Though our swords now are besoms, our targes are stanes.

We are sons o' the true men who bled wi' Will Wallace,
And conquered at brave Bannockburn wi' the Bruce,
Thae wild days are gane, but their memories call us,
So we'll stand by langsyne and the guid ancient use.

And we'll hie to the spiel, as our fathers afore us,
Ye sons o' the men whom foe never could tame,
And at nicht round the ingle we'll raise the loud chorus,
To the land we lo'e weel, and our auld Scottish game.

While at Rugby, Shairp kept up correspondence with all
his Scotch friends, as well as with the Houstoun circle ; and
in the following letter to the minister of Kilmalie, his
strong Jacobite sympathy, the minute accuracy with which
he remembered the places he had visited, and his passionate
attachment to his native land, are equally seen. There are
signs also of partial weariness with the work he had in hand,
and of a preference for the freer life he would have, were he
to leave it and return to Scotland :—

[No year given, but it was probably 1851.]

"RUGBY, 11*th September.*

"MY DEAR CLERK—I remember Druimchosie quite well. I saw it that day I walked from Glenquoich to Glenfinnan, as I lay on the top of Scour-corry-buy and looked at those piles of Scours which guard the passes down to the Atlantic. Druimchosie is not a Scour, but a long low ridge running westward, and a little south from the head of Loch Quoich, toward Knoidart—in fact, towards the head of Glen Barrisdale. If I live, I shall yet see with my own eyes Maamclach-archaig, and the ravine up which Charlie crawled.

If Mr. Macdonald of Hunett knows well the country over which Charlie wandered, could he tell you what line he took from Fruich-vein (the hill just over Glenfinnan) to Druimchosie, where he got through the sentinels?

You know that from Skye he landed at Malag, on the south side of Loch Nevish; thence to Bonadale; thence to Fruich-vein over Glenfinnan; thence (under the guidance of Glenaladale and Donald Cameron of Glenfean) to Druimchosie, where he cleared the sentinels. These are the main points; but if Mr. Macdonald knows the intervening points, or any incidents of this journey, I should be glad to know them. For to me there is none of his journeys more interesting than this—I don't think even the one with Flora. I have got a book of the Jacobite Memoirs, edited by Chambers from Bishop Forbes's MSS.; very interesting they are. They give a very detailed account of the cruelties that followed Culloden. History has almost forgotten to record them. I wonder whether Macaulay will. But there they stand, the darkest blot on the Hanoverian line. . . . Will you tell me on what principle these slaughters were carried on, for they seem to have slaughtered in cold blood all whom they knew to have been *out,* and many who stayed at home? Also in what districts was the visitation most severe? and how long did it last? Was it continued after Charlie had fairly sailed? These, and any

other traditions of that time—especially of his wanderings
—will be most welcome at any time. . . .

How well I remember, about fifteen years ago, your
repeating to me, for the first time, in the Greek class-room
at Glasgow, those lines, ' Or like a ship some gentle day.'
It was one of those evening meetings of the Peel Club, after
Norman had been holding forth to a full house. They gave
me a thrill of delight, such as I have seldom felt since—
rarely if at all since. Perhaps only when, from the high
hills of Moidart, I catch a glimpse of the blue Hebrides far
seaward. If we live, I would like to go over some of these
places with you. This is as prosaic a place as a man need
wish. Perhaps some day I may exchange it (how willingly
I would) for a Lochaber sheep-farm. . . ."

In a letter to Edward Scott (22d August 1859), he
said—" I used to repine at returning to Rugby, during this
bright autumnal weather, which seems to call only to the
hills and the sea, where they meet as in the West Highlands."

CHAPTER VIII

IN this chapter are some of the estimates of Shairp sent me by his many friends, and former pupils; and I must again thank those of them who have allowed me to divide their papers into sections, in order to make the biography more complete, while not overloading it with repetitions.

The Archbishop of Canterbury writes—

"ADDINGTON PARK, CROYDON.

". . . When I first went as a young master to Rugby, full of reverence and keenness for the place and its traditions, I found that I had come into a remarkable group of men. Besides Dr. Goulburn himself, Canon and Professor Evans with his intense keenness for Greek scholarship and his insight into its finest expression, Dean Bradley with his Latin prose and his devotion to history, Charles Arnold with his German literature, Charles Evans with his finished, elegant scholarship, Highton with sciences and electric telegraph, and other most interesting men, were all masters there together, as well as Shairp. And those were days not at all bad (as I venture to think) for the boys, when the masters had *time*, after Dr. Arnold's example, to have, and to pursue, studies of their own with some ardour. Among them all Shairp was a most delightful presence. Every one loved him, and felt the infection of his perfectly detached interests. His devotion to Scotland and all that was Scottish, his wide knowledge of poetry, and his memory

of it, and the quiet, appreciative, moist-eyed repeating out
of the very noble and pathetic passages, made him a holiday
in himself. He was most kind and warm to me from the
first, and for my six years there I knew him intimately.
He was very fond of riding a fine horse in the company
of a Scotch staghound of great power and beauty, which,
as we went along roads or through fields, cleared the
highest Warwickshire hedges of that time in steady succession. In these rides, as well as in walking up and
down the Close, he would get quite lost in discussing Coleridge, points about Wordsworth, defining Imagination and
Fancy, etc. etc.

Others told me of the surprise which was felt when he
accepted Dr. Tait's invitation to school-work, and he himself
told me how no known relation of his (I think) had ever
been anything else but a soldier; ' but I thought,' he said,
' that there was a manly strong work to be done among
English boys, and I love lads, and I never hesitated.' He
also, I think, had been keen to work where Arnold had
worked, and he was strongly attached to Dr. Tait. He was
unconventional in his look, with his cap far back, and his
gown carried, till he got into school, over his arm. And
besides, there was generally a look-out kept by his Form in
the hope that he might be a quarter of an hour late, at
which moment the tradition allowed them to depart in all
directions. His Form loved at once his genial, fresh, sunny
face, and fine stature, and fatherly tone, and the penetrating
reverence and gravity with which he spoke of anything
serious, or read the Bible with them. He was extremely
fond of 'Arthur Stanley,' and the Dean in his turn of him.
The Dean told me how once, on a visit to Shairp's home in
Scotland, before his father's death, he was taken by him to
see the ' graves of the Covenanters '; and while he was
himself conjuring up facts and traits of the time, Shairp
became quite silent, and when, among the graves, Stanley
turned to say something fresh, there was Shairp with his
hat held before him in both hands, and his face turned up
and tears streaming over it.

His exclusive love of Scotland was delicious when in England. I remember well being one of a committee of four to settle a history subject for our examination, in Dr. Goulburn's study. One suggested one period, and one another; but Shairp objected to a political period as full of the worse premature lessons for boys, and to the French Revolution as too horrible, and to the Great Rebellion as to two good causes overthrown each by its own badness, and to French periods as mad or selfish, and to the Conquest because nothing was known about it, and to others as badly or drily told, until we asked him to settle his own subject. When he said: ' So far as boys are concerned, the only real heroic history is the *History of Scotland*, and the best and most feeling narrative is the *Tales of a Grandfather!*' Similarly, when some one commended in his hearing a fellow-country-man who spoke English so purely, that there was not a trace of northern pronunciation or accent, Shairp said, in the broadest yet most polished of Scotch tones, 'I never (al-most niver) knew the man (almost mon) who deliberately tried to be rid of his natural brogue, but there was some-thing base in the man.' His delight was great when he secured a beautiful copy of Billings's *Scottish Castles*. We went through them, and the peculiarities of their architecture, most minutely; making every place live with tales and legends and family histories about them.

I wish it were yet lawful to tell many interesting reminiscences of his Tractarian experiences at Oxford. He had been at one time powerfully affected by Newman, and had known Ward very well. His stories of that time, and his views of its leading people, were as vivid, and as clearly put, as anything in his discussions of poetry and literature, so much of which he has since written out and published for all. He used to speak of Ward's ' sharp logic ever goading on leaders,' who were then ' stepping on, feeling the way, quietly and gently, but anxious to go on alone for a time.' He looked on ' the ideal of a Christian Church ' as having, through its author's impetuous nature and ruthless pursuit of logic, ' revealed tendencies much earlier than was intended.'

Of all this I give now no opinion—it was Shairp's interesting view and talk. At the same time, he admired the ascetic self-denying life of Ward, coupled in such strange combination with extraordinary merriment and enjoyment.

One day in arguing with him Shairp ended by saying to Ward, 'You consider your church and system the essence of Christianity. Now, if I've never seen a real Christian yet among my own Presbyterian relations, I never will see one; I'm sure of that.' Ward's reply was, ' Shairp—Newman tells me' ('he always drew on Newman,' said Shairp, 'for facts') ' that there are no *saints* to be found outside the Church,—no *saints* you see—no character that can lay claim to *saintliness*—to be the *saintly* spirit.'—' *Then*,' said Shairp, 'understanding what *he* meant by saintliness, I was overthrown, and could only hold by my own convictions unreasoningly. But afterwards, of course, I saw that if you give an ecclesiastical definition to saintliness, it is no wonder that you do not find saintliness outside ecclesiasticism.'

This story was very characteristic in all points of Shairp. With all his love for his boyhood's type of religion he had a very sincere respect for and love of English worship, and no face ever expressed more simple, manly trust and affectionateness than his always did, as he knelt, with his eyes closed, and his face upturned, and his hands hanging down clasped, before receiving the Holy Communion.

He was an admirable element in our very bright happy industrious Rugby life, with its spaces of recreation. Both his enjoyment of country and country life, and his interest in abstract discussions and in non-scholastic literature, came with great freshness over our own work and that of the boys, many of whom, before it was made a part of regular school-course, took a very vivid and original interest in books which then lay off the path of common teaching.

And, on the whole, I go back to saying that it was the whole man, which was very complete in its type, which impressed one more than any particular things he said and did.

I wish this fragmentary, broken memory of a most true-hearted friend and bright example were more worthy of him. . . ."

The Rev. Arthur T. Butler, of Oriel College, Oxford, writes—

" My first acquaintance with Professor Shairp was as a boy at Rugby, nearly forty years ago, when he came fresh from the University to be an assistant-master under Dr. Tait, and the kindness he there showed me laid the foundations of a friendship, which has been one of the precious things of my life. All old Rugbians of the time will remember the impression he at once created, as he stalked about, sometimes with a plaid around him, and a long crook in his hand, and a noble deerhound at his side, in earnest talk with one of the masters or older boys, often gesticulating, and unconscious alike of the games and of the curious eyes bent upon him by many beholders, for it was at once felt that he was something different from the ordinary schoolmaster. He did his work ; he went through the usual routine of school-teaching and discipline ; he was far too much of a man and a gentleman to fail in keeping a decent order and attention among his pupils, and in his Form ; but it was evident that his mind was often far away, and that the multitude of small details which make up the life of a schoolmaster was not to his liking. ‘ Boys,’ says an old pupil and friend of his, ‘ want regularity, order, being saved from their own exuberance ; in a word, method. Shairp admired method, but had it not. Inspiration was his gift. He was like a wave of the sea ; wherever he came he brought freshness with him.’ If, however, there was any principle of grammar or history to be enforced, or of poetic interest to be noted, there he could be eloquent and instructive, and to a few boys would give a new intellectual impulse in their school-life ; but for the steady, dogged, daily drill at grammar and derivations, as well as for the many devices calculated to keep indolent and inaccurate schoolboys in the path of school-learning, he had, it must be confessed, little taste by nature, and he never acquired it. He was rather a poet and a philosopher, with an intense love of nature and literature ; and he found it difficult and tedious, instead of carrying on his own and others' higher education, to be working only at elements, and giving almost exclusive care to turning a very small wheel in a great machine. It was this in part which led him to say to one of his older pupils that he felt it 'as a knockdown blow, when he reached Carlisle, on his way south.' It was due also, no doubt, to his intense love of Scotland, and his dislike of the tame scenery of an English midland county; but to a poetic mind like his, fond of brooding and leisure, I suspect that the real objection lay deeper. School-life, though full of other and deep interests, is too engrossing to allow of much thought or study, and the constant teaching of rudiments is a burden which to certain minds becomes intolerable. And so Shairp never took kindly to the life of a schoolmaster; it was drudgery; it was not in Scotland; the country round was poor and unattractive; and a schoolmaster is a dominie.

And yet it must not be thought that his work at Rugby was a failure. 'Every man,' said one of his colleagues, 'should be a missionary to his pupils: Shairp was a missionary to the masters.' If to this be added his influence among the older and more thoughtful boys, the picture will be complete. He was a missionary, a preacher, not only, or chiefly, of religious truth, but of whatever things 'are true and lovely and of good report.' And he would find a boy here and a boy there on whom his ardour and enthusiasm made an impression never to be effaced. It was through him that we first learnt to appreciate Wordsworth, Newman, and in a less degree Carlyle, as he poured forth his inexhaustible quotations in a fervent stream of affectionate remembrance ; and it is hard for any one who once felt the spell to think of certain passages in those great writers apart from him. His voice then had a fulness and a resonance which it lost in later years, and there was withal a depth of earnestness and inwardness in his recitations which made them (even while he himself was filled with the vision of St. Mary's pulpit, or of the poet's haunts at Rydal or at Yarrow) seem all his own. And so if his influence at Rugby be measured by a standard of quality rather than quantity, he did a work there in receptive minds for which many a more successful schoolmaster might sigh in vain.

With one pleasant reminiscence, sent to me by an old pupil, I will conclude this sketch of Shairp's life at Rugby. His great deerhound, whose name was Gruim, has been before mentioned. Gruim, it seems, was a thief, or at least from being a great favourite with the boys, and often invited to their studies to be fed, he would also go there uninvited; and, presuming on the affection of his friends, in their absence would help himself, especially to their pats of butter laid out for breakfast. Gruim, however, could do no wrong; and, loving the dog, the boys learnt, though not understanding him, to love the master. Every schoolmaster who is a poet and philosopher should certainly have a Gruim. I have seen the same dog, sitting beside Shairp at breakfast, watch the opportunity, when his master was talking earnestly to a neighbour, and take a cutlet from his plate and bolt it whole. After a time Shairp would look round, and, finding his meat gone, would glance at Gruim. The dog's gravity, however, was equal to the occasion, and instead of the miserable 'not proven' look, which a weaker dog would have exhibited, he stood boldly on his innocence, and was acquitted."

Mr. Butler has also sent me a characteristic story :—

"When he first went up to Oxford he hardly knew any one, and feeling lonely, determined to indulge himself with a day's hunting. Accordingly, he went to the best livery-stables, and demanded a horse. The proprietor was a knowing man, and, after a little conversation, concluded that Shairp was a safe man, and gave him a firstrate mount.

There were a great many 'men' out that day, and the

run was a severe one; and, as it happened, every one was left behind except Shairp and the master of the hounds—a young man very well known and much admired among the sporting members of the University. The two got talking, and Shairp proposed that, being near to Oxford, they should return together and dine in college. This was done, and great was the astonishment of Balliol to see the young Scotch freshman walk into hall, accompanied by the dashing young M. F. H ——, who was, at least to the sporting ones, the object of so much admiration.

That evening, Shairp said, one after another of these men dropped into his rooms, and he found himself at once introduced to as much of the college society as he desired."

The following is a continuation of the reminiscences sent by the Dean of Westminster, Dr. Bradley :—

" Early in 1846 I left Oxford, and entered on the work of a Rugby master. In the summer of the same year a valued colleague died, and as October drew near, the late Archbishop of Canterbury, then head-master of Rugby, asked me one day ' how I thought that Shairp would do as his successor ?'[1] I was startled for a moment, as I felt that Shairp's ignorance of English school-life, his probable deficiency in such parts of a Rugby master's work as the teaching of Latin and Greek verse, and even his entire and delightful unconventionality, and the freedom with which he would discuss all questions—philosophical, social, or theological —might prove serious drawbacks. On the other hand, I felt that his high character and active intellect, and his very originality and fervour, the *perfervidum ingenium Scotorum*, would bring a new element and a most valuable one into our society ; and on asking the opinion of a friend already named, was answered in the characteristic words, ' My dear Bradley, you will all take him to your bosoms.'[2]

---

[1] Dr. Tait had known Shairp well when himself Tutor of Balliol.

[2] Alas ! as I correct the proof of this letter, the grave is hardly closed over the Matthew Arnold whom I quote.

Dr. Tait, after consulting others who knew Shairp better than I, wisely carried out his purpose, and Shairp began his work, I think in October 1846, in lodgings close to my own house, and from that time we gradually became fast friends.

The anticipations formed of him by his friends were in the main thoroughly verified. Among his colleagues there was hardly one, I should imagine, who did not regard him with unusually warm feelings of respect and affection. I should think that there was not one among us who did not feel that his character, his personality, his conversation, his mode of looking at things, his very eccentricities and Scotticisms, had about them a savour of originality and freshness, which was of the very utmost value in a society of English schoolmasters; and his generous, frank, and chivalrous character, his outspoken contempt for all that was petty or ignoble, his genial humour, and his earnest and deep sense of religion won from us something more than respect.

Among the Rugby masters of Shairp's day I might name such men as Bonamy Price, George Kennedy, Richard Congreve, H. Highton, Charles Arnold, Canons Charles and Thomas Evans, the present Archbishop of Canterbury, and his Balliol friend, Theodore Walrond, over whom the grave has scarcely closed as I write these lines. But there was no one toward whom he was more closely drawn than an older colleague, in many respects singularly unlike himself, George Cotton, afterwards Master of Marlborough and Bishop of Calcutta; the close friendship between the two men was one that was and might well be greatly valued by each. If Cotton gained much from his younger friend's fervid enthusiasm and almost restless activity of mind, Shairp not only thoroughly enjoyed the quiet and unfailing humour of his older colleague, but greatly valued his calm and wise judgment, and felt imperceptibly, I think, his influence on subjects in which he was always deeply interested—the larger and more important questions of Christian theology. On these questions Shairp's mind, as was the case with most thinking young

men who had been at Oxford in the years between 1840 and
1850, was often much exercised. He had a strong aversion
to all 'tests and subscriptions,' as also to all oversubtle and
scholastic definitions of things that he thought undefinable.
I remember once, in Dr. Goulburn's head-mastership, his con-
fiding to Cotton and myself his determination not to read
the Litany when it came to his turn to do so (as it did in
those days to all masters, lay and clerical alike) in morning
prayers in the 'Big School'—not on the ground of any stum-
bling at the doctrine of the Church, but because he could
not use the fourth sentence, and address in prayer so abstract .
an idea as the Trinity. I cannot recall the exact solution
of the matter which made us both—Cotton and myself—
seriously uneasy for a time. But no doubt the present
Dean of Norwich—to whom Cotton undertook to speak—
had already found out how true and earnest a brother
Christian he had in a colleague, in whom he soon learned
to recognise something far different from a mere academical
sceptic, or bold questioner of accepted truths. I mention
the story as a not uninteresting trait in the history of one
whom many knew only in the full maturity and fixedness
of his religious convictions.

It was not, however, I need hardly say, to theological
questions that his interest was confined; least of all
to such an aspect of them as I have just indicated.
He was never tired of talking of poetry. It was during
his Oxford and Rugby days that Tennyson gained the
ear, and absorbed the attention of the rising generation
of Englishmen: and Shairp, though the first time that I
ever heard him speak 'upon his feet,' was as the upholder
of the superiority of Wordsworth to Tennyson before 'The
Decade'—a small debating society to which we both had the
honour of being admitted—was yet a devout admirer of the
younger poet. There was a story of some cricketing members of the school coming to a full decision that the Scotch
master 'must be mad;' for, in addition to other eccentricities,
he had walked across 'bigside,' and right through the game,
with a new book in his hand, which he was wrapt in reading,

quite indifferent to the momentous fact of a game being in full play. The book was *In Memoriam*, just published, and the temporary oblivion was characteristic of the man. And whatever may have been the merits of his writings or his lectures or his conversation in later life, it was in those days a real treat to hear him at his best on poetry and cognate subjects. Day after day, when he lived on the Hill Morton Road, before and after my own marriage, and before his own, he would come in after 'first lesson,' stand with his back to the fire, refuse breakfast, but 'prophecy,' as I used to call it, heedless of time, till I remember saying to myself—after seeing him out on his homeward way after one singularly interesting half hour—'better than all knowledge that in books is found is the talk of that half-inspired Wordsworthian.' I am speaking, it will be remembered, of days when he had as yet written nothing, and when his mind and spirits were still in their full effervescence of early manhood.

As was to be expected, he could never thoroughly reconcile himself to the tame and featureless scenery of a midland county. In this the Highlander was strong within him, and the 'voiceless streams and endless hedgerows,' and monotonous undulations of Warwickshire scenery had few charms for him. Though even here he found, as others have found, during a short period in which he occasionally followed the hounds on an excellent hunter, a certain charm in the great sweep of those widespreading grassy fields, and in the occasional old-world, time-worn, farms and granges, past which he would ride after the hounds, looking, he said, as though they had stood undisturbed in a quiet settled country for centuries. Nor could it be said that his work as a schoolmaster, though carried out with unfailing faithfulness and sense of duty, was entirely congenial to him. It was not, I think, that he cared in the least for the curious mixture of feelings, with which his holding such an office as that of 'a Dominie' was in those days looked on by some of his friends across the Border. Of this he used to tell us in his best manner amusing stories. One of these I cannot suppress.

It was a story of a small Scottish laird, who had
known the family of our head-master, who, on hearing
that Archibald Tait, Tutor of Balliol, as he then was, had·
been elected as Dr. Arnold's successor, exclaimed with a
groan, 'What! Craufurd Tait's son made a dominie!
Eh, sirs! that I should have lived to see it!' Once I
remember a touch of the same feeling taking a very different
shape on my dear friend's lips. As we came out of school
one morning in 1853, a troop or two of cavalry of, I think,
the 14th Light Dragoons, rode through Rugby on their
way southwards for the Crimea. Shairp got out his horse,
and rode with them two or three miles, and came back much
interested and excited with his conversation. He came to
me on his way to second lesson, and after telling me about
it, the old soldier's son gripped my arm, in his way, and
said, 'Eh, Bradley, it was as much as ever I could do when I
came back not to roll up this gown and throw it away!' But
in the main, he was for some time, at least, happy and interested in his Rugby life; and if some parts of his work
and of school routine were more or less irksome and distasteful to one of his temperament and habits of thought, his
strong common sense and entire conscientiousness preserved
him from failure. But valuable as his career at Rugby was
both to us, his colleagues, and to not a few of his abler pupils,
and much as I believe he himself gained from the discipline
and responsibilities of the place, yet others than himself felt
that he had a right to look towards a post of a different kind,
and that, with whatever grief at parting, we were content to
see him installed in the chair of a Scottish professor.

I will not enter into either the joys or the sorrows of
the later part of his Rugby life; his most happy marriage,
or the sad and trying loss of his first child, under which no
young mother could have suffered more than he. Both events
alike seemed to call him away from Rugby and towards
Scotland. His old yearning for his own country became
exceedingly strong within him; and the cares of life, and
more settled and decided views on questions on which he
had often wavered, took off something from the youthful

exuberance and freedom with which he would discuss the most momentous subjects.   It was a time also of decaying prosperity at Rugby, and, on the whole, some of his best friends judged with him that the removal to Scotland was a step from which we could no longer dissuade so staunch a Scotsman.

From that time, though we remained on terms of warm mutual affection, I saw him less frequently.   I need hardly say that I read with the greatest interest all that he wrote, and joined with others, who valued him as highly as I did myself, in doing all in our power to promote his election to the Professorship of Poetry at Oxford.

Many instances might be given of Shairp's unfailing readiness to act as the champion in central England of Scottish history, and of the Scottish Church and Nation : one may suffice.   Once, after dinner in my house at Rugby, at a time when Shairp was in an especially Scottish frame of mind, there sat near him a neighbouring clergyman (of Carlisle by birth), an able man, but rather given to promote controversy by saying disagreeable things.   He said to Shairp, 'Your aristocracy, till civilised by England and English force, spent half their time in murdering each other.'   I thought Shairp would have let something fly at him, but he merely replied, ' At all events, Mr. ——, we had a church which was not that of the squire and landlord, but went down into the very hearts of the people.'   Still I was rather afraid of an explosion, and was much relieved by seeing Shairp sound asleep (a weakness of his after dinner) in his chair, while my friend was still talking about the superiority of England to Scotland."

Sir Horace Davey's reminiscences refer both to the Rugby years, and to meetings in the Scottish Highlands afterwards.   He writes—

" I first made the acquaintance of Mr. Shairp when I entered Rugby in August 1848.   I was placed by my father in the house of the Rev. R. B. Mayor, who was a mathematical master ; and as Mr. Shairp had at that time no boarding-house, he acted as the classical tutor of the boys at Mr. Mayor's house. I was Mr. Shairp's pupil until I left Rugby, in October 1852. With his name are entwined the brightest memories of my school-life, and to him I owe the best influences of those four years.

Without being a great scholar, he had a good and quite sufficient knowledge of both Latin and Greek, and whether his heart was in it or not at that time, he spared no personal trouble or pains with his pupils. I cannot, of course, remember all the books we read with him as tutor, but I have a distinct and lively recollection of the *Agamemnon* of Æschylus. I have no doubt he conscientiously instructed us in the construction of the sentences, the philology, the proper emendations of the obscure or corrupt passages, and all the scholarship part of it. But what I remember is his enthusiasm for the poetry and the majesty of diction and rhythm of the masterpiece, and his endeavours to inspire his pupils (not always, I fear, with perfect success) with some appreciation of the greatness of the work we were blundering through, and some spark of his own delight in it. Sometimes, when one of us was wearying his soul with a painful schoolboy's translation of a fine chorus, he would break out and give us a vigorous rhythmical translation of his own. I remember also reading some at least of the *Idylls* of Theocritus with him. I suspect his heart was more in the poetry, than in what he used afterwards to refer to as the 'gerund-grinding,' quoting from Carlyle's *Life of Sterling*. Mr. Shairp always attached great importance to the writing of Latin prose, which he thought the best foundation for a good English style. He used to encourage me to make written translations from Cicero's letters, and put them by for some weeks, and then retranslate them into Latin. My own experience confirms his opinion. It was due to his teaching that I learnt to write tolerable Latin prose.

But it was as a friend, and not as a tutor, that I knew Shairp best. From the time of my first entrance into the school he began to make a friend of me, and I began to love him. We took long walks together, and when I grew

older we went expeditions beyond the limits of a walk on
half-holidays, and sometimes he took me for a ride. I have
no doubt we talked on all sorts of trivial everyday subjects,
for Shairp was never a pedant, or a prig; but he also
talked much of poetry, and he would recite to me whole
poems or long passages, chiefly from Wordsworth, Burns, and
Tennyson, and the songs from Scott's poems in a kind of
musical chant or lilt. One of my most valued possessions
is a copy of Wordsworth, which he gave me in the spring
of 1850. He was also, at that time of his life, full
of Carlyle, and was fond of quoting some racy or humorous
expression of his in conversation. Under his guidance I
read the *French Revolution.* I cannot remember that he
ever talked much of Byron or Shelley. He used to tell me
about his Oxford life, and friends—particularly A. H.
Clough,—of the influence of Newman's sermons upon him.
I do not remember that he ever talked much on contemporary politics, or social questions; but I have a distinct
impression that it was largely to Shairp's influence (I hope
I don't malign his memory) that I went up to Oxford a
youthful radical, ready to reform the world at a day's notice.

In walking in the flat pastures of Warwickshire, Mr.
Shairp would frequently talk of his beloved Scotland, and
to my delight he invited me to join him in a tour in the
Western Highlands, in the summer holidays of 1850. I
joined him at Oban, and thence we went up Loch Linnhe
and Loch Eil to Glenfinnan—the place (Shairp told me)
where Prince Charlie raised his standard in '45. I kept
no journal of our tour, and I have found it impossible to
trace our route on the map. Only certain parts of it
remain in my memory. It was like a new existence to a
boy who had been brought up for the most part in London.
At Glenfinnan we were joined by Mr. Edward Poste, and
Shairp's elder brother, and our first walk was to Arisaig.
We were in the country of *The Bothie,* and I then first made
the acquaintance of Clough's delightful ' Long Vacation
Pastoral.' In some part of the tour we must have gone up
the Sound of Mull, past Ardtornish, round Ardnamurchan,

and past the Scuir of Eigg by sea. I remember reading the *Lord of the Isles* for the first time on board the steamer. We visited Dr. Macleod, 'the High Priest of Morvern,' at his manse on the shores of the Sound of Mull, and spent a night at his house. I remember sitting up to a late hour, listening to his stories of Highland character and marvellous tales of second sight. Thence we crossed the Sound and the Island of Mull to the Isle of Alva; and from there we spent a long summer's day visiting Iona and Staffa, in a large rowing-boat which we engaged. Shairp had not been to these islands before. He would not go in the ordinary way in the excursion steamer with the tourists.

The next thing which lives in my memory is a walk along the southern shore of Loch Hourn, at the end of which we found that the expected inn at Kinloch Hourn had been closed. We were, however, hospitably entertained at Glen Quoich House by Mr. Ellice, whom we met returning with his friends from shooting. The next day we started under the guidance of one of our host's shepherds to walk over the hills back to Glenfinnan, but somehow we lost our way, and when night fell were still in the open hillside, far from Glenfinnan, and our guide had left us. We did not get to Glenfinnan till the early morning. I still remember the tender care which Shairp took of me in our walk through the night, and how I at length reached the inn worn out with fatigue. We spent a night at a manse on the shores of Loch Eil opposite Ben Nevis, which was covered with snow when we rowed across in the early morning to Fort William, where we met Mr. Theodore Walrond and a party, and went up Ben Nevis with them. From Fort William Shairp and I made our way southwards by Glencoe, Loch Lomond, and the Trosachs to his beloved home in Linlithgowshire. I stayed three days with him there, and thence returned home. I have visited Scotland since, but the memory and joy of my first tour, under my dear friend's care, have never been effaced. He was, of course, full of anecdotes of the adventures of Prince Charlie, in the

L

country where he landed, and whence he escaped; but I remember he was careful to tell me (so like him!) that he did not really think it would have been to the advantage of the country that Prince Charlie should have succeeded in his enterprise.

After I went to Oxford I regularly visited Mr. Shairp so long as he remained at Rugby, and on one occasion was laid up in his house by an accident, owing to the fall of a horse, when I received the kindest attentions from himself and Mrs. Shairp. But it became evident to me that his heart was no longer in his Rugby work, and his thoughts and hopes turned towards Scotland, the home of his affections. I was glad, therefore, when I heard that he had been offered, and accepted, congenial work at St. Andrews. The consequence to me, however, was that I almost lost sight of him. My work was in London, and from circumstances I was unable to pay visits to Scotland. I saw him, however, from time to time on the occasions of his rare visits to London, and later more frequently at Oxford.

Others can portray Mr. Shairp's character with greater knowledge and greater skill than I can. His relation to me remains that of an older brother and friend to a schoolboy, which is outside criticism. I can recall the elevation of his character and his tender affection; and his very prejudices added a charm and raciness to his conversation."

Dr. Jex-Blake, lately head-master of Rugby, writes—

"14*th September* 1887.

" My first recollection of J. C. Shairp was his appearance in Rugby Chapel as an assistant-master in the autumn of 1846. I was then a boy in the Fifth Form, seated very near him; and his slightly bald head led me to say to my neighbour, ' Much older than old Tait.' For some time I saw nothing of him; but towards the end of 1850 I was high in the Sixth, and along with Godfrey Lushington and J. H. Bridges—who, like myself, were not his pupils,—and with Shadworth Hodgson, John Cordery, and Horace Davey,

who were his pupils—was often at his house. There, or
strolling in the Close, he would talk of poetry, politics,
morals, and common things of our school-life in a genial
simple way; taking pleasure in a boy's talk, and putting at
the boy's disposal the resources of a man's reading and a
man's brain. The very day I left school, he said to me,
standing by the east end of the chapel, 'You will find
Oxford a place of wonderful opportunities; and there is no
place where real good nature and good temper will carry a
man further.' He also said, 'Oxford is a capital place to
teach you to ride. You have capital limbs for riding.' It
seemed at the moment an odd remark; for I had no idea
that I should do a good deal of riding there—to hounds
and to the drag—with little or no injury to work, and much
good in other ways. He had himself hunted a little at
Oxford, and had won repute thereby in college, and in the
county; from Sir Algernon Peyton among others. While
an Oxford undergraduate, I saw him from time to time at
Rugby and at Oxford; and in our many rides in those days
he would talk horseflesh or poetry with equal animation.
One talk I remember, that lasted from Hillmorton to the
Hempton Hills, seven or eight miles on horseback, wherein
he maintained the great superiority of local patriotism and
local sentiment over any cosmopolitan or humanitarian feeling, as inspiration for poetry. Burns and Scott were quoted
on the one side, Shelley and Keats on the other. He would
talk too of David and Isaiah, and the strong reverence of
the Scotch peasant for the Bible; but there was in those
days a tinge of Oxford Liberalism which wholly vanished
long before his death.

Just when I should have gone in for Greats, I had to
leave Oxford through some sort of fever; and Shairp asked
me to come to Rugby to recruit. I stayed a full fortnight,
and was treated with extreme kindness by both husband
and wife; meeting with sympathy and patience in perplexities which then befell me. I can remember no talk
except of a personal character; but I shall never forget the
visit. He was little at Rugby in 1858-68, while I was an

assistant-master; but I remember well the indignation
aroused in him by some cavils at the Books of Kings, urged
somewhat irreverently by a young Cambridge man. During
my own head-mastership he stayed with me three or four times;
and also stayed with Henry Rhoades and Edward Scott;
and in several walks and rides he spoke with earnestness
against the Radicalism of Oxford and the scepticism which
seemed to him rampant; taking too sad a view, I thought,
of men and things.

Altogether he was one of the freshest and truest natures
I have known,—sterling, loyal, kind; a man all over. He
believed in breeding, in inherited qualities, in poetry, in
Scotland, and he disbelieved in remorseless logic. He did
not find in all respects a congenial atmosphere at Rugby,
and did not possess all the points needed for dealing saga-
ciously with all sorts and conditions of boys; but he was
one of the best men, and, to capable boys, one of the most
inspiring men Rugby has known through the last half
century. As a writer he seems to me endowed with a fine
feeling for poetry, rather than a born poet; and perhaps
some of his prose criticisms on poetry are as good as any
poem he has published."

The following is by Mr. Edward A. Scott, one of the Rugby
masters, whose account of the visit to Clough, in Inverness-
shire, has been given in a former chapter :—

" I first knew Principal Shairp when he became a master
at Rugby in 1846.

I was a boy in the Sixth Form, not in any way especially connected with him; and for some reason unknown to
me became the recipient of unbounded kindnesses from
him. His house, his horse, and his time were always
offered for my use. ' Such intimacy between a master and
a boy, now not unusual, was then quite new; but it always
was Shairp's way. His greatest influence at Rugby was
exercised through these private friendships. I never had
a lesson from him, and only knew him as an inspiring

friend. What struck me most in him was the combination
of enthusiasm, and a certain precision of character, which I
may almost call severity. He repelled no question; gave
his opinions evidently with no reserve; but made me feel
that there were some questions which it was good not to
ask, for himself as well as for me. I do not think his
opinions were as sharply defined then as they became later;
but I felt even then that in the freest discussion he was
shaping an opinion, and would have me feel that discussion
for discussion's sake was useless. I remember particularly
conversations on Spinoza, Shelley, and Byron, if I can speak
of a conversation when I can only have been a listener; and
perhaps still more short turns, almost surprises, in which
his stern Presbyterian training came to the front, as if it
were the rock-substratum of his character. But Wordsworth
and Newman were his main themes. I can see him now,
and hear him, as he used to roll out lines of the one, and
declaim periods of the other: lamenting always that he
had not the memory qualified to retain words in their exact
order. More particularly Wordsworth's poems written during
his Highland tour, and the peroration of Newman's last
sermon, delivered in the Anglican Communion, were his
favourites. But it is hard to say what Scotch poetry, or
what English writing since 1800, was not opened up in
flashes, during walks, and rides, and breakfasts, or teas, to
which I received such frequent invitations.

It is not easy to describe, or even to recall, the novelty
of such companionship in a boy's life, extending itself over
the whole range of his interests, while it opened a new world
to him beyond them. Rugby was not a congenial place to
him, either then or later. But this uncongeniality only
made more attractive the freshness of the new life which he
opened to his pupil.

Nor was this freshening power felt only by his pupils.
It was as warmly recognised by his colleagues. Bishop
Cotton, whom I knew well, and under whom I lived for five
years as my chief at Marlborough, was full of this theme.
He spoke of Shairp as a unique force: a fountainhead of

originality. The present Dean of Westminster, who at that time exercised the most vigorous influence as a teacher, used to say that 'Shairp was a missionary to the masters.' As a form teacher he was never quite at home. Method was foreign to him, as he often said. At a later period, when Dr. Goulburn gave him work with the Sixth Form, his special powers had more scope. But I should expect to find that those who owe most to him have incurred the debt from conversation, or incidental remarks, throwing light into dark places, and kindling interests previously dormant, rather than from any systematic or complete map of knowledge laid down for them. The delicate appreciative power combined with firm and definite conviction, which marked his mature writings, I can now trace clearly in my recollections. At the time criticism, enthusiasm, sense of duty, and the warm glow of a poetical imagination drew me by a complex chain that I should not have cared to analyse, even if personal affection had permitted me to do so. I loved him all my life, and wish I could have loved him even more than I did. No man has ever done so much for me, or made me so deeply his debtor.

The charm of his presence only seemed to deepen, and to throw itself over all who came within its reach. His manner with women was perfect—having in it something chivalrous : a combination of freedom and self-restraint, which I have not seen equalled in any other person. He seemed to set value upon everything that was sincere and natural, and from my first acquaintance with him always imbued me with something of his distaste for people who 'could not be themselves.' This lay at the bottom of his frequently-expressed admiration for repose of character. It was not the repose of artificial superiority, but the repose of Nature, true to herself, of which he spoke.

To myself he remained to the last what he had been in 1840. When he was talking nothing was allowed to interrupt his flow, as nothing interrupted my desire to listen. I have often stayed with him as he was dressing or undressing. The last time he was in my

house I saw him almost into bed, as I had so often done
as a boy."

The Dean of Salisbury writes thus of the same period

"It was in 1847 that I spent an evening with Shairp at
Rugby, and saw for the first and only time the Close, the
Chapel, and the Library, all speaking of the remarkable man
whose life, through Stanley's admirable biography, was at
that time so often in the thoughts of Oxford men.
Shairp was full of the delights of his new life, and spoke
much of his intercourse with B. Price, Cotton, and Bradley,
in whose house I found him residing during Bradley's honey-
moon. He spoke with great admiration of the judgment
and skill with which Dr. Tait was managing the great school;
and told me, I remember, that all doubts as to his efficiency
had entirely passed out of Stanley's mind and other old
pupils of Arnold. With metaphysical questions he was
now much occupied. I think that he looked forward to a
Chair in some Scottish University, and we had a long conversation on Spinoza, and a remarkable article contributed by
J. A. Froude to the *Oxford and Cambridge Review*. Froude
had turned his back on his old Oxford friends, and though
still a Fellow of Exeter College, had begun to show his
sympathy with advanced German thinkers. During the
period of my undergraduate life, Shairp came occasionally to
Oxford, and as I was fortunate enough to enjoy the friendship of some older Balliol men, I had frequent opportunities
of meeting him, and enjoying his hearty and enthusiastic talk.
It was his custom to read some dialogues of Plato, and,
when he came to Oxford, to discuss them in walks with one
of his dearly-prized Balliol friends, the late C. E. Pritchard. I
remember he came to breakfast with me after one of these
walks. The only other person present was the late Sir
Alexander Grant. When breakfast was over, Grant, putting
on his gown, said, 'I must go to Jowett's lecture, but I
have had one from you, Shairp, already, on the Parmenides;'
and, indeed, Shairp had talked of little else. When Grant

had gone, he remained with me and recited a poem of A. H. Clough's, beginning with the words, 'I give thee joy.' I took it down from his lips, wrote it in a commonplace book, where it now stands, and I found it afterwards in the small volume of *Ambarvalia*, published in the same year by Clough and his friend Burbidge. It is almost impossible for me to say how much I owed at this time of my life to the healthiness and high tone of Shairp. I was passing through the period of Goethe worship, which I suppose came strongly upon many Oxford men of my generation, and I greatly wish I had preserved a short letter in which Shairp exhorted me to read an article in the *Edinburgh Review*, by Herman Merivale, on the Goethe festival. I obeyed his order, and when we next met in 1850 at Oban, he expressed pleasure at finding that I had, as he said, taken a turn for the better, and had begun to see that Carlyle's idol had some flaws in him.

It was delightful to see Shairp in the West Highlands. There were many Oxford men at Oban at that time. Some were reading, and among them the present Speaker, with Mr. Jowett. Sir M. E. Grant Duff and I were pupils of a great ethical coach, Mr. Palin; but we all met together frequently in a way which recalled something of the freedom of Clough's 'Pastoral.' Shairp and Mr. Poste, who had been his fellow-traveller, were full of their experiences in Morven, and we heard much of the simple and delightful life of the manse, where one well-known member of the Macleod family reigned like the spiritual chief of the district. It was the year when *In Memoriam* appeared, and there is an old churchyard not far from Oban, which will ever be associated in my mind with Shairp's recitation of the poem on 'Lazarus.' Jowett had preached a remarkable sermon to the congregation gathered, under the auspices of Bishop Ewing, in an upper chamber, and when the service was over, Shairp, with his plaid round him, walked with two or three others in search of this old burial-ground. As we returned there was a purple hue over Kerrara not unlike the glow on Olivet alluded to by Tennyson."

A pupil friend of Shairp's at Rugby, Mr. Shadworth Hodgson, sends me the following:—

"When Mr. Shairp came to Rugby as an assistant-master, it was my good fortune to be in the number of those who were assigned to him as pupils. From that time I date a stimulus and an influence which have been of the greatest value to me, and which were owing, I think, far more to the rare personality of the master than to any special feature in the classical instruction which he imparted in the ordinary course of school studies, excellent as that also was. The schoolmaster of typical excellence, I suppose it would be admitted, is he who is excellent alike in dealing with boys in school and out, alike in the class-room and in the cricket-field, in indoor work and outdoor sports; who encourages boys to work while at work, and to play while at play; feeding and developing their mental powers, while at the same time maintaining the due limit between the bodily and mental domains, and combining harmoniously the energies proper to both.

It was not, however, in this direction that Shairp's special excellence lay. To be a typical schoolmaster was not his ambition, though he fully satisfied the ordinary requirements of the type. His unconscious message to us schoolboys was a message from the world of life, not only outside school, but also outside even that larger world of ordinary careers of business or pleasure, for which school is the preparation—a spark or ray from the ideal life of man as a denizen of the planet Tellus, haunted and guided by the Eternal Mind. In one word, Shairp was a *poet*, a poet not so much by the accomplishment of authorship, as by necessity of nature. That great gift was his, by which, when adequately supported and subserved by technical skill, the painter, the sculptor, the musician, and the penman produce works in their several departments, which convey, and in a manner express, what is ineffable in the works of Nature, and (ineffable though it be) yet at the same time appeals to and awakens feelings of pleasure and delight, not transitory and modish, but permanent and continuously developable, from having their roots embedded and interlaced with the inmost fibres of the human mind.

This, I think, and have often thought, in looking back upon it afterwards, was the source and secret of Shairp's great moral and intellectual influence upon his pupils. But to describe, or even enumerate the various ways, and countless minute incidents, by which this influence oozed so to speak, and was communicated, is a far more difficult task. One chief mode perhaps was by his quoting, and reciting lines and fragments of poetry, which expressed his own feeling, and by the tone in which he would recite them. He was a great rider, fond of expatiating on the delights of riding to hounds, and of a burst across country. Often have I heard him repeat from a well-known song—I think I hear him now—as I accompanied him one day in a somewhat tamer ride, when staying with him at Rugby as his guest in my undergraduate days—

> When he leaves his care on his bed behind,
> And the world is all fresh before him.

One of his most marked and striking characteristics was the deep-seated chivalry of his disposition and temperament; and in perfect harmony with this was not only his delight in all country scenes, and especially mountain scenery, but also his strong nationality and love of Scotland. The mere outward and accidental vehicles of all this—such as were the two beautiful engravings from Turner (one of Loch Coruisk enveloped in cloud), which adorned his lodgings when first he came to Rugby, later on his great Scotch deerhound, and even the partridges cooked Scotch fashion on toast, with which he feasted us occasionally at breakfast—were all vivid and delightful impressions to us boys, and made us apt recipients for that influence which I have striven to delineate. Nor must I omit his keen pleasure and appreciation of physical prowess in any of his pupils, and indeed in any one, at cricket, football, or any kind of athletics. One instance I particularly remember in the case of a pupil of his, and then and since a very great friend of my own, whose name I may perhaps be pardoned for recalling, now that death has unhappily taken him from us, John Frederick Gosling, who at cricket, but chiefly at football, was superb; morally superb also, as I think Shairp then saw.

Naturally, however, the pupil-room, or ' Private Tutor,' as we used to call it, was the chief occasion and means of irradiation, the classical authors there studied offering the most frequent opportunities for genial criticism or illustrative quotation. He treated the ancients as our own flesh and blood, ancestors wise or unwise as the case might be, but always engaged on the same world of experience, the same problems of life as ourselves, though seeing them from different sides, and consequently seeing in some respects more, in others less, than equally wise moderns. Plato would be illustrated from Coleridge, and more especially from Wordsworth. I remember the impressive way in which he once read to us Shelley's *Hymn of Pan*, beginning

> From the forests and highlands
> We come, we come.

The Shelleyan word ' dædal ' was a great favourite of his, and he would enlarge gladly on its expressiveness. But Wordsworth was the poet from whom he chiefly delighted to quote, and whose meaning he brought out by his most impressive recitation. In those days, it should be remembered, Wordsworth was not the universally acknowledged classic that he now is. It was always the specially Wordsworthian passages in Wordsworth that he dwelt on. The shorter and less renowned was the piece, provided it was specially Wordsworthian, the more, it seemed, he was inclined to dwell on it. I remember one day particularly, in conversation, his reciting *Glen Almain* to me, and insisting on its wonderful charm, and on the combined depth and delicacy of its sentiment—

> It is not quiet, it is not ease;
> But something deeper far than these :
> The separation that is here

Is of the grave, and of austere
Yet happy feelings of the dead;
And therefore was it rightly said,
That Ossian, last of all his race!
Lies buried in this lonely place.

Several other instances I could recall were it desirable, but all that I could say would still leave my faint and fragmentary reminiscences utterly inadequate to give anything like a living picture of him whose teaching they are intended to commemorate. Still they may serve to add a grain to the heap contributed by others. Fortunately, however, I am able to conclude them by transcribing a letter which I received from him, I think in the year 1853, the subject of which is still of general interest, and which will do more to paint the true wisdom and sincere kindness of the writer than any words of mine could do. It should be noticed that when Shairp wrote me this letter I had left Rugby for some time, having gone up to Oxford after the Easter Vacation, 1851."

"HOUSTOUN, UPHALL, LINLITHGOWSHIRE,
"6th January [1853].

"MY DEAR HODGSON—I was concerned to see when you were at Rugby that your mind was painfully occupied with thoughts suggested by Carlyle's *Life of Sterling*. That this book, and most of Carlyle's, should suggest such thoughts to one of your temperament is nothing wonderful. Without thinking that I could answer all these questions, even if I knew them, I would wish, being myself *haud ignarus mali*, to suggest one or two practical considerations. I will not tell you not to read Carlyle, for I have read him myself for twelve years now, perhaps too eagerly. Almost everything he has ever written I know more or less. And perhaps no writer living or dead has ever so thrilled me. To this hour I cannot read him without having a thousand unutterable thoughts stirred within me. But he carries one off one's legs like a hurricane. While his power is on you, you cannot see nor think but in his way. Therefore one learns in time that if one is to judge fairly and not allow oneself to be quite overmastered by any one man, however strong, one must, after reading him through, lay him down, get out from under his shadow, and get calmed again. Then when he and others are removed to an equal distance from oneself, one may look at them fairly, judge of their relation to each other and to oneself, of Carlyle's relation to existing opinions, and to whatever other truth one has found in one's own experience to be true. If you feel that Carlyle does not put forth all sides of the truth equally—though no man puts his own large side so powerfully—then one should pause before giving oneself over to his entire guidance. And I think you will feel that there are some very needful tempers of soul which have no place in his thoughts.

The fact is, there are many difficulties, critical, historical, metaphysical, connected with religion which you cannot answer now,—which you probably will never be able to answer. Make up your mind to this at once. On the other hand, there can be no doubt at all about goodness,— about the Christian standard of life and temper, which rises before us in the New Testament. There is no speculative difficulty at all here,—none but the great practical one of realising it. If we could but keep this honestly in view, and do earnestly the good that is right before us, I think we would find all things simplify themselves. Then opinions would in time grow within us—what opinions are necessary— not as a system gathered from without by the head, but as the result, the reflex, of life.

I remember that at your age I had—what I daresay you now have—a strong desire for a consistent system, for some standard and principle of knowledge within, by which to measure and adjust all things without. Long one felt this, and searched philosophical systems in hopes of finding it. But now one feels that his knowledge is something far more fragmentary and imperfect,—that it would be enough if he were given not a consistent intellectual system of all things, but a consistent and single-aimed life—one that was at harmony with itself.

I should not have written to you thus, but that I have found, when in a like frame of mind to yours, some such suggestions as these from others give me some help and comfort.—Believe me, your very sincere friend,

J. C. SHAIRP."

A previous letter, written in June 1851 to the same pupil and friend, if not so characteristic, has an interest of its own. He speaks of being "knee-deep in examination papers," but refers to his friend's essays in *The Rugbeian*, which he praises, "not so much for the results at which they arrived, as from the marks they contain of patient thought, and the attempt to look at things from your own point of view, without repeating the sayings of books and men. This when natural, and not much striven after, is always good." At the same time he found the papers "incomplete and obscure. This I hardly regard as a fault in one of your age. It is almost the necessary condition of any attempt to think or write for oneself. Perhaps the Plato and Coleridge you have read encourage this, as in all those who take to them they call up 'thoughts beyond the reaches of their souls.' Therefore I never find· fault with obscurity, if a fellow really strives to speak as plainly as he can, and makes conscience of doing so. But if one lets oneself get into a habit of leaving things cloudy, from carelessness, or a belief that therefore they are grand and deep, this is a bad fault. Hence it is good for all those who love the idealists to read some of the hard definite realists, as Aristotle and Mill. This last, with much that is unsatisfying, has this great excellence, that whatever he has to say, he makes a duty of putting it as clearly as he can. It really amounts to a moral virtue in him, akin (ἀδελφά, as Plato would have it) to honesty and thoroughness of character. . . . I think if some time in your first year[1] you would finish *The Republic*, making a short analysis of it, you would find it an excellent introduction to the *Ethics* and *Politics* of Aristotle."

---

[1] At Oxford.

One important part of his work at Rugby was his Sunday evening Addresses to the boys in his house. They illustrate his own ideal, and are simple, direct, earnest appeals, going straight to the point as an arrow to its mark. There was nothing artificial or morbid in the style of these religious addresses. I select one delivered in November 1852—

"To-day, left alone while all of you were in church, and some were at the Holy Communion, the thought, often present, again recurred, whether five years hence, when you who are in this house now are scattered over the face of the earth, some of you perhaps in every quarter of the globe, you will be able to look back with thankfulness to this place and feel that it has indeed been good for you to have been here. By that time, of those who may be spared to see it, all of you will have fixed on, most of you will have already entered on, your profession. Probably many of you have fixed on it now. . . .

But on all of you, whether you have already chosen your profession, or whether you have yet to choose it, two things I long to impress—first, *the duty and the blessedness of work* for every human being ; secondly, the *right spirit* in which to enter on our appointed work on earth, and the encouragements so to enter, whatever may be its nature.

Now the duty of work the world is not slow to acknowledge, but when you go on to speak of its blessedness it will laugh at you outright. According to its view, they only are the blessed who inherit a fortune, and can be 'men of pleasure.' Work it regards as a hard necessity, incumbent on the many in order to get a livelihood, to be endured for a time till we can make ourselves affluent, then to be flung aside that we may live at ease. Is it to be wondered at that men or boys who hear such maxims from their childhood should soon become hard and selfish, mere money-getters or fortune-hunters, or at best wholly given over to ambition ? . . . But there is a higher and truer view of life than this. No man, whatever his circumstances, whether born to a fortune or born to nothing, can live long and not devote himself to some determinate line of duty without greatly injuring his own character. A profession, a fixed line of duty, is the moral framework in which our lives are cast. . . . It disciplines a man, brings him into intercourse with his fellow-men.

But we are apt to think of our profession as one thing, of our religion as quite another, as if these two things had each their own distinct sphere, wholly apart from and independent of each other. Christianity knows no such distinction. Nay, it is one of its chief objects to destroy this distinction. It tells us of a Kingdom not far away, and in eternity only, to be entered on when we shall have put off the body, but a Kingdom actually here and now, though we see it not ; a Kingdom which even you cannot see, but our hearts can feel and partake of : for it cometh not with outward show, but is among us and within us ; a Kingdom which, established on the earth by Christ Himself, has never failed, but has gone on leavening mankind ; a Kingdom not to be measured nor confined by this Church nor that, nor by all the Churches, but which will surely recognise as its own whatsoever is pure and good in humanity ; a Kingdom which rejects nothing but what is evil, but which claims for its own, to be used in its service, all gifts of body, mind, and spirit, all strength and health and manliness, all intellectual gifts, all moral force, all spiritual devotion and self-sacrifice. This is the Kingdom for whose coming we daily pray. . . . It is an awful thought, but at the same time a thought of joy, that every one here may, by his life and character, be either helping forward this invisible Kingdom, or by his selfishness doing what he can to defeat its advance.

Try then to think of this kingdom of God and of Christ, not as a poetic image, nor as a thing you merely read of in the Bible, but as a simple truth, and that every good deed, every holy disposition of yours, now and in time to come, is part of it, helps it forward, and that every selfish deed and worldly thought so far hinders it ; if you can but act on this, it will give a meaning and a dignity to all your work, here and elsewhere, which nothing else in the world can give.

If I were asked what was the best thing that this School in times past had done, I should at once answer, not that it has made scholars, nor literary men, nor clever professional men, but that it has sent into the world men impressed to the very core with the conviction that they had a work to do .in it, and that the way to do it was in the spirit of Christ. That great man who was so long the soul of this place, and whose memory is now its best inheritance, lived and laboured in this faith as perhaps none other in our time did, and from him many hearts caught the inspiration. There are many who were formerly boys here who could tell you that but for this place and Arnold, they had never known what were the duty and the blessedness of a life of earnest, unselfish labour. Why should not you go forth, as they have done, to live and labour in this same faith ? . . . "

One of the most interesting estimates of the Rugby period is by his old pupil, Mr. Godfrey Lushington, now permanent Under-Secretary in the Home Office, London. It is contained in a letter written shortly after the Principal's death, in 1885—

" I had many kind and good friends as a boy at school, but he gave me what no one else gave, and taught me what

I have never had to unlearn, but, on the contrary, wish to remember and to value more and more. I don't quite say that but for him I should never have cared for poetry, though certainly I was, more than others of my own age, dull and insensible to it; but it was he who kindly took me by the hand, and led me into what was then to me the new world of poetry, kindly and affectionately, like an elder comrade inviting me to come and enjoy with him the happy and beautiful things he enjoyed and prized so deeply.

But it was not poetry only, or even poetry chiefly. Rather, I should say, he kindled in me, as in others, an interest in the best things that appeal to feeling and the human heart—things which lie at the bottom of all society, and every individual human life, but which are apt to be forgotten or unheeded in the world of business or pleasure, or the pursuit of mere knowledge; and this he did, not by teaching or preaching, but by giving expression, with such a charming frankness and enthusiasm, to his own native feelings and meditations, and trusting to find a sympathetic response.

Everything about him interested and delighted me, his love of his own home, his own country, its nobility and its peasantry; his reverence for ancestors, and the Covenanters; his appreciation of native worth of every kind; his love of horses, and stories about them and their riders; his righteous pride, and complete unworldliness; his beautiful natural feeling; and all his natural and vivid expressions that laid hold upon me and many others, like Davey, and Hodgson, and Gosling (now no more), Arthur Butler, etc.

I remember with pleasure so many of the things he said to me: his description of his early terms at Oxford, and his making friends there—what he thought of Clough and Jowett;—his last words to me on my leaving Rugby—the old Scotch ballads, and passages from Burns, and Wordsworth, and Keats that he used to recite to me,—his discourses about Carlyle, etc. I can remember too very clearly, and always with pleasure, all my times with him at Rugby and elsewhere—his stay at Dresden with Bishop Cotton in

1849,—our visit with the Dean of Westminster to Yarrow, and Tibby Shiels, and Burns's home at Ellisland (and how he took up the ladle there, and said, '.Many a good bowl of punch has been in that, too many and too good'), and his visits to my father in Surrey, and how he enjoyed the rides we had together, and gave us the unexpected compliment that he had not known there was such beautiful scenery in the *South.*   Latterly I saw him, to my great regret, but very little; but I much enjoyed it when he occasionally looked in upon me, at the Home Office, when passing through London. . . ."

To this I may add the remark of another Rugby pupil, to whom, after Shairp's marriage, a large share in the management of the boys in his house was left.

" To him I am sure that I owe whatever success I achieved at Oxford, mainly owing to the strong taste for Latin prose composition with which Professor Shairp inspired me.   His plan consisted of making one translate Cicero into English, retranslate it back into Latin from memory, correct it by the original, and finally learn it by heart."

This is the more interesting from the fact that the writer says, in another part of his paper, "There was great sympathy between us, for which I can hardly account, for how could you look for much sympathy between a poetic Scotchman and an English public schoolboy, whose heart was in football, cricket, and athletics ?"

The following memoranda are from Dr. Tait's successor at Rugby, the present Dean of Norwich.   Dr. Goulburn writes—

" DEANERY, NORWICH, 18*th August* 1887.

" I am glad of the opportunity of bearing my testimony to the nobleness of a character, which no difference of early associations, views, and habits of thought at all prevented my appreciating.   One seemed, while in his company, to breathe a purer and fresher atmosphere, both moral and intellectual. . . . The only direct connection which I had with Principal Shairp was when he held an assistant-mastership in Rugby School, now more than thirty years ago. Judging from the general cast of his character, he would find the drudgery of instilling rudiments too irksome to do it well. . . . While I hardly think him to have been well qualified as a *teacher* of boys, he had high gifts as a *tutor* and moral guardian—that sensitive conscientiousness and deep religiousness of feeling which, in the intercourse of older people with the young, cannot fail to inspire, and to impress them.   I remember, even at this distance of time, his reporting a boy to me for some serious fault, it was so different from the common run of such reports, and was made with such unusual seriousness and earnestness: 'I have said to him the utmost I can say; and now I feel that I have nothing left me to fall back upon.'   Those who knew him will be able to imagine the intense earnestness of face and manner with which he said these words.   The incident will never pass from my memory.   I should add that the sterling worth and nobleness of his character transpired among his pupils and attracted them.   All the better and more discerning among them loved him.   'Dear old Shairp' was his constant and familiar appellation."

Archdeacon Palmer of Christ Church, Oxford, writes—

"When I came into residence at Balliol in Michaelmas, 1842, John Campbell Shairp had already been two years in Oxford.   What struck me most in those days was the enthusiasm with which he quoted poetry or spoke of high subjects.   Though he seemed to hold himself in, and attempt to put a restraint on the tones of his voice and the expression of his feelings, there was something about him which gave me the notion that he had the mind and heart of a poet.   I never knew a man in whose nature veneration seemed to play a larger part.   For great men, noble thoughts, noble actions, his reverence was unstinted.

He was no bookworm or recluse student. It is true that he was unknown in the cricket-field and on the river. But Shairp had established his character early in his under-graduate life as a fearless rider, and stories of his perform-ances in the hunting-field were current when I came up. It was in consequence, perhaps, of this that he was on friendly terms with the few Balliol undergraduates who hunted, as well as with those who lived a studious and economical life. His manhood was recognised by men who did not care for his literature or his enthusiasm. He had intimate friends who thought little of books or book-worms. Of course my awe of him vanished as I grew older; my admiration never diminished. I had become intimate with him just in time to regard him, and be re-garded by him, through life as a friend made in under-graduate days. But I saw him often enough to keep alive my feeling of intimacy with him, and to give me opportunities of observing the permanence of his early characteristics. Whether he came back to us as a Rugby Master, or as Principal of the United College at St. Andrews, or to lecture us on that subject which I had always thought peculiarly his own as our Professor of Poetry, he brought with him the same generous enthusiasm, the same love of all things noble, the same freshness and unworldliness which had distinguished him in early life. He was profoundly religious, but there was not a trace of formalism or of austerity about him. Perhaps it is for this last reason that I do not remember to have looked upon him as in any special sense or degree a religious man in undergraduate days; and to the end his religion was free alike from affectation and from narrowness. But, as years went on, his love of Nature saved him from being dried up by study and reflection, or hardened by experience of human folly and wickedness. We were very sensible of it in his lectures as Poetry Professor. It became almost a proverbial saying in Oxford that he seemed to bring with him a breeze from his native heaths and mountains. I could not refuse to contribute a stone to his cairn, as I believe that few loved him better, or more heartily mourned his death."

Mr. Henry Rhoades—once a pupil of Shairp's at Rugby, and afterwards warden of the College Hall at St. Andrews, and assistant-professor of the classical languages there, now a Master at Rugby—sends the following recollections :—

"RUGBY, 3d *September* 1887.

"You ask me to give you some of my recollections of Principal Shairp, and I will try to do so as far as his work at Rugby is concerned. I was his pupil there for ten years, and the impression he made on me as a boy is so vivid that I do not think I am in danger of confusing it with the more intimate knowledge I gained of his character in later life.

He was not perhaps especially successful as a form-master, but many of his private pupils must look back to their tutor lessons with him as giving the most stimulating and ennobling influence they ever received from the outside. Accurate work and preparation were always exacted, but we were early made to feel that beyond and above this we had to try to grasp the writer's thought. This was more and more enforced as we rose in the school. A boy must have been dull indeed, who did not catch some spark of his enthusiasm for poetry, history, and philosophy. It was like a revelation to read with him such books as the *Agamemnon*, the *Life of Agricola*, and the *Phædo*. Most valuable of all, perhaps, were the hours when some passage in the day's work stirred a train of thought, and the books were laid down, while he talked—as few but he could talk—or read to us from his favourite authors. In this way Coleridge's *Aids to Reflection* and *Biographia Literaria*, Scott's *Border Minstrelsy*, and, above all, Wordsworth, found places of honour on our study shelves. Once a week his Sixth Form pupils were required to translate at sight passages of Lucretius, or Cicero, or Plato, or Aristotle ; and though we were often floundering out of our depth, the practice in his hands was most useful, and many a great thought was thus brought home to us. When to this is added a high-bred courtesy, a lofty scorn for what was mean or base, a transparent unselfishness and unworldliness, deep reverence for sacred things, and a centering of thought and aim on all that was high and pure, his unique influence at Rugby becomes intelligible. This influence extended to his colleagues. More than one of them in after years has spoken to me of it. One in particular who has achieved distinction as a scholar and a teacher (I hope the Dean of Westminster will forgive my quoting him) said, 'It was not Arnold or Rugby or Oxford that educated me, but John Campbell Shairp.'

I cannot bring myself to write of the time when I was associated with him at St. Andrews, and enjoyed his intimate friendship. In many a walk on the sands, or 'twahanded fireside crack,' as he would have called it, he poured out his thoughts with such unreserve that I feel it would be a breach of confidence if I were even to attempt to play Boswell to his Johnson. Let me conclude by applying to him—to the man more than to the writer—the lines of his favourite Wordsworth—

> Blessings be with them and eternal praise,
> Who gave us nobler loves and nobler cares,
> The poets, who on earth have made us heirs
> Of truth and pure delight by heavenly lays."

Mr. Kitchener of Newcastle, Staffordshire, writes thus of Shairp as a Rugby Master—

"I first came under him in the Fifth at Rugby, then taken by Bradley (now Dean of Westminster). When Shairp took us in the Odes of Horace, we knew we would have an easy hour compared with the severe if stimulative rule of our ordinary master. Later Mr. Shairp took the lower Sixth, and I again came under him. All the boys liked him. His rule was genial ; but the idle fellows escaped him, and only the clever boys learned much. At one time he helped Dr. Goulburn with the composition (English and Latin essays) of the Sixth. Our essays would accumulate. Then the boy would have to go to him, and rapidly read essay after essay. They were as rapidly marked and done with, till some essay would suggest a train of thought, and then a talk might spring up, which, in my case, was worth more than all the essay-correcting he could have given me. Words dropped out by him, in his dry manner, seemed to work in one's brain, and set one thinking."

Another, who knew him well in his later Oxford and in his Rugby days, though he was not at Rugby with him, Lord Lingen, writes : " He was keenly alive to the beauty that there is in the world, whether of human character or of nature. Classical learning had produced that effect upon him which is happily described by the old academic word ' humanity.' In conversation he was simple and gentle ; but, through the impression thus conveyed, a certain Scotch humour and shrewdness were always coming to the surface. He was quietly but intensely attracted to everything Scotch ; fond of field-sports, and good at them. He was, according to my experience, universally popular among his contemporaries, and respected by them as one of the pleasantest of companions, and as a man in whose sense of honour the most absolute confidence could be reposed."

CHAPTER IX

IN November 1852 Shairp attended the funeral of the Duke of Wellington, and described that thrilling event, first in a letter to his father, which has been preserved, and secondly, in another to the late Dean of Westminster, which has unfortunately been lost, but of which Dean Stanley—who was also a spectator of the event—said, in replying to it, that it was "almost more impressive than the funeral itself."

This is the letter to his father—

" RUGBY, 22d *November* 1852.

" MY DEAR FATHER—Ever since Thursday last I have not ceased to regret that I had not tried to get you and T—— to come to London on that day. Had one been on the spot bedrooms and tickets could have been easier managed than seems, even at this distance. And for any trouble, you would have had overpayment in the intense interest. Even the dullest Cockney was thrilled by it, and what would you have been? It would have served you with recollections while you live, as I think it will serve me.

No one out of the Cathedral had a better place than I had. In the front nook of the front balcony of the Oxford Club, about fifty yards east of St. James's Palace, I could see them as far as Trafalgar Square. The procession and the funeral in the Cathedral were two distinct things. The chief interest of the one was military, the other more solemn and saddening, I suppose. There were four things which specially struck me in that long array, which took one hour and threequarters to defile past the place where I stood.

1. After long waiting, when no sign had been given except the faint far-off minute guns at starting, suddenly the advanced guard of 1st Life Guards wound slowly round the corner, close followed by the first band playing that most mournful music with their muffled drums. We had not been expecting them, and in a moment every voice was hushed and the music was almost too sad. It made you turn away.

2. When the car came with the coffin lying on the top of the immense pile, the bier strewn with all its decorations, and with palm-wreaths and laurel, which seemed all so useless now, there was a deep silence and every head unbared—you felt that here was the very last of him we should ever see.

3. The horse touched every heart—large, and upwards of sixteen hands, dark brown, like a powerful hunter; saddle and saddle-cloth of blue and gold; the field-marshal's boots, with their spurs in the stirrups reversed; and this fine animal as meek as a lamb, with his head drooped low to the ground, as though he felt it all.

4. When all was past, and the blues closed in the whole, as the car faded from sight down Trafalgar Square, and the last of that most mournful music died on the ear, there was a strange vague pain, for one felt that there was passing not only the grandest pageant one would ever see, but the last vestige of the greatest epoch of England's history was going down to the grave with him who made it.

One who was in the Cathedral described to me the thrilling effect of the sacred music pealing within, blended with the military music without, as each band successively marched up to the same spot outside and played the same dirge of the 'Dead March.' And then, as the coffin went down into the grave, he said he could distinctly see several of the old Peninsular generals in tears—Lord Seaton weeping like a child, Lord Anglesey and others holding up their plumes to their brows to hide their manly grief.

Of all the military in that long procession no cavalry looked better, hardly any so like work, as the Greys; no infantry marched half so proudly as the few representatives of the Highland regiments. Every one remarked these last; and in the Cathedral I heard that one tall Highlander was the most striking figure there. I would not have missed it for anything else in the world, for I never can see anything half so historical.

Only I do wish you had been just where I was, or in the Cathedral."

.   .   .   .

The following is Dean Stanley's reply to the lost letter of Shairp's to him, descriptive of the same event:—

"CANTERBURY, 23*d November* 1852.

"MY DEAR SHAIRP—Many thanks for your letter, which was to me almost more impressive than the funeral itself. By this time you may perhaps have heard that through night and day, by sea and land, horses and steam, foam and spray, I arrived at London at midnight on the 17th, passed in the grey dawn through those vast streets of amphitheatre, and fought my way by nine o'clock to the Deanery of St. Paul's! Under these auspices I was fortunate enough first to see the procession advance up Ludgate Hill from the balcony of the Cathedral, and then, entering, to share in the actual service from the galleries within the dome. I never have been so much struck by the estrangement from English feeling produced in travelling—partly for good, doubtless, and partly for evil—as on that day. Great as the pageant was, yet the long and varied succession of scenes which had passed before me, between it and the Duke's death, made it extremely difficult for me to look upon it, as I suppose many others did, as the climax of a long-sustained consciousness of one great event. It seemed to me a magnificent pageant—hardly the burial of a man.

Yet my reason every day convinces me of what my imagination still fails to convey—that I have indeed witnessed, as you truly say, a universal movement, such as we shall see no more again, in the heart of our country, and the close of a world-wide power and glory. For this reason alone I am thankful to have come—there would have been something painful in feeling that one had no share in such a celebration.

> Such honours Ilium to her hero paid,
> And peaceful slept the mighty Hector's shade.

I confess this thought of his shade did from time to time cross me during the service. It was the one feeling which was left unexpressed. 'Where—what—whither is he gone, for whom these tens of thousands are sitting round in grim and awful silence?' Has he indeed passed from us, and we from him, so that we have nothing to say or do for him henceforth and for ever. Λιάν ἄφιλον is the first impression, yet I know not. . . ."

In 1852 Shairp became a candidate for the Chair of Moral Philosophy in Edinburgh, then vacant by the resignation of Professor Wilson (Christopher North); and although he was not successful in obtaining it, the testimony borne to him by his numerous Oxford friends, twenty-eight in all, was a very remarkable evidence of how he had impressed them with a sense of power and originality, of freshness and force of character, and fitness for such a post. It is rare, indeed, that so many men, distinguished in so many different ways, unite in bearing testimony to any one. Their names, given in alphabetical order, were—C. T. Arnold, Balliol; Matthew Arnold, Oriel, Inspector of Schools; G. E. Bradley, now Dean of Westminster; Professor Buchanan, Glasgow; A. H. Clough, Oriel, Professor of English Literature, University of London; John Connington, University College, Oxford; G. E. L. Cotton, Rugby, afterwards Bishop of Calcutta; Professor Fleming, Glasgow; E. M. Goulburn, Head of Rugby, now Dean of Norwich; B. Jowett, now

Master of Balliol; W. C. Lake, Balliol, now Dean of Durham; H. E. Liddell, Head of Westminster School, now Dean of Christ Church, Oxford; R. W. Lingen, Secretary to Educational Committee of Privy Council, now Lord Lingen; Principal Macfarlan, Glasgow; Norman Macleod, Barony Church, Glasgow; C. Marriott, Oriel; F. E. Palgrave, Balliol, now Professor of Poetry, Oxford; Edward Poste, Oriel; Bonamy Price, Rugby; C. E. Prichard, Balliol, Vice-Principal of Wells Theological College; James Riddell, Balliol; W. Y. Sellar, Oriel, now Professor in the University of Edinburgh; A. P. Stanley, afterwards Dean of Westminster; A. C. Tait, Rugby, afterwards Archbishop of Canterbury; T. Temple, Balliol, now Bishop of London; T. Walrond, Balliol, afterwards one of the Civil Service Commissioners.

These testimonies are much more interesting than testimonials usually are, from the way in which they refer to that force and elevation of character without which the keenest intellect and the amplest learning are (for the purposes of teaching) of little use. From one or two of them quotations may be made. Mr. Matthew Arnold spoke of his " thorough knowledge of the subject, and a remarkable faculty for imparting that knowledge in an interesting manner." Clough spoke of his power of appreciating and mastering the theories of others, with original thought and feeling of his own, his careful study of Aristotle and Plato, and "the probability of his uniting in a rare degree knowledge of various and differing schools of mental and moral science." Cotton based his testimony on his being a thorough Scotchman, but educated partly in Scotland and partly in England, on his genius for ethical study, helped by classical knowledge, and by his imaginative and poetic power, on his power over young men, his unselfishness, his industry, and his strong sense of duty. Professor Jowett referred to his living interest in philosophy, and his power of communicating to others the freshness which its problems had to himself, and his power of personally attaching others to himself, " which is perhaps half the secret of success as a teacher."—" No one

can be with him without feeling that he has higher aims
and higher views than the majority of even good and able
men. His perfect disinterestedness, as well as his never-
failing enthusiasm for intellectual subjects, are very remarkable qualities." He would "add literary eminence to any
university in which he was appointed Professor. But I
should expect him to be more than a mere lecturer, and to
exercise, by his character, a lasting and beneficial influence
over the minds of his pupils." Dean Stanley wrote of his
"faculty of throwing life into dry systems, and of present-
ing in a vivid and intelligible form the thoughts and feelings
of past ages. Such a faculty, valuable in any department
of science, seems to me, when combined, as in his case, with
largeness of mind and patient industry, almost certain to
ensure success in a Professor of Moral Philosophy. I may
also be permitted to say that there are very few men to
whose teaching and influence I could look forward so con-
fidently as likely to guide young men rightly, through the
many complicated questions arising out of the relations of
philosophy and religion; because there are very few who
so happily combine the spirit of criticism with the gift of
imagination, true reverence for what is good, with an honest
inquiry after what is true." Others say that the lecture-room
is his true place for the exposition of the thoughts of the
great men of the past, and the discouraging of the conceit of
knowledge without its power; that he would promote the
study of ancient philosophy in the original authors, but the
spirit in which he would approach the study would be mainly
a modern spirit; so said Connington. Many others spoke of
what Wordsworth calls the first great gift, the "vital soul,"
that would give new life and freshness to familiar thoughts.
T. Walrond writes thus—"Great vigour and originality of
thought, imagination of a high order, habits of patient investigation, an ardent spirit of inquiry, tempered by reverence
for truth and consideration for the doubts of others, a power
of looking below words and phrases into the meaning that they
contain ; these qualities combined in Mr. Shairp with great
practical sense make me confident that he would, if elected

become really distinguished among the moral philosophers of the day."

On the 23d of June 1853, Shairp married Eliza Douglas, daughter of the late Henry Alexander Douglas, and granddaughter of Sir William Douglas, Bart., of Kilhead, Dumfriesshire. She was a sister of his college friend, Henry Douglas, afterwards Bishop of Bombay. The marriage took place at Bute House, Petersham. They went to Dumfriesshire for a short time, and spent the rest of the Rugby summer holidays in Scotland.

Just after their return to Rugby in September 1853 his mother, the Moira of *Kilmahoe*, died—she who, " through all the strain of life," was " strong to do and bear." The son's description of her last years at Houstoun, in the first section of that poem, entitled *Ingathering*, is so delicately drawn that some stanzas may be quoted here—

> . . . To all so loving; when, keen-eyed
> To other's faults, some hastened to condemn,
> Her kind heart still some hidden good descried,
>   And gently pled for them.
>
> And country people whenso'er they spoke
> Her name, by farmer's hearth or cottar's shed,
> Would call her " the Gude Leddy," and invoke
>   A blessing on her head.
>
> At length, as in a garden one night's frost
> Comes down, and blights the flowers in the fall,
> A sudden ailment fell on her; almost
>   She heard the angels' call.
>
> But God to her life's book one little page
> In mercy added, that her own might see,
> Who early seek him, in declining age,
>   How beautiful they be.
>
> As one, who long laboriously going
> Beneath a sultry sun up sheer hill slope,
> Finds the path easier, fresher breezes blowing,
>   Just ere he reach the cope.

Her sister playmate—earliest and latest friend—came

to her house to tend the evening of her days, and found in
her aged eyes

A far-off spiritual range,
A pensive depth of peace, a resting on
Things beyond time and change,
Yet full of human tenderness that drew
All hearts to her.

Of Shairp's outward life for the next few years there is not
much to record. Continuous labour through the school
terms at Rugby, and autumn holidays in Scotland, came
and went. His aim as a master at Rugby was to carry
out the spirit by which Dr. Arnold had governed and guided
the school, to perpetuate the traditions and the influence
of that educationist with whose name Rugby must always
be chiefly associated.

His Christmas holidays as well as summer vacations
were usually spent in Scotland. On the 13th of January
1854, writing from Grangemuir, Pittenweem, to Mr. Erskine
of Linlathen, he refers to a recent visit to that delightful home, where many kindred spirits were wont to
gather round one of the most remarkable Scotsmen of this
century. In September 1854 we find him at Loch Shiel
and Kilmalie (as Norman Macleod notes in his *Journal*).
Then, and ever afterwards, when Macleod mentions his meetings and occasional trips in the Highlands with his old friend,
it is of "dear Shairp" that he speaks. This was invariably
the feeling with which he inspired his friends. The following is part of a letter from Mr. Erskine :—

"SHANDON, 3*d September* 1853.

". . . You cannot think that you have been absent from
my thoughts during all this eventful time of joy and sorrow
in your history. . . . Your mother has left behind a most
sweet savour beyond the circle of her attached and devoted
family, of a most lovely and pure spirit. If ever woman
possessed the ornament of a meek and quiet spirit she did.
From my childhood I have associated her name with
singular beauty of face and form, which were in delightful

harmony with her character as wife and mother, which she inherited from *her* mother. My whole memories of her are perfect sunshine. . . . Thus rapidly, as we advance in life, does the majority on the other side increase."

In the beginning of the following year he wrote thus to Mr. Erskine—

[Postmark, 1854.]

"GRANGEMUIR, PITTENWEEM,
"13th *January.*

"MY DEAR MR. ERSKINE—I cannot longer delay writing to say how much I enjoyed my visit to Linlathen, and to offer my sincere thanks for your great kindness. It is not often that such a visit, and such intercourse, is allowed to us; but when it is, it revives and strengthens all that life within, which, from one's own fault and the worldly atmosphere we generally meet with, is ever ready to droop and die.

Linlathen I shall ever look back on as a resting-place beside the way; and I trust that the refreshment there received will not quickly fail, but remain to strengthen me to go on my journey with a more single will and more steadfast purpose.

Forgive me if I say that over that door I shall in thought seem to see inscribed those lines of Homer's, which I once saw applied to Bishop Wilson—

φίλος ἀνθρώποισι,
πάντας γὰρ φιλέεσκεν ὁδῷ ἔπι οἰκία ναίων.

I have often thought much over all the conversations I had with you. I do not think I ever heard from any one so much that recommended itself, as far as I could judge, to my feeling and conscience. There were, of course, some things you said, which I could not so entirely make my own as to know rightly whether I agreed.

With the main principle and starting-point of all you said—I mean the criterion of truth to every man within himself, as distinguished from outward authority—I think I entirely agree. The conclusion of your book you lent I have nearly finished, and I find it very valuable in recalling and fixing much of what you said.

This inward standard, which must apprehend the righteousness of any truth before the man can be said to believe it, is the thing which I had long been feeling after; but one difficulty always remained out of which I saw no escape. It seemed to end in making ἄνθρωπος μέτρον πάντων, as Plato accused some Greek Sophist [1] of doing; and this was confirmed by observing that so many who started from this inward principle ended by rejecting the teaching of the Bible and all other outward help, and by taking their stand (in a proud isolation) on their own shallow and hard sense of what they thought right and wrong.

But the answer to this which you give, I mean the finding in the Bible a historic record of conscience, and in Christ the universal conscience of the race, this—though I had caught some glimpses of it. before—was, in the broad, clear light in which you placed it, quite new. I trust I may go on more and more to apprehend it, and find it practically as well as theoretically true, and to turn it to some good use. . . . The remembrance of your kindly house will long be with me as a thought of peace.—Yours very sincerely,   J. C. SHAIRP."

Another letter to Mr. Erskine, written during the summer vacation of 1856 (which was spent at Moffat), may fitly follow the above—

[Postmark, 1856.]

"LANGSHAW COTTAGE, MOFFAT,
"27th July.

"MY DEAR FRIEND—If you will allow me to call you so, it is long since I have heard anything of you, but often during the long winter now past I thought of you, and wished but did not write. It has been a dark winter for us. Last autumn we were blessed with a son. For some

---

[1] πάντων μέτρον ἕκαστος, the maxim of Protagoras.

N

months he grew, and promised to be very healthy. He was a more than commonly beautiful boy, with a face of rare intelligence for so young a child. The blessing was great, and seemed to open new life to us both. All at once he was smitten with sickness, and for three months, the darkest of the winter, we had to watch his much suffering and gradual decline. He lived just till the verge of spring, and was then taken from us. A year ago I could not have imagined how great this trial would be. The months that followed were very dreary; and though we felt sure it was well with him, yet the sense of what we had lost and the remembrance of his long, mute, unrelieved suffering were very overpowering. Often I fear they have shut out 'all other light from my mind. The darkness I had seen was often stronger than the brightness I had not seen.

I know not why I did not write to you, except that I wrote little to any one; but certainly there is no one I should more have wished to converse with, during these long months of depression, as now, than you. We have retired to this very pleasing neighbourhood for our holidays, and have been both refreshed by the change from Rugby. As far as these outward things go, few places could have suited us so well. I have lately read Mr. Campbell's book.[1] Few books I have read are so suggestive, and have opened up so many *great*, deep, and true thoughts on that and like subjects. There is just one thing I don't feel quite sure of, that his view meets the full meaning of many of the Scriptural expressions; but I never have seen any book which opened up *so much* that the mind could dwell in on that subject.

I am sorry that from being so seldom in Scotland, I have so few opportunities of deriving benefit from conversation with you and with Mr. Campbell. If you and I are both well in winter, I shall hope that we may meet. . . .—Yours very sincerely,   J. C. SHAIRP."

The bereavement referred to in this letter gave rise to the following lines, which tell their own tale :—

---

[1] Doubtless *The Nature of the Atonement*, by J. M'Leod Campbell.

1st March 1855.

Violets on earth and laverocks in the sky,
    And children's voices on the vernal air ;
But our sweet darling all unheeding lies,
    While light and life are moving everywhere.

Around his new-born head fell last year's leaves,
    He did not stay to see them reappear ;
The swallows that last autumn left our eaves,
    Are flying back but not to find thee here.

Only one breeze that forward stole to tell
    The spring was coming kissed that wasted cheek ;
Only one sunbeam through the window fell
    Upon that pale face, meek.

Ah, darling sweet, the world impressed not thee
    Save with its primal pain—nor thou the world,
No more than blossom from some orchard tree
    This flowering springtime by the rough winds whirled.

Mr. and Mrs. Shairp went from Moffat for a two days'
change to Yarrow, and this visit gave rise to another poem,
from which one or two stanzas may be quoted. The first
stanza contains a sort of invitation to his wife to visit Yarrow,
after their " winter dark with dool and sorrow." He then
says—

It's not that these green hills are fair,
    And calm the lakes beneath them sleeping,
There's nothing there can e'er repair
    The sorrow we have long been weeping.

Though lambs are bleating far and near,
    And plaintive pipes the moorland plover,
A tenderer cry still haunts our ear,
    We shall no where on earth recover.

And yet, if any place has felt
    The mellowing touch of human sorrow,
And into woe-worn hearts could melt
    Like healing balm, 'twere braes of Yarrow.

There lies " St. Mary's," tranced and lone,
    'Mid the old hills, their darling daughter,
And songs of dim old ages gone
    Sing on for aye in Yarrow water.

During this visit to Yarrow, Shairp first made the acquaintance of one who afterwards became a very close friend, Mr. John Veitch, now Professor Veitch of Glasgow University. He has supplied me with a specially interesting paper of reminiscences, which, with his permission, I have used in the same way as I have treated Mr. Sellar's.

Mr. Veitch says—

"In the early part of July 1856 I met him for the first time at Tibbie Shiels's cottage. He had been making that charming spot—as rich in natural beauty as in associations with the best Scottish poetry and life of the last half-century, with Scott, Wilson, and Hogg—a residence for some days. He was then one of the masters of Rugby, and would be in his thirty-seventh year. I had come up Moffatdale, by Birkhill and the Loch of the Lowes, through a day of sunshine, and by hillsides flecked with shadow, and it was now the 'gowden afternoon.' Passing through the gate which leads to the arbour of peace and quiet beauty,—to me an oft-resting haunt, known as Tibbie Shiels's,—the friend who was with me, pointing to a figure before the door, said, 'There is Shairp.' I had in my ear dim rumours of him, but had not met him before. A fair-haired, ruddy-faced, and manly man—with open light gray-blue eyes—frank and affable, with ready recognition. But what attracted me most was that he was very wet—trousers, stockings, and boots all fairly soaked. There was no waterproof trash of gearing in those days, or more probably he despised it. He had just come in from the upper hills, and had waded from one glen to another, with a delightful sovereign contempt for the plashing of the burns through which he had made his way. This went to my heart at once. I was not generally at that time inclined to respect a Rugby master. But looking at this Rugby master, I said little, but in my soul thought this must be a good fellow, and he was. This was my first sight of and introduction to Shairp, and, though I spoke but few words with him, I marked him inwardly as a congenial and lovable man. Yet how little can we judge

of the inner feeling of a man from outside appearance and
casual greeting ! After that time—long after—I learned that
he was under the shadow of a family sorrow. Mrs. Shairp
was with him—brought, I imagine, for the first time to
Yarrow,—a hope in him, I suppose, and well founded, that
she would share in its spirit—in the inner chord of sympathy
with the pathetic feeling of the place—perhaps find some
solace there."

Remaining at Moffat for the summer, in the following
month Shairp paid another visit to Yarrow with his sisters.
The following extract from an occasional journal kept in
the year 1856, tells of a drive to St. Mary's and a meeting
with Dean Stanley and Mr. Godfrey Lushington :—

" 20*th August* 1856.— Started up Moffatdale 10
minutes to 10 A.M.—Helen riding—Grace in dogcart with
me. Strong east wind blowing against us all the way.
Sunshine till we got to Polmoodie—then darker. Reached
St. Mary's about 12.30 or so. Waited more than an hour
for Stanley and Lushington. They did not come, so we
three started for Chapelhope, up the burn, till we came to
the cleaving of the burns, up the ' South Grain till,' a sheep
round, near which we got a view of the moss hags out
towards Loch Skene. I gathered blaeberries. Then Grace
returned the same way. Helen and I up the hill towards
the head of the North Grain. Came among a flock of *cloud-
berry bushes* on the hillside ; found only four or five berries
really large and fine ; pulled many leaves ; crossed the
burn ; a gleam of finer sunshine for about half an hour
on to near the top of the Summerhope Hill. Looking
back, a grand view up the head of the south branch of·
Chapelhope burn, spread the wide moor of the moss hags
in which the Covenanters lay ; behind this wide dark
wilderness a grand screen of mountains—the mountain-heart
of the south of Scotland—shutting it in ; the Loch Craig at
the head of Loch Skene sloping down to the Talla north,
and a precipice over the loch to the south, then the Mid

Craig, then the Great White Combe, and beyond it, to the left, Black Combe, separated from White Combe by a hollow down which comes Polmoodie Burn. The Mid Craig, on the west side of Loch Skene, bounding it, separated from it by a burn called Moodlaw Burn; as fine a mountain view as any in the south of Scotland. The brown, dusky moors with dreamy sunshine over them, 'the wilderness wherein there is no man,' and the thought of the Covenanters singing psalms and praying there, present as we gazed over that wilderness. The Watch Hill, out towards Loch Skene, was visible by a cairn, though it only seems a little rising ground in the moor-wilderness, and in a line south it ends in the Broad Law beyond it, seen on the tops of the mirk side of Polmoodie. Started from where we had the view in haste, ran down the brae by Ox Cleuch, and met Stanley and Lushington. Dined and left St. Mary's. Stopped and saw Dobbs's Linn. Home here 9.30 P.M."

On the following day Shairp left Moffat, with Stanley and Lushington, on a visit to Dumfries. Their interest in this place was both historical and topographical. They also doubtless wished to see the spot where Burns spent his last days. The visit was one of great delight, often referred to afterwards, although no detailed record of it survives.

In writing to his friend Edward Scott about his child's grave at Rugby, and the tombstone over it—the erection of which Mr. Scott took charge of—he said he desired some permanent creepers put round the rails : " only do not think of keeping up a supply of flowers : for, sooner or later, that must come to an end, and it is well to put it as nearly as possible in the way it will permanently remain."

CHAPTER X

FIRST HOME AT ST. ANDREWS, AND THE PROFESSORSHIP
OF LATIN

SHAIRP must have got leave of absence from Rugby in the late autumn of 1856, for in the November of that year he taught Professor Lushington's class in the University of Glasgow. For some time his mind had turned towards the subject of the Scottish Universities; and his friend, the head-master of Rugby, having spent an autumn holiday in St. Andrews, thought of the Latin Chair in the College of St. Salvator and St. Leonard as one for which Shairp was admirably suited. It was through Dr. Tait's influence that this chair was afterwards secured to him. If Shairp cherished any dominant ambition during his Rugby life, it was that he might ultimately work, in some capacity or other, in one of the Universities of his native land. Meanwhile, in October 1856, he wrote a pamphlet entitled *The Wants of the Scottish Universities, and some of the Remedies*. This pamphlet was published before the reforms in the Scottish University System were carried out by the Commission, over which the present Lord Justice-General presided. It is an elaborate and admirable discussion, and although it has long since shared the fate of every pamphlet for the hour, one or two extracts from it will be interesting—at least to University men—since it deals with a question of no temporary or trivial interest.

"During the last fifty years Oxford and Cambridge have made such rapid progress as greatly to alter their relative position with regard to Edinburgh and Glasgow Universities, and within the same period the

London University has come into being. Doubtless there was more to be done,—greater need for change in the southern ancient seats of learning than ever existed in our own. But, perhaps, one chief cause of our altered relative position is, that while we have been complacently calling ourselves the best educated people in Christendom, and therefore not careful to improve what we thought so nearly perfect, England and other countries have fully confessed their defects, and striven honestly to find the remedy. We may well be apprehensive lest, in our case, the old fable prove true, and while the hare sleeps the tortoise win the race. For if at the opening of the century the English Universities were asleep and the labouring population unable to read or write, no country ever did more in the same space to take away such a reproach. Within the last twenty years the efforts made for the education of the English people, in town and country, have been vast, and are ever increasing; while within the same time the old Universities have sprung to life, and have thrown down, and are daily more throwing down the old encumbrances, and now combine the venerableness of many centuries with fresh vigour as of yesterday.

.   .   .   .

What is that weak point? you may ask. Not any want of mental vigour and activity in our students. Of a loose, discursive intelligence, which can deal readily with things in general, there is abundance ; of power to write plausibly on almost any subject in a fluent, semi-metaphysical, semi-rhetorical way there is no lack : but it is when brought to book that our weakness comes out, when not crude views of things in general are called for, but accurate knowledge of some things in particular, combined with careful reasoning on these ; when some accuracy of scholarship and some definite historical knowledge is required, it is here that our students fail. And without a groundwork of these, which few of our schools afford, and which the professorial system alone cannot supply, no man, however great his natural powers, can ever do well in any examination. Yet this arises from no inherent defect in the national intellect. The character of the Scottish mind is definiteness, exactness, even rigidity.

.   .   .   .

'University Reform' is not a cry that will ever be heard from the hustings. There is absolutely no political capital to be made out of it.

.   .   .   .

A country which, from the first, amid many natural and material hindrances, has held her own mainly by the moral energy of her people, energy which, in the old warlike times, made of them hardy unconquerable soldiers; in peaceful modern times, solid workers and intelligent thinkers ; such a country more than any other ought to prize highly, and dread decay in, her places of education, and most of all in those central ones from which the life-blood of the others flows.

.   .   .   .

But it has been the honourable characteristic of our Universities, that from them no class has been excluded, but that they have opened their lecture-rooms to the humblest and poorest of the people.

Indeed, in Scotland, more than any other country, the vast majority of the men whom we remember with pride, have risen from the lowliest places, and they have owed their rise scarcely more to the sterling stuff they are made of than to the institutions in which that stuff has been moulded and tempered.   So it has been in past times.

It is the interest of every Scotsman, the humblest as well as the highest, indeed of the humblest even more than the highest, that our Universities, while they preserve their unexclusive character, should also do something in an age of change to maintain the pre-eminence that formerly was theirs.

For the lower and more general education of any country must needs follow in the wake of its higher intelligence.

If the springs on the high hills are dry, what will become of the streams in the valleys ?
These springs of Scottish thought, let us hope, will never dry, although they may be suffering at present from a protracted drought.

A pause no doubt in the succession has come, but why should this be the prelude of perpetual barrenness ?

Leave the literary circles in the towns, and visit the farms and cottar-homes in corn-growing, and especially in pastoral districts, and see if the men you find there are less muscular in body, less vigorous in mind than their fathers were.   If they are, then we may well despair.

It was in the homes of the peasantry that in past times many of Scotland's best and greatest were reared ; and from them as education spreads wider and strikes deeper, we may look for a still larger and richer harvest—not of men like Burns and Scott, perhaps even Chalmers and Wilson.   Such men education cannot create, and can do but little to foster.   On them has fallen that diviner fire, which men call genius and inspiration, because they feel that it cannot be forged in their workshops, but it is in some peculiar way the direct gift of God, bestowed by Him, for purposes of His own, on certain men in certain generations, according to laws which we cannot fathom.

Genius is exceptional.   How and when it will come no man can divine.   Talent is calculable.   You can trace the process of its formation almost as certainly as you can any natural growth. The stuff out of which such men are formed is around us in abundance.

* * * * * * * *

That in the special faculties many branches are unrepresented by professors is not denied ; and even in the literary department it is obvious that some most needful subjects are wholly omitted. There is, practically, no study of history, either ancient or modern, in any of our Universities,—a fact almost incredible in a country which has produced so many good historians.

* * * * * * * *

Whatever other changes it may be desirable to introduce, there are four main points which cannot be passed over in any thorough scheme of University improvement. These are—

1. The standard of admission to the Universities must be raised, or rather a standard of admission must be, for the first time, instituted.

2. The professorial instruction must be supplemented by the appointment of sub-professors or tutors to do that part of the work which the professor himself cannot overtake, but without which his teaching cannot thoroughly educate.

3. A final examination for literary degrees must be established, which shall be imperative on every student preparing for any of the learned professions ; and this examination must be made such that it shall guarantee some substantial education, some real mental training.

4. It is 'much to be desired that if possible the four Universities should combine for the purpose of granting literary degrees, and only for this purpose ; and that one board of examiners be appointed from among the professors and graduates of the four Universities, who shall preside over the yearly examinations and grant all Scottish degrees.

* * * * * * * *

For philosophy, the best of all preparations is the thorough study of language; and this to be thorough, and accurately grammatical, must begin with the dead languages.

* * * * * * * *

Classical preparation is, I believe, the best; classical, with the addition of a due portion of mathematical.

* * * * * * * *

No doubt, the professorial is the highest form of teaching. A function it has of its own, not to be accomplished so well by any other agency, to stimulate thought, to open up larger, more far-reaching views than either the school or the study can suggest ; by the living voice of a gifted man to awake within the heart fresh springs of interest, which the words of a dead book can never reach. This is the prerogative of the professor ; this function our Scottish professors have fulfilled, and still fulfil, and with it no change should be allowed to intermeddle. Taken as a body, our Scottish professors have been, at least, as eminent as any other educational corps in Europe.

* * * * * * * *

Indeed, in classical learning, if either were to be dispensed with, the professor could be omitted with less loss than the schoolmaster.

. . . .

If the function of the classical professor is to open up the life and thought of the two great nations of antiquity, and to illustrate and give interest to their literature and their history, how can he do this to any save to those who have won some solid footing on ancient ground, by having mastered the whole, or, at least, large portions of some of the greatest classical authors ?

. . . .

Compared with this 'impudent knowingness,' this intelligence from the teeth forward, the blankest ignorance, the densest impenetrability to all such inquirers is an excellent gift.

. . . . . .

And even without getting to this extreme of emptiness, are we not all prone to accept without question the abstractions handed down to us by former thinkers, to take them up into our minds unrealised, and, adopting them into our vocabulary, to reason on them as if they were facts of nature or necessary first principles ? " [1]

. . . . . .

For the causes which led to Shairp's removal from Rugby to St. Andrews, and the details of his earlier years there, I have recourse again to Professor Sellar's paper of reminiscences—

" Though he found in his Rugby life a sphere of usefulness, and had much enjoyment in his intercourse with his colleagues and his older and abler pupils, yet he longed for more freedom to develop the speculative and poetical faculty within him. I had heard him say long before that he would rather use his practical power of work in Scotland than anywhere else. When, accordingly, in the year 1857, Dr. Pyper, the Professor of Latin in St. Andrews, was permanently disabled by bad health, Shairp, though at a great pecuniary sacrifice, applied for and accepted the position of his assistant. The position which had held out most attraction to him when he was at Oxford was that of a Scotch professor ; but he thought then more of a Chair of Moral Philosophy, for which he was admirably qualified, had he been appointed to one while the speculative impulse

[1] *The Wants of the Scottish Universities*, pp. 4-30.

was still strong upon him, than of one of the classical chairs.

He had a genuine appreciation for the great Greek and Roman writers, and he held that there was as yet at least no other equally humanising discipline for those who were able and willing to profit by it. Still the classics were, as he said, not 'his first loves ;' and I have heard him humorously complain of the weariness of the daily round of 'vocables,' —a word much in the mouth of one of our colleagues in looking over the papers in the Bursary Competition, at which lively occupation, which he keenly enjoyed himself, he used to keep us out of bed, though hardly awake, till four in the morning. But he recognised and availed himself of the greater scope afforded in a professorial class for vitalising the reading of the classics, developing the literary interest of the subject, and for that unsystematic ethical teaching,—the teaching of 'humanity' involved in it. The work of teaching the language in a sound scholarlike way, I need hardly say, he performed faithfully. I think the Professors in the Arts Faculties of the Scottish Universities would feel along with me how much the pleasure and usefulness of their work depends on their colleagues in the subject cognate to their own ; how it takes half the heart out of their work if their yoke-fellow pulls the other way, teaches what they feel called on to unteach, and unteaches what they feel called on to teach ; or if he is one between whom and himself there exists no personal or intellectual sympathy.

I had gone to St. Andrews three or four years before Shairp came there, as assistant to the Professor of Greek, who was incapacitated for work for several years before his death. Shairp and I worked together for six or seven years first as assistants, doing all the work of the Professor and afterwards as professors : he of Latin and I of Greek. It would have been impossible to have had a colleague more loyal and sympathetic, one with whom one could work in more perfect harmony and mutual confidence, —an advantage which, if I may be allowed to say so here, I again enjoy in the fullest possible measure. None of his colleagues took a warmer personal interest in the students than Shairp, especially in some of the poorer among them, and those who had enjoyed fewest previous advantages, in whom he recognised some finer traits of character. From his sense of responsibility and from the influence of his English experience, he wished to exercise a more direct moral influence among them than was in accordance with the traditions of student life in the Scotch Universities; and this had a tendency to rouse in some of the rougher set the *nemo me impune lacesset* sentiment, which is perhaps stronger in the Scotch student than in any other members of the community. With the same view he co-operated most cordially with Principal Forbes in the establishment of the College Hall, which for two or three years, under the first Warden—who had the happy tact of hitting the right mean between freedom and restraint, and of being himself both the companion and the guardian of those under his charge —promised to be a most successful experiment, an experiment which, for some reason or other, failed to maintain itself; and which, though often talked of, has never been renewed in any of our universities. Perhaps the much-dreaded danger of the 'Anglification' of our indigenous customs and manners is an obstacle to the introduction of such alien institutions.

We were most fortunate in our colleagues, and in the social circle which their families and other families in the town then formed. There was first the veteran Scottish representative of science, Sir David Brewster, who to us newcomers, though we were quite unfit to enter into his special pursuits, was always the most simple and delightful of associates. When he removed to Edinburgh, his place was filled by another representative of science, equally illustrious, Principal Forbes. Between him and Shairp there was for a time some friction, arising chiefly out of difference of opinion about College matters. They were both men of a pure and disinterested type of character, but they were essentially different in temperament. Shairp was, beyond almost all other men, warm and open; Forbes was outwardly cold and reserved, perhaps even suspicious, till he knew well those with whom he was dealing. Gradually, however, as they worked together in College business, Shairp came to recognise the single-minded devotion to duty, and the warmth and sensitiveness of feeling which lay under that outward reserve ; and, with the generosity native to him, he grew into an appreciative admiration and trust, all the warmer and firmer because he had at first misjudged him. Tulloch was Principal of St. Mary's, still a young man, in the vigorous prime of his intellectual force and genial companionship. Not to speak of some others among the professors, with whom Shairp was always in friendly relations, we had for one year among us the eminent Cambridge mathematician and discoverer, Professor Adams. The Logic Chair was filled at first by Professor Spalding, an earnest and successful teacher of his subject, and a man of fine literary accomplishment ; but his bad health, though it did not prevent his doing his work faithfully till the last, prevented our seeing much of him socially. He was succeeded in 1860 by Veitch, now Professor of Logic in Glasgow, and he soon became one of Shairp's most valued and sympathetic friends. The intellectual bond of sympathy between them was partly, I suppose, speculative agreement, though Shairp's speculative interest was directed mainly to ethics, and to some ultimate problems of metaphysics connected with theology, and not much to the province of logic and psychology ; but the chief and most lasting bond was a common love of ballad-poetry, and the Border country, both of which were probably better known to them than to any other men of their time.

But the centre of all the intellectual and social life of the University and of the town was Professor Ferrier. He inspired in the students a feeling of affectionate devotion as well as admiration, such as I have hardly ever known inspired by any teacher; and to many of them his mere presence and bearing in the classroom was a large element in a liberal education. By all his colleagues he was esteemed as a man of most sterling honour, a staunch friend, and a most

humorous and delightful companion.   Shairp, though he
had no pretension to original humour, had a great enjoyment in it, and in all lively and harmless fun; and there
certainly never was a household known to either of us, in
which the spirit of racy and original humour and fun was
so exuberant and spontaneous in every member of it, as that
of which the Professor and his wife—the most gifted, and
brilliant, and most like her father of the three gifted
daughters of Christopher North—were the heads.   Our
evenings there generally ended in the Professor's study,
where he was always ready to discuss, either from a serious
or humorous point of view, with him or any one else (not
without congenial accompaniments) the various points of
his metaphysical system till the morning was well advanced.
Grant too was much there in those days, taking his part
in the philosophical, literary, and humorous talk of his
future father-in-law, and bringing to us reports of the
latest developments in the ever-shifting phases of Oxford
taste, opinion, and educational machinery.

One source of pleasure in the life Shairp felt I think
more than any of us—the delight in the place itself, in its
picturesque shores and ruins, and its historic memories.
During his summers he continued his wanderings over the
more familiar and some of the wildest parts of the Highlands, and it was chiefly in these wanderings that he had
gradually shaped the poems, expressive of the characteristic
sentiment, both as regards outward nature and the spirit
of the people, of Highlands, Lowlands, and Borders, which
were given to the world in 1863 in the volume called, from
the principal poem, *Kilmahoe*."

It was in October 1857, after eleven years' school work,
that Shairp finally left Rugby, and settled in St. Andrews.
Professor Sellar has referred to the great pecuniary sacrifice
involved.   The income of the assistant to the Professor
of Latin was only £200 a year.   This obliged him to
take private pupils for some years, and his work, both
in and out of College, was laborious.   If the taking of pupils,

however, was a necessity, it was also very interesting to himself, and of real service to the University; and he had the promise of the Chair,—whenever it should become vacant,—from the Duke of Portland, in whom the patronage was vested.

On the death of Dr. Pyper, in 1861, he became Professor of Latin, and the most important part of his lifework began. He held the Chair for eight years, doing admirable work, which made no noise, but which enriched the lives of many students ; and on the death of Principal Forbes, in 1868, he was appointed Principal of the United College of St. Salvator and St. Leonard, which office he held till his death in 1885.

His introductory lecture as Professor of Latin in the United College, delivered in November 1857, was on *The Uses of the Study of Latin Literature,* and was published at the request of the students, and dedicated to them.   It is a clear, forcible, and fair-minded appeal, not advocating an education in classical scholarship as the best for every student, but only for those who have scholarly aptitude ; yet vindicating its claims on the ground of the highest utility, as well as the intrinsic excellence of the discipline itself.   It is to be hoped that this lecture, as well as the paper on Oxford and the Scottish Universities, may yet be republished.   The following is one paragraph from it :—

"Here on our foam-fringed promontory, withdrawn in some measure from the hurry of to-day, and looked down on by those many-centuried towers, breathing a very atmosphere of antiquity, and hearing for ever that roar of ocean, which whoso hears,

Must think on what shall be, and what has been,

whatever others may do, we surely cannot forget the past. There is enough here to remind us how greatly our lives are the creation of foregone civilisations, that we are of such stuff as the past has made us, and that, if we would understand ourselves, we must learn to know ourselves in our causes, not only in our own immediate Teutonic and Celtic forefathers, but in those who stamped on the youth of Europe the impress of their language, their customs, and their laws. No need for us to insist on these things here to those who are already convinced. And small chance of any argument reaching those busy but shortsighted politicians, who, dazzled with the material achievements of to-day, find more mental food in one edition of the *Times* newspaper than in 'all the works of Thucydides.' . . . Three things, then, will occupy our special attention in this classroom ; each so far distinct, yet all mutually connected, —the Language, the Literature, and the History of Rome— and each of these will yield its own special gain, which gains I shall now attempt briefly to indicate."

The most important letter, which the publication of this lecture called forth, was one from Dr. John Brown of Edinburgh (the author of *Rab and his Friends*), then unknown to Shairp, but who soon became one of his best friends. He wrote as follows :—

"EDINBURGH, 23 RUTLAND SQUARE,
"*27th January* 1858.

"MY DEAR SIR—Let me, though a stranger to you, thank you from my heart for your noble lecture. I have not been so moved with any words for months. You took me by the heart, and held me there from first to last. It is an odd sort of praise, but it is at least an honest one, when a man says to another man, 'These are exactly *my* ideas!' I cannot help saying for myself this much that it was almost ludicrous, the nicety with which some of your thoughts, and, indeed, the whole scope and spirit of your argument and its enforcement, was felt by me to be the expressions of my own old but somewhat amorphous convictions. I trust the lecture will be largely circulated. I meant forthwith to send forth a covey of the pamphlet to all sorts of people. I said to myself, and you must pardon me for repeating it to you, 'Give me twenty such

o

men in our Scottish Universities, and I'll engage to " reform " them, without much more of public meetings and commissions.' *This is a Scottish Arnold*, the real spiritual son (not the ape or imitator) of 'Black Tom,'—like yet different, being more like himself than any one else. May God spare you for much good. I was specially delighted with all you say about *style*. That is a fine bit of French from Buffon, and involves the whole truth, 'The style is the man.' Good writing, like good breeding, comes from keeping good company. Excuse all this. It is your own fault. You have kindled me up, and set me a-thinking. . . . —Yours very truly,   J. BROWN."

Professor Shairp, corresponding with an Edinburgh friend as to the publication of his Inaugural Address, said : " The University has suffered of late years from having been taught by old or infirm professors. But they are now laid aside ; and I sincerely believe (not to speak of my own Department) that in none of the Scottish Universities are the Greek, Logic, and Moral Philosophy clearer and better taught than here." [The professors were Mr. Sellar, Mr. Veitch, and Mr. Ferrier.] " The place, too, has far more of a University air and aspect than any other town in Scotland. I thought so long before I thought of coming here."

His first literary work, during the years of his professoriate, was a series of historical papers on St. Columba, Queen Margaret, St. Ninian, and Kentigern, written for *Good Words*. Then followed a more important series of articles in *The North British Review* on " Wordsworth," " Coleridge," " Keble," and " The Moral Motive Power," afterwards republished in his volume of *Studies in Poetry and Philosophy*. Three years after his election to the Chair, he published his one volume of Verse, though not his sole poetical work, which he called *Kilmahoe, and other Poems*.

His work, as Professor of Latin, left its impress on many minds ; not on the mass of the students, so much as on the select few, who came under his more immediate personal influence. It is thus that one of them, Mr. Bayne, now at Helensburgh, wrote a few weeks after his death, in 1885, in a magazine article in *Merry England*, in memoriam of his teacher—

"Those who studied under him when he was a Professor of Latin knew him at his very best. They can hardly forget his acute and suggestive expositions of Horace, his vigorous and impressive criticisms of Lucretius, and above all his delicate, keenly appreciative and altogether masterly prelections on Virgil. It will always be matter for regret that many of these did not take permanent form, as they would certainly have constituted a valuable addition to the literature of standard criticism. It is not too much to say that many a youth, in these ten years, learned for the first time what is implied in a truly generous culture. Professor Shairp was anything but a mere etymologist. He did not rejoice in roots for their own sake, nor find exclusive pleasure in the mechanical process summarily comprehended in the expression 'gerund-grinding.' He disliked dwelling over the mere dry bones of scholarship. There was always a vitalising process at work in his teaching; he felt, according to his own lights, that he too, like Socrates, was privileged to enrich the present by means of the past, as a preparation for the onward journey. If, indeed, his professional work was defective at all, the weakness was due to the energetic quality of his special philosophical bias. Yet it has to be said that there are now among the foremost scholars in England men whose pure scholarship owes much to what they imbibed in the sixties at St. Andrews. And let it be put on record here also that there are others who, while caring less for the mere technicalities of philology, can point to Professor Shairp as the man that first gave them stimulus towards the study of comparative literature. This will become intelligible to those who did not know him, if they will read carefully his *Culture and Religion*, and such a suggestive and vigorous essay as that entitled 'The Homeric Element in Scott.' Few men had a better sense of literary definition and comparative literary method. Just two years ago a casual reference to the minor Scottish poet, Hew Ainslie, drew from him, on a railway journey, a disquisition on the poet's three distinct styles, with apt quotations, delivered in the fervid, emotional way peculiar to him.

.   .   .   .

His volume of poems came as a revelation to those that knew little of the man. It was not that he had written poetry; he was generally believed to be capable of that, and the wonder was that he had not published sooner; the surprise was due to the novelty and strength of what had been at last produced.

.   .   .   .

The real outcome, however, was both in the manner of Wordsworth and at the same time something other and different. It was found that the poet, with all his reverence for the master he had long followed, was able to speak for himself and to sing in his own way."

The same appreciative writer says—

" Students entering College for the first time naturally made the acquaintance of Professor Shairp before coming to know any of his distinguished colleagues. The hour at which he met his junior class being early in the day, gave him the opportunity of introducing the new ' citizens of the University' to their academical routine. Those who were privileged to listen to the wise and weighty introductory addresses, with which for several years he began the work of the session, cannot fail to have a vivid and a grateful recollection of the strict and manly purpose with which he strove to inspire his hearers; his earnest appeal, his strong admonition, and the stirring note of his encouragement. He stood there a comparatively young man, addressing younger men, charged with a deep and noble sympathy for them in their new position, and ready to help them on the path he had just trod before them. It needed but a small penetration to discover in the speaker a tender and sensitive observer, a wise and anxious adviser, and a true and steadfast friend. . . .

The highest qualities Principal Shairp displayed in the Professorial Chair—his rare power of exposition, his ready appreciative sympathy, and his consistent moral earnestness —are likewise the qualities by which he will continue to be known in literature.   Curiously enough, there is but little trace in his writings of that vein of genuine humour from which he could pleasantly draw, both in his lecture-room, and among his friends.   When he took pen in hand he was almost invariably dominated by the deep serious-ness of his deliverances.   He hoped that his published lectures and essays would reach 'some of the thoughtful young.'   He never forgot the lessons impressed on him by Wordsworth that we are all steadily 'stepping westward.' This generation probably recognises less fully than its successor will do how much the doctrine of 'plain living and high thinking' owes to the earnest advocacy of Prin-cipal Shairp. . . . It is astonishing how closely and minutely he knew the writers who had really attracted him."

Again—

"When Principal Shairp was Professor of Humanity in the College at St. Andrews, one of the points of his teaching most valued, next to his range and accuracy, was his extem-pore translation, into glowing English prose, of some flowing *ore rotundo* passage from one of the poets.   Lucretius, Horace, and Juvenal were all thus covered with glory; but the charming metaphors and the tender descriptions of Virgil were treated with special sympathetic touch and deli-cate grace.   As an instance, we may mention the simile in the fifth book of the *Æneid*, line 215, where a pigeon is described as fluttering out of a cave, and then skimming away through the air on outstretched noiseless wings—

Fertur in arva volans, plausumque exterrita pennis
Dat tecto ingentem, mox aere lapsa quieto
Radit iter liquidum, celeris neque commovet alas.

There is an echo of this passage in Principal Shairp's poem *Kilmahoe*, in the lyrical division entitled *The Glen*—

> With laughter and shout the rock-doves will flout,
> Till, flapping the loud cave-roof,
> They 'scape overhead, and their poised wings spread
> To the calm heavens aloof." [1]

In a letter to the writer of the article, from which the above is an extract, Principal Shairp said, in December 1875—

" In really good translation, whether into English prose or verse, there is quite an education in itself. The longer I live the more I value the rendering of the best Latin and Greek authors into English, at once accurate and idiomatic, nervous, elegant, and refined."

The following extract from the letter of an Oxford tutor, once a St. Andrews' student, written after Shairp's death, bears alike upon his work at St. Andrews, and afterwards :—

" I have never known any one like him. Every time I saw him he raised my mind above the dull routine, to show me the nobler side of life, to put a more living interest into questions. When we talked to him we got beyond platitudes and party cries. He seemed to give to others for the time some of that spiritual insight which he had himself so deeply. . . . He filled a place which none of my other teachers ever approached. . . . His most endearing side was his wide sympathy. Those who drank of his spirit could not be narrow partisans. We seemed to lose our passions, our prejudices, our factious aims when he spoke to us. We found good in opponents, and even when we still contended, all the bitterness of conflict seemed to be taken away."

The present Lord Aberdeen was a student in the United College at St. Andrews under Shairp, and speaks,—as all his friends do,—of the " healthful and breezy freshness " of his teaching and influence.

[1] *St. James's Magazine*, November 1875.

"The charm and benefit of his personality," he says, "was always within reach, not only because he was ever accessible as a sympathetic adviser and friend, but from the tone and method which characterised his teaching in the lecture-room.

It may be thought that to a man of his poetic and eager temperament the teaching of Latin, so far as regarded his junior classes, would sometimes seem irksome. Whether this was so or not, I have little doubt that those who attended his lectures would join with me in testifying that his treatment of classroom work never became a thing of drudgery or dull routine. There was plenty of animation, and, not seldom, playful humour. With all this, and in harmony with that true and high keynote of his teaching and motives to which allusion has been made, he occasionally introduced (when it would naturally and appropriately occur) some helpful word or suggestive thought in relation to the spiritual and religious aspect of life.

I recollect, for example, how, when in the course of our reading we had gone through a passage where Tacitus, alluding incidentally to the subject of death, deals with it in the somewhat cynical style of his period and school, the Professor asked us to contrast with this the words of another writer, and then read to us the well-known passage in the last chapter of Ecclesiastes. Whilst writing this I can almost fancy I hear the rich tones of his voice as he walked to and fro, reading with solemnity and pathos the words, 'Or ever the silver cord be loosed, or the golden bowl be broken. . . . Then shall the dust return to the earth as it was: and the spirit shall return unto God who gave it.' "

The following letters from Shairp to his old Rugby friend, Edward Scott, tell their own tale :—

"ST. ANDREWS, 28th January 1859.

". . . A Scotch Chair, though not very lucrative, is a very nice thing, to my taste the most desirable of all educational posts. . . . As to schoolmastering, the worst of it is that, unless in the case of a head-mastership, all the best comes first, and before you are thirty-five you find yourself drinking the lees. . . . We like our life here, on the whole, very much. Latin and Roman history which I teach, is by no means my pet subject; but I greatly prefer a university, and that in my own country, to any school. Here we have no Donnism, nor any stiff academic air, but quiet easy family life. The University is too small, the place too retired, and Scotland altogether not the soil for Donnism to flourish. This is great gain, for the more we cease to see men and things through academic blinkers the better. Scotland this week has been in wildest most enthusiastic uproar about Burns. There never was such an outburst of love for any poet in any land; and that because no poet ever so took the heart of a whole people, from the highest to the lowest, and the low more than the high. There is but one other worthy of being named with Burns; of course I mean Shakespeare. And Burns thrills *me* more than the Englishman. The *Times*, I see, has been scoffing and jeering at it. It won't jeer us out of our nationality 'for a' that and a' that, and *twice as much as a' that.*' The Crystal Palace affair, I grant, was vulgar and cockney enough; but that was only a catchpenny travestie of what was real earnest here. The day was a holiday from Tweed to Johnny Groat's, and not a village but kept festival."

"St. Andrews, *6th May* 1859.

" I was delighted to hear of your transplantation to Rugby. . . . The intimate playfellow relation with boys may be very natural for a few years after leaving College, but it cannot last. It must needs pass, just as our child-hood passes, and our teens, and all beautiful things. You may feel Rugby cold and chill after the warm companion-ship with coevals at Marlborough. But that too must needs be. Rugby is the place for middle life. Our friendships lie all on the other side of thirty; and what life has of warmth and love this side thirty is to be found by one's

own hearth, and by making a home of one's own. . . . Make
the best of all men.   Bear, as much as you can, with
blemishes, and be as hearty as you can be.   Analysing and
fastidiousness, which all University men are prone to, makes
life painful, wounds us at every turn.   The best way of
getting over the *disagréments* of life is to flood them with
as much heartiness as we can pump up—something that will
turn the small ills of life as a duck's back does the rain.
This is in great part the secret of the abundant and life-
giving strength that Temple bears with him wherever he
goes. . . ."

Again, in January 1860—

". . . It is so good to pick up and carry on the thread
of old friendships.   And really this is best done by meeting;
because, as you get on, the power of really keeping up communion by letter leaves one. . . ."

To the same friend he wrote in May 1860 about the
materials he had collected for a series of papers on Scottish
Song.   His wish was to contribute to a magazine, such as
Macmillan's, "three short papers, five or six pages each,—
the first, 'Scottish Song before Burns'; the second, 'Songs
of Burns'; the third, 'Scottish Song since Burns.'"   These
were not published.[1]   In the same letter he states his
opinion of the volume of *Essays and Reviews* just published.
It is characteristic, and may be quoted: ".I have only
read Temple's, which I greatly like.   It had been better
elsewhere" (than in the volume). . . . "Jowett's is probably
the only other I shall care to read.   Williams's seems
feather-headed.   Of B. Powell we know what he has to
say already. . . . However, it is a great thing, the free
ventilation of opinion.   No honest belief without it.

---

[1] In a subsequent letter (in June of the same year) he speaks of another
division of the subject of Scottish Song.   "Smith's essay would by no means
clash with mine.   His subject was the historical Ballads, mine the *Songs*—quite
another region ; the one speaking of the chivalric time, the other of later
more rustic life ; as different, in fact, as 'O a' the airts' is from 'Sir Patrick
Spens.'"

> Say it, all ye who think it,
> Say it, and never blink it.

Say it, only don't compel me to swallow more of it than I see to be wholesome."

In the year 1860 Professor Veitch became a colleague of Shairp's in the University of St. Andrews, and renewed the acquaintanceship which was begun in 1856 at Yarrow, and which soon ripened into an intimate friendship. Mr. Veitch filled the St. Andrews Logic Chair from 1860 to 1864, and writes thus of the years he spent with Shairp as a colleague—

" In those years, from 1860 to 1864, talks and walks with Shairp were constant during the winter months, on the sands, and by the eastern shore, and of an evening—say Friday or Saturday—there were delightful quiet dinings and discussions when the lamps were lit,—now but gleams in a far-back memory. He was one of the most copious and richest talkers I have known. It was a kind of talk at the same time ever fresh and interesting, with keen insight, pointed speech, frequently happy summary phrase, suffused with feeling, and often glowing with imagination. The range of topics was widely varied. At this time, as I remember, he would discuss Newman and Keble, Walter Scott and Scottish story—especially the history and fate of the Douglases,—the old ballads, and the Minstrelsy of the Border especially—chanting with fine feeling stanzas of the best. Then passing perhaps to Kant and the Relativity of Knowledge, but luxuriating with fullest soul in Wordsworth. The influence he had caught at Oxford seemed to me to have come, not so much from the studies of the place, as from the accident of the Anglican Church movement, which had been going on there from 1834 to 1843. During the latter part of this period Shairp had been an undergraduate, and seen the notable men who were the leaders of the new ecclesiasticism. . . . Scotsman and Presbyterian as

he was by birth and training, these men touched him on
the moral and imaginative side, which was far stronger in
him at all times than the power of any definite theological
creed, or set of formulæ, for which I rather think he had a
distaste.

It occurred to me also that there was in him a
sympathy with Newman in his early restlessness and grop-
ings—in his despairfulness regarding human reason in the
theological sphere,—his refuge and solace in Authority, his
reverence and submission, and his love of Spiritual Order,
for History and its teachings, the accepted results of struggle
through generation after generation with the problems of
man and God, especially the work and lives of men who
had passed through the highest and noblest spiritual trials
and experience, formed always a strongly modifying and con-
straining power in Shairp's intellectual and moral convictions. Moral truth—moral rules of action consecrated by
history and time,—the continuity of this truth, its having
been shared in by successive generations of men, touched
him, and bent him to the side of Church authority and
order. Yet I never observed that Shairp had accepted any
distinctive part of Newman's final creed, or indeed of what
is known as Anglican High Churchism. It was the spiritual
character of the man, the form of the transcendent truth
that was in him, which mainly influenced Shairp, just as
it happened in other cases. He had a curious catholic
sympathy for different sides in Church and ecclesiastical
discussions—a desire to find what was good, true, inspiring,
in the varied views and systems. It was thus that he would
be found in partial sympathy with various, even opposite
men in the Churches, from Newman and Keble to the fervid
Highland preacher, and representatives of the diverse sections of evangelical dissent. Towards the close of his life
his sympathy was certainly greatest with the doctrines of
Atonement and Redemption, as these have been put in their
less extreme forms, and with a recognition of a moral basis.
Hence his attraction towards the person and writings of his
friend, the late Thomas Erskine of Linlathen.

But there was another line or rather series of cognate subjects—on the imaginative side—in which Shairp took the strongest interest. He had been drawn in his early youth even to two great men, opposite in several respects yet truly concurrent—Walter Scott and Wordsworth. He seemed to me to be as strongly attracted by the robust sense, the graphic picturing, and the chivalry of Scott, as by the naturalism, the meditative depth, and the spiritual symbolism of Wordsworth. Shairp was an intensely patriotic Scot; but he always seemed to me to look at Scotland through the eyes of the author of *Waverley* and *The Lay of the Last Minstrel.*

At the same time, looking back on the Scottish life of the past, he saw more fully into its religious element than Scott ever did, and had a greatly more enlightened appreciation of it. He has touched the subject only slightly in several of his poems, as in *Thrieve Castle,* and *The Good Lord James.*

One suggestion from Scottish, more particularly Border history, and Scott, was a theme to which about this time he used frequently and fervently to refer—the House of Douglas, and its tragic story, the family whose ' coronet for long counterpoised the Crown.' This he thought afforded a subject for a drama, or dramatic poem, unequalled in our history. Its feudal splendour, its heroic episodes, its tragic close, and the unworldly ending—all earthly ambition foregone—in the retirement of the last direct representative of the earlier line in the Abbey of Lindores. These stirred him as no other historical themes seemed to do. Somehow the ideal never took shape in performance."

CHAPTER XI

IT was after his settlement in St. Andrews that Shairp became personally intimate with Mr. Erskine. He had been
at Linlathen during the Rugby Christmas holidays of 1854,
and they had occasionally corresponded since then. He
now visited frequently at Linlathen, and the friends met in
Edinburgh, where Mr. Erskine usually lived from December
till April, down to 1870.

His winters were devoted to the teaching of his class ;
his summers to literary work, and visits to friends, or
residence in Highland retreats. The summer of 1859 was
spent, with pupils, under the Ochils at Montague Cottage,
near Blairlogie ; that of 1860 at Pitlochrie, from June to
September ; that of 1862 between London, Houstoun, and
Dumfriesshire. Later on he spent a week by himself in the
Highlands, of which the only record in his Journal is " went
to Fort William and Corpach, September 30 ; stayed one
week." It was a checkered year. His brother-in-law,
Colonel Hugh M. Douglas, had returned from India, and
died in the prime of life. His Journal is full of allusions
to the happy childhood of his son Campbell, and to events
connected with it.

In 1861, on hearing of Arthur Clough's death, he wrote
thus—

" Heard of the death of A. H. Clough, first by the paper
in the forenoon, then in the evening by letter from his
wife, dated 17th November. How many unspeakable

thoughts this calls up. One of the noblest men of his time, so true, so deep, yet gentle-hearted too, and tender. And then what a battle! what a sore spiritual struggle his has been."

" Monday, 16th December 1861.

" This day at ten o'clock in my classroom Thomas the janitor told me of the death of Prince Albert.[1] The College and Church bells tolled from eleven to twelve o'clock noon on Monday. All day the thought was with us of the great loss to the whole nation. It has been felt with a hearty home-sorrow such as I never before remember for any public man. A fine afternoon and sunset."

" 22d August 1862.

" Started from Linlithgow at seven o'clock for Stirling. Met Stanley and Mr. Pearson in Gibb's Hotel. Rain cleared at 10.30. Then drove out to Bannockburn. Went over the field, and on to the well, and mill where James III. was killed. Stirling Castle; views to the Bens so blue; one yearned to be among them. Parted at 5.15. I back to Lithgow, where I had a most pleasant evening with Donald Macleod."

The mention of Shairp's growing intimacy with Mr. Erskine of Linlathen will make way for a further portion of the Dean of Salisbury's reminiscences, and for some of the letters from Mr. Erskine to Shairp.

Dean Boyle writes—

" I must pass over various occasional meetings, but I remember well, very shortly after Shairp had begun to know Mr. Erskine of Linlathen, I met him accidentally in Edinburgh, and he poured into my ear many most interesting particulars of his intercourse with Erskine. He was delighted to find that in consequence of Maurice's dedication of one of his books to Mr. Erskine, I had begun to read all that

---

[1] Compare his poem on *The Death of Prince Albert.*

Erskine had written with avidity, and he told me many
interesting details of his conversations on various doctrinal
subjects. When I read Shairp's recollections of Mr. Erskine,
first published by Dr. Hanna, I recognised at once the old
conversations with which Shairp had made me so familiar.
He used to say that Mr. Erskine enabled him to put things
in their right place, that his culture was always subordinated
to his religious feeling, and he often expressed a wish that
Stanley, who, he said, had much in common with Mr.
Erskine, could see him frequently, and learn to love him.
In after years it is well known that wish was fully gratified.
Lady Augusta Stanley had a most tender affection for the
laird of Linlathen, and the Dean has recorded in his own
delightful style his own appreciation of Mr. Erskine's varied
gifts and delightful character. After I had taken orders, my
visits to Scotland were necessarily brief, and for many years
I saw little of Shairp. Whenever we met, however, he was
at once ready to take up the old familiar strain. I think
that his feeling regarding Bishop Cotton increased and
strengthened. His intercourse with his brother-in-law, the
lamented Henry Douglas, Bishop of Bombay, had a marked
effect on Shairp's character. He began by degrees to distrust some of the tendencies of his old Oxford friends. He
makes no secret of this in his remarks on Matthew Arnold
in his *Religion and Culture.* But I confess that, in all my
intercourse with him, I hardly ever saw anything like
asperity, and the heat and din of controversy were odious to
him. When the Essays and Reviews battle was at its
height, he spoke of the way in which Dr. M'Leod Campbell
had lifted the whole question in his *Thoughts on Revelation*
into a diviner air, with a degree of delight I shall never
forget. Is it wrong in connection with this to say that he
sometimes regarded the comprehensive schemes of Dean
Stanley as utterly ' unworkable ' ? and that he would sometimes say, ' Dear Stanley is doctrine-blind, as some people
are colour-blind.' Shairp was as intense in his feeling about
religious questions as in all literary matters. Some who
heard him speak with real enthusiasm upon Scott or Words-

worth, might be led to fancy that he was opening out his whole nature. But it was only in moments of most familiar converse with old and trusted friends, that he gave indications of the intense occupation of his inner spirit with the deepest problems of faith and speculation. A relation of mine had offered a prize for the best knowledge of Scott to Harrow boys, and I had the pleasure of being associated with Dean Stanley in the work of examination. This led to a visit to the present Master of Trinity, and when I arrived at Harrow I found to my delight that Shairp, who had now become Principal of St. Andrews, was at Harrow, engaged in the general examination of the school. There are very few persons who are capable of treating a younger, who has owed much to their encouragement as an equal, when the time of youth has passed away. Shairp was, however, one of these. I had at one time looked on him as a mentor, but during the last few years of our intercourse I found that he was always ready to forget any difference of age. We generally met in Scotland in autumn, and I have the pleasure of remembering many and many a conversation on the books and men we had a common interest in.

From the year 1872 until the year of his death my occasional intercourse with Shairp assumed a deeper and more interesting character. He used often to say that to two men—Thomas Erskine and Arthur Stanley—he owed much of the same influence which he had derived from the writings of Wordsworth and Coleridge. What attracted him most in Mr. Erskine was the delightful harmony between his deep spiritual nature and the thoughts of the great writers who were Mr. Erskine's constant companions. Stanley had always had a great delight in Scottish history, and no one admired and loved the genius of Walter Scott more than he did. This made a strong tie between him and Shairp. They had explored together the region where Scott delighted to wander in his early days, and Shairp was fond of telling how thoroughly the spirit of the Borderland had penetrated Stanley. It would be unfair to omit mention of a growing disinclination on Shairp's part during his latter years for some of the Dean's expressions and opinions in theology. I especially remember one long conversation, as we wandered on the banks of the Almond, near a house with which I had been very familiar all my life, and where I often in later years had the privilege of meeting Shairp during my autumn holiday, when he lamented what he called a departure on Stanley's part from the position he had maintained, as the biographer of Arnold and the champion of a form of Christian belief, apart from the ecclesiasticism of Oxford, 'a debtor,' as he said, 'to German theology, but not a slave.' Cotton he looked upon as a more true exponent of Arnold's thought and belief than Stanley. But although there was this growing difference, his delight in Stanley's company was as fresh as ever, and on the evening of the day I am calling back into memory, when the Dean arrived at Methven Castle, I spent such an evening as it is now almost mournful to recall. Stanley had the delightful faculty of imparting to others his keen interest in all literary and historical subjects. The old castle at Methven led him to talk of the story of Mary Queen of Scots. From one topic of Scotch history to another he and Shairp passed rapidly, and the evening was concluded by a most interesting review of the influence exercised by J. H. Newman during the days when the sermons at St. Mary's were making their marks on the minds of many Oxonians. I do not think it is too much to say that the two men exercised upon each other a sort of subtle fascination, so that all that was highest and best in the natures of both, seemed to be drawn out in vivid conversation. One remark about the power of Scott as a novelist and writer I well remember : 'After all,' said Stanley, 'if he had only given us Jeanie Deans and Bessie Maclure, I think it is enough to put him very high, indeed, as a great Christian writer.'—'Yes,' said Shairp, 'to make sisterly unselfishness delightful was even better than to write *Marmion*.'"

A very interesting letter of Shairp's to Mr. Erskine has been already printed at p. 176. Mr. Erskine replied to it as follows :—

P

"LINLATHEN, 4*th October* 1859.

"MY DEAR SIR— . . . Let me say a few words on the subject of your letter. I never intended to say that our confidence toward God was to be grounded on anything which we could discern in ourselves, or any agreement, for example, between our own consciousness and the feeling expressed in the concluding verses of the 139th Psalm. I meant to say that the confidence expressed in these verses was evidently founded on the belief that God was a Father whose desire with regard to us was to train us into a participation of his own character and blessedness, and that such a belief must produce such a confidence. If I know this purpose of God toward me, if I know that it is his unchangingable purpose, I cannot but trust him. I cannot but invite him to look into my heart, and do his gracious work there, delivering me from everything that is evil, and leading me in the way everlasting. The difficulty is when the evil within us has got so close to us, and has sent its roots so deep, that the removal of it must necessarily be most painful, when we have come to love our sin and to disbelieve in any love that should separate us from it—*and it cannot be removed without our will.* Our will must be gained to God's side. But I believe that God will strive with us till he succeeds.—With much regard to Mrs. Shairp, ever truly yours,

T. ERSKINE."

The following letters from Mr. Erskine have not been published, and since they are as characteristic of him, as illustrative of his friend, they are now given in series, according to date.

[Postmark 1863.]

"POLLOK, GLASGOW, 2*d June.*

"BELOVED SHAIRP—I thank you for your love, which I return with my whole heart. I knew that you wished to see me, and that it was only by the frustration of your plans

that you did not come to *tryst*. I hope we may meet
quietly some time this summer or autumn, and talk easily
and freely over matters which are better understood by ourselves, when we have uttered them to another. One of my
earliest convictions, when I first apprehended the meaning of
Christianity, was that, however much we might learn truth
from the Bible, as soon as we had learned it, we found that
we held it on a much deeper and more unshakable ground
than the authority of the Bible, namely, on its own discerned
truthfulness. This idea was the origin of my first publication on ' The Internal Evidences of Christianity,' although I
failed in bringing it out, because I did not fully understand
my own thought. This is really the question of the day,
and the right answer to it is the only true defence against
Essays and Reviews, and Colenzo and Renan, and all the
tribe of pickers and stealers.

I am paying a visit to my friend, Sir John Maxwell,
who is a great sufferer from pains and aches, produced by
long past falls in the hunting-field, which have left their
mark, although they were smoothed over at the time. It is
like sin, which never goes away of itself. Every sin committed must be deleted by being brought under the action
of the sin-condensing love of God. It may be forgotten, but
it remains till that operation expunges it.—Yours ever truly,

                                        T. ERSKINE."

[Postmark 1863.]
                        "13 CHARLOTTE SQUARE, 24th *December*.

" MY DEAR MR. SHAIRP—I did not answer your last
letter in proper time, as I ought to have done, waiting for
some definite and distinct information as to the days of
Stanley's sojourn with us. These days, however, still remain amongst the unrevealed things, and may remain so
for some time longer, although, in his new circumstances, I
am sure such mistakes are not likely to happen again. . . .
He was married yesterday, and he has got a wife who will
do him good, and not ill, all the days of his life. I had a
call from your friend Lushington to-day, inquiring about

you. I could give him no information, but his inquiries stirred me up to write, and to keep up habit and repute with you.

Have you looked into Renan's *Life of Christ?* It is a curious book, worthy of being thoroughly considered, as pointing out the way in which men of the present thought are to be met. I should like to see it fully met.

Theism is something distinct from the laws of Nature. Free Will belongs to a *province* distinct from the laws of Nature. Miracles are not the external evidences *à la mode de* Paley, but declare a Being who deals with us in that higher province. They declare what we call a Personal God. But I must stop. Happy Christmas and New Year to you and Mrs. Shairp.—Ever truly yours,

T. ERSKINE."

"13 CHARLOTTE SQUARE, 27*th January.*[1]

"MY DEAR SIR— . . . I read every word of Keir's address, and with much pleasure. It was cordial and earnest, and evidently connected with personal consciousness, and personal history, without which all such addresses must be false, just as pulpit discourses ought to be, and yet are not, except very rarely. His concluding counsels and warnings to young theological students show that he has not thought of these things so much as the other parts of self-education, and he evidently views them and speaks of them as an honest man who feels the importance of not making engagements which he cannot keep. If I had in youth entered into any church, I should certainly never hold myself in the slightest degree fettered by such engagements, so as either to restrict my speculation or preaching as to make me feel that I ought to leave the church to which I had joined myself. I should have considered that I did it wrong if I did not believe that it would be ready to adopt any truth, however alien from its articles, if they were clearly set before it. It

---

[1] The year was probably 1864, as Sir W. Stirling Maxwell of Keir was elected Rector of the University in 1863, and delivered his rectorial address in January 1864.

might depose me, but I would press upon it that it professed, above all things, that it was a Church of Christ, more
a great deal than of England or Scotland, and that those
who entered into it had engagements to God, paramount to
any he could make with it, as it had also engagements to
Eternal Truth. . . .

I liked Tulloch's little pats of butter exceedingly.
They were discriminating, and not overdone.—Yours always,
T. ERSKINE."

[Postmark 1864.]
" LINLATHEN, DUNDEE, 8th September.

" DEAR MR. SHAIRP—How I should like once more to
smell a Highland mountain and breathe its bracing breeze,
but I feel as if all that were past for me, and ' Lochaber no
more' must be enough for me, as substitute for Lochaber
itself! I have got some heavy weights upon me too—an
accumulation of deaths—beyond common—so that 'I go
mourning all the day long,' as King David said a good
many years ago, and as many have said and done since.

Your letter to Mr. Stirling has been forwarded,—though
it had been preceded by one from Jowett in favour of
another candidate, Mr. Green, whom I had seen in Edinburgh this winter, and who paid me a visit a few days ago.
I rejoice that there are amongst the Scotch clergy such men
as you describe Flint to be. I shall hope to know whether
he is elected or not. I am the better of meeting with right
men, especially if they have that interest in their own subjects which leads them to seek sympathy from others. All
my metaphysical interest is really theological. I care for
metaphysics simply as an instrument; but our relation to
God and his spiritual kingdom is the true *Supernatural*. . . .
—Ever truly yours,   T. ERSKINE."

" MOORE'S HOTEL, 2 FORRES STREET,
" 22d November 1867.

" . . . I am now in my eightieth year. It is wonderful to
myself to discover that I am so old. I seem all at once to

have made a start forward, without passing through the intermediate stages. I know, however, that I am on the boundaries of the unseen world, and that I must soon enter that untried state. . . .

There is much' of cloud and weakness in human life, and we need to have something in which we can always rejoice. There is that something, but we do not seem always able to rejoice in it. When you come to town, look in upon me.—Ever affectionately yours,

T. ERSKINE."

[Postmark 1867.]

"MOORE'S HOTEL, 2 FORRES STREET,
"28th *November.*

"MY DEAR MR. SHAIRP—I hope you will dine with me one of these days, and I shall try to get Dr. Brown to meet you.

It 'is a great duty to cultivate an habitual state of hopefulness, founded on the assurance of the fatherly character of God, and of his purpose to overcome evil with good in everything. . . . —Yours affectionately,

T. ERSKINE."

[Postmark 1868.]

"2 FORRES STREET, 18th *February.*

"MY DEAR PROFESSOR—I have an answer from Keir, saying that his name is at your service as Patron, or rather one of the Patrons, of the Ramsay Scholarship. . . .

So —— is at last withdrawn from this scene of things, and his end seems to have been a peaceful one. I had never known him intimately, but I had been acquainted with him above fifty years. His energies had chiefly gone out in scientific speculation, but he seems also to have, at least latterly, waged a successful war with the difficulties of his temper. However, no one can tell what internal wars are carried on by another. Without such wars no real advance is possible, and if the asperities of temper are merely softened by age, little is really gained. . . . —Yours affectionately,

T. ERSKINE."

The following letter of Shairp's to Mr. Erskine is sent to me by his nephew, Colonel Erskine of Linlathen :—

" *3d December* [Year not given].

" MY DEAR MR. ERSKINE—The last two times, as I have said good-bye to you, you have told me that you would be glad to have a line from me. I have not written, mainly because my reflections contained nothing I thought worth writing about to you. But I have lately read two papers by Matthew Arnold, my old friend, on St. Paul's doctrine, which, I am sure, would interest you, and on which I should much like to have your judgment. They occur in the *Cornhill Magazine* for October and November, entitled 'St. Paul and Protestantism.' Arnold has not hitherto paid much attention to theology. A man of great ability, Goethe and the Greek Poets have been his chief studies. . . . 'The old faiths are welcome, the new faith has not yet been born'—such has been the burden of his song. . . . Now he grapples boldly with St. Paul. . . . He is not wanting in admiration for the great Apostle. He thinks, however, that Protestantism has claimed him as its founder, but has sadly distorted, indeed wholly misrepresented him. With you, he lays his hand on righteousness as the central thought of all the Apostle's teaching, the longing to be really intrinsically right in heart and will, not with a forensic or artificial rightness, but with a rightness real and deep as the universe. So far I think you will agree with him in that he discards, with much impatience, all the glosses and substitutes of a merely forensic rightness, as altogether below and apart from the thing St. Paul longed for. In his positive statement as to what St. Paul considered rightness to be, you will find some defect, because he regards it as harmony with the eternal order, but does not, I think, recognise this harmony as consisting in sympathy with the nature and will of God. . . .

But I need not describe these papers at greater length. . . . To me it has been a great pleasure to find an old friend, generally believed to be more Hellenic than Christian, and to care for none of these things, yet a man of evident 'culture,' and looked up to by all the young men of so-called culture, at last recognising, and stating in his own eloquent way, that St. Paul saw further into, and spoke more to the Reality, than any one of all the poets and philosophers. . . . —Ever very sincerely yours,

J. C. Shairp."

None of the character-sketches written by Shairp are finer or more discriminating than that which he supplied to Dr. Hanna of their common friend, Mr. Erskine. The following are selected portions of that sketch :—

" Although it was as a spiritual teacher working by voice and pen that Mr. Erskine was known to the world, yet one cannot fully understand his mind and influence without taking some account of his human temperament and earthly circumstances.

.   .   .   .

He himself would have been one of the last to underrate what he owed to his ancestry. On either side he was sprung from a far-descended and gracious race, and among these, his kindred, he passed a childhood and youth sheltered from those early shocks and jars which probably lie at the root of much of the unkindness and asperity there is in the world. Equally on his father's and his mother's side he came from what the late biographer of Walter Scott used to call, with so much satisfaction, ' a fine old Scottish family.'

.   .   .   .

Out of the carse of Falkirk, that great dead level plain that stretches from Falkirk to Stirling, which, as the great battlefield of Scotland, holds in Scottish history, as Dean Stanley has suggested, the same place which the plain of Esdraelon held in the history of Israel, —out of that carse, about a mile inland from the Links of Forth, rises a scarpment or ridge of sandstone abruptly breaking from the surrounding flats. On the edge of that scarpment stands the old castle, originally a square peel tower with pent-house roof, like those common all over Scotland. To that tower has been built, on a long high line of building, with crowstepped gables, a steep roof, and dormer windows projecting from it. This range of building forms the later dwelling-house,—all that was there in Mr. Erskine's childhood ; though since then there have been made quite modern and not very congruous additions. This long building, flanked on the west by the older tower, looks down, over a small precipice, on a quaint garden beneath, and

beyond the garden are old trees and a lazy stream lingering towards
the Forth. The house fronts southward, and across the dead level
carse the windows look far away to the rising ground of Falkirk muir,
the scene of two great battles. Contiguous to the house, on the north-
east side, is the old churchyard, full of ancient graves and grey tomb-
stones. A church must once have stood there, but it has disappeared.
Behind the house, to north and west, long straight avenues and park
trees stretch on towards the grounds of Dunmore Park. It is almost
an ideal abode of an ancient Scottish family, like those Walter Scott
loved to picture. Such outwardly was the place and neighbourhood
where Thomas Erskine drank in his first impressions of a world in
which he was to abide for fourscore years,—for the associations of a
mere town-house in childhood go for little compared with those of·
the first country home.

. . . .

Airth, Kippenross, Keir, Ochtertyre, Cardross, with occasional
visits to Ardoch, his grandmother's home, and to Abercairney,—the
summers of childhood and boyhood spent in these melted into him
with associations of beauty and ancestral repose which were indelible,
and the warm atmosphere of human life that then surrounded him,
sweetened his whole nature to the core. It had, no doubt, much to
do with drawing out that deep and tender affectionateness which made
him all life through the much-loving and much-beloved man he
was.

In this he was very unlike most men. Hearts more or less, I
suppose, most of us have, but we keep them so close-cased and padlocked, we wear an outside so hard or dry, that little or none of the
love that may be within escapes to gladden those around us. And so
life passes without any of the sweetening to society that comes when
affection is not only felt but expressed,—for to be of any use to others
it must be expressed in some way. Mr. Erskine was in this happy
above most men, that, being gifted with a heart more than usually
tender and sympathetic, he had brought with him from childhood the
art of expressing it simply and naturally. So it was that the loving-
kindness that was in him streamed freely forth, making the happy
happier, and lightening the load of the sorrowful. It was as if inside
his man's understanding he hid, as it were, a woman's heart. And
though this is a thing no early training could have implanted, yet
when it was there the warm affection that surrounded his boyhood was
the very atmosphere to cherish and expand it.

If this had been all it might have led to softness, but the society
of his childhood, though based on affection, had enough of the old
Scottish verve and intellect in it to keep it from degenerating into
sentimentalism. His own busy intellect, too, was early stirring, and
the winter home of his mother in St. David Street was pervaded by
that old-world simplicity and frugality which is so bracing to character.
Besides, even if the boy's early years had been too tenderly nurtured,

school-life, as it then existed, especially in the rough old High School of Edinburgh, was sure to give scope enough for the hardy virtues.

Although I had long known Mr. Erskine by reputation and through mutual friends, it was not till the year 1854 that I became personally acquainted with him. As I happened to be in Scotland in the winter of that year, his cousin, Miss Jane Stirling, wrote to him that I was anxious to meet him, and he at once invited me to visit him at Linlathen.

It was, I think, on a Saturday afternoon, the 7th of January in that year, he received me in that library in Linlathen which his friends so well remember. I had not been any time with him before he opened on those subjects which lay always deepest in his thoughts. Often during that visit, in the library, or in walks after dark up and down the corridor, or when the weather allowed in walks about the grounds, those subjects were renewed. The one thing that first struck me at that time was his entire openness of mind, his readiness to hear whatever could be urged against his own deepest convictions, the willingness with which he welcomed any difficulties felt by others, and the candour with which he answered them from his own experience and storehouse of reflection. He exemplified that text which he often quoted, 'The heart of the righteous man studieth to answer.' This was a characteristic of him which is not found in men so religious. Commonly the statement of any view, very unlike that which they have been accustomed to hold, shocks them; and younger inquirers, seeing that they are thought impious or give pain, cease to reveal their thoughts, and intercourse is at an end. With Mr. Erskine it was just the reverse of this. His whole manner and spirit elicited confidence from younger men. No thought could ever have occurred to them which, if they were serious about it, they need have hesitated to tell him. And it would seldom be that they did not find in his replies something either really helpful, or at least something well worth their pondering.

·   ·   ·   ·   ·   ·   ·   ·

It would be no inadequate representation of Mr. Erskine, as he appeared among men, to conceive of him as confining all his conversation to religion and theology. Yet these, no doubt, were his favourite subjects, those that lay nearest his heart; and when he met with a sympathetic listener he poured himself forth unweariedly. It was not any mere speculations about theology, any mere dealing through the intellect with what is called scientific theology. That was to him the mere outwork, the shell of something far more inward and vital. In that inner region that lies beyond all mere speculation you felt that his whole being was absorbed,—that he was making it his own, not with the mere understanding only, but that his heart, conscience, and spirit were wholly in it. And whether his listener understood all he said—for sometimes it was hard to catch for its subtlety—and whether he agreed with it or not—for sometimes it was novel and even startling—no one, who could feel what spiritual-mindedness was, could come away from his converse without feeling that in his society they had breathed for a while a heavenly atmosphere. To return from it to common doings and everyday talk was like descending from the mount of vision to the dusty highway.

It used to be a strange feeling to walk about his place with him, wearing, as he did, to the outward eye, the guise of a Scottish laird, while all the while his inner spirit, you felt, was breathing the atmosphere of St. John. It was something so unlike anything you met with elsewhere in society.

. . . .

For when left alone to himself he was a man absorbed in the thought of God.

. . . .

And combined with this went another tendency—I mean the absolute conviction that all true thought about God would be found to harmonise with all that is truest and highest in the conscience and the affections of man. It was the desire himself to see and to make others see this harmony, to see that Christian doctrine was that which alone meets the craving of heart and conscience,—it was this desire which animated him in all the books he wrote, and in all the many conversations he carried on.

Over the social circle that met within his home at Linlathen his Christian influence showed itself in many ways, and though differing according as it met with different characters, yet was always in harmony with itself. Among the many relatives of all ages and characters who visited him, and the guests who, especially during summer, were welcomed to Linlathen, there were of course those who could not sympathise with him in his deepest interests. If, however, they cared for literature, in Mr. Erskine they found one who was at home in all that was finest and most soul-like in literature, ancient and modern, and his bright and sympathetic remarks or questions drew out the stores even of the most reserved. The Classics he knew and loved to speak of, Shakespeare he knew only less well than the Bible, and his conversation was edged with many apt quotations from him. Even when sportsmen were his guests, men whose chief delights lay at Melton Mowbray, he found some bond of sympathy with them, something that made them take pleasure in his society. He had a wonderful art of setting every one at ease, and drawing out the best side of every character.

. . . .

I remember calling one summer afternoon at Mrs. Paterson's house in Morningside, about the year 1863 or 1864, I think. Mrs. Paterson, Mrs. Stirling, and her sister-in-law, Mrs. James Erskine, were alone together in the drawing-room. For an hour I sat while they talked of the things nearest their own hearts and their brother's,

in a natural yet most unworldly strain, such as conversation seldom
attains. Mrs. Paterson perhaps spoke most, but all three took part.
It was early summer, and the western sun was shedding a soft light
along the green slopes of the Pentland Hills, visible from the drawing-
room window. When the hour was ended I came away, but a soothing sense remained long after as though for a brief while I had been
allowed to overhear a high pure strain of heavenly music. I felt
that all three were, not by natural kinship only, but by the kinship
of the heart, spiritual sisters of their gifted brother.

With any of his guests at Linlathen who cared for it, Mr. Erskine
used to continue his talk, not only in his library and along the corridor, but in walks about the place, or in a longer walk to the
bare bleak links of Monifieth, where the outlook was on the eastern
sea.

. . . .

During those winters his appearance, as he passed along Princes
Street to and from his afternoon visit to the New Club, must have
struck most passers-by,—with his broad hat or wide-awake, and his
quaint, antique, weather-fending guise. Walking with him on one
such occasion, I observed that he stopped and spoke very cordially
with a distinguished ecclesiastical leader of the time, who was well
known to disagree with him, and strongly to disapprove of his views.
'You seem very cordial with Dr. ——.' With a smile he answered,
'He tries to cut me, but I never allow him. I always walk in
before him and make him shake hands.' On another occasion as I
walked with him, we foregathered with Dr. John Brown, and we three
stood talking to each other for some time. When Dr. Brown passed
on he said : 'I like him; he is a fine vernacular man; he can speak
to you in a whisper. Have you ever observed it is only Scotchmen
who speak in a whisper? The English cannot do it.'

. . . .

Among the last occasions on which he was allowed to receive his
friends in Edinburgh was in the spring of 1866, when his old and
much-valued friend, Mr. Carlyle, after a long absence, revisited Edinburgh to be installed as Rector of the University. Many will still
remember the wise and gracious courtesy with which he then performed the duties of hospitality,—on the one hand securing for his
guest the repose he needed and desired, on the other, according to as
many as possible the coveted privilege of meeting the sage of Chelsea.
On the day on which Mr. Carlyle addressed the students in the large
Music Hall, Mr. Erskine, knowing how great was the effort for a
retired man of Mr. Carlyle's years, and anxious how he might feel
after it was over, had asked no one to dinner for that day. When the
address was well achieved, and Mr. Erskine found that Mr. Carlyle
was none the worse but rather the better for the deliverance, he asked
two or three of his intimate friends to come and join a quiet dinner-

party. That evening Sir William Stirling Maxwell sat at the foot of
the table, and with nice tact gave such turn to the conversation as
allowed fullest scope to the sage who has praised silence so well, but
fortunately does not practice it. Released from his burden, Mr.
Carlyle was in excellent spirits, and discoursed in his most genial mood of his
old Dumfriesshire remembrances, of the fate of James IV., and other
matters of Scottish history, and of the then Emperor Napoleon, of
whom, as may be imagined, he was no admirer. Those days when
Mr. Erskine received Mr. Carlyle as his guest were among the last of
his hospitalities in Edinburgh.

. . . .

The last visit which I remember having paid to him at Linlathen
was on the sixth day of July 1868—a beautiful summer day.

. . . .

It was a day of delightful sunshine, and as we drove to Mains the
genial air seemed to touch the springs of old feeling and memory with
him. He went back in retrospect to early companions—the large
cousinhood who used to meet at Airth and Kippendavie.

. . . .

After we had returned from our drive, we sat for some time on
the lawn just over the Dighty Water, which ran underneath the bank
on the top of which the house stands. It was about six o'clock P.M.,
and the sun was shining warm on us as we sat, and beautifying the
landscape near and far. After talking for some time, he asked me if
I remembered Mr. Standfast in the *Pilgrim's Progress*, and his words
when he came to the bank of the stream : ' The thoughts of what I am
going to do and of the conduct that waits for me on the other side
doth lie as a glowing coal at my heart.' . . . And then looking across
the Dighty to its farther bank, he added, ' I think that within a year
from this I shall be on the other side.'

He then, I think, spoke of the awful silence of God, how it sometimes became oppressive, and the heart longed to hear in answer to its
cry some audible voice. Then he quoted that word, ' Be not silent to
me, O Lord, lest if Thou be silent to me, I become like them that go
down into the pit ;' and then I know, he added ; ' but it has not always
been silence to me ; I have had one revelation. It is now, I am sorry
to say, a matter of memory with me. After it I did not know anything which I did not know before. But it was a joy for which one
might bear any sorrow,—*Joie, Joie, Pleurs de Joie*, as was the title of a
tract I used to read at Geneva. I felt the power of love, that God is
love, that He loved me, that He had spoken to me,'—and then, after a
long pause,—' That He had broken silence to me.' As he spoke he
touched me quickly on the arm, as if to indicate the direct impact from
on high of which he had been aware. As he walked away, leaning on
my arm, round the west end of the house, towards the door he added :
' I know many persons in the other world, and I would like to see

them again.' This was, as far as I remember, the last visit I paid him at Linlathen." [1]

. . . .

As the notice " In Memoriam " of Mr. Erskine in the *Scotsman* of 31st March 1870 was written by Principal Shairp, the following extracts from the letters of his physician friend, Dr. John Brown, referring to the closing hours of Mr. Erskine's life, have a special interest.

On the 16th March he wrote : " God only knows what an awful thing it is to be so near Heaven as I am when near him. He is past all fear and darkness. He is falling asleep, as a child in its mother's bosom—perfect peace—and speaks out his dreams, such utterances of love and tender and subtle thought; bits of his essential self, the perfected flower of a life with God. . . . It is, indeed, àn awful thing to be privileged so to see the spiritual movements of the soul, and *such* a soul, in its supreme time. When he dies, it will be a heart dying. He was a power among men to make them *feel.* You knew and loved him ; and he loved you, as he loved few. He said to me often, ' He is a vernacular man, I love him.' I think he will hardly get through the night, and he is fain to go. He is cared for, as if he were a weaned child.—Ever　　　　　　　J. B."

" 19*th.*—Our dear friend still lingers ; at times saying kind deep words—' thoughts that wander through eternity.'"

" 21*st.*—Half-past ten. He is gone. I have just been with them. Nothing could be more gentle. . . ."

Dr. Brown and others had urged their friend to write a memorial notice of Mr. Erskine for the *Scotsman;* and on the 30th March, after it appeared, Dr. Brown wrote of it : " It was well we were importunate. Nothing could more greatly express his nature and manner of man. It is perfect in form, expression, turn of thought and feeling. I have read it at least four times over. . . . No one could

---

[1] *Letters of Thomas Erskine of Linlathen,* pp. 347-378.

have said it as you have; and you will be glad all your
days that we got you to do it.   That word 'inwardness,' is
the very word.   The whole has the specific flavour of his
very essence.   It will give a deep and tender pleasure to
those to whom he was a man greatly beloved, loved because
loving.   That is fine about the spoken doctrine being made
lucid, and revealing the immediate God; but it is all fine.
You have done nothing more full of truth and beauty. . . .
I know it is in the very key he would have liked.   J. B."

   Amongst the friends of later years mention should be
made of the Rev. John Smith of Ecclesmachan, the parish
adjoining that of Uphall.   He was one of those somewhat
remarkable men whom the Church of Scotland has numbered amongst her rural clergy,—a calm, reflective, unam-
bitious, self-abnegating man—full of interest in many
things, intellectual, literary, and religious.   Conversations
with this clergyman were a great resource to Shairp when
at Houstoun, and he was much missed when he passed away.
A reference to him occurs in one of the Journals written
during a holiday visit from Rugby.[1]
   Of all the friends, however, whom he numbered in his
later years—friends not of his boyhood or early manhood—
by far the most intimate was Dr. John Brown, the author
of *Rab and his Friends*.   With such a colleague as Professor Veitch, he may have been (and doubtless was) more
familiar, than with a man of kindred genius and originality
such as Dr. John Brown.   But the radiant friendships of
middle-life are rare ; and one that began when both men
had crossed the watershed of life, and were going down the
western slopes to face the sunset, deserves a special mention.
The best way to record it is to give some extracts from the
letters of Dr. Brown, unique as a literary genius among the
modern physicians of Scotland, and one of the truest and
best of men.

   Writing on 28th February 1875, after the publication

[1] See p. 124.

of Mr. Erskine's letters, Dr. Brown said : " Yes, Mr.
Erskine's letters are wonderful—noble in their very incon-
sistency and halfness. He had an intense rather than a
wide mind, and brought the rays of his intellect to a focus,
making one thing very bright, and the *next* thing very dark,
—as with a burning lens.   You will make a book as
delightful as Alexander Knox's *Remains* (more so, for there
is more genius).   Do you know the ' Cherry and the Sloe ' ?
I was struck with this stanza—

> Leave sin, ere sin leave thee, do good,
> And both without delay—
> Less fit he will to-morrow be
> Who is not fit to-day."

Going back, however, to an earlier date, Dr. Brown
writes thus—

" 23 RUTLAND STREET, EDINBURGH,
" 17*th June* 1861.

" MY DEAR SHAIRP— . . . Thanks for what you say
about the *Saturday Review*.   Four years ago this would
have mortified and vexed me.   Now it does not.   This is
one of the uses of a great steady calamity—it sobers a
man, and keeps him from being depressed or uplifted by
passing things. . . .

Do you know —— ?   If not, you should introduce
yourself upon the strength of knowing me.   Things that
are equal to the same are equal to one another. . . .   What
are you doing about your Poems ?   Don't hang back too
long. . . .   Did you see my blast against that idiotical
Wallace monument ?—Yours ever truly,   J. BROWN."

[Postmark, *6th January* 1862.]

" *Wednesday.*

" I like this more and more.[1]   It has an unspeakable
charm,—the true pastoral melancholy of the region—and
these long satisfying lines, like the stride of a shepherd

---

[1] *The Bush aboon Traquair.*

over the crown of Minchmoor. Why not send it to
Thackeray for the *Cornhill?* I will be its godfather. I
wish you had another word than 'winsome' for the
summer. . . . Thank you again for this exquisite song. I
would rather have been the man to write it than Gladstone
with all his greatness and goodness.—Ever yours,

J. B."

Again (5th February)—" My dear Poet, do let me send
the ' Buss '[1] to Thackeray for the *Cornhill!*   J. B."

" 11*th August* [No year given].

" I' had a walk yesterday with Syme across Minchmoor
from Kailzie in Tweed to Yarrow. Such a sweet Sabbath
among the hills. The immense landscape, dappled with
sunshine and shadow and white clouds, as it were the very
tabernacles of light. It is a place to be thankful for having
come under the power of. Now you must write out that
song for me to show to Syme, who is as romantic and soft-
hearted as you or I. I think you say 'high' Minchmoor.
Now how would *dark* do? It is the special feature of the
hill. It always looks swart, or swarthy, among the other
green fellows—indeed it looked almost black. . . ."

" 4*th March* 1863.

" *Ecce iterum* Minchmoor! You will laugh at my
inveteracy, but it haunts me like a ' mission,' and you know
me too well to care a straw for saying No in the most
decided manner. The cause of this fresh and final outbreak
is that Edmonston and Douglas have induced me to get up a
new volume of Odds and Ends, with ' Pet Marjorie ' in it,
and ' Minchmoor.' Now it would be delightful to end the
piece with ' Will ye gang wi' me ?' telling of course where I
got it, and a word or two more, which would not displease
you. . . ."

[1] *The Bush aboon Traquair.*

Q

Again—

"14th *October* 1863.

"I had hoped to be where you are, but this is impossible. There are so many people very ill. I don't say I envy you, much less do I say I don't. What a wonderful Highland cateran and his wife you are living with. . . . I was at the Physicians' dinner to the Prince, Lord Brougham, . . . Mr. Gladstone, and the other Sauls. The Prince is a modest, manly, happy fellow, with much more capacity than his elder brother. Gladstone made a short but most beautiful speech, in which he referred to the Prince and Brougham, who were sitting together, as the Dawn and the Evening of Life. Spoke of the Association as a congress of love, emanating from the ever blessed God, the fountain of all love and goodwill. It was simply but greatly done. I was much with him on that Monday. There is a wonderful intensity and sincerity about him, and a sort of boyishness. . . ."

The following extract is from an undated letter to an Edinburgh correspondent, evidently belonging to the year 1862 or 1863. Shairp had been urged to become a candidate for a Chair in another University :

"The whole spirit of the Town-Councillor mind is so antipathetic to mine that I never wish to have anything to do with it. I mean that I should never volunteer myself for a contest in which they or their delegates were the electors."

His correspondent was about to visit the English Lakes, and Shairp alluded to Wordsworth thus: "He was one of my earliest and profoundest loves among the poets. This of course increased my interest in his country. Hardly any scenery has such soothing beauty. He was, as it were, those old dumb fells become articulate."

To the same correspondent he wrote of Macaulay: "The man who spoke, as he does in his letters, of both Scott and Wordsworth, deserves the truth to be said about him, namely, that he was the lineal representative of Jeffrey, and all that tribe of Edinburgh reviewers, who to all that is

best in our highest poetry were simply blind as moles. . . .
As for the critics, I don't care what they say. I fear there
is something in me that would rather enjoy setting their
backs up."

Again, speaking of some of his papers, which he preferred
sending to a magazine, rather than making a book of them:
" They are very far from my standard of a book style, too
flabby, flashy, lectury, not condensed, simple, and sober, as I
think a book style should be;" and, in the same letter,
referring to a biography which his friend had, or was to
have in hand, " Oh! don't be too diffuse. Everything nowadays errs this way. Nobody condenses, because the steam-
press goes so fast. If you wish the Life to be read, don't
let it be a line longer than ——; and for his works, don't
sweep his writing-desk, but only publish what is really good,
and likely to be permanently read."

It is not the part of one who is writing a Memoir to
give a critical estimate of the works of the author whom he
is trying to memorialise. Some account of successive writings may be given, but the judicial appraising of them must
be left to others. This much, however, may be said of
Shairp, that it is with his volume of *Studies*—devoted to
Wordsworth, Coleridge, Keble, and the Moral Motive Power
that his name will be chiefly associated. It is the belief
of the present writer that no estimate of Wordsworth written
within this century can be compared with Shairp's, for com-
prehensiveness, fairmindedness, and adequacy. Wordsworth's
place in literature is now so well defined, as one of those

> Stars pre-eminent in magnitude,
> Which from the zenith dart their beams,

that appreciative estimates of him are now less needed than
once they were; but no one,—not Clough, nor Henry Taylor,
nor Lowell, nor De Vere, nor Stopford Brooke, nor Leslie
Stephen, nor Hutton,—has given so full, so thorough-going, or
judicial a study of him as Shairp has done. It is a study not
for contemporaries only, but for the generations of the future.

The essay on Coleridge is also one of the best reviews of his philosophy and poetry that we possess; while, in point of finish and delicacy, the study of Keble is perhaps the richest of the three.   It deals with much besides the poet of *The Christian Year;* it touches the whole religious movement, of which Newman was the preacher, and Keble the poet.

There is little doubt that Shairp was greater as a critic of the poets than as a writer of verse, and that as a delineator of character he was better than either; while as himself the embodiment of one of the finest types of modern character, he was best of all.

To say what he contributed to Ethics, in his essay on the Moral Motive Power, would lead me too far a-field from the path of biography.   Suffice it to say that if the sphere of Ethics be divided into four provinces—the first unfolding the facts of our moral motive, the second tracing its ancestry and evolution, the third determining its authority and credentials, and the fourth essaying to explain the process by which its ideal can be realised—there is no contribution to the last of these problems in our English Ethical Literature that is more suggestive or helpful than this one.

Of the article on Wordsworth, his old Rugby pupil and friend, Vernon Lushington, wrote to him—

"12 King's Bank Walk, Temple, E.C.,
"14th October.

"My dear Shairp—I read in one of the newspapers that the article on Wordsworth in *The North British* was yours, and this afternoon I read it.   Thank you for it! Thank you also for reminding me, though indeed I little wanted the reminder, that it was by you I was first led to read Wordsworth, and to drink joyously of his pure stream. It was at Rugby, years now ago ; one of those lucky moments which lead to much, one of those kind gifts which bring so much more than the giver or receiver contemplates.

. . . I recognise in the quotations passages you have
quoted to me; and surely the stranger in the plaid, who
turned and took his gaze at the Poet, was no other than
J. C. S.

I heartily agree in your view of Wordsworth's noble
character and noble work. The only serious disagreement
I have is with your last two pages. That lies rather deep;
but it seems to me indisputable, and full of deep meaning,
that not only Wordsworth's later orthodoxy was dull, almost
lifeless, but his general poetic power became deadened
thereby; and this, too, in the very prime of his life as a
man. I rejoiced in your full reference to *The Prelude*, which
I have read and re-read many times, admiring it beyond
The Excursion. I also welcomed all your passages and
references to poems. If I missed anything, I knew so well
that want of space must have been hampering you at every
moment; and yet I did miss a fuller reference to the
Matthew Poems, *The Brothers*, and *Michael.* And if there
was anything unsaid, which I wished particularly to be
said, or said which I wanted to be said more, it would be,
I think, these three things: (1) That Wordsworth's feeling
for landscape is essentially *manly ;* Nature, he always insists,
gives gladness to the glad, comfort and support to the
sorrowful, of which numerous instances must occur to you.
(2) The wondrous depth of his feeling for the domestic
affections, and more especially the *constancy* of them.
(3) That he must be considered a leader in that grandest
movement of modern times, care for our humbler brethren;
his part being not to help them in their sufferings, but to
make us reverence them, for what they have in common
with us, or in greater measure than ourselves. But all this
is carrying coals to Newcastle. . . .—I am affectionately
yours,   VERNON LUSHINGTON."

In 1864 Shairp published a small volume of verse, which
was immediately recognised as a distinct contribution to the
literature of Scotland, and which gave him a place of his
own amongst the minor poets of the Victorian age. In the

first and longest poem in the book, *Kilmahoe*, which gives its name to the volume, we have a bright picture of west Highland scenery, of the moorlands, the hills, and the shores of Kintyre; and it is all indigenous, a native growth of the Scottish muse, and much finer than the story contained in the poem. It may be that in *Kilmahoe* we miss the magic touch, and the high ideality of these poems that are for all time, and for all men; but we have the strong breeze of the western sea, coming to us over heathery moorlands, and we hear the burns rushing down the corries to the shore, and the living creatures of the earth and air are around us —a sense of life and joyousness everywhere diffused. Along with these touches of pure nature, we have pathetic stories of old Highland life, a strong affection for antique customs, and the simple ways of a past state of things. The life of a bygone time is reproduced for us, alike in the laird's house and in the cottar's sheiling, at gatherings for worship on the hillsides, and at the haymaking in old Kintyre; and throughout there is no strain, and no affectation of simplicity. It is all perfectly natural, and it is national (Scottish) from first to last.

Shairp's dedication of *Kilmahoe* to his Father is noteworthy every way: "To my Father, this poem, intended to illustrate a manner of life which prevailed in ·the lower Highlands during his youth, but has now passed away, is dutifully and affectionately inscribed."

The following is a sample of the poem, taken from the opening of Canto VI., entitled *The Glen :*—

In the glen by the shoreland
It is blythe to-day,
O'er ocean and o'er land
In flows the May :
Come, sisters, sweet sisters, with me !
The burn from the hillside is falling
Down the deep dell from linn to linn ;
Merl and mavis aloud are calling
From the heart of the hazels within.
Come, children, to our green home !
And the cuckoo wandering from height to height

Thro' the hills is shouting his lone delight,
Come, children, for Spring hath come.

The mixture of Scotch and English phrases in this poem
is, however, not always successful ; and it is the way in which
they are woven together in the poem that makes *Kilmahoe*
inferior in many ways to the shorter lyrics in the volume.

It is in *The Bush aboon Traquair, The Moor of Rannoch, The
Run, The Bonspiel, The Dream of Glen Sallach, Lost and
Found,* and *The Blue Bells,* that Shairp is seen at his best.
Of *The Bush* Dr. John Brown wrote : " It is a tidy little free-
hold.   We would wish to live as long after we are dead
as the author of this felicity is sure to do ;" and of *The
Moor of Rannoch* he wrote : " That touch of the pipers com-
ing up Glen Etive at midnight is of imagination all compact."

In these Scottish lyrics, the distinctive feature is not so
much a description of Nature, as the subtle way in which
human feeling is introduced and dealt with.   We find in
them impressive traces of the way in which the spirit of their
native land has impressed itself upon the character of the
Scottish people, giving to the latter an indelible shape and
form.   It may certainly be doubted if any poet has felt the
whole sentiment of Scottish scenery more truly than Shairp
has done, or even as truly ; and especially if any one has ever
inwoven the traditions of the land with the peculiarities
of its scenery more deftly than he did, or recognised the
spirit of the past lingering on in the present.

The following are extracts from letters of Dr. Brown in
reference to the volume of Poems :—

" *Sunday Night [January* 1864].

" MY DEAR FRIEND—I am delighted quite with *The
Moor of Rannoch,* with *The Run,* with *Lost and Found,*
and *Balaclava* (both of them like trumpets), with *The
Losing Time,* with *Prayer, The Weird Wife* (magnificent
and *weird*), and many others.   Indeed I think we have had
nothing since Wordsworth and Campbell,—for there is a
curious mixture of these two, or rather *likeness,* with far

more of your own,—nothing so fresh and caller, with the strength of the hills, the sweet music of the burns, and the native wood-notes wild, for many a long year, so open-air and *native.* God bless you for them, and above all for *The Moor of Rannoch.* My *Bush* remains exquisite and perfect. —— is delighted with Rannoch and the pipers coming up Glen Etive. . . .   J. B."

In a subsequent letter he said : " I have kept down my enthusiasm sternly, perhaps too sternly. The book will give great pleasure to all it is worth pleasing."

Again—

"17*th March.*

" MY DEAR POET—. . . In *The Bush aboon Traquair,* I prefer ' high ' to ' dark,' and I like ' down to the Tweed ' better than ' to the Vale of the Tweed,' both for the euphony and for the idea. It is the Quair singing down to the Tweed, not to its vale ; but in all this you are lord paramount."

" 23 RUTLAND STREET, EDINBURGH,
" 22*d October.*

" MY DEAR SHAIRP—I have read *Kilmahoe* — parts of it over and over, and I need hardly tell you I like it, that it has held me, and that it made the old Laird and them all, from the sisters to ' Shepherd Colin, canty carle,' come into my ' study of imagination,' and live and move and be. By my mild markings you will see the bits I least liked. What I least like are *Paul Jones, The Garden,* and *Moira to Marion ;* what best, *The Sacramental Sabbath, The Glen, Marion to Moira* (as finely touched and as musical as *The Bush*), *Ingathering,* and *Return,* especially its later stanzas. I don't like ' doth ' and ' goeth,' and some of the lines are rugged, even harsh, and some obscurish ; but it is delightful altogether, and as autochthonous, as original in the true sense, as your own voice and tone, or as

the glorious Bens and Glens you sing.   I heard your voice
through it all.   As to its being popular, if the public were
a vast conduplication of *me* there could be no fear, and I
would risk £2000 on it if I had it; but it is too simple,
too unforced, relies too much upon the deep, constant affections, is too virtuous, too humble and unsubjective for the
jaded public.   I would greatly desire, however, to see it
tried.   I send you this rich note.   I had a great critique in
my hat (where my head was) all day, but it was not worth
giving you.   *Macte esto tu!* . . .—Ever affectionately,

J. BROWN."

In a letter from Mr. Theodore Walrond, to whom *Kilmahoe* was sent in MS., the other side of Shairp's poetic
faculty was acutely noted : " I have read your poem twice,
with great and increasing interest.   I would certainly say,
Publish it.   You must not expect a very large public.   It
is too peculiar in subject, tone, and language for that.   But
its fulness, truth, originality, and beauty will be sure to
charm many.   There are, however, a great many roughnesses,
both of diction and of rhythm, which it would be well to alter.
You poets get into the habit of crooning lines over to yourselves, till you have found them to run smoothly as read by
yourselves.   But when they get away from their master's
tongues they are as rough as ever."

Another Rugby friend, Mr. Shadworth Hodgson, wrote
thus of *Kilmahoe* in March 1864—

" The poem is certainly a new thing, a subject treated in
a new way, because in a more complete way than I remember elsewhere.   Family life, the life of the family centred
round a home, exhibited with sufficient detail, and carried
out into several branches. . . .

I should think you could not have found a country or
a time in which such a life existed in such completeness,
under such favourable conditions, as those of the poem.
Sheltered from the distractions of the ordinary social life of
modern crowded society, the family life develops itself in its
full glory. . . ."

To this letter Shairp replied—

"St. Andrews, 23*d March* [1864].

"My dear Hodgson—. . . . It was a great pleasure to see your handwriting once more. It is a pleasure, too, to find that you like *Kilmahoe*, and so entirely understand its meaning and aim. I don't think that any one has expressed this, either of those who have reviewed it, or of those who have written to me privately about it. Some of the inner harmonies of structure which I had hoped were there, you seem to have caught in a wonderful way. On the whole, I have good reason to be well content with the way the little book has been taken both by friends and by reviewers. One thing (I may say to you) I shall always remember with gratitude, my father was allowed to see it and read it and find much pleasure in it, before his illness came."

Of all the press notices of *Kilmahoe* that in the *Scotsman* of 18th February 1864 was the most discriminatingly just. "This is a spring of genuine poetry — not a cistern or a pump. It is of Nature's own gift and cunning workmanship. Mr. Shairp's strains are as native and unforced, as tunable as the notes of a lark or mavis. It is not philosophical or intense poetry—much less does it belong to the convulsive or the Satanic schools. It is the expression of the imaginative affections—of the heart of a refined, fervent, and leal-hearted Scotchman. Sometimes there is a little overmuch heart and expression, the head having at times hardly its due ; but it is a delightful book —fresh and ' halesome,' sweet, strong, and gentle as its own men and women, and as the moors and glens, the mountains and ' fairy water-brooks that murmur on for ever,' the unspeakable solitudes he wanders through and sings. . . . He does two things, either of which few men do well, and fewer better,—he is a passionate pilgrim through God's beautiful world . . . and he makes his readers share his love for the Great Mother, for he is a genuine child of Nature, with Wordsworth for his master."

During the years that followed the publication of
Kilmahoe, Shairp's Highland wanderings gave him material
for fresh poetic work, while many contemporary events
stirred the fire within him ; and from time to time fugitive
verses appeared in the magazines—in *Macmillan's* and *Good
Words.* The best of these have been gathered together and
recently published under the editorial care of the present
Professor of Poetry at Oxford.   Mr. Palgrave's Preface deals
so admirably with the features of Shairp's poetic work and
genius, as to render further comment almost superfluous.
I would only remark that we have sometimes to forget
the political, or politico-economic teaching of the poems,
in order to appreciate to the full the imaginative beauty,
and truth which underlie them.   *Glen Desseray*—the longest
of the poems in the new volume—should not, however, be
read as if it were meant to teach any truth as to the clearances in the Highlands.   In one of his letters to Dr. Clerk,
Shairp wrote, " Tory as I am, the native people don't owe the
lairds much."   There is no doubt that the emigration of the
hardy peasants of the north has, in the immense majority of
cases, been by far the best thing for themselves, for the
colonies they have entered, and for the mother country they
have left ; but one who believes this may still recognise
with Shairp the element of sadness that mingled with the
clearances.   It is the present solitude of the glens, and
the few memorials that now survive of the hardy race that
once peopled them, that is the very source of the pathos with
which that region is now invested in the semi-elegiac poem
of *Glen Desseray.*   We need not now wish these glens re-
peopled by a starving peasantry, while we recognise the many
stern virtues of the forefathers of the clans.

When the *Cry from Craig-Ellachie,*—composed after
travelling for the first time in the Highland Railway to
Inverness,—was published in the *Scotsman* newspaper, Dr.
John Brown wrote to Shairp as follows:—

" MY DEAR SHAIRP—You are a sweet-blooded man.   I
was just going to sit down to tell you how poor and shabby

I felt my notice to be, when in comes your note. The truth is that I was not in a condition to praise or relish anything. I had got out of my blessed state of thankfulness, and into one of harsh discontent. Man delighted me not, nor woman, nor poetry, nor any pleasant thing, and certainly not poetry as yours, spoken of out of the fulness of the heart. . . . My small quarrel with your ' head ' is in the matter of the railway and Killiecrankie. You hold with Wordsworth. I hold with what is called ' the spirit of the age,' the locomotive with its glorious trail of steam, its wild scream, its resounding thundering roar ; and I think it is as needless to lament the injuring the beauty of an apple in eating it, as to do the same by the birks and braes. Besides, it is amazing —as in Cumberland now—how Nature repairs and beautifies her wounds. I am rejoiced at the notices I have seen. Never you fear. Yours is a book to go into the hearts of men and women, and live there, and make you beloved and remembered. . . .   J. B."

In connection with this *Cry from Craig-Ellachie*, those who think that the Highland Railway has not really injured Speyside may sympathise with the underlying spirit of the protest contained in it, viz. the ruthless invasion of Nature's solitude by the noise of steam engines, and all their et cæteras. Shairp was always ready to join the ranks of those who opposed such desecration, whether in the district of the English Lakes, or down Glencoe. One has only to imagine a railway to St. Mary's Loch, and a station at Tibbie Shiels's, to realise the irreparable injury that would be inflicted on a district where the whole secret of the charm is

> The silence that is in the starry sky,
> The sleep that is among the lonely hills.

Similar in character, though totally different in result to his *Cry from Craig-Ellachie*, was Shairp's indignant protest in the *Times*, against the introduction of tramcars in the High Street of Oxford, and the changes it necessitated, in the removal of old Magdalen Bridge. His deep conservative instincts were outraged; but whatever may be said in reference to the latter change—whether it is to be a permanent improvement as well as an immediate utility in Oxford—the consensus of all educated opinion throughout the country is with him in the effort he made to preserve the national sanctuaries of the land unviolated by the roar of machinery, and unpolluted by the atmosphere of great cities.

There are several of Shairp's poems left in MS. undated, which we cannot connect with any special year. The following must have been suggested, if not composed, at St. Andrews; and although written in a Scottish dialect, it has some characteristic qualities, which warrant its reproduction. It shows its author in a light that may be altogether new to some of his friends :—

THE FISHWIFE'S ADVICE TO HER BAIRN.

Ken the kintra,[1] Kirsty,
    Ken it wide and weel,
Ere ye cry a codlin,[2]
    Ere ye back a creel.

Mim [3] be wi' the leddies—
    Words are easy spaired—
Selling flukes [4] or haddies
    Bargain wi' the laird.

Cosh be wi' your kimmers,[5]
    Whether auld or young ;
But wi' flyting limmers [6]
    Mind your mother tongue.

Let the auld and needy
    Ken ye hae a creel ;
But the grippen [7] greedy
    Pit it [8] to them weel.

Freely birl your bodle [9]
    Whan the wark gaes weel ;

---

[1] Know the country.
[3] Silent.
[5] Be quiet with your gossips.
[7] Avaricious.   [8] Put it.

[2] A young cod-fish.
[4] Flounders.
[6] Scolding women.
[9] Spend your money freely.

But ne'er lade[1] your noddle[2]
'Till ye've toomed[3] your creel.

Learn to blaw[4] and blether[5]
Baith wi' lad and lass—
Gie your tongue nae tether,
Lang's it brings the brass.

Sae ken the kintra, Kirsty,
Ken it wide and weel,
Ere ye cry a codlin,'
Ere ye hack a creel.

The summer of 1865 was spent at Luib Inn, Perthshire, where the article on Coleridge was written. Dr. John Brown wrote to him thus in the autumn—

"*21st August* [1865].

"I have been away in Warwick and Derbyshire, and finally at Ambleside, where I had not been for thirty-three years! 'Oh, for the change 'twixt now and then.' I was in Wordsworth's house, saw the room he died in. . . . I drove to Grasmere, saw the grave, and went into the church, and called on Lady Richardson, and then drove down along the other side of the Lake, by Red Bank, into Langdale. Glorious! It is a holy land all that region, and you have helped to make it still holier. I read the conclusion of your paper[6] on Saturday with gladness, and deep joy, and much thankfulness. Douglas tells me Coleridge is quite as good. . . . You must see Dovedale before you die. . . . Happy fellow, falling asleep under the shadow of Ben More!"

In 1866 the Chair of Ethics in the University of Glasgow became vacant by the death of Professor Fleming, and while still Professor of Latin at St. Andrews, Shairp became a candidate for it. The testimonials he now received were not less interesting than those sent to him fourteen

---

[1] Load.   [2] Head.   [3] Emptied.   [4] Brag.   [5] Chatter.
[6] The paper on Wordsworth.

years before, when a candidate for the same chair in the
University of Edinburgh while still a master at Rugby.
In his own application to the electors he speaks of Moral
Philosophy and its kindred subjects as what have "always
been my favourite department of study," and of his endeavour, if elected, to bring that great subject to bear "with
power both on the minds and characters of the students."
Mr. Matthew Arnold's testimony may again be quoted in
full :—

". . . My acquaintance with Mr. Shairp began many years
ago at Balliol College, Oxford. He had brought there from
Scotland a familiarity with philosophical writers and subjects which is not common among University students in
England. By the warmth of his interest in these matters,
by his energy in discoursing of them, and by the living and
stirring aspect he made them wear, he certainly gave a new
and beneficial stimulus to their study in the circle of young
men amongst whom he was thrown at Oxford—a circle
which included the greater number of the most promising
students then at the University. All of these who are now
alive would bear witness, I am sure, to the fruitful and
stimulating effect of Mr. Shairp's companionship in awakening or promoting in their minds an interest in the great
men and great matters with which Moral Philosophy deals.
    Since that time Mr. Shairp has pursued other studies
also, and has thus given more firmness to his hold upon his
main study, Moral Philosophy. His recently-published
essay on Coleridge seems to me as remarkable for its clear
and well-ordered exposition of a very difficult subject, as for
the ardour—the same now as Mr. Shairp's friends remember it in his more youthful days—which gives to that exposition attractiveness and vitality. I think that, both as a
writer and as a teacher, Mr. Shairp would fill with distinction
the Moral Philosophy Chair at Glasgow."

    The present Bishop of London spoke of his having
"the true fire of genius which would give animation to

whatever he touched." The present Archbishop of Canterbury said, "Whatever doctrines he held were absorbed into his life, and that which he lived he could not help uttering;" and Sir Alexander Grant, the late Principal of the University of Edinburgh, wrote: "There are peculiar capacities which he possesses far more eminently than most other men, which render him in an uncommon degree fitted to be a Public Teacher of the Abstract Sciences. The faculties I allude to are those of imagination and of expression. It is known to all how intimately philosophical thought has been in many cases connected with poetical imaginativeness, and how the abstract letters of Plato, Bacon, and Coleridge have received light and beauty from the forms with which they have been invested. A similar faculty to that possessed by these great men I venture to attribute to Mr. Shairp. There is no man I have ever known to whose mind a poetical imaginativeness is so habitual and natural. Connected with this is his peculiar power of diction, and his great charm of oral delivery, which has caused him to be looked up to with reverence by a large number of those younger than himself."

As it is a well-known fact, in some academical elections, that the unsuccessful are as worthy of office as those who win,—I do not say more worthy,—it is often extremely interesting to note who the defeated candidates were, in the light of their subsequent work ; and, as Carlyle was a candidate for the Moral Philosophy Chair vacated by Chalmers, and was supported by the recommendation of Goethe, it may be interesting to note the grounds on which Carlyle's friend, Thomas Erskine of Linlathen, supported Shairp, more especially as his letter deals with questions of greater import than an election to a University chair.

Mr. Erskine wrote several letters to his friend about his candidature—one on 3d May, and two on 6th May— apparently telling him to use the letter he preferred. In one of them he said—

"Most assuredly my appreciation of your fitness to fill

the Chair of Moral Philosophy is high, and I shall endeavour to write down what the grounds of that appreciation
are.   In the first place, since ever I have known you, your
tastes and speculations have all been in that direction.   All
your reading, whatever the subject, has been made to
minister to it, and these cogitations have not been without fruit, as your articles on Wordsworth and Coleridge
testify.

In the second place, I would say (what may appear to
some minds almost insignificant, because in their estimation
absolutely to be assumed and taken for granted, with regard
to all candidates for such an office) that you have a *real
faith* in the existence of such a thing as Moral Philosophy,
and that your interest is in it still more than in general
metaphysics.   This is, I conceive, rather rare; and the
proof that it is so lies in this fact, that the lectures in
Moral Philosophy classes are generally occupied very little
with the proper subject of the class, but fall away into
metaphysics, or logic, or rhetoric.   Men for the most part,
even thinking men, take it for granted that the knowledge
of what is right, together with the honest desire to do it,
is all that is needed, and indeed all that is to be had, in
order to enable any one to do it.   And yet their own experience might have taught them that there are many
things within them which they not only feel to be blots
but miseries, and which they therefore wish to get quit of,
but cannot by the most conscientious efforts.   They can,
by effort, shirk the experience of almost any evil, *but they
cannot cast it out.*   Now I would say that if there is no
remedy here, then there is no real philosophy of morals.
And certainly the man who believes that there is no resource in such cases, beyond earnest effort, is not the man
for the Moral Philosophy Chair, as he really has nothing
available to say on the subject.   I think you believe that
there is a remedy, that there does exist a moral centre of
gravity and a moral law of gravitation, which are equal to
any emergency of the kind.

These I conceive are considerable qualifications, and I

R

would merely add that you have always appeared to me to possess a remarkable capacity both for giving and drawing out sympathy, which I conceive to be of the very essence of what is required in any teacher, but especially in a teacher of Moral Science.—Wishing you success, I remain yours, etc.   T. ERSKINE."

In the second letter he speaks of the belief "that there exist relations and principles in the spiritual world corresponding to the centre of gravity and the law of gravitation in the material world, which, if known and accepted, would produce order and harmony in that higher sphere, but which remain powerless until thus known and accepted," as saving a teacher of Ethics from "making his class a class of rhetoric and eloquence;" and he speaks of the subject-matter of "this branch of teaching—if it can be called a branch, and ought not rather to be considered the stem, and trunk, and root of all true knowledge."

In the third he says : "Although you may have read and understood what Aristotle, Butler, Adam Smith, and others have written on the subject, you will not consider that you are really teaching your class when you repeat over what the thoughts of these men have been ; but you will feel it necessary, in the first place, to arrive at something which satisfies your own mind as reason and truth in the matter ; and in the second place, you will make your students understand that they have to go through a similar process, to use lectures and books not as substitutes for, but as helps to, their own knowledge of Moral Philosophy."

Dr. John Brown wrote of his candidature thus—

"When I say that it has long been my conviction that Professor Shairp was better fitted for the Chair of Moral Philosophy than for that of Humanity, I perhaps express as fully and strongly as I can my sense of his remarkable qualifications for the honourable place he now aspires to, for we all know how excellently and efficiently he has fulfilled his St. Andrews duties, and how much he has influenced for the best his attached scholars.

Professor Shairp, as is well known to his friends, has long devoted himself to the study of Ethics. They of all others have to him the deepest and most abiding interest. As he thinks and feels, so would he speak; his person, cordiality, freshness, and deep seriousness of nature could not fail to make his discourses, and all his intercourse with his students, most successful with young men, by not only instructing them in the whole doctrine of duty, but impressing on them their own deepest obligations to themselves, to their fellow-men, and to their Maker.

He has already, in his profound and exquisite essays on Wordsworth and Coleridge, given evidence of the true philosophic faculty, and of his power of discussing, at once with depth and clearness, the great problems of moral obligation.

He likewise has had long experience of, and a singular aptitude for, the Socratic method of teaching by questioning, and by the frank reaction of thought between master and pupil. I earnestly trust his great powers may find their full exercise by his being made Professor of Moral Philosophy in his old and much-loved University.

JOHN BROWN."

Writing from London (30th May 1866) Brown said to his friend: "I am sorry, and indeed surprised; but not altogether sorry, as it gives *us* a chance of you now; and if you were to lose, you could not have lost less than by Caird getting it. I am kept in this huge and prostrating place. . . . Yes, we must get into the solitudes and be comforted. This place excites and depresses me. I shall be glad when I turn my back on it. I was at Stanley's on Monday, and had a long visit at Carlyle's. He was prostrate and dumb at first, but soon revived, and got quite cheery and full of talk. It was wonderful to hear him."

Several letters from Principal Shairp to his old Rugby

friend, Shadworth Hodgson, have reached me while these sheets are passing through the press. As they refer mainly to the philosophical aspects of experience, and are a series in themselves, I place them together at the end of this chapter. But a letter from Mr. Matthew Arnold, belonging to the year 1866, and referring to his own poem *Thyrsis*, must precede them.

"*2d April 1866.*

". . . It gives me great pleasure that you and Sellar like *Thyrsis*. *Multi multa loquuntur : ideo fides parum est adhibenda*, says Thomas à Kempis; but the voices I do turn to are the voices of an old set, now so scattered, who, at the critical moment of opening life, were among the same influences, and (more or less) sought the same things as I did myself. What influences those before and after us have been or may be among, or what things they have sought or may seek, God knows. Perhaps the same as we, but we cannot know, cannot therefore be sure of understanding them and their criticisms on what we do.

Thyrsis is a very quiet poem, but I think solid and sincere. It will not be popular, however. It had long been in my head to connect Clough with that Cumner country, and when I began I was carried irresistibly into this form: you say truly, however, that there is much in Clough (the whole *prophet* side, in fact) which we cannot deal with in this way; and one has the feeling, if one made the poem as a memorial poem, that not enough is said about Clough in it. . . . Still Clough had this idyllic side, too—to deal with this suited my desire to deal again with that Cumner country; any way, only so could I treat the matter this time. *Valeat quantum.*"

"St. ANDREWS, 14*th December* 1865.

" MY DEAR HODGSON— . . . Your Aladdin's Lamp is a precious document, not only as containing your answer to that grave question, but also as containing the starting-point of your philosophy in a nutshell. If one grants your

main premiss, the rest follows of necessity. But I still
demur to your main principle that the ' lamp ' or any other
object consists of feelings and nothing else. As at present
advised, I accept the duality given in every perception, and
believe that the *non ego* given in perception (the lamp) is
something independent of me. I do so for two reasons :
that if one explains away these ultimate distinctions given
in consciousness we cut away all ground of certainty about
everything.

(2) Because your out-and-out phenomenalism, if one
were to believe it, would make one walk about as it were in
a nightmare world of shadows that have no substance—
no meaning. However, though not accepting the first principle of the solution, viz. that external objects are feelings
and nothing more, yet I must compliment you on the
clearness of your exposition and the vivacity thereof—a
vivacity that puts one in mind of Ferrier. Do you know
that I think it would be a great thing if you could introduce more of this style into your philosophic writing. The
philosophy would not lose one whit in exactness, and would
gain greatly by the added vividness and impressiveness.

Then as to what you say of Coleridge. I grant that he
was not great as an analyst—a weakness in which I
share. But still though analysis is required in philosophy
I do not allow that it is everything, or even the greater part.
Coleridge did great service to philosophy by calling attention
to facts long forgotten. The nature of the will as opposed
or different from physical sequence, and the existence of the
Reason, of something, call it what you will, which brings us
into contact with spiritual truth. The latter, no doubt,
needs further analysis, but as to the former, the will, I doubt
whether analysis can get much further. When you have
eliminated all that is intellectual, and all that is emotional in
an act of will, there will still remain over that which is τὸ
ἴδιον in the act of will, which must be, I take it, an ultimate
and unique element. At least it can never be accounted for
by Time and mere feeling. It contains in itself an ultimate
and peculiar element, and in fact I believe that when

analysis has done its utmost, it will, instead of reducing thought to fewer elements than the old division of faculties, resolve it into more numerous. Then again, after analysis has done its work, there is surely another work remaining for philosophy—the synthetic—to exhibit the working of the several elements in combination. In fact it would seem that it is in order to see this more fully, intelligently, and discriminatively, that the preliminary work of analysis is chiefly valuable.

Don't, please, reduce all philosophy to analysis, or I fear I must abjure it. For oh it is

> Life, not death, for which we pant,
> More life, and fuller, that we want.

. . .—Ever most sincerely yours,

J. C. SHAIRP."

"HOUSTOUN, UPHALL, LINLITHGOWSHIRE,
"2d *June* 1866.

"MY DEAR HODGSON—The Glasgow attempt has miscarried; but my thoughts have been set for some time on the primary questions of morals. And knowing that you have been investigating these, I want to have a chat with you about them. No doubt you will *more tuo* treat them in the most thorough analytic method; but I hope your analysis will not be so abstract as to be unintelligible to my more round-edged and concrete mind. I hope that though we get the matter reduced to its last elements, there may yet remain in it the vital power.

What I want to ask you is, If you have determined what it is that makes an action what we call 'right' or 'good.' Or to put it in a more practical way: As actions are the result of character, and from this must take their colour, what is it that constitutes the righteous man, the virtuous character? You remember, I daresay, how Adam Smith, at the end of his book, classifies the possible answers to this last question. He says they are three. The virtuous

temper, he says, may consist either: (1) In a proper balance
and government of all the affections and impulses, making
a well-adjusted and rightly-subordinated whole. This is
Plato's δικαιοσύνη, Aristotle's μεσότης, and Butler's Constitution. (2) There is the theory which places the virtuous
character in Benevolence on the proper exercise of the unselfish affections. Such was Hutchison's and others. (3)
There is the prudence theory, which makes virtue to consist
in the judicious pursuit of our own best happiness.

Now, whichever of these theories be the true one, there
is one practically fatal objection to them all, except perhaps
the last. They, none of them, have any dynamic power, and
they don't show how men are to get it. They are like a
perfect clock, which, however, won't go.

It may be quite true that the virtuous character is an
even balance of the affections. But my affections are all
disordered, and what is to put them into order? Where
am I to get the power adequate to do this?

Again, it may be that the self-forgetting temper, self-
sacrifice, is the only right one. But I am a most selfish,
self-centred dog. What is to make me forget this self, and
learn to love others, and think of them? Above all, whence
am I to get the power really in heart, and not in act only,
to love those who do not love me—who perhaps in themselves are not lovely?

The prudential theory of virtue, no doubt, has the
dynamic power ready-made to its hand. There is an
abundant supply of self-love in all men. It requires no
stimulant, only right information, enlightenment, to know
what will make for one's own happiness.

When this theory, however, is transformed, as it is in
Mill's hands, to the wider form of making the greatest
happiness of all men the end of all action, then the want
of the dynamic force is felt as strongly as in either of the
two first. The simplicity and plainness of the utilitarian
theory disappears, and you are involved in as many hard
questions as in any of the other systems.

My questions, then, resolve themselves into three.

1. What does your analysis give you as the element or elements which constitute rightness in actions and in character ?

2. What do you say as to the dynamic power which seems to me the great *desideratum* in almost all philosophical moral systems ?

There are some good thoughts in one of the chapters of *Ecce Homo* as to the need of an inner heat—an inspiration to make morality vital.

3. Can you tell me of any portion of Comte, or any French or other modern writer, which would be helpful in these inquiries ? . . .—Yours very sincerely,

J. C. SHAIRP."

"ST..ANDREWS, 26*th July* 1867.

"MY DEAR HODGSON—I have been a great defaulter, and must confess it with contrition. For your long and valuable letter on Ethics last summer deserved other treatment. I have read it and re-read it, over and over. . . .

But I am now trying partly to give you some reply in a paper I am writing for the *North British* on the "Dynamic Power" in morals, or on "Morality and Religion." I am not sure which it will be called. It is an effort to throw together into something like shape many thoughts I have long had. It will contain a survey—perhaps too tedious a one—of the motive power which some of the greatest moralists have offered, and then will proceed to my own theory, which finds the true dynamic, mainly by opening a passage from morals into religion, and letting in the living powers of the latter into the hard and somewhat empty forms of the former. In the way I slightly touch on your view that Pleasure is the universal dynamic. I cannot agree with this view. I wish I could mention you by name in adverting to it, but as you have not published on it I cannot. If I have misapprehended your view you must tell me. . . . Probably I may have committed some mistakes from not having read many modern books on these subjects, for I think more than read about them. I hope, therefore, you will accept this paper, which will, I trust, appear in the next *North British*, as in some sort an answer to your letter. For as I told you, I could not answer it by a common epistle, but only by a treatise. It was so wide and so systematic. Merely to take up small points in a letter seemed of no use. And now before the *N. B.* article appears give me a line to tell me of yourself and your work and doings. How far has your ethical *opus* advanced, and when shall we have it in our hands ? I look forward to reading it with pleasure. For Ethics, especially in connection with Religion, are more interesting to me nowadays than Metaphysic pure. I think that while Ethics require further analysis, they also require much to be brought back to life and nature, and to be enriched by new facts taken straight from life and experience, and not repeated from books. Also they ought surely to be so far practical as to afford men some help in the many practical moral problems that meet men, and will meet them more and more in our highly complex modern life. . . .

I read Godfrey on strikes, and thought him excessive. No doubt the working-man ought to have equal laws, but there is no use making a god of him as has been done lately. He is just as selfish as the rest of us, with less check to it from cultivation and restraints of society. . . .—Yours most sincerely,   J. C. SHAIRP."

"ST. ANDREWS, 23d *December* 1867.

"MY DEAR HODGSON—You must put down my seldom writing to the great exertion which I find it to be to carry on a philosophic discussion by letter. Indeed, I seldom can get myself up to the sticking pitch to do so. And yet I greatly relish having your philosophic thoughts, which always set me a-thinking. Your last argument to prove that pleasure is the universal motive power does not satisfy me.

You say that a man is benevolent for the specific pleasure of being so, and in being so he secures the more general pleasure of a good conscience. But I should deny that a man is benevolent *for* the pleasure of being so. The pleasure is the result and not the cause of his being benevolent. If he is benevolent for the pleasure of being so—that is, if it is the pleasure thus to be gained that urges him to be benevolent, then I should say he is selfish, not benevolent. I quite accept Butler's account of the outgoing emotions. If you say that a man is urged to be benevolent by the feeling of pain at seeing objects of compassion, I should reply that this may be part of his motive. But then that the feeling of pain arises from an anterior judgment of conscience that he ought to relieve misery.

I greatly like your name 'Newman's Law,' and agree with you that his beautiful statement of it deserves that it should be so named. You will find it in his volume of sermons called *Sermons on Subjects of the Day*. The sermon is entitled 'Sanctity the Token of the Christian Empire,' and in my edition, which is the second, it occurs at p. 276.

I still adhere to what I said about analysis not being the whole work of philosophy. The LIFE in every analysed entity which escapes you in the analysis is surely to be taken account of. If this is a real element which the analysis fails to catch (as it does), then after the analysis, let the whole matter be placed before the reader in synthesis, and then the living nexus which held all together will in the synthesis reappear.

I do wish you would in your Ethics try to give this side as well as the other. If you give merely analysis, your book will be read by the few professional metaphysicians— there are somewhere under 100 in Great Britain. If you throw the life into your book, it will probably be read by all thinking and educated men.

Another way of giving interest and vitality to your book is to take care that you apply it to actual problems of the time, to the felt needs of men. You won't be the worse philosopher if you give us some of the poet too. I know there is the poet in you, if you did not keep him so sternly under. Plato was not worse philosopher for giving his imagination (which is the truth-realising faculty) play.

Do thou likewise. All good things of this season be with you! A great shadow is thrown over our Christmas by our expecting to hear every hour of the death of my brother-in-law, and that under very distressing circumstances.

Write to me. I do like your letters, though my long intervals of silence scarce deserve them.

I heard you were recommending Maudesly's *Mental Pathology*. I have only seen a review of it. It seemed too materialistic to much interest me.—Ever yours,

J. C. SHAIRP."

"ST. ANDREWS, 20*th March* 1868.

"MY DEAR HODGSON— . . . I shall look forward to reading your thoughts on Space and Time. Though I have given up Metaphysics as a primary study, I still take great interest in them. We much need some more spiritual philosophy than Mill's, which the *Saturday Review* vaunts as all-sufficient, and which (along with Grote) Oxford teaches as its one modern book. If I had had your leisure time I should have probably spent a good deal of it on Metaphysics. But Rugby work made that impossible for more than ten years, when the appetite for these subjects is keenest. When more leisure came, I found that I was past the age when I could ever become really learned in philosophy.

By that time, too, I had come to feel quite distinctly that there is that within us which Metaphysics cannot satisfy—that in the pressures of life they are cold and distant; that one needs something nearer to us, more intimate, in which the heart may find its home. This at least was what I felt.

But if this central stay for our being has once been found elsewhere than in philosophy, then philosophy may render great service by introducing harmony into all one's thoughts and aims, and helping out consistency of life. I

mean that philosophy, as I understand it, cannot originate
the first truths, the foundations on which our being must
lean. These it must receive from faith, or from the moral
and spiritual side of our being, call it what you will. It
may, however, take them up, show their reasonableness,
make them good intellectually, and so be of great
service. What I mean is that philosophy is not τὸ
ἡγούμενον of life, but must work in subservience to this.
Of course it must be a reasonable service. It must satisfy
itself that it is the right ἡγούμενον which it serves. But
I prose, and so shall stop. Do you see much of H. Davey?
I should like to know about him, and how far he is on his
road to the woolsack. Tell me, too, about Gosling.—Ever
most sincerely yours,   J. C. SHAIRP."

CHAPTER XII

THE Glasgow election over, Shairp seemed to realise that to St. Andrews the remainder of his lifework was to be chiefly confined. In May 1866 he removed from Gillespie Terrace to Edgecliffe,[1] then just erected on the Scores; and in the late summer he took an excursion with his friend, Professor Veitch, to the Braemar Highlands. Of this expedition one vivid memorial remains in a letter written to Mrs. Shairp. The Wells of Dee have nowhere been more accurately described.

> "BRAEMAR, 25th July 1866.

" . . . We started at half-past eight o'clock—the day fine, with a nor'-east wind, just enough to make it not sultry. By eleven o'clock we had reached the highest house in Glenlui, and there we left the pony carriage. We then started to walk up through Glen Derry, a regular forest of pine, some fresh, many decayed, many broken over with the storms, many bleached skeletons. After this the ascent began, and lasted for two hours. About 3.15 we reached a great field of snow, and lunched at the bottom of it, by a fine cold granite well.

It was four when we reached the top. A mist was coming over Cairngorm and hid Strathspey and all the north. But south and west we saw the whole mountain group of Scotland, from Ben-y-gloe to Ben Nevis. *He* was clearly visible. Afar to the nor'-west high peaks, which I took to

---

[1] I believe the word was originally spelt without the final *e*, but when I became tenant of the house I found that the landlord had changed it as above.

be the Sgor-nan-Ciche at the Head of Loch Nevis and Loch Hourn.

At half-past four we began to descend, not as we came, but in exactly the opposite direction. . . . We were determined to see the Wells of Dee. A sheer descent over granite boulders it was. Very strange they were. It would take long to describe them. Suffice it, they are four little cup-shaped lochans which are fed by one cataract that comes sheer down from Ben Muichdhu out of wreaths of snow. This torrent falls right over a precipice, then disappears from sight, runs for a quarter of a mile under granite debris, reappears in the first cup or lochan, which is about twelve feet in diameter; then comes another mass of debris, the water from the first well is lost under this to reappear in the second lochan or well, and so on through all the four wells. It then bursts away down a wild glen between Ben Muichdhu on the east and Braeriach and Cairntoul on the west, joined at every few yards by new feeders, and before it has got ten miles down its glen (Glen Dee) it is a full river. I should say that the first well is at the very head of Glen Dee, just before you come to the watershed, down to Rothiemurchus and the Spey.

Coming down the glen from its wells for several miles we had to the east the great summit of Ben Muichdhu, red with bare granite, on the west side the rugged corries and awful precipices of Braeriach and Cairntoul. I have never seen anything in Scotland more awesome than these last. Out of Glen Dee, about four miles below its Wells, we crossed a ridge, got into the pines of Glen Luibeg, and reached the keeper's house by nine o'clock. . . ."

An undated paper amongst Principal Shairp's MSS., which gives an account of a September walk in that magnificent moorland and mountain country between Ben Alder and Ben Nevis, may follow this—

"To those who can from morning till sunset support its weight, it has a stern delight which awes the soul yet kindles the imagination, nowhere else to be found. I have heard one who had travelled much among mountains, and felt them deeply and truly, say that it was these great mountain moors and their peculiar character in which the Highlands most excelled Switzerland, and which to his mind more than made up by their utter solitariness for the want of glaciers and peaks of eternal snow.

It is well before undertaking a long solitary ramble to have been for some little time in the Highlands. It takes time before your mind gets attuned to their spirit, so different from that of the rest of the world. To plunge at once from the throngs of men, and the hurry of some great capital or commercial centre, into these calm and idle solitudes is too sudden a transition. The sights and sounds and thoughts of the streets and the railways are here only a hindrance. We require to get rid of these, to let the scent of the wild myrtle, the cry of the curlews, and the sighing of the wind through the long muir grass, enter into us, and put out the others. 'The world' must not be 'too much with us' if we are thoroughly to take in the mountain spirit. That world is full of a busy, changeful present, and an anxious future. These solitudes are given over to leisure, the same yesterday as a thousand years ago. Only the present speaks of a past— of old battles now all but forgotten, of songs of a ruder more primitive time, and of sheiling life and pastoral virtues now for ever vanished.

Before our minds can open themselves to these things they must have sloughed off the film of a too pressing present.

Many such rambles I can call to mind, undertaken during the summers or autumns of the last twenty years. One of the latest I shall now try to put on record.

It was a clear bracing September day, the wind blowing from the north-west—that clear bracing wind that with most gives promise of steady weather and strings the frame to its fullest vigour — that I left the west end of Loch Rannoch, and held away nearly due north. The region that lay before me was quite unknown to me. I had

never travelled it before, though I had looked on it far off
from the hilltops. All I knew was that some twenty miles
to the north lay a loch, whose name occurs several times in
old Gaelic songs of four hundred or five hundred years since,
and that at the south end of that loch I should find shelter
for the night in a keeper's house. The whole way I was
told I should pass no human dwelling but one shooting-
lodge lately built there. After climbing the low heights
that skirt the upper end of Loch Rannoch, and starting the
black cocks and gray hens that shelter in the natural woods
that fringe it, I lost sight of the loch, and found myself in one
of those vast, seemingly boundless, rolling moors of which I
have spoken. Near the head of the loch I loitered for some
time in one of those old half-deserted burial-grounds, so
common in the Highlands, called by the name of the primitive Inch or Iona saints who have left their names all over
the Highlands. The people still bury there, though the
chapel that once hallowed it is gone—the graves are many
of them centuries old, with no inscriptions or headstones—
there is generally a blue stone or two with a warrior and
broadsword roughly sculptured on it; and some of them
—the more modern—have Gaelic inscriptions and verses
legible on them. All the names one saw were Highland—
Stewarts, Macgregors, Robertsons, and MacDonalds of the
neighbouring hills. Once on the open and expansive
elevation of the moor the view on every side was most
exhilarating. Near me for miles lay the wide storm-gashed
waste, with its moss hags of every shape and size, over-
strewn with countless gray granite boulders.

   .   .   .   .

The tops of its mounds and knolls were covered with
mosses, which the storms have bleached from green to gray.
All round this vast moor was girdled by great mountain ranges. Far to the south-east was the peak of Schihallion, like a craggy speck thrust into the deep blue sky,
westward from him the hills that close Glenlyon with their
sheer precipiced summits, westward still the long line of the
Brae Lyon mountains, ending in the three-topped Ben Douran.

Of these three the most nor' westerly, which terminates the whole range, is the most peaked, and between the tops lie, in deep shadow, three great corries or hollows, loved of the deer, in which doubtless Duncan Ban many a day plied his deer-hunting, and which he has sung in that matchless poem beginning—

> Honour o'er all Bens
> To Ben Douran be,
> Of all hills the sun kens
> Beautifullest he.

Very far west, down on the farthest horizon, in intensely clear and spiritualised blue, the three peaks of Cruachan so distant now, looking up as if peering in on us from another world. West and a little north Corrie-Ba, the highest peak of the Black Mount Deer Forest, with its great dark corrie turned toward it, and the cataract down its side gleaming white in the sun; and farther north the Buachaill' Etives, 'Shepherds of Etive,' and the mountains thronging round the head of Glencoe. Nearer mountains, immediately to the north of me, shut out Ben Nevis and all his range. One great mountain only to the east, the southern precipices of the lonely Ben Alder towering over Loch Ericht, one long white cataract falling sheer down his precipiced side. On the nearer and southern edge lies the cave, the last that sheltered Prince Charlie in his wanderings, where, when hunted and banished from every other place, he found quiet with Cluny MacPherson and Lochiel for two months before he sailed from Scotland for ever. The northern side of Ben Alder runs away till it loses itself in a wilderness of glens and corries infinite."

This September excursion is doubtless the one referred to in the following letter to Dr. Clerk at Kilmalie :—

"TIGHNAULT, ABERFELDY, 17*th September.*

"Your *bis dat qui cito dat* cuts me to the quick. I fear you will say now *Haud semel dat qui tarde dat.* But your

letter found me at Inveroran, where we are for a week.
'The power of hills' was far too strong in me then to read
anything, excepting Donach Ban's songs, for it is his
country. I sat with reverence in the 'Carach,' where his
house once stood.

Bha mi 'n dé 'm Beinn Dorain.

Yes, I clomb to the top of it, through Corrie-dhu, and looked
for and found many of the places named in the great poem.
Then I learned by heart almost all the names of the peaks
and corries of the Mona Dhu, that the most glorious brotherhood I have ever made the acquaintance of. I also found
one of the old foresters there, a man of about sixty-eight,
who is a poet full of 'Dana' of his own making. They say
they are only second to Donach Ban's. We must try some
day to get him before you; and if you find them good, we
will get them written and printed. It was a glorious time.
From one of the hills I saw your Ben, and Scour Eilt,
. . . and all the rest of them. Don't be daunted by
what Norman says against 'Bens.' Use it; only using
your own discretion. Norman wished me to substitute
'Sacramental Sunday' for 'Sabbath' in *Kilmahoe.* And
now even Englishmen have told me it would have been
a great blunder. Don't desert literality; only add what
smoothness and music you can, consistently with this. Be
sparing of your *'s,* in the genitive, and never use it with an
abstract noun, as compassion's smile."

An undated letter, also written to Dr. Clerk, after a visit to
Kilmalie, and a walk south by Loch Treig to Rannoch, supple-
ments the description of that district.

" WEEM HOTEL, ABERFELDY.

" Here is a ' latha fuasach fluich,' which has kept me here
instead of leaving the hiclan's for the lowlands to-day. . . .
Whenever I get into Lochaber the power of hills comes on
me so strongly, and makes me so filled with the love of
them, and eager thirst after old Celtic lore, that after I

come away I often fear that I have been selfishly absorbed
in my own subjects. To me, coming fresh to them, every
old hill and corrie, itself and its name, has an indescribable
charm; and by knowing their names I feel that I have
fairly got acquaintance with them, so that when I return
and meet them once more, we meet as old friends. . . . Of
all my Highland splores none beats this last, unless it be
that one by Loch Hournhead, Barrisdale, and Màm-clach-
ard. . . . After leaving you, Angus M'Intosh, a shepherd,
a nice youth, quite a gentleman in manners, walked with
me up most of the east side of Loch Treig, and told me the
names of all the hills and corries visible on each side the
loch. By the side of Allt-coire-mheadhu (pronounced
vōēar) I saw the remains of the Bethana-n-àiredh of the
olden time. It is a burn coming out of a corrie on the east
side of the loch, and within one and a half or two miles
from the south end. A shepherd at the end of Loch Ossian
gave me all or most of the names of the hills visible thence.
Reached Corrour just at the darkening. Adam M'Intosh,
the head keeper there, a tall handsome man (Roman Catholic),
having heard of my being a night at his house, received me
like an old friend, offered me all refreshment, and sent his
brother with a pony three or four miles to see me across
Allt-eäch, which is hard at times to cross. He wished that
I should not give him or his brother any money, as he
meant it as a compliment. There are three brothers of them
employed as keepers in the Corrour ground—Adam at the
head of Loch Treig, John lives all year at Corrour, and
Donald at Coire Chreagaidh on Loch Ossianside. Another
brother is young, and is a gillie there. I made friends of
them, and they are fine fellows. They both, the one at
Corrour and Adam at Loch Treig, offered voluntarily to put
me up if I came that way any summer before the shooting
begins. . . . I walked over the Moor of Rannoch, east side,
under clouded moonlight; a more utter loneliness, more
weird and eerie place to be in at night, I don't believe Scotland
holds. About half-past ten I got down to the west end of
Loch Rannoch. . . ."

In the course of these solitary Highland wanderings his interest in the moors and mountain corries was not greater than his interest in the people, in the shepherds and gillies and their families. He would sometimes write minute accounts of them to his friends, and take trouble to benefit them afterwards.

Much later, in May 1880, writing to the same friend— Dr. Clerk of Kilmalie—from Rannoch Lodge, he says : " I had several fine looks over my old friend the Moor of Rannoch, with Cruach, Loch Loyden, and as far as Corrie-Ba. Mrs. Shairp and I thought at one time of going on ponies to Loch Treig, and so coming down on Glen Spean and the Braes of Lochaber. One day by way of pioneering I rode to Corrour, and was most hospitably received by Mrs. Lucy (the late Monzies's daughter), who promised to do all they could to help our journey. I had a grand view over the dusky wilderness, saw the lochs of the black water glistening over the desert down to Kinloch Leven, my old friend Beinn-a'-Chreich and Creag Cruach (so often mentioned by the old bards), at the head of Loch Treig. It is certainly the greenest, loveliest hill in the Highlands."

Shairp's appreciation of the distinctive features of the West Highland scenery, and of the great Central Moors and Bens of Scotland, comes out in these letters, and in many of his poems ; but his appreciation of the Border country was no less thorough and intense. In a former chapter we have seen how he drank in the spirit of the south, of Yarrow and Moffat, in other years. To this district he returned in the autumn of 1867, when he rented the farmhouse of Castlehill in the Manor district of Peeblesshire. In a poem written in that year, his *Song of the South Countree*,[1] he has caught the spirit of the place, and embodied it in memorable lines—its scenery, its still chastened beauty, its pathos, its weirdness, its historic charm, the witchery of dale and stream and holm and lea.

The subtle interchanges " of sunshine and of shadow " in

[1] See *Glen Desseray, and other Poems*, p. 198.

autumn, over the hillsides and the meads of that "enchanted ground," with the "sheen" of the bracken, and the heather on the heights, are described in another poem on *Manor Water*, also included in the recent volume. But the poem which deals most deftly with this region is as yet unpublished, and which from its minute topographical detail is perhaps unsuited for publication *in extenso*. Much of it is in the realistic strain of the *Polyolbion ;* but the following extracts are as characteristic of the poet as they are of the country he describes :—

THE HERSTANE OF BROADLAW.

This morn the great south-west wind is alive,
Blowing sunshine and shadow down the vale.
Come, let us take the morn, and rise, and go
To the great summits where the streams are born.

.   .   .   .   .   .

One hour of straining limb and panting breath,
Past the last heather, past the highest streams,
And we are out upon the great heights, free
Of those broad-backed long level altitudes
That league on league sweep endlessly away,
The central barrier of the Border land.
   The bent grass grows not here ; only the moss,
The short smooth moss, all weather-bleached to gray
Was soft beneath our feet, as miles on miles
We walked, companioned by no living thing
Save startled plover, and the shearing wind.

.   .   .   .   .   .

One more brief ascent, and we have won
The supreme summit of the Border land !
No soaring peak, but a broad ample round,
A table, whereon heavenly guests might dine ;
How meet for beings more than man to tread,·
Majestic amplitude, reposeful strength,
And meekness that amid his great compeers
Would rather hide than vaunt his majesty.
O Sovereign Hill ! us children of a day
Thou from thy heights one moment dost allow
To look abroad, and the great Vision take
Which thou inheritest since the hills were born.

Before the blast the moving Heavens stooped
Nearer the hills, and gave them majesty,
In solid blackness brooding far to south.

.   .   .   .   .   .

But all between, the flanks of cloud outspread
Tweed's upper Vale, even to his moorland springs,
With all his multitude of vassal glens.
Ridge rolled on ridge tumultuously away,
Dusky and desolate, with some stray fleck
Of sun on hillside, here and there a glint
Of the great river, wan beneath the gloom.

.   .   .   .   .   .

In all that mighty round, but one sole Life
One Presence, the vast movement of the heavens
With the answer of the sympathetic hills."

Professor Veitch,—than whom no one better knows the
Border country,—writes thus of his friend's first introduction
to its recesses—

"It was in this same summer (1867) that Shairp first
became acquainted with what may be called the inner and
highest reach of the Tweeddale hills. One day in July of
this summer, he and I passed up Hall Manor Glen, and
reached a point beyond the Scrape on the shoulder of Pyke-
stone. Here we were allowed, through a passing rift in the
mist and rain, to see for a few seconds the Polmood Crag,
which flanks Broadlaw to the east. Gray-gleaming and
grand, it stood silent and motionless beneath the hurrying
black driven rack of the sky overhead. He seemed unaware
that our hills enclosed so rugged and impressive a crag.
He stood for some moments with a rapt look in his face,
then said, 'We must be there, another day.' The 'other
day' came soon afterwards—and more than once in subsequent years. On the first occasion, the ascent was made
from the Manorside, by Kirkhope and Long Grain Knowe ;
on another, from Tweed to the Crook and up Glenheurie—
'The Dark Glen.' One of these walks—the earlier, I think,
in the autumn of 1867—impressed him powerfully, and led
him to express his feeling in some lines, which, though left
in their original rough state and unfinished, are worth quot-

ing to show how well he could catch, in a single day's walk, the characteristic features of a scene. They give a full and highly realistic picture of the walk, the Law itself, and the wondrous waves of hills to be seen from its summit—2764 feet above sea-level." (The lines referred to are those on *The Herstane of Broadlaw.*)

In another part of his papers of reminiscences, Professor Veitch remarks—

"Above all . . . he sought out for himself constantly the scenes of Scottish song and story, legend and tradition, got a familiar knowledge of them, through long and ever-recurring days and nights of walking amid the Southern Uplands and the Highlands of his native country. This was his holiday work and delight, and it was for him the truest and most natural education. It was those scenes, met face to face, acting on a poetical soul, and strong historical and patriotic sympathies, which, by their own features and their power to such a mind of an ever-thrilling suggestion, made Shairp what he truly was, as poet and even prose writer. It was perhaps this side of him, which, while I knew him at St. Andrews, drew me towards him with the strongest attraction. Of the strength of this influence, and the moulding of him through Border scenery and story, he was himself well aware. He felt, as others have done, that the Border land comes, to the dweller in its midst, closer to the heart— less sensuously grand, no doubt, but more pathetic in its solitude and suggestions than the scenery of the Highlands. After he had fixed his summer residence near Aberfeldy, I have known him, with all his love for that district, allow a half-articulate regret to escape him that he had not readily found a spot in which to settle in the valley of the Tweed or the Yarrow. . . . No one in this century has loved that land with a more intense love, and no one, I believe, has from an early period of life, and even down past middle age, walked its glens, moorlands, and hills more frequently, and with a finer eye for its natural beauty, and a heart more attuned to its stirring traditions, and the music of its ballads and songs. In his wanderings over the Border country, he took in the breath of song which pervades it all, as naturally and rejoicingly, as he did the breeze of the hills."

Although it may have been on a year considerably later than this, an excursion which Shairp took one September day with a party of three friends, including Dr. John Brown, may be mentioned here. They started from Abington up Camps Water and went down Glen Breck into Tweed. Dr. Brown has recorded it in his paper on " The Enterkin,"[1] " a gray demure day, gentle and serious, ' caught at the point where it stops short of sadness,' the clouds well up and curdled, lying becalmed

> O'er the broad fields of heaven's bright wildernesse.

What of sunshine there was lay on the distant hills, moving slowly, and every now and then making darker the depths of some far-off *Hope*. There is something marvellous in the silence of these upland solitudes. The burns slip away without noise ; there are no trees, few birds : and so it happened that day that the sheep were nibbling elsewhere, and the shepherds all unseen. There was only the weird sound of its own stillness as we walked up the glen. It was refreshing and reassuring, after the din of the town, this out-of-the-world, unchangeable place."

They went over to Tweedsmuir and down to Bield, by Logan Water and Mossfennan "yett," on to Broughton. Dr. Brown relates that, as they walked on, Shairp recited to the party his *Cry from Craig-Ellachie*, referred to in a former chapter.

In a letter to Shairp in July 1872, Dr. Brown wrote thus of a visit to Dumfries, and of a journey he had just taken from it back to Edinburgh past Abington : " Sweetheart Abbey[2] is really a glorious protest by the past against being forgotten. What a wonder it must have been when

---

[1] See *Horæ Subsecivæ*, vol. iii. p. 361.
[2] The Abbey, near Dumfries, sometimes called New Abbey.

it stood all by itself within its Cyclopean precincts, with its
full ministry. But ours is a more excellent way. . . . I
swept past Abington, and thought of us four taking to the
hills, and you reciting the lament of the 'majestic solitudes.' . . .—Yours ever,   J. B."

It was when Shairp was staying at Castlehill, Manor,
Peebles, in September 1867, that his article on "Moral
Theories and Christian Ethics" appeared in *The North
British Review*, the article afterwards republished in his
volume of *Studies*, under the title of "The Moral Motive
Power." On reading it, Dr. John Brown sent him the
following letter :—

"I have just finished your noble paper. . . . It is just
what was needed; it justifies your claim as a moral philosopher in the true sense. It shows you can apprehend
the very life of the theories of others, and *develop your own*,
so as to stand in the front of those who assert that mind
is higher than body, that duty is higher than either, and
that love is highest of all, is the fulfilling of them all. This
resolution of all morality into love—Godlike love—seems
to me to give a true originality to all you have now written.
I don't know any nobler piece of thought and expression
than the thirty-ninth page. I wish the paper had been much
longer, and that you had taken up Cudworth and Hutcheson,
and some others. I think all upon Kant is wonderful for
elevation and appreciation of the grandeur and solitude and
skill of the categorical inspiration. I am sure this will do
good. All true morality merges in, runs up into, religion :
all true religion blossoms and breathes out into morality,
and practical immediate goodness and love. What is the
whole duty of man, but his entire special morality, and
what is man's whole duty—love to God and love to
man, not excluding himself as being a man. But I have
written more than enough. . . . The language strikes me as
very wonderful, expressive, homely, elevated, easy, earnest,
unaffected, impersonal ; full of sudden felicities, 'empty of
context,' 'penetrate into Nature, whenever he may, Thought

has been there before him.' All upon M. Arnold is most
admirable, perfectly true, and infinitely important, and just
(indeed generous) to him. . . . Perhaps after all the most
sincere praise any one ever gives, if not the highest, is
when an author, exactly, and infinitely more beautifully and powerfully expresses your own most cherished
thoughts."

As Mr. Arnold is referred to in this letter, another undated fragment from the same pen, bearing on his work and
on other things, may follow it—

"I think Homer is untranslatable, and should now be
left in peace to his own majesty, and simplicity, and perfect-
ness. Did I tell you how delighted I was with M. Arnold's
Arthurian poem, *Tristram and Iseult?* It is as Homeric
as I suppose the nineteenth century can make itself, and
fuller of native and open-air free strength and sweetness
than anything of Tennyson's."

A letter from Lord Coleridge, enclosing one from his
father, on the article on Keble, which was published in
the same volume of *Studies*, may close this chapter—

"HEATH'S COURT, OTTERY ST. MARY,
"24th September 1866.

"MY DEAR SHAIRP—On my return here from Wavetree
I brought with me your article on Keble, which I read
and then handed on to my father, who read it also. It is
capital—quite the best thing I have seen about Keble; and
the introduction about J. H. N. is delightful. To me, at
least, there is not a syllable too much, and it says (much
better) what I have been saying all my life as to his influence and the effect of its withdrawal on the University.
. . .—Ever affectionately yours,   J. D. COLERIDGE.

My father sends you his paper and a note with this.
Keble was younger than my father in years, though senior in
University standing. I think Keble was seventy-three when
he died in March—my father was seventy-eight in July."

"Heath's Court, Ottery St. Mary,
"30th December 1866.

"My dear Professor Shairp—I have to thank you very sincerely for your kindness in sending me a copy of your essay on the author of *The Christian Year*. I need not tell you again what I think of it. I am very glad that it is put into a form in which it may not only obtain more general currency, but a sure enduring place in our literature; it deserves the latter, and may do much good in the former respect. I hope you will not give up your design in respect of the papers on Wordsworth and Coleridge—the Keble, besides its own independent importance, has an interest of a temporary kind which a publisher would be very much alive to; but those two papers, in a critical point of view, and with reference to our general literature, have an enduring importance, which makes it desirable that they should be disinterred, and appear by themselves.—Believe me, truly yours, and much obliged,

J. D. Coleridge.

P.S.—Should you be preparing the two papers I speak of for publication, if you would let me know, I might be able to suggest something—and if I could, I gladly would."

In the *Life of John Coleridge Patteson*, Missionary-Bishop of the Melanesian Islands—who was an old Oxford friend of Shairp's, and whose death at the post of duty was so tragic—we find a letter, dated 8th March 1871, in reference to the *Studies*, which had been sent out to him, in which he says—

"I am delighted with Shairp's Essays. He has the very nature to make him capable of appreciating the best and most thoughtful writers, especially those who have a thoughtful spirit of piety in them. He gives me many a very happy quiet hour. I wish such a book had come in my way while I was young. I am sure that I have neglected poetry all my life for want of some guide to the appreciation and criticism of it, and that I am the worse for it."

The last letter the good bishop wrote was to Shairp. The next day, 20th September, he was killed by the Nukapu (Polynesian) Islanders—

> "*Southern Cross* MISSION SCHOONER,
> "IN THE SANTA CRUZ GROUP, S. W. PACIFIC,
> "19*th September.*

". . . You won't remember my name, and it is not likely that you can know anything about me ; but I must write you a line and thank you for writing your two books (for I have but two) *Studies in Poetry and Philosophy*, and *Culture and Religion.*

The *Moral Dynamic* and the latter are indeed the very books I have longed to see ; books that one can put with confidence and satisfaction into the hands of men, young and old, in these stirring and dangerous times.

Then it did me good to be recalled to old scenes, and to dream of old faces.

I was almost a freshman when you came up to keep your M.A. term ; and as I knew some of the men you knew, you kindly, as I well remember, gave me the benefit of it. As John Coleridge's cousin, and the acquaintance of John Keate, Cumin, Palmer, and dear James Riddell, I came to know men whom otherwise I could not have known, and of these how many there are that I have thought of and cared for ever since !

You must have thought of Riddell, dear James Riddell, when you wrote the words in page seventy-six of your book on *Culture and Religion*, 'We have known such.' Yes, there was indeed about him a beauty of character that is very, very rare. Sellar is in the North somewhere. I think I have seen Essays by him on Lucretius. . . .

Indeed, you are doing a good work, and I pray God it may be abundantly blessed.—I remain, my dear friend, very sincerely yours,

J. C. PATTESON." [1]

---

[1] *Life of John Coleridge Patteson*, vol. ii. pp. 336, 377, 378.

CHAPTER XIII

ON the death of Principal Forbes, John Campbell Shairp was elected by the Crown to the Principalship of the United College at St. Andrews. He was urgently requested, however, by · a majority of the Professors of the United College, not to · resign the Chair of Latin, but to continue to hold both offices for a time.[1] He had been an excellent Professor, and there were some doubts as to the consequence of his resignation of the Chair, which was not by statute obligatory. It is unnecessary to refer to any incident connected with this matter, or to the steps taken by others in regard to it, which should be now entirely forgotten, and which the Principal was the first to forget. It ought, however, to be said that Principal Shairp acted— throughout a somewhat painful and lengthened case—with an exclusive eye to the good and the honour of the College over which he presided.

Many things came under my own notice after I became one of his colleagues in the University (and others have been told me by senior colleagues, and by our excellent and ever faithful janitor, Mr. Hodge), of Principal Shairp's special interest in the students that came to St. Andrews. It is one of the advantages which a small University has over a large one, that the students come into much closer personal relations to the teaching staff; and, when he ceased to teach, Shairp did not cease to care for, or to interest himself in the students. He had a special regard for Highlanders, and

[1] See Professor Campbell's remarks on this at pp. 381, 382.

sympathy with them; but it was his aim to get to know and to help all whom he could benefit in any way. Of course it was impossible to know all of the 150 to 200 students who spent the winter in St. Andrews equally well, or even to see them all at his house or elsewhere. Over and over again, however, Principal Shairp asked me to give him a list, not of the cleverest or most promising students, but of those who would be most encouraged by being asked to his house, and who would be most helped by means of it. It was those who were least likely to be asked elsewhere, whom he desired especially to befriend.

In after years it fell to Principal Shairp to write the larger part of the Life of his predecessor, Principal Forbes; and as the preparation of that Memoir led him to speak at some length of St. Andrews itself, and of incidents and events in which he had himself to take a prominent part, a portion of one of its later chapters, descriptive of the University and its work,—and of the College Hall, which Principal Forbes was the chief instrument in founding,— may be given here. The personal part of this Memoir of Forbes will be referred to at a later stage :—

"The University over whose oldest and largest College Principal Forbes was now called to preside, is one of the few fragments which survived the wreck of the Scottish mediæval Church. Whatever the shortcomings and corruptions of that Church for two centuries before the Reformation may have been, it ought not to be forgotten that it is to her that we are indebted for our Universities. Three out of the four Universities of Scotland had Catholic Bishops for their founders. This was pre-eminently true of St. Andrews, the most ancient of them all. A Bishop it was—Henry Wardlaw—who, near the opening of the fifteenth century, founded that University, and the accomplished First James smiled upon its infancy. Each of the three Colleges which were successively incorporated into it owed their origin to a separate prelate. The oldest of the three Colleges, that of St. Salvator, was founded and endowed by the successor of Wardlaw, Bishop James Kennedy, kinsman of the king, and the wisest man of his time both in Church and State ; a prelate of such pure and beneficent character that even George Buchanan, prelate-hater though he was, has no word but praise to speak of him. To him, in the old sea-tower at St. Andrews, his cousin, the Second James, turned for counsel when the violence of the three banded earls, each almost a king, had all but driven him from his throne.

The next College in order of time was that of St. Leonard, founded by the youthful Archbishop of St. Andrews, Alexander Stewart, and by John Hepburn, prior of the monastery. One of the charters of the foundation was signed by the young archbishop, and confirmed by his father James IV.—the year before they two, father and son, fell together on the field of Flodden. The foundation of St. Salvator's College by Bishop Kennedy was one of the many efforts made by that prelate to counterwork the corruptions of his Church, and to reform those abuses which he saw were eating out its life. . . .

This last College was scarcely founded when it became the nursing mother of many of those ardent spirits who bore a chief part in working that Church's overthrow. To have drunk of St. Leonard's Well was another expression for having adopted the principles of the Reformation. When the Reformation had got itself established, George Buchanan became Principal of St. Leonard's, which he adorned by his scholarship more than by his character. He received one pension from Queen Mary, and a second from Queen Elizabeth for slandering his first benefactress; so that, as has been said, though he did not serve two queens, he at least took wages from two.

With the Reformation these two Colleges, which had been founded mainly for the rearing of clergy and the teaching of theology, were so far secularised that they were devoted exclusively to instructing students in classical literature, science, and philosophy. Instruction in theology was handed over by the Reformers exclusively to the younger College of St. Mary's, which, having been founded and endowed chiefly for this purpose by the last three Roman Catholic Archbishops, James Beatoun, David Beatoun, and John Hamilton, was soon after the Reformation presided over by those two stout anti-prelatists, Andrew Melville and Samuel Rutherford.

The two older Colleges, restricted to the more peaceful pursuits of classics, mathematics, and philosophy, were less heard of in the turbulent conflicts of the seventeenth century than their younger theological sister.

About the middle of the eighteenth century the finances of St. Salvator and the tenements of St. Leonard's having fallen equally into disrepair, the more flourishing finances of the one were transferred to the better buildings of the other, and the two Colleges were by Act of Parliament conjoined, under the prosaic name of the United College. From that time, 1747, there have continued to be two instead of three Colleges in the University; and at this time St. Andrews remains the only place in Scotland where native Scots have an opportunity of learning the distinction between a College and a University. . . .

These historic details are not out of place in the account of the life of Forbes. For him the ancient records, monuments, and traditions of his newly-adopted University possessed a peculiar charm, and called out a faculty and taste which had hitherto lain dormant within him, only because it had nothing to feed on. Among the predecessors of Principal Forbes for more than a century, no distinguished name is to be found till we reach that of the venerable Dr. Hunter, famous in his day as a scholar and philologist, who, after filling with great success the Humanity Chair for nearly sixty years, was, towards the close of his long life, raised to the Principalship of his College. Him followed, after a brief interval, Sir David Brewster, who, during his twenty years' tenure of the office, if any remains of the family system still lingered, scattered them, somewhat turbulently, to the winds. The reputation of Sir David's name was, of course, an honour to St. Andrews as it would have been to any University ; but he laboured under a delusion, of which he could not dispossess himself, that it was the peculiar calling of St. Andrews to train practical men of science, especially engineers, for the whole nation. So illusory was this idea, that it may be doubted whether so much as one student ever came to St. Andrews in quest of training for this profession. Principal Forbes, devoted though he was to his own subjects, did not share this delusion. He saw clearly enough that in St. Andrews these could have no special prominence ; that it must continue, as in the past, to give a general education to young men meant for any one of the professions, and that if it had a specially professional calling at all, it was to prepare ministers for the several churches, and teachers for the borough and parish schools. But to Sir David's unflinching opposition to all jobbery in choosing Professors, and his determination to elect the best men that could be found, Principal Forbes owed it that he found his College equipped with a staff of Professors not then surpassed by the staff of any other Scottish University. Prominent among these was the late Professor Ferrier, who, by his subtle philosophic genius, expressing itself in a perfect style, not only adorned his own chair, but maintained for another generation his country's ancient fame for metaphysical genius. . . .

Just before leaving Edinburgh to reside at St. Andrews, Principal Forbes had wound up a letter to a friend with this remark : ' All things become solemn when the past perspective of life is the predominating object. . . .'

The time at which he entered on his new sphere was a momentous one for St. Andrews as well as for all the other Universities. The Scottish University Commissioners were in full session, busily framing ordinances which should control the course of study, the University finances, the library privileges, and the Professors' salaries for a long time to come.

To supply the Commissioners with the information they required, and to offer his own suggestions for their guidance, was one of Forbes's earliest tasks.

The finances of his own College he found in a confused and

dilapidated state; and to understand these, and devise measures for their restoration, he first addressed himself. At whose door lay the largest share of blame for this confusion need not now be inquired. Suffice it that it mainly arose from a long habit of dividing among the Professors the annual rents of the College lands, without laying by a reserve fund adequate to meet the necessary outlays for repairing farm-steadings or other such contingencies. To unravel the tangled mesh Forbes applied himself with characteristic diligence, method, and business faculty; and it was mainly owing to his exertions that the Commissioners were enabled to place the finances of the United College on a footing which, if somewhat burdensome to the present generation of Professors, promises to provide for their successors ampler incomes than those now living are likely to enjoy.

The next subject he had to tackle with was the University finances, or the contents of the University chest. These he found in a much more flourishing condition than those of his own College. But this prosperity was mainly owing to a source of revenue which the Universities' Commissioners were understood to regard with no friendly eye. This source was the granting of medical degrees—a function which St. Andrews, though it possessed no thoroughly equipped medical school, had yet, in virtue of its original charter, been accustomed to exercise time out of mind. It is said that there had been a time, extending down to the early years of this century, when these degrees had been granted, without sufficient examination, to persons but poorly qualified.

This practice, indefensible if it ever existed, had, however, long ceased, and under the able management of the late Dr. Reid and the late Dr. Day—successive occupants of the Chair of Medicine in the United College—a system of examination had been instituted in which the candidates were thoroughly tested, and the granting of degrees to none but duly qualified persons was adequately secured. With the St. Andrews Medical Professor as Chairman, a Board of able examiners, sanctioned by the University, had been got together, consisting of the best of the extra-academical medical lecturers in Edinburgh and Glasgow. . . .

In later years the candidates were numbered by hundreds, of whom, while a sufficient percentage were rejected, not a few out of the majority who passed now stand high in the medical world of London and elsewhere. . . .

The result in the end was, that the Commissioners sanctioned a compromise, limiting greatly the exercise of the right in future, but allowing it to continue under certain very definite restrictions, which, while they meet an acknowledged need in the medical profession, are still a source of some revenue to the University.

A third project which early engaged the attention of Principal Forbes was the founding of a College Hall. In St. Andrews, as in other Scottish Universities, it had long been customary for students to live where they chose in lodgings in the town. All that the

T

University requires of students is regular attendance at the Professors' lectures, good conduct within the College walls, and without them to keep the peace. In old times St. Andrews had been resorted to as a place of education by the sons of many persons in the higher ranks. Indeed the shields attached to the silver arrows in the old College attest how largely it was frequented by the sons of the oldest and most honourable families in Scotland. This had, however, almost entirely ceased more than thirty years before Principal Forbes's advent to St. Andrews. The Professors who had once been in the habit of taking boarders had ceased to do so, and the general set of the educational tide southward had borne from St. Andrews to England almost all who could afford to go thither. It seemed to Principal Forbes and others, that the idea of a University, as originally held in Scotland, was not fulfilled unless it contained students of all ranks ; and it occurred to them, whether by providing a fitting place of residence under proper superintendence, some of those who had left it, to the loss of the University and of themselves, might not be lured back. St. Andrews, with its noble historic memories, its academic aspect, its healthy climate, and its fine Links, which have been for ages the elysium of golfers, seemed to offer peculiar outward advantages for the trial of such an experiment. But for the energy and business talent of Principal Forbes, this idea of a College Hall might have continued till now only a dream. As soon as it was mentioned to him, he adopted it with all his energy, and less than his usual caution, and straightway set himself to realise it. The result of his exertions was the formation of a company, whose members subscribed for a sufficient number of shares to set the institution on foot. Within two years from Forbes's appointment the College Hall was opened, with twelve students in the first, and an increasing number in the following session. These lived in a hired house, one of those which occupied the old site of St. Leonard's College. Over them was a warden, an Oxford graduate, who superintended the discipline and management, presided at the common meals, and assisted the students in preparing their College work. During the first four or five years the College Hall prospered so well, and attracted so many desirable students, that Principal Forbes conceived the more ambitious project of building a large Hall, which should be specially fitted for its purpose, and should accommodate a greater number of students. As the institution itself possessed no funds except those necessary to carry it on from year to year, and as no University revenues could be used for this purpose, the venture was a bold one. There were some who thought that it was too bold— that the institution had not yet struck its roots deep enough to warrant so large an experiment. But Principal Forbes was not to be turned from his purpose. By his almost unaided advocacy the old shareholders were induced to take more shares, and new shareholders were added, and by the joint contributions of these a sum was raised which proved nearly sufficient to erect a large and commodious Hall within what was the ancient Garden of St. Leonard's. The completion of this structure will be noted in due time. Whether the venture was altogether prudent or not, is a question which time has not finally answered.

A fourth project which deeply interested Principal Forbes was the restoration of the College Chapel of St. Salvator's. This chapel is not only the oldest unruined fragment of ancient St. Andrews, but, along with the noble tower of St. Salvator's, which rises above it, forms the earliest piece of University building still extant in Scotland. Tower and chapel had both been built by the good Bishop Kennedy, and are the only remnants of his workmanship. The original roof of the chapel is said to have been of a peculiar and rare construction —massive blue stone, deeply engroined. Within the chapel is the tomb of the founder, a Gothic structure wrought in Paris, of blue stone, in the middle of the fifteenth century, which originally must have been of wonderful beauty, since even in its cruel defacement it still shows so fair. As the old stone roof is said to have been nearly flat, the Professors, about a hundred years since, either themselves conceived, or were persuaded by some architect, that it would one day fall in and crush them. They therefore resolved to have it removed, and a common lath and plaster ceiling placed in its stead. So solidly, however, was the old roof compacted, that the workmen in order to remove it had to detach it from walls and buttresses, and let it fall *en masse*. The fall is said to have shaken the whole city. But however this may be, it is only too certain that it shattered the richly-wrought columns, canopies, and pinnacles of the founder's tomb. A maimed and mutilated fragment that tomb now stands, beautiful still in its decay, proving that Professors of the eighteenth century could be more ruthless and insensible to beauty than were the ruder Reformers of the sixteenth or seventeenth. But besides the mutilated tomb of which no restoration was possible, parsimony and Philistinism had combined to make the rest of the church hideous. High bare fir pews, an unsightly gallery at one end, lath, plaster, and whitewash, floods of harsh light from many windows,—ugliness could no farther go. To the removal of these deformities and the restoration of the church, not to its ancient beauty—that was not possible —but to somewhat greater seemliness, Forbes gave his undivided attention for one whole winter. . . .

As the result of all these exertions the College Church, if it has not re-attained its pristine beauty, has certainly lost its former repulsiveness, and been rendered one of the most soothing and attractive places of worship in which Presbyterians at this day meet."[1]

As the years of his Principalship advanced, while engaged in various literary labours, Shairp not only watched over the

[1] *The Life of James D. Forbes*, pp. 394-404.

fortunes of the College which he adorned, but took part in many wider educational movements. He became President of the Educational Institute of Scotland, and in that capacity delivered a brilliant lecture in Edinburgh. He addressed University Clubs, and Literary and Scientific Societies in provincial towns. He delivered a course of lectures, in connection with a University-extension movement in Dundee. He made speeches, of no trivial or passing interest, at meetings in Edinburgh, in connection with the Border Counties Association for the encouragement of students, and at gatherings of old Edinburgh Academy pupils and friends. To some of these detailed reference will immediately be made. There are two short papers, however, with which I have been favoured, that may here find a more appropriate place, in the first instance. The one is the reminiscences of a Highland student, now a parish minister in Scotland ; the other, a very characteristic sketch by Mr. Cotterill, of Fettes College, Edinburgh.

The Highland student is the Rev. Mr. Sinton of Glengarry, Inverness-shire. He helped Professor Palgrave with some notes to his recent edition of Shairp's Poems ; and the following remarks are the concluding part of an address which he delivered to the Gaelic Society of the University of St. Andrews :—

" In addressing you, it would be strange indeed were I to omit all reference to one lately passed from our midst, who, by his writings and personal influence in society, did much to awaken renewed interest in the race, language, and literature of the Gael, at a time when it seemed as though they were about to sink into oblivion. . . .

In the Highlands, Principal Shairp felt completely at home. He had visited many glens and corries where few tourists find their way. The solitudes of Loch Arkaig, and the wild grandeur of the remote Loch Treig, with the great Moor of Rannoch—treeless and houseless—stretching beyond, supplied to his mind solemn and never-to-be-forgotten thoughts. He frequently surprised students from the north by showing that he possessed a much more accurate and extensive knowledge than themselves of the scenery and lore of districts in which they had been reared. One incident of his life, although but a trifle, was so entirely·characteristic of the man, that I cannot forbear relating it. Near twenty years ago when wandering among the Grampian and Monadh Liath mountains, he entered an old-fashioned parish school—mindful that it was then presided over by a St. Andrews student. I shall never forget that tall and stately stranger who slowly made his way among the crowded forms. We all felt that he belonged to the great mysterious world, of which as yet we had no experience. On the same day he met one who, though a considerable tacksman, was still a shepherd in all his tastes, and whose forbears, like many of his class in the Highlands, had herded on the Teviot. The poet's eye had no doubt been arrested by the gray plaid, the hazel crook and the collie, without which accompaniments that excellent yeoman rarely went abroad. In the course of conversation he alluded to these, and spoke in glowing terms of the striking situation of a solitary farmhouse which he had passed that morning far up in the country, and which he soon discovered was the home of his companion. The latter, proud of the interest taken in a place very dear to himself, gave the Principal his crook, and the two went their several ways never more to meet. But long afterwards, when Principal Shairp discovered among the first year students of St. Andrews a son of that farmer, he at once became the lad's friend, and never ceased to manifest the kindliest interest in his welfare. He took the first opportunity of showing his protege the simple gift of a parent then dead ; and related the manner in which it had come into his possession many years before. That student will always retain as a cherished memory his intercourse with this good man, the kindness he received at Edgecliffe and in that beautiful home in Strathtay, and the holy counsels to which he listened there. Nor will he ever forget how, within an hour of leaving St. Andrews, he was guest for the last time in the house of his benefactor, when, with an assurance of continued friendship, and a warm shake of the hand, he bade him farewell. When his young friend was far away in a beautiful Highland parish—classic ground in Gaelic song and lore —he wrote to him repeatedly, and proposed a visit, which year after year was still fondly looked forward to, until the end came.

The saintly Archbishop Leighton wished to die in an inn, and so it was at length granted unto him to depart. The scene where Principal Shairp breathed his last was strangely appropriate. In death surely he had his desire. In a district whose quiet pastoral spirit so harmonised with the tenor of his soul, where in early life he had wandered and communed with nature, within sight of the hills he loved, and near the wild Atlantic that rose and fell around many an isle his ancestors frequented of yore, after life's work was done, and with the simple faith of a child, he ' fell on sleep,'

et dulcis moriens reminiscitur Argos."

The following extract from a letter from the late Dr. Irvine of Pitlochry will be read with interest in connection with Mr. Sinton's paper—

" He took the most lively interest in poor students, about several of whom he from time wrote to me. I can recall occasions when he accompanied me to visit some of them, and I was much touched with the warm sympathy and kindly words of encouragement he expressed. These visits were an evident satisfaction to the poor invalids, and are among the pleasantest incidents of my long professional life."

Mr. Cotterill writes—

" My acquaintance with Principal Shairp began in 1872, when he sent his son to my house at Fettes College. The acquaintance thus begun soon passed into an abiding friendship. I became very intimate with him.

The impressions of his character left upon my mind by this intimacy are very clear, as I now review them. First and foremost, penetrating and permeating his whole nature, stands the instinct of poetry. No estimate of his character can, I believe, be other than misleading which is not based upon this as its primary conception. His attitude towards all questions was, primarily, that of the poet. His character was portrayed with singular faithfulness in his countenance and his whole bearing, in the very movements of his body, in the tones of his voice, and the pronunciation of his words, and even in his dress. This is, of course, true of all men, to some extent, but it was so, I think, of him to a very unusual degree. All his features were eloquent. In his long, large forehead there was evident the habit of brooding thoughtfulness which he brought to bear upon all subjects. In his mouth was to be seen a set determination—which at times was apt to pass into something very like obstinacy—the same characteristic being shown in the square and resolute jaw. His mouth also, when he smiled, revealed a peculiarly winning attractive sweet softness, such as which of us that has seen it can forget, but who describe? But not in one or in all of these lay that which made him what he was. This lay in his eyes. The real man, the inner man, was there. The dreamy, far-away, wistful gaze of them ; their unworldly innocence and gentle goodness ; here at last was the real man. You could be with him but for a little while, if you were in sympathy with him, before he told you through the mute and unerring eloquence of those wonderful eyes that though he might on occasions here and there be this or that, he was always and everywhere destined to see all things as they are seen only by the poet. Such a poet too as might, perhaps, be best described in the words used of the poet whom he most loved—

Friend of the wise, and teacher of the good.

Such I believe Principal Shairp to have been ; and as such we must always regard him, if we would regard him rightly. I will try to illustrate some of his characteristics by a few examples.

It must at once be said that, socially, he was extraordin-

arily sensitive to his surroundings.   If he was not sure of
sympathy, he could not utter himself, otherwise than con-
ventionally.   But, given sympathy, I have heard no such
conversation from any man.   He had not a ready tongue,
and this made his conversation all the more extraordinary.
The thoughts slowly worked themselves out, coming from
his very soul, every word adding weight.   It was rarely
monologue ; it was true conversation.   Sometimes, indeed,
he quite forgot his surroundings, and, with real inspiration
upon him, would deliver himself of some great thought that
had been pent up within him, with a kind of solemn awe that
all who have been intimate with him must recall.

One such occasion I specially remember.   We were walking on the Links at St. Andrews, and our conversation was upon
deep things.   He became more and more possessed by his
subject, it worked within his soul, and the burden of it was
upon him, until at length with that swift and sudden pause
in his step, so characteristic of him at such moments, he
came to an abrupt climax, with one of those instantaneous
utterances of deep solemnity.   His spirit was unburdened,
and his voice was still.   And it was all natural, unconscious,
inevitable.   It came from the fire that was always smoul-
dering within him.

He was fond of saying that his Scotch descent and his
early training had given him a bent towards metaphysics.
And this was quite true.   It was a part of his very
nature to dwell constantly and habitually upon the Ideal.
But united with this tendency there was within him an
equally deep-seated tendency to look at all things from the
practical and concrete side.   All his friends must remember
how often, during a conversation upon the deepest questions,
he would say, ' Give me an instance.'   And to the test of
' an instance ' he would bring everything.   Nor would he
hesitate to bring forward instances from his own life, even in
cases where many men would have shrunk from putting the
matter to a personal test.   I well remember his bringing
forward such an instance, to prove the extreme difficulty of
practically shaping one's life according to the ideal standard.

It may be thought that my particular relation towards him gave me special facilities for hearing his views upon educational questions, and we certainly frequently discussed them. I believe I am right in stating that his general views both as to subjects and methods of study were essentially conservative.

Two points stand out with special prominence in my recollection, upon which he felt very strongly. First, in the education of boys he was for ever insisting upon the necessity for *thoroughness*, and used to detail to me the minuteness of his own method whenever he taught his son. Secondly, regarding English University education, he set his face strenuously against the bringing of everything to the test of the *class*, and used to say, with much fondness of reminiscence, that in his days at Oxford *character* was what a man was judged by, and that they were not then in the habit of enquiring *what class* he would take.

He was in all matters, great and small, penetrated with the sense of duty, and with the determination to let nothing interfere with the performance of it. Once let him be thoroughly convinced that his duty lay here or there, and no amount of opposition from others, or inconvenience to himself, could prevent him from holding to his resolve with the utmost tenacity. All his friends could give examples of this. I will permit myself to record only one, as possessing some particularly pleasant features.

When Carlyle came to Edinburgh in 1866, to deliver his Rectorial Address, Principal Shairp was asked to meet him at a small dinner hastily got up at the house of a friend. But he had a previous engagement to what he said was, he knew, likely to be a very prosaic dinner, and he was eager to meet Carlyle. He knew, however, that there would be disappointment among his friends whom he had promised to dine with, if he asked to be excused; and so, with much disappointment, he held cheerfully to his engagement. 'And,' he said, 'I heard that Carlyle was in a specially delightful mood .that evening, overflowing with pleasant and mellow conversation.'

For many of us the name of Principal Shairp stands in constant association with that of Wordsworth; and that this is so, is due, I think, not only to the fact that he did perhaps more than any one to introduce Wordsworth to many readers and to interpret him to them, but, along with this, to the fact that there was an undoubted similarity of nature and character between them, which amounted to a kind of innate and primal sympathy. In interpreting Wordsworth, he was often interpreting himself. And perhaps this may have given him that sensitiveness, which he certainly possessed, to Wordsworth's defects. But all that was greatest and truest in Wordsworth he embraced as a kind of natural good, and it was a very part of him—it was himself. This could be abundantly illustrated by a reference to much that is most characteristic of Wordsworth's utterances on the deep things of life. I will take a somewhat different example.

Wordsworth's views, so consistently enforced in practice, on the subject of literary style, are well known. To Principal Shairp a style that seemed artificial or redundant was positively painful. I remember well his talking to me about a small biography of Wordsworth that had lately appeared, striking, indeed, and meritorious from many points of view. But it seemed to Principal Shairp somewhat copious in style. And this he could not get over. It seemed to him a sort of indignity to Wordsworth that his life should be written in any style that was not very simple and almost severe. And he expressed himself about this with something like a really personal feeling. He was personally almost pained about it.

This similarity between Wordsworth and his interpreter extended, as I have often thought, to another feature of a very different kind. There was about Principal Shairp an inherent love of plainness, extending even to his dress. He did not move easily in the ordinary everyday get-up of a professional man. He always preferred a tweed suit to a black coat. I met him one morning at one of the great public breakfasts, given by the Moderator of the Church

Assembly in Edinburgh, who that year was his colleague at St. Andrews, Principal Tulloch. After breakfast we walked out together. The first thing he did was to go straight to his tailor's and divest himself of his society black coat, and put on his ordinary tweed suit. Then he was comfortable. All this was thoroughly characteristic of him. The clothes were part of the man. He was studiously careful to conform to all reasonable social usages, whether of dress or other things ; but for himself, in all things, of all kinds, and under all conditions, *he preferred homespun to broadcloth.*

I do not think I ever saw him more overflowingly happy than on the occasion when Dean Stanley delivered his inaugural address, as Rector of the St. Andrews University. And perhaps both men were seen at their best, as we walked round inspecting the old ruins and buildings of that most deeply interesting place, so rich in those ancient historical associations in which each of them loved to move.

I saw Principal Shairp for the last time, as he passed through Edinburgh on his way to Oxford to deliver one of his lectures as Professor of Poetry. He was to lecture upon Virgil, and it was upon Virgil mainly that we talked. It is fitting perhaps that it should have been so. For with so much superficial and real difference between the two, there was a yet greater and deeper likeness. Upon none has lain more constantly a sense of 'the burthen of the mystery' of what is here, and what is beyond. And each, according to his capacity, has looked into the depths, and has helped us to look. Of Virgil's strain of sad and ironical pessimism, I think Principal Shairp had little. But with that subtle wistfulness, that penetrates Virgil, to lift the veil—*ripæ ulterioris amore*—with this those who know the writings of Principal Shairp, and knew the man, know that he too, as Virgil, was penetrated to his very soul. Rarely, I believe, absent from him was the thought, expressed over and over again in one form or another in his own writings and words—the thought expressed in these words of his—'there remains more behind.'"

In the year in which he was appointed Principal, Shairp
gave a course of lectures to the students of St. Andrews
on the subject of " Culture and Religion." These were
afterwards published in 1870. The remarks of Cardinal
Newman and of Dr. John Brown upon them are much
more important than any critical estimate; but, before
quoting them, one point may be noted. Though the Greek
ideal is happily described and dealt with in these lectures,
they are mainly devoted to the notions of culture that
govern the modern scientific mind on the one hand, and
are the outcome of the modern literary spirit on the other.
An accurate understanding of the laws of Nature, and an
implicit deference to them, may be said to be the scientific
theory of culture. The possession of a highly-educated
and perfectly-balanced nature, — a nature developed all
round to the utmost possible extent,—is the literary ideal.
Principal Shairp is much more satisfactory when he is
criticising the scientific than the literary view of culture.
The end of education, according to the former (of which he
takes Mr. Huxley as the representative), is to learn the
rules of the mighty game of life, and to conform to them
with unerring accuracy, remembering that we play the
game with an unseen antagonist, who never makes a mistake, and who never overlooks one. It is a fine simile;
but it will be seen at a glance that, in such a universe, the
only passive virtue will be that of submission, and the only
active ones possible will be those of worldly wisdom and a
selfish struggle for existence. And what of those who *do*
occasionally make mistakes in the playing of this mighty
game? Must they inevitably go to the wall? and sink
inevitably out of view? So far as these laws of Nature
are concerned, that is their fate. They cannot receive any
aid from a source higher than themselves. Principal Shairp
points out, with force and clearness, that the scientific study
of the universe cannot reveal to us a supernatural Deity;
and therefore that, by this pathway at least, we can never
reach the realm of the spiritual. But he condemns the
literary theory of culture (of which he takes Mr. Matthew

Arnold as the representative), no less than the scientific one. He holds that if Religion is made a part of universal Culture it is immediately degraded, if not surrendered, and that if it be not allowed to be *supreme over all culture* it will vanish away; in other words, that the literary view of culture makes that primary which should be secondary, and relegates to a subordinate position that which ought to be supreme.

His contention here is, however, open to some counter criticism. Religion may be looked at either as the distinctive life of *one part* of our complex human nature, or as the action of the whole of that nature turned *in one special direction;* either as one out of many tendencies equally valid and necessary to the life of the whole, or as a supreme and supernatural influence, emanating from the Fountainhead of existence, and intended to pervade human nature, in all its parts, root and stem and branch together. It is a question of definition; and there is a way in which the view taken by Mr. Arnold may be reconciled with that of his friend and critic. Every one must feel, however, that this is an eminently genuine and helpful book, whether they agree with its conclusions or not; that it is clear and direct, as are all the writings of its author, and that it stimulates the higher nature from first to last.

Of these lectures on "Culture and Religion," Dr. John Brown wrote :—

[Postmark, 12*th December* 1870.]

" The first I read when driving and screaming through the once Drumshoreland Moor, past the dear old steading and chivalrous woods and house of Houstoun, standing stark and strong in the pallid moonlight, as I journeyed to my dying uncle at Crofthead. I have now finished them, and though it is like the voice of him who saw the Land of the Blessed, across the great gulf fixed, I cannot help thanking you for these words,—for their heavenly majesty, as of a strong, simple, humble, faithful soul, one who has more of the mountain air, and stride, and clear vision, than of cultured fields, and fat pastures, and oil-distilling productiveness and payingness. . . ."

Cardinal Newman [1] wrote of the Lectures as follows :—

"THE ORATORY, BIRMINGHAM,
"18th *December* 1870.

"MY DEAR MR. PRINCIPAL—I have been much gratified in receiving your volume from you. It is not the first kindness which you have done me, nor the first thanks I have to pay you. Your volume is on a most interesting subject, and I shall have pleasure in reading it. It is almost *the* subject of the day. In cutting open the leaves I am pleased to see that you urge the view of conscience, which has ever seemed to me so important. Were I a wider reader, I daresay I should not have found so much cause to be anxious about it, or so much reason to insist upon it. I have done so again and again in print, because, to my perplexity, I have not fallen in with those who have sympathised with me in it. I mean, I have not found those who considered it as much an act of reason to believe in God as revealed in Conscience as to believe in Him as revealed in physical nature. For myself (without denying the argument from final causes), my reason would not lead me to Him from the phenomena of the external world.

It pleased me also to find that you agreed with me on another point, at p. 87 ; and to read your quotation from Mr. Davies. A striking passage to the same effect was shown me lately in the Preface of Cardinal Wiseman to the works of St. John of the Cross.

I am quite persuaded that in this way alone religious men will ultimately arrive at unity of thought and worship. Not that it will be attained in our day, but the first step is

---

[1] In giving me permission to publish this and other letters, Cardinal Newman has kindly added one or two sentences to the original.

to lay the foundation, or rather to prepare the soil. It
would be a great thing if certain theses could be drawn
up, such as the two to which I have referred, which all
would be willing to subscribe, not to speak here of the all-
important question of dogma. It is the way with men of
science to grant us a great deal, sense of beauty, moral
sentiment, greatness and height of principle, a great history,
abounding in romance and heroism, and so on, but not mere
logical *reason*. Spirituality is thought something distinct
in kind from rationality. To show that there is a true
philosophy of religion is the first step in the development
and reception on a large scale of Christian and Catholic
truth.—Most sincerely yours,

JOHN H. NEWMAN.

P.S.—On reading over your letter again I find I have
not thanked you half enough for the great encouragement
and consolation it gives me."

With none of the younger clergy of the Church of Scotland was Principal Shairp more intimate than with Mr.
Robertson, the parish minister of Whittinghame. He had
been a student at St. Andrews when Shairp came as Professor, and had acted as tutor to some young men who
boarded at Gillespie Terrace while preparing for Oxford,
and afterwards became a familiar friend. Mr. Robertson
has sent me a long and valuable paper, containing fragments of letters, and relating conversations on religious
subjects. It exhibits a side of Principal Shairp's character
which perhaps none of his friends knew so well. Mr.
Robertson writes :—

" I had the privilege of an intimacy of acquaintance
with him which grew with years. It became a habit that
I should pay a yearly visit to St. Andrews during the
session. . . . The feature of these visits, for which above all
others I cherish their memory, was my conversations with Mr.
Shairp at his house, and especially in long daily walks with

him across the Links, through the grounds of Strathtyrum, and through the old Castle and Cathedral precincts. These conversations were always religious. His talk might take a wide range, and I often delighted to draw from him reminiscences of his College friends at Glasgow and in Oxford, so many of whom have since become famous ; but all his conversations were penetrated deeply with religious feeling, and continually returned to thought and inquiry about Christian truth and hope. I know not how better to indicate what those days were to me than as the yearly realisation of what has been called a spiritual ' retreat,' with, however, a breadth and varied light in them like the ample, airy, and historic spaces in which they were spent.

I should not feel that I was giving any fit impression of Principal Shairp if I merely set down, so far as I know them, the articles of his creed. A man so catholic that he gave unstinted reverence to men so differing in creed as Newman, Arnold, M'Leod Campbell, and Thomas Erskine,—whose culture of spirit as well as of mind was the result of the finest Scottish along with the finest English nurture and opportunities—such a man is not known by having a few of his opinions set down. What I felt so rare and elevating in him was the tone and emotion of his spirit. It is this which I would wish in these lines chiefly to recover. And when I begin by asking myself what most constantly and deeply characterised his spirit, I find I must name these two things together,— high Christian aspiration and profound sense of sin. He had that deep sense of sin which belongs to all characters of high devoutness. It showed itself in the tender reverence that penetrated all his conversation on religious subjects. It showed itself in his tones of voice and aspect even, and now and then it was uttered in words of deeply humble self-estimate. It gave to his piety a certain subduedness, even with its enthusiasm, that reminded one less of the joyousness that is distinctively Protestant than of the graver devotion which has been called Catholic. And when he himself. writes of ' that refinement of feeling and that deep and sober piety which seems to have descended to us from the Catholic ages,' he is describing one of his own affinities. His life had been from the beginning an unusually pure one, and there had been no crisis in it. He was accordingly not burdened by any special recollections from past years. But he was so ideal in thought and aim, and so sensitive to saintly memories, that his own spiritual shortcoming was much in his thoughts. He longed with great desire to be a profitable servant and do good in his generation, and no good seemed to him comparable in value to spiritual good.

He would have marred relentlessly the art of anything he ever wrote, prose or poetry, if otherwise there would have been the least hazard of its Christian influence. The question whether he had so handled his subject as to subserve the highest ends was never long out of his mind. He had a keen sensitiveness of conscience about what he undertook to write.

Another main characteristic of Principal Shairp was his belief in light and help from the unseen world.[1] This was not merely a belief which he accepted and defended. What was unusual was the degree to which it possessed him, and controlled all his thoughts and conversations about religion. Often I have noticed in going out for a walk, hardly had he gone a few steps when he seemed, even in bodily attitude, to place himself reverently under the unseen powers. To an idealist such as he, familiar with the feeling that visible things are but shadows, and spirit the only reality, the unseen was solemnly near, and his conversation went on as if partly in commerce with it. . . . He believed that the universe cannot be construed by mere intellect, that this can carry us but little way in divine things, that these are to be apprehended by the whole man, more by the conscience and affections than by the intellect. . . . He seemed always to distrust argument, and to wait for truth to be felt in the spiritual instincts quickened from the great source of truth, and to be yielding up his own natural reason, conscious of its weakness, with the prayer, 'O send out Thy light and Thy truth : let them lead me !'

[1] Compare his address on Religion, delivered at Aberfeldy, pp. 308, 309.

U

In regard to help from the eternal world, he looked for it through many channels. His hope was not in putting forth the strength in us, but in receiving impulse from above. I remember speaking once of *truth* as the invariable instrument of the Spirit of God. He interponed emphatically to say there might be, there were, *unconscious* influences of the Spirit. All Nature and the ordinances of life he thought of as an organ through which God reaches our souls,—as indeed in a manner sacramental. . . . His thoughts may be judged from his writing as follows:—

' You said something in your last letter about inability to apprehend the sacramental view. My thoughts on it are not formulated, but I rather think that something of this kind is part of the teaching of St. John's Gospel, and that by refusing to take it in we miss much that is deepest in that Gospel. Is it not a cardinal image of that Gospel that He took upon Him our flesh, that we in and through His flesh (flesh spiritualised by the Divine Spirit that dwelt within it), might pass to His Spirit, and to God the Father who is Spirit? It often occurs to me that Presbyterianism by denuding the truth of all its material side,—by making the whole of it into doctrine and into spirit,—has never fully realised the whole meaning of that truth " The Word was made flesh." I am not satisfied with any Presbyterian or purely Protestant view of these things which I have ever met with.'

I have spoken of the deep expectant belief he had in help from the unseen world. Yet in one of the most impressive letters I ever had from him, a passage occurs in which he seems to seek for this and not find it. . . .

' " Toiling in rowing for the wind is contrary," is the experience of so many, it is so much my own. With my understanding I see clearly that there is no happiness but to believe with the whole heart and mind that God's will and way are good—are the best for us—and to acquiesce. This is very easy to see, to acknowledge, but how to attain to it I find not. To love the will of God (however it crosses one's own will) better than anything else in the whole world, this is the only true peace; one sees this. But really to do it is a very different matter. Often one feels inclined to say, I have rowed long enough against the stream; I will row no more—the current may bear me where it will. A little ease, a little rest before the grave, this one often craves. It is not so much the struggle against the winds without—though this is often sore—as against the strong tides within. . . .'

Another thought constantly present to Principal Shairp was the mysteriousness of our life, the fragmentary character of our knowledge, and the consequent impossibility of complete intellectual system in our beliefs. . . . A passage in Canon Mozley's sermon on the Atonement — as well as much more by that theologian — Principal Shairp found quite to his mind, and he quoted it with the emphasis he was accustomed to give to favourite passages.

'Have we not in our moral nature a great deal to do with fragments?   What is mercy itself but a fragment which we do not intellectually understand, and which we cannot harmonise and bring into consistency with justice? . . . Justice is a fragment, mercy is a fragment, mediation is a fragment,—all three; what indeed are they but great vistas and openings into an invisible world in which is the point of view that brings them all together?'

I recollect his pointing out two verses of Keble's hymn for Monday before Easter (the fourth and fifth), and telling me of a saying of Mr. Erskine that they were 'worth more than all the Calvinistic theology.' . . .

I do not suppose that Principal Shairp took this saying of Mr. Erskine after the letter, but the preference of one thought that stimulated reverent devotion over doctrinal system was quite to his mind.   He regretted that theology in Scotland had been reduced so much to mere logical propositions.

Ecce Homo he read with great interest and appreciation.   I may mention this expressly, because in his published writings what has chiefly appeared has been, I think, criticism or objection.   But I well recollect calling

on him when it first came out, and finding him much stirred
by it.   He began at once to give me an idea of its scope
and character.   Oddly enough, while he was in the act of
doing this, a letter was handed him, which after glancing at
he read aloud.   It was a letter from the publishers asking
if he had written the book.   The MS. had come to the
Messrs. Macmillan through a third person ; they themselves
were as puzzled as others to know who could be the author,
and they had come at length to guess that Mr. Shairp
might be the man.   'No,' he said to me.   'I have not
written it ; it is not in me to write it.'

He had a ready interest in all practical Christian work,
at home and abroad, but shrank from ecclesiasticism, and
belonged himself to the Church Universal.   In spite of his
sacramental leanings, he had no place in his mind for the
doctrine of apostolical succession, and once gave the following emphatic utterance publicly on the subject :—

'Scottish Presbytery has a witness to bear in Christendom and a work to do at home, and the witness it has to bear
is against all sacerdotalism and priestly notions.   If there
is one thing for which more than another I, in common
with many others, value Presbytery, it is for the protest
which its very nature contains against sacerdotalism.   With
my whole heart I believe with Dr. Arnold that the separat-
ing of the clergy from the people as a separate caste, endowed with some mysterious and mystical functions, was
the first and most fatal apostasy—a thing which more than
anything else has paralysed the power of Christianity in
the world.   Presbyterianism rightly understood is a protest
against this sacerdotal notion—not merely a negative protest,
for negatives have no power ; but it is and ought to be a
positive protest, by asserting that the only priesthood on
earth is the priesthood of every true believer, a priesthood
in which the humblest layman shares equally with the
highest clergyman.   The truth it has to witness to is that
every true believer who is united by faith to the one
heavenly High Priest is the only priest on earth, that
ministers are not priests of the congregation, but merely

office-bearers and instructors in it, and that they derive
their functions from God in no other sense than the humblest
layman derives his functions. . . .'

In Scotland, however, he seemed to miss the nobility of
form and embodiment which Christianity had attained to in
England. Presbyterian worship whenever it had not the beauty
of fresh spontaneousness (to which he always responded in
the humblest meeting), and the mundane tone of Presbyteries,
exaggerated as it is by the selections given in newspaper
reports,—these repelled him, as indeed all denomination-
alism did. 'I look forward,' he wrote, 'to a time not far
off when all the present organisations will be broken up.
The whole apparatus of Presbyteries, Synods, and Assemblies
rather repels me. Excuse my saying it.' The helpful
sense he felt in the Church of England service of a larger
catholicity and of the communion of saints is expressed in
the following extract from a letter :—

'To-day being Good Friday, I ask myself whether we
have not cut ourselves off from an enormous fountain of
spiritual life, by having turned our back on this day as a
historical commemoration. How much of the spiritual
virtue that lies in the crucifixion may we not have lost by
giving up the historical remembrance of it ? Then, too, we
cut ourselves off from the sympathy of all the rest of
Christendom by neglecting it, and this sympathy I hold and
feel to be a very real support. The services of the English
Church, from last Sunday to next, I have always felt to be
of inestimable value, quite the most precious inheritance
the Church of England has retained. Yet I don't like any
mere imitations of the Church of England, especially as
fashion enters so largely into this. And fashion is not
religion. . . . I do long to find in myself, and see in others
in our land, a quickening and a broadening of spiritual
energy. Mere revivals are not enough. We need a deeper,
firmer, more habitual grasp of unseen realities,—a theology
that shall pervade our whole being, intellect, heart, will, and
spirit.'

In writing of Principal Shairp one cannot omit the tinge

of sadness that belonged to his prevailing sense of the mystery of life. He never *gave in* to melancholy; but there was a strain of it in him which had much to do with the sympathetic depth of feeling which was so great a charm of his character. He had naturally keen capacity for enjoyment. His early life abounded with this, and his Oxford time and years of Border excursion must have had in them an extraordinary spirit and fulness of enthusiasm. But this temperament has also deep sensitiveness to the sadness of life. He wrote once: ' As time goes on one does feel ever more deeply how sad a place earth is— how deeply inwrought into the very texture of life sorrow is. This is the case apart from all religion,—the actual experience of life to all who have hearts to feel it whether they are religious or not. And it seems a great verification of the reality and divinity of the Christian faith that it recognises this fact, takes account of it, and without seeking to lessen it, meets it with truths which fit into it, and elevate the sorrow into peace and the promise of ultimate joy through sorrow.' . . .

One naturally keeps to a grave and pensive strain in writing of Principal Shairp. Yet it would be an error if this led to a conception of him as too sad for humour. He was no mere dreamer. His eyes were perfectly open to common life. He saw the ridiculous side of character, and could exchange talk with men he met on sport or any miscellaneous topic; but this was all in the outer court of his mind, and his humour did not bubble and swell continually, but gleamed or 'glinted' across the pensive landscape of his thought.

The conservatism of his political leanings, his tenderness to the Stuarts, and his honour for the Great Montrose, are known to his readers. In politics, however, he seemed to me to speak less guardedly, and often somewhat beyond the actual balance of his conviction. He did so, I felt, in impatience with the conceit of democracy, its ignorant depreciation of greatness in the past of which it does not know, its susceptibility to flatteries, and its frequent hostility to the finer and more cultured side of life. . . . Principal Shairp's interest in humble lives of true worth and dignity, his fellowship with them and sense of what was to be learned from them, were such as belonged to one who was at once a Scotsman and a scholar of Wordsworth. But if his handling of politics seemed sometimes an impatient reaction from extremes of the hour, to his conversation on religion, on the other hand, his whole being was summoned, and he placed himself in an attitude of reverent self-doubting and ready subjection to any one who seemed to be at all taught of God. I have heard him read in his own family circle, where he was most entirely himself, the sermons of a student of his own, who died early in life (Mr. Forrester of Port Elizabeth), and the respect with which he sat at the feet of his former scholar, and his earnest recognition of a true authority in that scholar's words, seemed tô me beautiful then, and are still more pleasing now in retrospect.

Few men I have known had a more habitual sense of the rapid passing of life. Years ago his links of friendship to so many eminent contemporaries had entailed on him the duty of contributing, in the case of one after another, reminiscences to their published Lives. He felt himself, he said to me once, becoming a *literary undertaker*—he had assisted at so many burials. This helped to call up again and again the thought expressed in lines of his favourite Wordsworth—

> And I, whose lids from infant slumber
> Were earlier raised, remain to hear
> A timid voice that asks in whispers,
> Who next shall drop and disappear ?

. . . Still it came to me with a great sense of unexpected loss, —my life deprived of a great stay and of a trusted landmark,—when I read in a newspaper of the death of Principal Shairp. My reverence for him, and my sense of indebtedness for influences of the very highest kind which one can receive in life, increase with distance. . . . One feeling especially is deepened by this effort of remembrance ; one word expresses the most characteristic influence of con-

tact with him—*aspiration.* Whatever else he did, even in
short converse with those who knew him, he plucked them
aside from the vulgar commonplaces of life. The 'high
humility' of his spirit stirred in them the feeling—

> Our only greatness is that we aspire."

Shortly after he became Principal, Shairp took up his
summer residence in Strathtay, near Aberfeldy, and during
the remainder of his life that district became very intimately associated with him, and he with it.

What he did for his College, his University, and his
Country, is to be measured not only by the record of attend-
ances at meetings of the *Senatus Academicus,* and its
numerous committees, or at meetings of his own College,
by his work in connection with the business part of a
Principal's duties, his annual addresses to the students,
his occasional lectures, and his literary work. It is to be
estimated also by elements not so easily seen, or weighed
in the balances of educational utility, by the influence he
wielded in Society, as representing his College and University—whether in the homes of the poor, or amongst the
schools and schoolmasters of his native land, or in private
meetings of literary men, or in the professional gatherings of
Scotsmen from other University seats, or in his frequent intercourse (where he was always a welcome guest) with the
larger academic circles of the south. Whether at St.
Andrews, Dundee, or Aberfeldy, in Edinburgh, Oxford, or
London, at his ancestral home, or at Linlathen, or Megginch, or Methven, he wielded an influence, which helped
his University, and spoke for it, wherever he went. This
was due not so much to his scholarship, his intellectual
resources, or the charm of his conversation, but to that
undefinable *atmosphere* which he carried with him—which
moved on as he moved amongst men—whether of high
or low degree. In judging of the work which the Principal
of a Scottish University does, or is expected to do, people
sometimes forget to take this latter element into account.

No direct teaching duties are associated with the office, but the indirect duties,—the work of superintendence and organisation, which habitually call for tact, prescience, and consideration for others,—these are quite as important qualifications in the head of a University as the gifts of scholarship and oratory.

In these respects Principal Shairp's indirect influence was quite as great, and as fruitful of good, as his direct administrative work. The help he rendered to many a poor student, his social influence in St. Andrews, and in Scotland generally, his loyal attachment to the Institution of which he was the head, and his firm faith in its future— when others were doubtful or faint-hearted—the prestige which his literary work carried with it wherever he went, above all the kindling touch of his personality, these things must be taken together, in any just estimate of him, as Principal of the United College.

His sympathies were not shut up, however, within the academic groove. There was no movement for the educational benefit of his native land—whether it concerned her Primary, or Secondary Schools, or her Universities—in which his interest was not keen, and his advice suggestive. He became President of the Educational Institute of Scotland, and in that capacity delivered a most stimulating address, from which an extract will be given later on. He took a special interest in the movement for the establishment of a great secondary school in Scotland, on the plan of the English public schools—Fettes College—not as initiating a rival movement to the old High Schools, or Burgh and Grammar Schools of Scotland, but as providing a much-needed supplement to them. He often spoke of the educational work that was done in that school all round, the training of mind and character together, as being of rarely admirable quality; and, during the time of his residence in the Riviera in the last winter of his life, when a memorial was prepared for Parliament bearing on the work of Fettes College, no one wrote more kindly or enthusiastically in reference to it.

All the Parliamentary Bills for the improvement of the Scottish Universities had his most careful attention and helpful criticism; and the expression of his views had an appreciable weight in the discussions that took place. Those who went with him in deputations to the Home Office, or to the Treasury, know how much importance was attached to his opinion on academic questions.

Another point of importance in connection with his official life in St. Andrews has reference to his membership in the University Court, to which he was elected as delegate from the *Senatus Academicus* in 1876. I have often heard Principal Tulloch,—who, as Vice-Chancellor, was, in the absence of the Rector, Chairman of the Court, —say, that though he might differ from Principal Shairp in his views of public policy at times, he was invariably the most conscientious in the discharge of his duties as a member of the Court; and I remember when such matters as the election of a Professor, or of a University Examiner had to be considered — so far as he conferred with his colleagues in the Senatus—how minutely careful he was in his collection of evidence, and invariably candid in his judicial estimates.

Shairp's correspondence with his early college friend, William Clerk of Kilmalie, was continuous, and very varied. We find him at one time sending a kindly remembrance, in the form of a post-office order, to some old Highland shepherd, whom he had known in Glen Desseray, or with whom he had wandered by the head of Loch Hourn; at another time, introducing a Roman Catholic priest to be befriended in the hospitable Highland manse, and guided on his travels; now asking for Gaelic songs, and old traditions of the district; again inquiring as to the precise meaning of local Celtic terms. He revised his friend's Preface to his Translation of Ossian, while that friend revised *his* notes to the Lectures on Gaelic Poetry he had delivered at Oxford. It may surprise some to find that Principal Shairp was able to express a critical as well as a literary judgment, upon these translations of Ossian, to so competent a Gaelic scholar as Dr. Clerk; but what his Celtic scholarship may have lacked in linguistic range, it gained in intuitive accuracy. There is a great deal in his letters to Kilmalie Manse, about the Ossian controversy and M'Pherson. He says in one of them that he felt "the Gaelic fever" coming on him whenever he saw the heather in bloom, or climbed to such a height as Farragon, and saw the great circle of the hills to north and west. He asks his friend all about the clearances in the glens, and the emigrations; where the people went to? and whether it was a voluntary exile? There is also much in these letters to justify what Mr. Erskine and John Brown called him, " a vernacular man."

The modest way in which he looked on his Gaelic studies, is seen in the following undated letter to Clerk.

After asking for some Gaelic songs, with words and music, and mentioning his efforts at translating Gaelic, he says, " How I wish I had begun Gaelic when we were at Glasgow. I might have made something of it. But life is too short now to do more than play at it. However, I'll stick to it as a recreation, after the necessary works are done, and do you so too. Use some of your leisure in writing into large common-place books all the oldest most characteristic legends, antiquities, songs, poems, you can get your hands on. Use plentifully the quarry that lies in old Kate Keith's memory, and then you may be sure that either in your own hands, or those of your children, these things will come into good service. All Gaelic lore is now on the rise, and will rise, perhaps just because the old life is receding so fast."

The two following letters are also imperfectly dated, but they belong to this period:—

" UNITED COLLEGE, 20th *January.*

" MY DEAR CLERK—. . . The more I study your Preface, the more I perceive how honest and moderate it is. It disproves Johnson's two strong assertions: (1) that there was no Ossianic poetry in MSS.; (2) that oral tradition could not preserve such poetry, and that none could repeat any amount of what M'Pherson had pretended to translate. Another point also I am arrived at—that M'Pherson took his MSS. and what he had written down for oral recitation, and out of these two sources, pieced and patched together the Gaelic as it now stands. This he did that winter in Badenoch, after his return from his collecting tour, and did it with the help of Strathmachie, Gallie (and Morrison perhaps). Whether they added any of their own to piece the fragments together, and if so, how much, this there seems to be no materials to show. . . .—Yours most sincerely,   J. C. SHAIRP."

"UNITED COLLEGE, ST. ANDREWS,
"11th February.

"MY DEAR CLERK—. . . The conclusion I have come to as the most probable one is, that whatever distrust belongs to M'Pherson belongs to Strathmachie and Co. equally, that if he had a secret they shared it with him, and that therefore if blame attaches to M'Pherson they share this too.

And the opinion I regard as most probably the true one is that M'Pherson, along with Strathmachie, Gallie, Morrison, etc., made up the Gaelic text, as we now have it, that winter in Badenoch—that the materials out of which they patched it were the old MSS., the fragments taken down from recitation which they had brought back with them from their tour. Whether in piecing these together M'Pherson put in any connecting lines of his own, and if any, how many, this, I believe, can only be ascertained, if ascertainable, by a very careful and critical examination of the Gaelic text by the most accomplished Gaelic critics. I am inclined myself not to think that M'Pherson added much of his own—if he added any.

The discussion of the evidence in bringing out this view will occupy almost all my paper. . . .—Ever yours,
                                   J. C. SHAIRP."

In June 1871 he contributed an article on Ossian to

Macmillan's Magazine, which was a review of Dr. Clerk's two volumes on the poems.

To the same friend he writes (20th January 1871): "You ask whether I am still teaching the Latin classes. I am, and what between this and my College duties, it is only half-hours every second day I can find for 'Ossian.' You must not expect anything good from this broken kind of work. If I ever do anything worth while, it is when I have had time to brood and muse till the fire kindles. During session time this is impossible."

Again, in February of same year: "A Professor's work and a Principal's correspondence and business are, I assure you, a heavy load."

A year later (2d January 1872) he says: "I am now rid of my Professorship; and though it curtails me of some incomings, it also cuts off great and vexing annoyances.

This year I am to try to lecture on the early Scottish history—Celtic Scotland, in fact, before Malcolm Canmore's time. These old Pictish times are intensely interesting, though very hard to make clear. Yet Skene, Robertson, and Stuart's *Book of Deer* have thrown a good deal of fragmentary light on them."

During the winter of 1872 he was gladdened by a visit in St. Andrews from Norman Macleod, who came to address the students of the University on the subject of Missions in the month of February. It was one of Macleod's last addresses, and Shairp wrote of "his worn and flaccid look; he seemed so oppressed and nervous when he was going to address only a few hundred people in our small University chapel." Macleod wrote to his friend in March 1872—

"MY DEAREST JOHN—More dear than ever as friend after friend departs, and as we feel ourselves every year like the remains of an old Guard whose comrades have almost all left us—all who could speak, not of the old wars, but of the old times of joy and hope, of struggle and of victory."

Again he wrote : " I feel as if the winding-up were coming soon."

When his friend died, Principal Shairp was asked to write his Life, but very wisely declined the task. His contribution to the work, however, his ' study ' of his friend's character, is, like all his studies, admirably real and vivid.

Some time after Macleod's death he sent the following unpublished lines to his widow, which may be compared with his elegy on Clough :—

1.

For one more day,
Thy name survives upon the lips of men,
The sport once more of every tongue and pen—
Then let them say their say.

2.

And every one is free
To make their best or worst of thy dear name ;
Many will doubtless praise, and some will blame,
But what is that to thee ?

3.

Within the old kirkyard,
Beneath the sod where thou art lowly laid,
Wrapt in the kind folds of thy Highland plaid,
It wins not thy regard.

4.

A small thing 'tis in sooth
How men may judge thee, now thou hast to do
Only with judgment that is wholly true—
With Him who is the Truth.

5.

Thou gavest to thy kind
The full outpouring of a noble heart,
And of their love did'st long some little part,
Some small return to find.

6.

Some gave it, some withheld :—
There is no more withholding there where thou

At the full-flowing river drinkest now
Of God's love freely welled.

7.

There now that thou hast met
Just men made perfect, and with them dost share
The larger vision, breathe the 'ampler air,'
Dost thou at all forget ?

8.

—Surely thou dost not—those
On earth so dear, but with love more intense
And wiser lov'st them, albeit dark and dense
The veil doth interpose.

In a letter written by Shairp in March 1876, to Dr. Donald
Macleod, the biographer of his brother Norman, the following occurs : " The last years saddened me a good deal, not
only from the impression that he was greatly overburdened
and depressed, but the impression that he felt all things to
be breaking up is so omnipresent as to be painful. You
hardly feel that he was seeing the relation in which the
Rock beneath his feet stood to the general break-up going
on around him."

It is a misfortune that all Shairp's letters to Dr. John
Brown have perished; but the following are fragments of
Brown's letters to him, belonging to this year :—

" *9th July* 1872.— . . . Last night at 10.30 the heavens
were lucid and luminous, and a great wing as of an arch-
angel—its feathers and great ' pens ' white and glistening—
lay across the whole north-west, a mighty angel's wing.—
Yours,   J. B."

" *14th July* 1873.—It feels a long time since our minds
met. I have been in Skye since, and have seen things it is
impossible for a man to utter."

Of Sara Coleridge's *Memoirs and Letters* Brown wrote :
" I have just finished a most delightful book. It is wonderful
for understanding, for critical and imaginative faculty, and

womanly tenderness, and now and then true fun. Her notes
on Wordsworth, and Tennyson, and Keats, and Talfourd are
quite worthy of her father.   She was a great theologian.
Her thoughts are the spontaneity of true poetry, a true
warbling of native woodnotes wild, setting (artist-like) the
imagination agoing like a mill."

When Macleod and Erskine had both passed away,
Principal Shairp found increasing solace in the friendship
of John M'Leod Campbell of Roseneath.   In sending
him a copy of his *Lectures on Culture and Religion* he
said : " There is no one to whom the book is more
due than yourself, for the suggestions I have derived
from your works.   I tried to acknowledge them in the
book, but sometimes it comes over me that I ought to have
acknowledged my obligations to you more fully still. . . .
I often wish that occasions took me more into the West,
that I might have an opportunity of seeing and conversing
with you.   I feel this all the more now since dear Mr.
Erskine has been withdrawn.   You know how much I prize
your work on the Atonement, as the only one I have ever
met with, which enabled me really to think and see some
moral light through that mysterious fact and truth.   Especially I feel the value of what you call the ' Retrospective
aspect.' . . . Yet satisfactory as is your teaching on the
retrospective aspect, *so far as it goes*, I still feel that neither
it, nor any thought as yet uttered by man, has gone down
to the roots of the matter. . . . Till we fully understand
the whole mystery of evil, can we expect fully to understand its antidote ? "

On receiving a copy of the *Reminiscences and Reflections*
of M'Leod Campbell, in 1873, Shairp wrote thus to his
friend's son, the Rev. Donald Campbell: " I shall read it
slowly, page by page, pausing over it ; for it is not—and
nothing your father ever wrote is—to be read otherwise
than with much meditation.   It is impossible to say all
that the few pages I have read awaken within me : thoughts
of the hours of intercourse with him—precious hours, but

brief, and at wide intervals. Then thoughts of his dear
friend, and mine too—Mr. Erskine. Lastly, thoughts of
another very different from both, yet worthy of them both—
dear Norman Macleod. What great gifts they were to their
generation, and to think that, having known them, we
are such poor beings as we are. If Norman's soul owed
allegiance to any other human soul, it was to your father.
. . . The last night I ever spent with him, in a railway
carriage travelling to London, in March last, Norman was
full of all your father had been to him."

Of his own contribution to the *Memorials* of his friend,
Shairp wrote to Mr. Donald Campbell : " It has now been
so often laid on me to record my memories of the departed
that I feel every new call to do so a heavier burden. It
would more please me to think of them in silence. But I
would like to put down the notes I have of one interview."

The following is an extract from his contribution to the
book :— ·.

" . . . From early days in our family the name of Mr. Campbell of
the Row was familiar. At that time, the fourth decade of this century,
'The Row Heresy,' as it was then called, was everywhere spoken
against. But through some members of the Stirling of Kippendavie
family who used to visit in our immediate neighbourhood, and who
were devoted to your father and his teaching, sermons and addresses
by him and his friends found their way into our household. They
were read by some and produced their own impression ; and that was,
that however they might be discountenanced by the authorised teachers
of the day, they contained something more spiritual, and more appeal-
ing to the spirit, than was at all common at that time. One small
book that was especially valued was *Fragments of Exposition,* which
contained notes taken of discourses delivered by your father after he left
the Church of Scotland. I well remember about the years 1845 and
1846 at Oxford, after having heard and read a good many of Mr.
Newman's sermons, and being much impressed by them, turning to
this small book of your father's discourses. Though they came from
a different quarter of the doctrinal heavens, and had no magic in their
language, as Newman's have, yet they seemed as full of spirituality,
and that perhaps more simple and direct. They seemed equally removed from the old orthodoxy of Scotland, and from the spiritual
teaching of the best Oxford men, confined as that was within a sacerdotal fence. Perhaps I do not rightly express it, but I remember very
well how soothingly many of his thoughts fell on me during those years.

Again, when I used to visit Norman Macleod at Dalkeith during the years from 1843 till 1850 he always talked much of your father, and of the refreshment of spirit he found in converse with him. For during those years Norman was very isolated and lonely in his church relations.

.   .   .   .

After I came to St. Andrews, and began to visit the late Mr. Erskine at Linlathen and in Edinburgh, he too spoke even more of Mr. Campbell than Norman Macleod had done. Often he would revert to the time of their first acquaintance, and tell me about their experiences then.

.   .   .   .

But of two days' visit he paid me at St. Andrews in July 1868 I have a very distinct remembrance, though I took no notes of what he then said. As we walked about during these two days he talked of many things besides theology—indeed he did not enlarge on this subject unless when questioned, and this I did not then do. I remember his speaking of St. Columba with great interest, and quoting a Gaelic verse said to be by him. I put it down at the time and have it somewhere. What especially struck me of his conversation at that time was the extent to which during recent years he seemed to have opened his mind to subjects of general literature and philosophy. In all his remarks on these there was a weight and originality one seldom meets with, as of one who knew nothing of the common and wearisome hearsays that pass current among the so-called educated, but as if everything he uttered had passed through the strainers of his own thought, and came thence pure and direct. Whatever he said bore the mint-mark of his own veracity, and commended itself as true—true that is, not only as regarded him, but true in itself. All his judgments of things and of men, while they betokened that subtle and reflective analysis which belonged to him, had a scrupulous justness and exactness. Penetrating inwardness there was, and watchful conscientiousness of thought, but at the same time eminent sanity of judgment. Above all, you felt that all his thoughts and feelings breathed in an atmosphere of perfect charity."[1]

Shairp's Highland home in Strathtay was built in 1872, and entered in the month of July. It was built on a feu from Killiechassie, the property of his brother-in-law and his wife, Mr. and Mrs. Edward Douglas. In April of that year he wrote to Dr. Clerk, from Tighnault, Aberfeldy—

". . . I have just run up here for a day to see about our new cottage. It occurs to me to settle now about its

[1] *Memorials of John M'Leod Campbell, D.D.*, vol. ii. pp. 338-344.

name. It is a 'nook,' and it has a lovely view. Therefore Cuil-aluinn has been thought of. Cuil is appropriate both to the spot, and also the farm in which it lies is called Cuil. If it is to be Cuil-aluinn, I wish you to write me out the exact Gaelic spelling which must be retained. Cuil-asgadh has been suggested. It is well sheltered. Again Beul-na-bruaich is the original name of the field on which it is built."

Cuil-aluinn was the name finally chosen, "the bonny nook," and from it the view westwards to the crags of Weem, above Castle Menzies, is one of the finest in the Strath. Here it was that for thirteen summers a resting-place was found by Shairp, in a beautiful spot, within hearing of the murmur of the Tay, and within sight of Ben Lawers—a Highland home where much fruitful work was done, and honoured rest enjoyed.

In a letter to Mr. John Boyle, asking him to visit Aberfeldy, he speaks of the changes which time had wrought in the neighbourhood, and of the losses of near relations which some households had experienced. " Still the old hills remain. Schihallion and Ben Lawers are as fresh as ever, though we and ours change and decay. If you come this way we must try to get some breath of their eternal freshness."

He interested himself in all the life of the district, and took his share in various bits of work for the benefit of the people in the Strath. His sympathies were most catholic, and he wrote thus to his friend Clerk of the Free Church minister at Aberfeldy—

"Yesterday I was at the Free Kirk. A man of your name is minister there. He is a remarkable man, very fervent and strong, and clear-seeing, very realistic, hitting the nail of fact on the head in every sentence. He may be in a state of tension, but there was no visible excitement in his sermon, but calm, strong earnestness. . . ."

The following is part of an address which Principal Shairp delivered both to a young men's society at Aberfeldy and to the students of St. Andrews who came out to a religious service on the Sunday evenings. It is greatly contracted, but even a few extracts will illustrate one side of his character, and will recall the addresses he used to give on Sunday evenings in Rugby School.

" The religious life has two sides, which we may contemplate separately, but which in practice can never be divided. One side is individual, personal, I may almost say secret, involving the personal relation of each with God. The other is active, social, outgoing, and involves all our relations with our fellow-men, our influence on others, and the influence we receive from them.

On each of them I would say a word, and on the importance of trying to preserve something like an even balance between them ; for, on preserving it, our spiritual health and wellbeing depend.

1. As to a man's inward or individual life. . . . Pardon and renewal are the two most essential needs of man. But in order that these two things may be to us not words, but realities, we need to know ourselves. It is not by merely reading religious books that we come to know our need of these things. We may admit as a matter of course that we need to be made better. But it may be to us no more than a truism, admitted readily, but without influence on our life. If we are to know it for ourselves, and not at second hand, we must go below the surface. . . . Can any one of us honestly say that the first and deepest desire of his heart is that ' God's kingdom may come, that his will may be done in earth as it is in heaven,' that he would prefer this to any personal or selfish object ? In looking back can we truly say that there is any one thing we have ever done without an admixture of a self-interested motive ? If we try thus honestly to examine our characters, and to scrutinise our motives, we shall learn how true is our need of pardon and renewal. . . . Just in proportion as we strive thus honestly to know ourselves, we shall learn that there is in each of us a double nature, ' a twofold moral personality,' what St. Paul calls ' a law in the members warring against the law of the mind.' . . . Further, let us try to learn that other truth, that there

is a strength not our own, out from us, above us, on which
we can cast ourselves, which can deliver us.

These two things pervade all Scripture as a deep undertone which runs through all its varied music; and they
are not two separate distinct things, but parts of one great
process. These are two continually recurring needs, forgive-
ness and the influence of a power not our own to purify
the inner springs of character, so that we may act, not with
the spirit of a slave, but with that of a child. Just as we sur-
render ourselves, with a single mind to be guided, is our growth
in character, and we are brought into a purer atmosphere,
a diviner life. Doublemindedness is our great hindrance,
from which we need deliverance. It is a hard struggle; a
fight it is, and must be. The struggle is to overcome the
selfish life; and yet we attain to peace not by struggle, but
by receiving the gift, by entering into the divine life. Thus
all heavenly powers are on our side.

In all this there is nothing new. They are the most
obvious points in the personal, individual life. But by going
over them anew, we may stir up our hearts by way of remembrance.

2. But as soon as this inward life begins, the outward
manifestation of it should follow. It has often been brought
as a reproach against the religious life of Scotland that it is
too isolated, too individual; that each man's religion is shut up
within himself, double padlocked—a padlock on the lips and
one on the heart besides. If this is so, it may arise partly
from the natural reserve of most Scotchmen about everything
that most deeply concerns them. But Christianity is above
all things an expansive and diffusive power. If we try to
bottle up our religion, and keep it to ourselves, it will surely
die. For the law of spiritual wealth and the law of material
wealth are directly opposite. The more openhanded a man
is with the wealth of this world, the less he has to himself;
but with spiritual life, the more it communicates itself to
others, the more it is strengthened and enlarged."

In 1873 the household at Cuil-aluinn was saddened by

a fatal accident to a near relative, Henry Douglas, at the
Moness Falls. Shairp wrote thus of it to Clerk at Kilmalie: "We have had in our family circle here an awful
visitation. Our nephew and niece, Henry and Mary Douglas,
were by a falling rock swept down a great waterfall in this
neighbourhood. He perished. She escaped as by a miracle.
It has taken all the light out of our autumn, and has indeed
saddened all this Strath. The father, Henry Douglas, is in
Bombay. You know he is Bishop there."

In this same year—1873—in conjunction with Professor
Tait of the University of Edinburgh, and Mr. Adams Reilly,
the geographer of Mont Blanc, Shairp wrote the Life and
edited the Letters of his ` predecessor in office, Principal
Forbes of St. Andrews. By far the larger and more important section fell to Principal Shairp. It was fitting that
it should be so; and his part of the work—his account of
Forbes's early life, of his professoriate, and especially of his
work in St. Andrews in directing the affairs of the United
College—is admirably done. It is bright, genial, and appreciative. He was quick to recognise the value of work done
in spheres where he had no special knowledge of detail.

A philosophic man of letters is usually more successful
in writing the life of a scientific specialist, than a student
of pure science is in dealing with the career of a poet or a
philosopher. This is simply because it is part of the vocation of the former to appraise excellence in every sphere of
genuine human activity. In 1866 it fell to Principal Forbes
to write some sentences about Principal Shairp, then a
candidate for a chair in a sister University of Scotland. It
is interesting to compare the respective estimates by the two
men of each other's work and genius. In his Biography
of Forbes, Shairp describes his aim from the outset as an attempt to indicate "what manner of man James Forbes was."
He says that "almost all men fall into one of two kinds.
In the one, the intellectual or professional interest is so paramount that it pervades the man's being to the very core.
Withdraw this, and little else is left. The domestic feel-

ings occupy but a small niche apart, and do not really colour and rule the life. In the other kind of man, affection is central and paramount; the mental and scientific habits, whatever they be, seem external powers or capacities, clothed as it were upon the deeper affections, which are the tower itself. To this latter kind Forbes belonged."

In the fifth chapter of the book he writes thus: "The life of recent Scottish professors was then, as now, divided into six months of unbroken work in College, and six months of vacation. To strangers unacquainted with the ways of Scotland and the habits of its students, so long a vacation appears a strange anomaly. But there are reasons enough, grounded on our social facts and habits, which have justified it for generations, and which satisfied the late University Commissioners when they carefully inquired into all the bearings of this question. It must not be supposed that these six months are either to student or professor times of idleness. The former is often employed in some useful work for self-support, as well as in carrying on his College studies. The latter, when he has recruited himself after the toils of the session, finds full employment in preparing new lectures or recasting old ones for the approaching session. Besides this, whatever Scottish professors have done for Science, Philosophy, or Literature, has been the fruit of their summer leisure. No man ever employed his summers more methodically and energetically than Professor Forbes. Indeed, it is probable that the world has received fully as much advantage from what he achieved during his summers as from his regular winter labours" (p. 107).

If this was true of Forbes, it was equally true of Shairp. Again he says: "Nothing can be more uniform than a professor's winter course—so uniform, that to lookers-on from without it may appear monotonous. But from this it is saved, at least in the case of a vigorous and advancing teacher, by the deeper insight and wider range, which he is year by year obtaining in his own field of inquiry" (p. 112).

In his further estimate of the professorial life of Forbes, he says: "Forbes never shrank from collisions, however

painful, if he met them in the way of what he conceived to
be duty. But he was by nature no polemic. He did not love
the battle for its own sake ; indeed, it cost him more than
most men to enter into personal conflicts. Though he never
flinched from opposing men when he thought he ought to do
so, he felt very keenly the hard words and severe blows
which such encounters call forth. . . . It was in the intercourse of the classroom, and of private life with like-minded
students, that he found the field most congenial to him "
(p. 135).

Shairp's Memoir of Forbes gives the picture of a brave,
devout, adventurous man, neither afraid of obloquy on the
ground of narrowness, nor of the effect of any discovery in
the realm of fact. It is admirably written.

A literary question which interested him much during
the same year (1873), was the authorship of the Scottish
poem on " The Cuckoo "—whether it was written by Michael
Bruce, or by Logan, on which subject he wrote a paper.
The following letters to Shairp from Sir William Stirling
Maxwell of Keir, and Mr. John Bright, refer to that controversy :—

" KEIR, DUNBLANE, N.B., 31st *August* 1873.

" MY DEAR SHAIRP— . . . I thank you for kindly undertaking the Latin of my English, which I enclose. It is to
commemorate an incident in my family history which I
think worth recording *in situ*. I shall now read your paper
on the Bruce-Logan Cuckoo with much interest, if you will
tell me when or where it appears. The question of the
authorship can be solved only by a much more close
attention to small scraps of evidence than I have given. I
have not Grosart's book commented on by D. Laing, and
know the Bruce side of the story mainly from Mackelvie's
edition of Bruce (Edin. 1837). The chief pieces of evidence
in favour of Bruce seem to be the statement of Birrel,—
Bruce's letter (which D. Davidson, *fils*, says his father Dr.
Davidson said he had seen) in which Bruce says ' he was

writing a poem about a gowk,' and Principal Baird's change
of opinion on the matter—going over from Logan's side to
Bruce's, on the evidence, *inter alia*, of a MS. of the poem
in Bruce's handwriting (Mackelvie, p. 117). All these,
however, seem themselves open to some suspicion. It is
odd too that the folly of Logan, in his treatment of the
matter (supposing ' The Cuckoo ' to be his) should have been
repeated by Baird, in printing as Bruce's a poem which he
himself had formerly believed to be Logan's, and which he
must have known was a subject of dispute, and adding no
note of the evidence which had induced him to transfer it
from one author to another. I had the good fortune to
pick up the original editions of the poems, both of Bruce
and of Logan, a few months ago—Believe me, yours very
truly, WILLIAM STIRLING MAXWELL."

"*3d December* 1873.

"MY DEAR SIR—I thank you for sending me your
paper on Michael Bruce, which I read with much interest.

From an error in your paper, I suppose you have not
visited Kinnesswood, and the shores of Loch Leven recently,
or in connection with your researches or reading about the
poet. He was not buried at Portmoak, where his friend was
buried, but in the graveyard of the church, which is on the
road leading from Kinnesswood round the loch, and where
there is a simple tombstone and monument to his memory.
I think it is very difficult not to admit the claims of Bruce
to the authorship of 'The Cuckoo,' after reading Mr.
Grosart's book. Dr. John Brown of Edinburgh sent me a
copy of it, and I think he considered it conclusive. In my
opinion Bruce's ' Cuckoo ' is superior to Wordsworth's, or
any other lines or verses on the same subject. But I do
not pretend to be an authority, and must leave it to others
better qualified to judge.

. . . I have much pleasure in the fine passages of some of
our poets, and only regret I did not study them more when
young, and when the memory is more retentive.—Believe
me always, very truly yours, JOHN BRIGHT."

In 1874 Shairp edited Dorothy Wordsworth's Journal
of the Tour in Scotland, which she took with her brother
in 1803. This Journal had lain for seventy years un-
edited, and very little known. Its publication revealed to
the students of Wordsworth what few were aware of before,
that the sister's eye was fully as delicate as the brother's
in its appreciation of natural beauty, and the varied phases
of human feeling. The fragments, which had been quoted
by the Bishop of Lincoln, in the *Memoirs* of his uncle, had
raised expectation, and excited curiosity; but scarcely any
readers were prepared for what the whole Journal contains,
viz. a minute and continuous unfolding of the distinctive
features of Scottish landscape and Scottish character. The
same thing is true of the as yet unpublished Journal of the
Tour on the Continent, which Wordsworth took with his
wife and his sister in 1820 ; and still more emphatically of
the sister's Diary of their life, both at Alfoxden, in Somer-
setshire, and at Dove Cottage, Grasmere. As a record of
the plain living and high poetic thinking of that Wordsworth household, in their Highland rambles, as well as in
their Westmorland cottage, these *Recollections* have a value
for all time. The book is full of delicate insight, of
much humour, descriptive grace, and happy characterisa-
tion. The editorial part of the work is a model of what
such editing should be. A brief sketch of the life of the
poet, and his relation to his sister, introduces the volume ;
and only a few notes are given, here and there, when anything calls for explanation.

Dr. John Brown wrote several letters to Shairp about
Miss Wordsworth's Journal of the Tour in Scotland.

"*9th April* [1874].—Isn't this of Dora delightful,
delicious, like the fragrance of thymy braes, or the cool
sweetness of fruits? It will be a poor soul that will not
relish it. Could you not write a *poem* as well as a *preface*,
setting forth, in your own way, William, Dora, Coleridge,
and the idea of their Tour? Try. It would be a great success, if that Great Beast—the Public—had heart, and taste,
and greatness of mind. Where in England, at that time,

would bare-legged boys be found careering to school to read Virgil and Homer? Will that, under our new Administration Act, be the case seventy years hence? The boys may be stockinged; will the mind be clothed and fed? Will the soul be awakened? When do you go north?—Yours,

J. B."

Again, " 15*th April.*—I am sure all the quotations from Wordsworth should be incorporated in the text within brackets. . . . It is exquisite, just like Nature's self, and soul, and smell. . . . I think at the close of the Tour you should break forth into song thus." [He then gives some lines and adds]—" This verse is the mother liquor uncrystallised."

On another page, some days later, he wrote—" Crystals forming—feebly—on finishing Dora's Tour."

I close the book, I shut mine eyes,
I see the three before me rise.
Loving sister, brooding brother,
Each one mirrored in the other.
Mighty ' William,' artless ' Dora '
Who was to the very core, a
Lover of dear Nature's face,
In its perfect loveliness.
Lover of her flowers and mountains,
Of her glens, and of her fountains,
Of her tears, and of her smiles,
Of her quaint and winning wiles,
Nor less the human face divine—
Brightening yours, and brightening mine.

Again on 9th June 1874. — " I have read it all. I knew what it would be, and yet it has surprised me with its fulness, its penetration. There is not one thing amiss; it is sustained throughout, and continues with increasing power what you long ago began so nobly,—the commending and unfolding Wordsworth to the world. You must do more in this line yet before you die; and you have added to his power and sweetness a fulness of Christian insight and

articulate Christian confession. . . . It is delightful to
have you associated with this quite unique Journal.—Yours,
J. B."

And on 10th June 1874.—. . . "The Preface or
Prelude please me more and more. . . . I don't think you
have done better work, and it was work not easily done,
and only by a man saturated with Wordsworth. . . . I wish
you would, having so well introduced the Journal, part
from it with *a blessing in verse.* Try this. Go up towards
Farragon, and let the winds blow and shout, and the *fang*
will come.—Yours,   J. B."

Again, "11th June 1874.—This Preface has taken a
great grip of me. I have just finished my third reading,
and I am so impressed with the majesty, the purity of that
third, I feel as if surely such a well of healing will
never be shut up. But you must dedicate yourself to a
larger work, and interpret Wordsworth to the world. What
a specific for the present feverish, godless, vain lines of
thought and feeling. Think of this. . . .—Yours,   J. B."

In the winter of 1874, at the Jubilee dinner of his old
school, the Edinburgh Academy, Principal Shairp made a
remarkable speech. Dr. Tait, then Archbishop of Canterbury,
presided, and amongst the 170 who were present, almost
all were former pupils of the Academy. In proposing his
toast, the Principal remarked—

"It is sometimes said by our southern critics that the fondness and
persistence with which we Scots revert to the literary eminence of this
northern capital during the past generation is a proof of our barrenness
in the present—that it is the wail of the land for a glory which has
departed. Now, whether this taunt be true or false, all must feel that
if ever there was an occasion on which we might naturally look back
with affectionate remembrance to that galaxy of great men, that occasion is to-night. It is not natural pride, but 'natural piety' that
makes us do so, for these men were the fathers and the founders of
that school whose birth we are to-night met to celebrate.
There is not probably a man in all this company to whom those

honoured names have not long been household words. Among those whom I address, some there are who knew these men as they walked in the flesh—who can feelingly recall the expression of their countenances, and the tones of their voices ; some, perhaps, who were bound to them by the still more endearing ties of kindred or of early friendship. We have all heard—some may even be weary of hearing—of that day when, on the top of one of the Pentlands, the idea of a new classical school first flashed on the brain of Henry, Lord Cockburn. It was a fitting birthplace for a large and beneficent idea. Not in the retirement of the lawyer's study—not under his wig in the Parliament House—but under his rustic hat, with the free Pentland winds blowing about his comely and expressive face, that idea was born. And what Cockburn's brain first conceived, his hand was not slack to execute. From that day to the latest of his life he gave to the young school all the aid of his ever-youthful enthusiasm, and regarded it as ' his only child.' With himself he generously associates Leonard Horner as the joint-originator of the conception, but probably the greater share, if not the whole of it, was due to Cockburn himself.

This idea, of which Cockburn was the father, Sir Walter Scott eagerly took up. He not only found for the new school its first rector, the Vicar of Lampeter, college friend of his son-in-law Lockhart, and the tutor who prepared for Oxford his only son Charles,—but he also presided at the opening of the new institution, and in a long and thoughtful speech, which still survives, explained in unadorned and kindly language what was the aim and the nature of the new school. You have told me, my Lord Archbishop, of that opening day, and you and others here to-night can probably still remember the feeling tones in which he expressed his hope that ' his words, poor as they were, would sink into the hearts of his young hearers and remain in their memories, long after they had forgotten the speaker,' as though they could ever forget him. Him followed on that memorable day the venerable Henry Mackenzie, the Man of Feeling, then in his eightieth year, the sole remnant and representative of the sentimental literature which flourished in the generation that preceded Scott.

Nor less zealous in his advocacy of the nascent school was Lord Jeffrey, whose eloquent, if somewhat artificial, accents were often heard within its walls. That venerable clergyman who, on the opening day, invoked God's blessing on the future of the school, was Sir Henry Moncreiff ; and his son, the late Lord Moncreiff, not only lent the advocacy of his voice, but contributed to its earlier years the ability of his several sons, and of him especially whom we rejoice to see here amongst us, and who so ably maintains the tradition of his honourable house. Nor must I omit to mention the less brilliant but not less useful service of the first Honorary Secretary, Mr. John Russell, who gave his legal knowledge to organise its beginning, and continued for many a year to watch over its interests with most disinterested zeal.

Time would fail me to enumerate all the others who co-operated with those I have named to launch the school on that course on which it has now held for fifty laborious and prosperous years. Enough, however, have been recounted to show that we can look back to a not undistinguished ancestry. It is one of the most benign influences of Learning and Literature that they can unite those whom nothing else can. And so it is pleasing to find that in the foundation of this our school, the great Sir Walter joined heart and hand with Cockburn and Jeffrey and others, to whom in most other public questions he had stood in lifelong antagonism. It was a pure and generous impulse which made those great men, in the prime of their powers, pause to think of the coming generation, and to provide for them what they hoped might prove some better learning than they themselves had enjoyed. Themselves but rough Latinists—and guiltless, most of them, of Greek — for Scott, though himself the true modern Homer—the poet who, of all others, for the last two thousand years, breathed most of the spirit of the old Ionian rhapsodist—never, I suppose, after his schooldays read a single line of the Homeric poems in the original language ; yet they generously desired that we who came after them might drink more deeply of Hellenic fountains than they had done. That the Academy did much for raising the standard of general scholarship, and especially of Greek, in Scotland, one cannot doubt. That it did not succeed in leavening the whole educated community with Greek lore, that it did not stem the strong currents setting in other directions, that it could not turn back the native bias towards mere utilitarian objects, is no discredit to it. Sir Walter in that opening address adverted to that saying of Dr. Johnson's, that ' in learning Scotland was like a besieged city, where every man had a mouthful not a bellyful,' and, sturdy Scotchman as he was, he could not gainsay its truth. He expressed his hope that the Academy might do something to wipe away this reproach ; but we must in candour admit that as far as deep scholarship goes we are like a besieged city still.

We all know that the Academy has trained, during the last fifty years, not a few very eminent Greek scholars ; but they, with the sure instinct of our race for the main chance, have for the most part carried their wares to southern and more lucrative markets. Scotland has been when it was a poor country—it continues now when it has become a rich one—a land in which scholars are few. But to produce great scholars is not the only, or even the chief, work of a large school : rather to train boys so that they shall become upright, honourable, intelligent, industrious men in all the walks of life.

Tried by this test, I believe that the Academy has abundantly fulfilled its mission. Of those, her pupils, whom it has been my lot to know in after life, I can recall many a one of whom she may reasonably be proud ; hardly one of whom she need be ashamed. In organising their plan of the new school, our founders kept their eye on utility—little or nothing on amenity. The situation they chose, the building they erected, the six hours' continuous work by day, with nearly as many more by night, required from the boys who stood near the top, made the existence of most boys of my time somewhat too unrejoicing. In vain you would look there for the green playing fields of Eton by the shining Thames, or even for the green close of Rugby with its venerable elm-trees, and all the pleasant associations that gather round these. These things the Academy did not affect. But it aimed at and affected careful grounding, sound learning, and a most laborious work. And the result has been that no Academy boy ever learned any part of scholarship there which he had afterwards to unlearn, go where he might. Ten continuous months of as faithful teaching and as hard a grind as any school in Britain ever knew, this is my impression in looking back to four years spent within the Academy walls. And if, when the year closed with the annual field-day, the spirit in which the orators year after year addressed the head boys was somewhat too mundane ; if mere worldly ambition and preferment were too exclusively set before them as motives of action ; if the higher spiritual elements which have since that day entered into the aims of the best English teachers were wanting ; yet those founders and patrons who addressed us spoke according to their then lights. They gave us of the best they had to give ; and the fault is ours, not theirs, if we have not something of the more self-forgetting spirit and Christian chivalry which has animated the best men of more recent times. It would be well if we, with our later lights, could hand on to our descendants any institution which could confer on them as substantial and lasting benefits as the Academy has conferred on her numerous sons."

Every movement for the promotion of the higher education in Dundee had the Principal's warmest support. In 1873, a University Club was formed in that town, consisting of the graduates in Arts, Law, and Medicine, who resided in Dundee or its neighbourhood, including the old students of any University, British or foreign. Principal Shairp became one of its members, was elected its President, and took much interest in its prosperity. When Dean Stanley delivered an address to that Club, and to the general public of Dundee under the Club's auspices, Principal Shairp presided, and introduced him. In February 1875 he himself delivered an address to the Club in the Albert Institute Buildings, from which extracts are given in the appendix to this volume.[1]

[1] See p. 443.

During his later years in St. Andrews, the chief interest
to Principal Shairp was the maintenance of the efficiency
and dignity of the College over which he presided, the
development of the University, and the extension of its usefulness.

Year by year, for many years, he opened the winter
sessions of the United College by the delivery of a lecture
to the students and the public. Many of these academical
addresses were weighted with wisdom, their subject-matter
was always important, and the treatment never commonplace. As reported in the newspapers of the day, they
served to keep before the public mind the work which the
University was doing, and the function which it fulfilled in
the academic life of Scotland. They were dignified addresses, dealing with varied themes, both national and local ;
and, whatever other features characterised them, their main
note of distinction was their elevated tone, and their ideal
touch.

In his efforts after University extension, however, Principal
Shairp's work was not carried on alone. He had the assistance of his colleagues in St. Andrews in many schemes which
had for their sole object the development of the University,
and the diffusion of its influence in the district of Scotland
to which it had been so long an educational centre. In the
month of March 1864, when a committee of Senate was
appointed to organise a system of University Local Examinations, he was a working member of it. He took special
interest in the educational work of the Dundee High School,
when its classical department was under the care of the late
Dr. Low, a man for whom he had a warm regard, and on
whom, at his instance, the Senate conferred the honorary
degree of LL.D. He used frequently to visit the High
School, and carefully to note the teaching of the Latin and
Greek classes in it.

Principal Shairp's chief relations with that commercial
centre—which has now its College, partially affiliated to
St. Andrews, and destined, let us hope, to be permanently united as a branch of the University—arose out of a

movement which originated in Dundee, but which was carried out by the St. Andrews Professors, for the delivery of University lectures in the former town. The story of the academic relations between the two places is a long one, and this is scarcely the place to tell it, as it may yet be done in a more detailed and formal manner. It may be mentioned now, however, that there were many in Dundee who sympathised with the local aspiration to have a College situated in the town itself, but who thought that whatever branches of learning were taught in it, the Arts and Science faculties in St. Andrews should be strengthened, and that the best way to help Dundee to develop a distinctive College of its own —having an academic right to live and grow strong amongst the other institutions of Scotland—was meanwhile to bring the two places into closer and more living accord. A Dundee Committee was formed to promote this end, and a request was addressed to Principals Tulloch and Shairp, and to Professors Heddle, Nicholson, and Pettigrew, to deliver courses of lectures in Dundee. A Guarantee Fund was raised, and thirty lectures in each subject were delivered in the evenings in the largest classroom of the High School. During the first year of the experiment the subjects of lecture were Chemistry, Natural History, and Physiology respectively; while two shorter courses were delivered on the Saturday afternoons, one by Principal Tulloch on "St. Dominic, St. Francis, Pascal, and the Port-Royalists," and the other by Principal Shairp on "The Poetic Interpretation of Nature." What Principal Tulloch did to promote an object, in which he was so profoundly interested as the union of St. Andrews and Dundee for educational purposes, will doubtless be told in the story of his Life. The share which Principal Shairp had in it, if less explicit in the way of organisation and business detail, was no less valuable.

He came down one day from Cuil-aluinn, and spent it with a Dundee citizen who was deeply interested in the work of the University; and of this visit he wrote home to the following effect: "The Lecture Scheme seems to go on well. Went with —— to —— (who is a representative

Y

man in Dundee, a sort of business king). He reports that 'the whole intelligence of Dundee is unanimous in favour of the lectures,' that a Guarantee Fund of £400 has been already raised, and when one or two more are asked it will be £500. He was very strong on the impetus that would be given to the movement if the two Principals would give four or five lectures on Saturday afternoons in connection with the more regular teaching lectures."

Accordingly, Shairp delivered a course of Saturday lectures. If his one gift to Dundee had been these discourses on " The Poetic Interpretation of Nature," it would be no small one. As was so often the case with those who listened to his spoken words, a desire was then expressed by several that an opportunity might be given them of reading the lectures leisurely. They were published in 1877, and so greatly were they appreciated in America that an edition was soon afterwards reprinted there.

In estimating these lectures their original aim must be remembered. They were meant to be popular, and to illustrate a side of Nature, different from that on which his scientific colleagues had been dwelling, but not less real and necessary to be known; especially so in an age of material success and utilitarian aims. Had they entered into minute scholarly detail, they would have been unsuited to the audience originally addressed, as well as to those whom their after publication was meant to interest and stimulate. There is in them all the freshness of Nature, the old breath of the mountain and the heather. Readers may see statements from which they differ, but they will be instructed by these differences. The relations between Poetry and Science are suggestively drawn out; and the eight different ways in which the poets are said to have dealt with Nature (chapter VIII. pp. 90-124), if not all fundamentally distinct from one another, are each real and important.

Cardinal Newman wrote thus on receiving a copy of the book—

"THE ORATORY, 6*th July* 1877.

" MY DEAR PROFESSOR SHAIRP—I saw the advertisement of your volume, and thought how interesting the subjects were which were contained in it, little thinking I should have the pleasure of receiving a copy from the author.

I thank you very much for it, and for the very flattering notice which you have introduced of me at the page you name.   However, I had seen it before your letter came and without setting to read the book formally, had enjoyed many detached portions of it.   I was particularly pleased at your remarks on Cowper.   He has always been dear to me ; and I never could acquiesce in Keble's judgment of him, which I do think was partly owing to Cowper's being a friend of John Newton's.

Thank you also for what you say of portions of my essay on Assent.—Very truly yours,

JOHN H. NEWMAN."

It should be added that the historical section of this little book (chapters IX. to XIV.), outlining the way in which the poets have contemplated Nature, from Homer and the Hebrew bards to Tennyson, is specially good, in particular the part dealing with the English poets.

Shairp's knowledge of, and delight in, the scenery of the Borders has been already referred to, but we have no record of it—not even in his poems on Yarrow, and Manor, Traquair, and Broadlaw—finer than the speech he delivered at the annual dinner of the Border Counties Association at Edinburgh in January 1877.   In proposing the toast of " The Literature of the Borders," he said—

" It is now with a feeling of strangeness and wonder that I look around and find myself in this gathering of Borderers —I who am no Borderer, but born in Lothian.   And yet I cannot call myself altogether a stranger here, for I have a dash of Border blood in me.   My great-grandmother was Anne Scott of Harden, the last female of the oldest branch

of that of Harden's line.   In virtue of this I never look on
Dryhope Tower, where Harden woo'd and won the Flower
of Yarrow, without something of a family feeling.   Besides
this, I have other more recent and nearer ties to the Border
which I need not name now.

Moreover, if not by birth, I am in heart a Borderer.
There is not here present one, I believe, who has wandered
longer, or more lovingly over that delightsome land.   In
long gone summers I have wandered on foot over almost
every dale of the Borders—from Stitchell and Smailholm
Tower to Leader Haughs and Cowdenknowes; from Leader
Haughs to Ashiestiel and Williamshope.   Over all Yarrow,
high and low, I know every hope, and holm, and howe; I
have sought out the site of every one of its long-vanished peels.
Up Ettrick I have travelled by Rankleburn and Timah
Water; seen the cleuch where the buck was ta'en; looked
from the top of Ettrick Pen far down Annandale to Niths-
dale, over the whole of that song-enchanted land; wandered down Craigmichen Scaurs, by Moffat Water; up
Carriffren Scaurs, by Gameshope and Whitecoomb Edge;
down by Meggat Water and Talla Linn, past Tweedsmuir
Kirk; by Kingledoors to the Tower of Lamington.

And as I wandered how often have I paused and asked
myself, What is it that makes the charm of this wonderful
land?   No doubt, the land is beautiful, with a quiet unobtrusive beauty of its own—with its soft, green, mammy hills,
with their soft-flowing outlines, and its secluded hopes, with
their clear burns—

> The grace of forest charms decayed,
> And pastoral melancholy.

But other lands are as beautiful, even more striking in
their beauty.   What, then, is its charm?   It is the atmosphere of tradition and of melody by which it is overspread
and glorified.   This seems to be the special inheritance of
the Borders, their peculiar gift.   No doubt, to create that
tradition and that melody centuries of wild and adventurous
deeds had first to be lived by the Border people.   The

whole line of hills that sweep from St. Abb's Head to the mountains of Galloway and Loch Ryan stood like a rampart between the two rival kingdoms, and to the Border men it fell to man that mountain wall, and roll back the tide of southern invasion. A grandly exciting time it must have been when, as soon as his board was bare, and the cattle stalls were empty, the Border chief sprang to horse and rode into England to drive a ˙prey more gleefully than their descendants to-day ride forth to the hunting-field. And then they had the sense that, while they were taking their pleasure in harrying our 'auld enemies of England,' they were doing good service to their own king and country. But this sport of cattle-lifting was too much to the Borderer's mind to be confined to his foes besouth the Tweed. When there was no raid over the English Border, he could turn with as little compunction, and harry his next neighbour's land, and drive off his herds.

This side of Border life and habits Sir Walter knew well, and many a turn he has given it in his poetry and romances. For three centuries, from the time of King Robert Bruce till the union of the Crowns, that fierce warrior-life of the Borders went on. But all that life of Border raid and battle, of wild adventure and romantic love, would have perished from memory, had not the nameless minstrels of the Border condensed it into those many ballads, and left them as the record of that 'war-wounded past.' And the ballads themselves, scattered here and there through the dales, would have been swept into oblivion had not Sir Walter Scott, just before the coming of the modern era, been born into the world. I may speak of the mist of tradition and melody spread over the face of the land. Like many another morning mist, it would have disappeared had not Scott been the sun that looked over the eastern hills and turned the mist to gold, and fixed it there for ever. Sometimes as I croon over these ballads a suspicion crosses me that here and there I can discover the hand of Scott re-touching them. In the song of the outlaw Murray, for instance, there is one verse where I cannot but feel as if

Scott had added a touch of his own. As it is about the
family of Buccleuch, will our noble chairman forgive me if
I quote it? The King, James V., had resolved to put down
the great freebooters of the Border. Foremost among these
was the outlaw Murray, who dwelt in his castle of Hanging-
shaw, on the Yarrow—

> The king was cuming thro' Caddon Ford,
>   And full five thousand men was he;
> They saw the derke foreste them before,
>   They thought it awsome for to see.

Lord Hamilton proposes that the king should meet the
outlaw and settle matters in conference—

> Then spak' the keen laird of Buchscleuth,
>   A stalworthye man and stern was he,

and told the king it was unbecoming his state and dignity
to meet an outlaw in conference—

> The man that moves yon foreste intill,
>   He lives by reif and felonie!

> Wherefore, brayd on, my sovereign liege!
>   Wi' fire and sword we'll follow thee;
> Or, gif your countrie lords fa' back,
>   Our Borderers sall the onset gie.

> Then out and spak' the nobill king,
>   And round him cast a wilie e'e—
> Now haud your tongue, Sir Walter Scott,
>   Nor speik of reif and felonie,
> For had every honeste man his awin kye,
>   A right puir clan thy name wad be.

I have never read this last stanza but a strong suspicion
has come over me that we have Walter's own hand here—
that it was he that added to the original ballad this wily
side-hit at his own clan and chief. A like suspicion has
often crossed me as to that grand Homeric touch in the
ballad of 'Jamie Telfer of the fair Dodhead':—

> But Willie was stricken oure the head,
>   And thro' the knapscap the sword has gane;

> And Harden grat for very rage
>   When Willie on the ground lay slane.
>
> But he's ta'en off his gude steel cap,
>   And thrice he's waved it in the air—
> The Dinlay snaw was ne'er mair white
>   Nor the lyart locks of Harden's hair.
>
> 'Revenge! revenge!' auld Wat gan cry;
>   'Fye, lads, lay on them cruellie;
> We'll ne'er see Tiviotside again,
>   Or Willie's death revenged sall be.'

That Homeric touch about Wat of Harden, who could have given but our own Scottish Homer? What a subject for a painter, could one be found to render it worthily! But all these long ages of wild battle and raid, and romantic adventure, love and sorrow, might all have passed into oblivion and been utterly forgotten ere now, but for the local ballads that preserved their memory. And these ballads themselves had all vanished from the dales ere now, unless—just before the modern age with all its changes set in—Walter Scott had been born to gather them up and give them an immortality in that wonderful *Minstrelsy of the Scottish Border.*

These raids after the ballads were what trained and made him. What college classes and erudition do for other men, Liddesdale and The Forest, with their old tales and ballads, did for him. Great and precious as are his poems and other works—his *Lay,* his *Marmion,* his *Guy Mannering,* and his *Antiquary,* his *Abbot*—I know not if there is one of them which we would not willingly spare, rather than lose that earliest of them all, *The Border Minstrelsy,* which, in his unknown days, he gathered and preserved. Lockhart has said that the minstrelsy was the great quarry out of which the materials for all his after works were dug—that there is hardly an incident or adventure or character in any of them the first hint of which may not be found in the three volumes of the *Minstrelsy,* either in the ballads, or in the prefaces and notes by which he so grandly illustrated them. This is the great storehouse out of which came the materials of all his subsequent creations.

The Borders received his first and best songs—'The Eve of
St. John' and 'The Lay.' They secured, too, his latest
love, when, as all remember, he roused him from that last
lethargy as he heard once more the name of Tweed. But
if the Borders were the centre of his inspiration, his gift has
overflowed and glorified the whole of Scotland—

> For thou upon a hundred streams,
>   By tales of love or sorrow;
> Of faithful love, undaunted truth
>   Hast shed the power of Yarrow.

But while we hail Scott as king of Border melody, we
must not forget the many other gifted spirits who sang their
songs, and each added some lyric contribution to their native
region. Leyden, Allan Cunningham, the Ettrick Shepherd,
Laidlaw, poor Smibert, and many more; Lady Grizell Baillie,
Miss Jane Elliot, Mrs. Rutherford—these flowers of the
forest who have each enriched their native minstrelsy with
at least one deathless song. And one poetess still lives,
worthy to be named with the best of these—Lady John
Scott, with her wealth of most characteristic minstrelsy.
While we do all honour to Scott, let us not forget those
genuine though lesser singers, whom he himself with his
large generosity would have been foremost to acknowledge.
If the volume of his song was as Tweed river, those other
singers were the affluent streams and burns and hopes that
fed its volume, without which he never could have been
what he was. And just as every tributary burn and hope
has an individual beauty of its own, and is worth tracing
up to its remote well-head, so each of those minor Border
poets has his own felicities to repay the loving student of
them.

I say nothing of other forms of literature produced by
the Borders—history, science, philosophy, etc. These may
be produced anywhere as well as in the Borders. It is your
minstrelsy, your rich inheritance of heroic tradition, em-
balmed and glorified in song—this is your peculiar, your
matchless possession, ye sons of the Border. Preserve it,

cherish it, love it; hand it on to posterity; be yourselves worthy of it. Once let go or be forgotten, it can never be restored. We who, in the heyday of youth, have wandered over these dales so delightedly, feel now that

> Yarrow through the woods,
> And down the meadow ranging,
> Doth meet us with unaltered face,
> While we are changed, or changing.

We pass; that romantic land remains. Preserve it, and hand it on to the coming generations, that they may drink from as deep delight as we have done. Keep its green dales, as far as may be, by needless railways undesecrated, its pure streams by factories unpolluted, and its solitary places by staring statues unvulgarised. If you preserve it as it is, the consecration of its beauty will deepen with every new generation of human eyes that look on it; and he, its great poet, much as you have thought of him, future men will think of him still more—his reputation and his fame will grow with time—as century follows century, and no second Scott is born into the world."

Two months later we find Shairp as full of the spirit of the North as in this speech he is in sympathy with the South. Writing to his friend Clerk at Kilmalie in March, he says—

" . . . Will you point out to me two or three of the passages in your translation of Ossian, which you consider most characteristic of Highland scenery ?

(1) Of the dreary monotone of mists, and moors, and ghosts, and voices of the wind.

(2) Of the more happy aspects, the breaking out of sunshine after the storm. . . . I wish some samples of Ossian's peculiar treatment for a book I am getting ready." He added, referring to *Glen Desseray*, " You have got the last but one of the instalments of the poem ;" and mentioned his being a candidate for the Professorship of Poetry at Oxford.

CHAPTER XIV

IN June 1877 Shairp was elected Professor of Poetry in the University of Oxford.

During his candidature many interesting letters were received by him from friends in the south.

Mr. Matthew Arnold, the former occupant of the Chair, wrote him : " Unless either the Bishop of Derry claims me, or the angel Gabriel, or some equally unforeseen personage stands, I will vote for you. I have a conscience in these matters, so if I thought ―――― the best candidate I should vote for him, though I like you best. But I do not think him the best candidate, though he has more accomplishments (I suppose) than you. I think he would be sure some day to run amuck at somebody or something; and this is just what a Professor ought not to do. . . ."

After the election he wrote : " If you had stood an election and won, I should certainly have written to congratulate you. And still more do you deserve congratulation on the peaceable entry upon office by the flight of your competitors. I am most thoroughly glad that you are to be Poetry Professor, and I congratulate you most heartily on the warm and appreciative feelings towards you, which have appeared right and left since you were first announced as a candidate. Cicero says most truly that the *benevolentia civium* is one of the best instruments of usefulness that a man can have. . . ."

Mr. Palgrave, his successor in the same chair (who withdrew in Shairp's favour in 1877), wrote expressing his great pleasure at the kind words Shairp had used in regard to his withdrawal, and stating that he had written to many friends to ask them to support him, and that he hoped he would "walk over." He said he did not know if "human nature" allowed one to rejoice quite so much at another's success as in one's own; but that if it ever did, it really did so now in his case.

The Bishop of Derry wrote wishing him success, and speaking of his criticisms "at once reverent and refined." He added, "You *feel* Keble, as no one else does."

His old Rugby colleague, the present Dean of Norwich, wrote : "I will vote for you against any man in the world. . . ." And the late Dean of Rochester, Mr. Robert Scott, said the same.

His election led to a pleasant renewal, in the closing years of life, of his old connection with Oxford, while retaining his position as Principal at St. Andrews. The duties of the Oxford Chair of Poetry are not laborious, although —when the post has been held by a distinguished man of letters—the lectures delivered have often been brilliant, and usually an addition to literature. The result of such lectures is never to be judged by their immediate effect. Their subsequent publication, by which a far wider circle is reached— as in the parallel case of lectures by the Slade Professor of Fine Art—may be regarded as more important than their oral delivery.

Shairp's first lecture on "The Province of Poetry" was given in Michaelmas term 1877, when he was the guest of an old Rugby friend, then Master of University College, and now Dean of Westminster. The fact that his son had matriculated, and was resident at Oriel, added greatly to the pleasure of these Oxford visits, when he went up once a term to deliver a new lecture. It was also a peculiar pleasure to meet the few survivors of his old circle of Oxford friends, and occasionally to make the acquaintance of new ones. The interest he took in all Scotsmen resident in Oxford, and especially in those who had gone up from St. Andrews as Guthrie scholars, was unabated. Before giving the reminiscences of the Dean of Westminster, and others, of these Oxford visits, portions from two of his own letters may be quoted. One was written three months before his election to the Chair of Poetry, and the other during a subsequent visit to the city. They both refer to his journey south.

Of his journey south to Oxford he wrote—

> "THE LODGE, BALLIOL COLLEGE,
> "*23d March* 1877.

". . . As we passed through the Border Hills between Clyde and Annandale, they were robed in snow till near the foot, and looked grander than I ever saw them, with the sunlight on them. As I came down Annandale, and looked out on all the old places that we have not seen for a number of years, it seemed so strange, like the meeting of friends long unseen. Moffat and its hills, the Dryfe, and the old *House of Lockerbie*[1] smoking away in the sunshine, as cheerful as if all its own people were there.

Then, as we passed over Shap Fells, I sighted far off the old Langdale Pikes, white with snow, and thought of past years. . . . To-day I travelled through a beautiful English country, Worcestershire, with its orchards all dressed, and newly-engrafted trees, waiting the touch of spring to bring them into bloom. It undulates beautifully, and the Malvern Hills and Breedon Hills, and far off the Cotswolds, take away all sense of tameness and monotony. As we neared Oxford we passed along the margin of Watchwood Forest, which I knew in old days, and saw the first primroses coming out beneath the oaks. . . ."

During another visit to Oxford he wrote from Balliol College: " I never saw a finer evening than last as I came from Crewe to Oxford; glorious glow of golden sunset over all the western sky, and the very thin young crescent moon in it set off the English landscape and fresh green swards so well. . . . Chestnuts fully out, all the different kinds of May blossom, and laburnums full out, and refreshing the air as I passed to my lecture."

[1] Mrs. Shairp's brother's house.

The Dean of Westminster writes—

" I was deeply interested in Shairp's election as Professor of Poetry at Oxford, which took place during my own residence as Master of University.   But I shall not attempt to enter into any estimate either of his writings or his lectures.   The man himself seemed to me, in his brief visits to Oxford and later on to London, at once unchanged and greatly changed.   The thirty odd years, that had passed since he left Oxford, had done their work on the general tone of the University, and on himself; and the course of intellectual and spiritual training through which Shairp had passed, since he took his B.A. in 1840, had carried him in many respects in a very different direction to that in which the University was travelling when he from time to time revisited it.   There was still the same earnestness, the same fund of enthusiasm, the same rich store of illustration from all the poetic side of Scottish history, tradition, or legend; the same keen interest in poetry, much of the same humour.   But there was much also in the feelings, opinions, and tendencies of young Oxford which was distasteful to him.   The attitude of his own mind had become, as life went on, essentially conservative. . . .   And remembering, as some of us did so well, the John Shairp of our own youth, there was something half-saddening and half-amusing in seeing that by the young generation he was looked on as a critic who belonged to an age that had passed away, and as only partially in sympathy and harmony with that which had succeeded.   For myself, who like my friend had long ceased to be young, I found his conversation, if not as stimulating and suggestive, yet scarcely less interesting and attractive than I had found it in years gone by.   His interest in religious subjects was uppermost; he retained of his former self a large and hearty and catholic sympathy; he still felt as much at home in the worship of our own Communion as of the Scottish Church; he still felt equally drawn to Keble, to Newman, to Arnold, and to Norman Macleod.   The name of Arthur Stanley was still as dear to

him, as to myself; but he was no longer in as much sympathy
as he had once been with what would be called the more
advanced section of the Broad Church, in either the Scottish
or the English Churches, and looked with quite as much
uneasiness to a further development of views in that direction,
as in that of a revival of mediæval tenets and practices. Many
questions also which he would once have keenly brought
forward and discussed, had lost their interest to him. In
politics, too, he had become, as it seemed to myself at least,
somewhat stiffly conservative, and lacking in readiness to
enter into the point of view of the other party. On the
other hand, in many respects he was in more advanced life
just what he had been in youth. On the subject of Scottish
history, life, or scenery he was always fresh, always delightful.
After a visit to Ross-shire in 1884, I remarked to him that I
had found little use there for the *History of Scotland*, which
I had found so delightful a companion farther south. ' True,'
he said, ' history there is a mute history, never put into print.
Plenty of it in tales and memories, and in songs if they could
only find a singer.' We tried hard to meet if possible, as we
had once done to our great delight, at his sweet little home,
Cuil-aluinn—which he taught me carefully to spell—near
Aberfeldy, on my return through the Highlands; but to our
mutual sorrow we were prevented. I saw him once more in
town, far from well, but suffering, as I hoped, from a passing
ailment; and later on was greatly gratified at being able to
co-operate in paying him the welcome compliment of admitting
him, by an Act of the Committee, as a member of the Athen-
æum. He was then leaving England in the early months of
1885 for a visit to the Riviera. In the following September
on our return from Germany, as we stood waiting for a boat
at the bottom of the Drachenfells, a newspaper was placed
in my hands with the news of his death, unexpected and
saddening beyond all that words can say. I can add no more.
Few men have been more deeply lamented; few passed through
life who have left behind them richer and more delightful
memories. As I look back and recall all that I have learned
from him, my life seems indeed the poorer; and no better

wish can I frame for our children's children than that they
may form in opening manhood such friends as I and others
found in the Shairp who has gone before us."

Mr. Butler of Oriel College writes—

"I pass on to the Oxford life, when Professor Shairp
returned to occupy the Chair of Poetry. It is needless to say what delight it gave him to come back.
Oxford was still hallowed to him by the memory of
old friendships, as well as of the great religious movement which he has so sympathetically described. Or, as
he wrote, combining both these memories into one, 'Those
who remember the fine spirits whom it touched, the noble
characters which it moulded, how deep they were, how pure,
how tender-hearted, how unworldly, can never look back on
the Oxford (religious) movement with anything but affectionate and pensive recollections.' Oxford, it is true, had
greatly changed, and he knew it. It was no longer dominated by a single movement, a great religious influence,
exercised by a master-mind; it was become cosmopolitan,
reflecting all the beliefs and unbeliefs, the interests and aims
which agitate England; but still it had for him that attraction which is common to all feeling minds, and to none in
a greater degree than to the author of *Culture and Religion*.
The duties of the Professor are not onerous, consisting mainly
of a lecture three times a year on some subject of art or poetry,
the task of looking over the University prize-exercises, which
are recited at the Encænia, and the delivery of a Latin
oration on the same occasion every second year. The position is one which is much coveted, and has been considered
as a kind of Blue Ribbon for the man who combines, in the
highest degree, critical and poetic power.

Now it will be seen at once that the Professor may, if
he please, live in a serene and ideal world apart from controversy, or he may come into conflict with some of the
deepest likings and prejudices of his hearers. The *odium
theologicum* is proverbially bitter; but it may be doubted

whether there is not quite as strong an *odium* between the
Naturalistic and Purist schools of criticism—the one admiring
'Art for art's sake; Beauty for beauty's sake'; the other
exacting from the poet the same self-control in expressing
emotion that it does from other men. There is doubtless a.
happy medium here as in other things; but it is one difficult to attain, without suspicion of either too great laxity or
severity, and a lecturer's views on some vexed question, such
as the merits of Burns or Shelley, are awaited with somewhat
of the same interest and curiosity as the delivery of the
first Bampton lecture on some vexed question of theology.
Young men naturally incline to the more indulgent school.
Professor Shairp was already, when he came to us, a well-
known advocate of the moralists. Moreover, 'Æstheticism'[1]
was just then rife in Oxford among those who most cared
for poetry, so that the elements of antagonism were not
wanting.

Unfortunately the Professor's voice was not equal to
the strain of lecturing to a large audience. He began
with spirit and animation, but soon, owing to the weakness
of his throat, the voice grew faint and indistinct, till he was
audible only to those close about him. Had he retained his
old Rugby fire and power of elocution, he would, I believe,
have had a great following. For young men admire a strong
and eloquent personality even where they differ; and the
lectures were in themselves of a high order. When published under the title *Aspects of Poetry*, they were met by a
chorus of approval. 'Full of interest, showing wide and
varied sympathies, fresh as his native air and heather,' they
at once silenced most of those objectors who had regarded
him as the narrow moralist and preacher. Some, it is true,
were irreconcilable. His lecture on Burns might be con-
doned, owing to the ardent praise and admiration with which
he qualified his censures; but that on Shelley could not
be forgiven. Here it was felt even by many of his friends

---

[1] " Æstheticism " was a very ephemeral movement here, as elsewhere. Just
now, Oxford, like England generally, is in a far sterner mood, girding itself
to try and find an answer to the problems of Democracy and Socialism.

that he was severe and unsympathetic. He took small account of the poet's circumstances and education, of the times in which he lived, and against which he revolted, or of the early age at which he died, just when his splendid powers were showing signs of growing restraint and self-control. He regarded him as the representative of poets of mere emotion, and, prevented by the tradition of his office from speaking of living writers, he made this protest against one great source and origin of the mischief. And yet he loved Shelley, and would at times quote his great lyrics with a power and pathos which showed how deeply they had stirred him. And his criticism on Shelley's well-known 'Lines Written in Dejection,' on the Bay of Naples, shows that he had felt the truth that the vivid expression of sorrow may help to lighten others' sorrow. 'So sweet they are,' he says, 'that they seem by their very sweetness to lighten the load of heart-loneliness.' In other words, melancholy and gloomy thoughts have their hour in all sensitive natures, and 'the sadness of the poet's strain,' like that of music, may be one means of giving these feelings vent, and cleansing the bosom of that 'perilous stuff,' which else would stifle it. But Professor Shairp felt strongly that the æsthetic school, then numbering so many adherents in Oxford, was full of danger; it was morbid, plaintive, pessimistic; and at a time when it was being seriously discussed whether 'life was worth living,' it was well to warn men that in loving Shelley, and other poets of emotion too well, there was 'poison in the air'; and that poetry was meant to brace, not enervate, to cheer to noble action, not to sadden and dishearten. Consequently he strove to turn them to the spiritual teaching and lofty optimism of Wordsworth, and the healthy manliness of Scott; but, as sometimes happens with our Professors at Oxford, he was out of tune with the rising generation, and his words, I fear, too often fell upon rebellious ears.

The same conflict between the Professor and the poetic tendencies of the time showed itself also in a more amusing manner in the adjudication of the prize for the Newdigate prize-poem. Here there is a restric-

tion that the poem shall be in heroic metre; but in
their treatment of the subject the successful poets had
come to be anything but heroic, and the verse, running into
the opposite extreme from its old rigidity, had grown slip-
shod and undignified.   This triumph of the æsthetic party—
I use the term for want of a better—was a constant grief to
the Professor.   At last, however, he thought he had secured
a more manly treatment by setting for the subject the most
heroic battle of ancient times.   Here it would seem that
man in his bravest, most sacrificing, mood was everything,
and Nature, sighing, sympathising Nature, nothing.   Both
parties seem to have understood the challenge, and girded
themselves for the contest; and there was considerable
interest in the result even outside the circle of the candidates' friends.   But here again the weaker side had the
stronger man, and the defeated champion of the heroic
school had to be content with two of his lines being much
quoted in the University—

> Is life worth living?   Yes, if truth be true,
> Life is worth living, death worth dying too.

This was at once a protest against the pessimistic side
of æstheticism, and a not unworthy tribute to the heroes of
Thermopylæ.

One more story may be told of the Professor's last
appearance in the theatre, when delivering the Latin oration
on the events of the past year.   The theatre is a large
place, and he was ill-heard and constantly interrupted by
the time-honoured jokes customary on that occasion.   One
small knot of tormentors, unusually annoying, was just above
his head, and at last, losing patience, he turned round upon
them, and, drawing himself up, shook his fist at them with a
good-natured smile.   They at once cheered him, and allowed
him to finish his speech without further interference, which
moreover was delivered with unwonted ring and fire.   This
little scene was characteristic of his relations to undergraduates, when brought face to face with them.   He won
them at once, partly from his own delight in young men,

and the deference and courtesy with which he treated them ;
partly also by his own native manliness and simplicity.
Sympathy is ever fresh and young, and he was full of sympathy; and men of all kinds were charmed with his conversation, so various, so original and full of humour. Who
indeed could resist that conversation's charm ? It needed a
small circle to bring him out, but given the right time and
place, his talk would flow on in a delightful stream, rich in
anecdote, on occasion elevated, abounding in humour. As
with all good talkers, you never felt you had come to an end,
even of any single subject. The stream flowed on ; the
source was inexhaustible. For his range and width of interest and sympathy were as remarkable as his fulness and
depth. He had known, or knew, most of the great leaders
of religious thought, and chiefs of literature, and liked to talk
of them ; not in a light gossiping way, but of their influence
on one another, and on their time. Sometimes it was a grief
to him that men to whom he owed much had known but
little of one another's writings, as, for instance, Newman and
Wordsworth. The great masters of thought live alone. He,
on the contrary, which is perhaps rare in men of strong
character and principle, was universal (if I may use the
word) in friendships and admirations. No matter who the
man was, an Erskine or a Keble, a Stanley or a Newman, a
Tory or a Liberal, if he recognised goodness and greatness in
him, he reverenced, he loved him. Perhaps the explanation
is, that he was a Tory-Presbyterian, educated at Balliol, in
the time of Newman. So, as I have heard from those whose
guide he was, he trod with reverence the place where
Dundee fell at Killiecrankie, and would stand bareheaded
before the tombs of the Covenanters.[1] And again, though a

---

[1] The following story is communicated by a friend :—
"There is a little island off the western coast of Scotland, called Eilan
Mhor. It is a lone spot; a few sheep from the mainland find summer feeding
there, but now it is uninhabited by man. It was here, in early days, however,
that one of the missionaries from the Isle of Saints fixed his abode. Here
still exist the ruined chapel where he lies buried, the cross on the rising
ground where first he preached, and the cell which was his dwelling-place.
Even for the ordinary mind Eilan Mhor possesses a strange fascination. But

staunch upholder of lords and lairds, he was eloquent in bewailing the wrongs of a peasantry expropriated to make sheep-farms and deer-forests. And in his heart, I think, he loved the people of Scotland far the best of all. In the highest and best sense, quite apart from political intrigue, he combined the spirit of Toryism and Democracy. And thus, having this breadth of sympathy, he had friends everywhere.

And what a friend he was! how kindly when present, how tender in recollection! Once I remember his stopping suddenly in Holywell, in Oxford, opposite a small house, and saying solemnly, ' Clough lodged here.' And he was silent for some time after, before resuming the broken conversation. And yet he did not idealise any one. He was too shrewd, too just an observer, to miss the flaw, or fault in a man or system. But he was, with all that it implies, a perfectly true friend. And speaking of many of his own friendships cut short by death, he loved to quote the beautiful lines of Wordsworth—

> Like clouds that rake the mountain summits,
> Or waves that own no curbing hand,
> How fast has brother followed brother,
> From sunshine to the sunless land!

Or again, those lines of Uhland, as translated—

> Take, O boatman, thrice thy fee !
> Take, I give it willingly:
> For, unwittingly to thee,
> Spirits twain have passed with me.

Or again, to quote his own words upon his old friend-ships—

> Since then, through all the jars of life's routine,
> All that downdrags the spirit's loftier mood,
> I have been soothed with fellowship serene
> Of single souls with Heaven's own light endued.

Principal Shairp was quite carried away by the associations of the spot, and was heard by his friends murmuring to himself, ' Holy they were ; holy they are ; holy it is !' And often afterwards he would refer to it as a hallowed place."

But look where'er I may, before, behind,
I ne'er have found, nor now expect to find,
Another such high-hearted brotherhood.

Full as he was of present living interests, he lived more
than most men in communion with the ghosts of the past.
And could he have brought himself to undertake it, he would
probably have been a great biographer, for he was greater, I
think, in construction than in criticism ; but, on the other
hand, he would have felt it his duty to criticise, which would
have been trying to him, at least in writing of a friend.

It would be easy to multiply stories and recollections
of a man whose character showed itself so transparently,
and in such interesting ways, in all his words and actions.
But I have already wandered from my subject, which is his
work in Oxford. It must not be thought from anything
here said that the antagonism between him and those of a
different way of thinking was a thing open and expressed.
Academical differences in these days are not very intense
or outspoken. But when occasion called for it he could
speak out plainly and unmistakably. As Professor Farrar of
Durham said of him in the University pulpit after his death :
' His mind was of the prophetic order.' Not a prophet, he
was of prophets' kin. And so, though it cost him much to
do it, just as he had done before in Scotland in attacking
the idolatry for Burns, so here also he felt it his duty ' to
make a strong protest against the fatal doctrine that men of
genius hold a charter of exemption from the obligations of
divine law.' But if, on the two occasions before alluded
to, he seemed to assume the functions of the preacher rather
than the art critic, they were the marked exceptions, not the
rule. Had he lived, he was meditating some lectures on the .
' Poetic aspects of Scottish History,' especially of the struggle
between the Stuarts and the House of Douglas, resulting in
the downfall of the latter. ' Even Shakespeare,' he said,
' never found a nobler subject for a tragedy.' Of his power
so to treat history he had given an earnest in a very interesting lecture on James I., the poet-king of Scotland. He
also meditated lectures on the Royalist and Jacobite poetry

in England and Scotland. But all these schemes were cut short by his untimely death. When the sad news reached Oxford it was received with universal regret. Even those who knew him little felt the charm of his simplicity, his kindliness, his most interesting and varied conversation, and his chivalrous and lofty tone of mind. He was, moreover, a connecting link with a past, which most Oxford men regard with reverence. What the loss was to his friends I will not attempt to describe. So charming a companion, so true a friend, will not come again.

Of his lectures, I think that some at all events should be saved from the oblivion which generally is the fate of work of this kind. Like his other writings, they are thoughtful, earnest, elevated, showing a pure and lofty mind, and with a thorough mastery of his subject; and though not striking in the way of paradox or epigram, or brilliancy of expression, there is in them a freshness and naturalness, as well as beauty of language, which make them delightful reading. Above all, he has a happy gift of selection from his author, and so letting him illustrate and explain himself."

The following is the concluding part of Professor Sellar's letter on his friend :—

" From the time I left St. Andrews in 1863, though we saw much less of one another, there was no abatement of our friendship. . . . His talk was always delightful, and was always about the things and subjects which really interested him. We met him once or twice in Oxford on our visits to the Master of Balliol, during the summer terms, when he used to give his lectures as Professor of Poetry. He had great pleasure in his life there, in the beauty of the place, in the revival of old and the making of new friendships among the younger men. Once, on their way back to their summer home in Perthshire, he and Mrs. Shairp passed a few days with us here in the Glenkens of Galloway. This was one of the few among the picturesque parts of Scotland which had hitherto remained unknown to

him.   I have never seen any one enjoy this country more.
His historic feeling was touched by a visit to Kenmure
Castle, by the sight of the pictures of the men and women
of 'Kenmure's line,' who played a bold part in the first
Jacobite rising, and also by seeing the desolate hills and
moors around Carsphairn, among which there still linger
memories of the Covenanters.   With these two antagonistic
causes he had an impartial sympathy.   Like Scott, he was
attracted by what was chivalrously daring or grimly earnest
in our national history, to the disregard of what was politic and
economic.   He was present at our Tercentenary Celebration
in the spring of 1884, when, on the proposal of his friend,
Sir Alexander Grant, he, among many distinguished men
from all countries, received the degree of LL.D.

The last time I saw him was in December of that year, when
he and I walked together in the sad and solemn procession at
the funeral of our old Balliol and Oriel friend.   The thought
occurred to both of us, as we talked over the past, how strange
it would have seemed to us if, some forty years before, when
we were all three young men together, with an uncertain
future before us, we had had, while all the intervening years
remained unknown to us, a prophetic vision of that spectacle
of which we formed a part, and some intimation of its
meaning.   He came back with me to my house, and I remember, as I was somewhat ill at the time, how kindly and
earnestly he urged me to get leave of absence till after
Christmas, offering to come and do my work for me himself.
I mention this because it was one among several occasions in
my life in which I had proof not only of his kindest sympathy,
but of his most active friendliness.   On one important occasion I now know that he acted towards me with a magnani-
mous disregard of his own interest, of which very few men
indeed are capable.   Though I could not specify these services
without entering on details which concern myself alone,
there are none ever rendered to me by any one for which I
feel a more lasting gratitude. . . . My last association with
him was of walking, along with old college friends of his
and mine, and friends and former colleagues from St. An-

drews, in the garden and the fields about his home in Linlithgowshire, on the morning of the bright autumn day on
which he was borne to the family burial-place. It seemed
then that there could have been no more pious and beautiful
close to a pious and beautiful life—none more fit to leave on
the mind, in the words of a poem which was a great favourite
of his, 'happy thoughts about the dead.' . . . He realised his
poetry in his life.

The biographies of men of genius show that sometimes, along with high aspiration and heroic effort, there co-
exists a 'seamy side' in their lives, and that the fame they
enjoy is counterbalanced by something unhappy in their
lot. Those most intimate with him never saw any 'seamy
side' in Shairp's life; and his lot was eminently a happy
one. He had not, and he never desired, great worldly success. He may have had at times, more than many of his
friends and social equals, to feel the strain of the *res an-
gusta domi.* But it came naturally to him to realise the
precept of his first teacher, and to combine ' plain living with
high thinking.' I remember when the St. Andrews revenues
were, owing to the agricultural depression, at their lowest,
his saying with a kind of gallant pride, ' It is nonsense making a poor mouth about these things.' He received from
Nature a combination of the courage and independent spirit
of a man, with the refinement and ready sympathy of a
woman. And this natural endowment was tempered into
a consistent character by constant watchfulness against any
assertion of self, in the way either of indulgence, or interest,
or vanity. He was eminently happy in his early home-life,
and in the home of his later life ; and the happiness
of his later home did not weaken his tie to the older
one. He was also most happy in the number and quality
of his friends, and while he went on till the end of his life
adding to their number, he never, I am sure, lost one through
any fault or neglect of his own. He was by no means too
facile in forming friendships, but when once he trusted a
man, it would have been no light cause that afterwards
alienated him.

He was, I think, a true discerner of character, and
what he looked for in any one he cared for was that
he should be genuine — his real self. He regarded with
good-humoured amusement all affectation and pretence, and
all ambition in a man to appear or to be greater or more distinguished than nature and circumstances fitted him to be.
For anything false and base in the relations of men to one
another he felt an indignant scorn ; and he would have been
more charitable in judging of it if the wrong were done to
himself than if it were done to a friend or even a stranger.
As he had a quick sense of personal dignity, and a generous
impetuosity of spirit, it was possible that he might sometimes take, and sometimes, though rarely, give offence ; but if
this happened, he was always prompt to receive or to make
acknowledgment; and the matter was never afterwards remembered.   At no time of his life would any one have said in his
presence anything essentially coarse or irreverent; or if he had
done so once, he would not have repeated the experiment.
But not to speak of the specially Christian graces which adorned
him, there were in his human relations two qualities prized
equally by Christian and Pagan, especially conspicuous, candour and generosity.   Dr. Newman, in the *Grammar of
Assent* speaks of the way in which, in our youth, we read
some of the classical writers, and think we understand them,
and he shows how different that understanding is from the
truer insight we gain into their meaning when we have had
experience of life.   It seems to me, in thinking of Shairp,
that I only now understand the full human feeling and
human experience compressed into the ' sad earnestness and
vivid exactness ' of lines often read and often quoted with
perhaps an incomplete realisation of their meaning,

Incorrupta fides nudaque veritas
Quando ullum inveniet parem ? "

To Mr. Sellar's paper may be added the remainder of the
Dean of Salisbury's—

" In 1877, when Sir Francis Doyle had concluded his

second term of office as Professor of Poetry at Oxford, it occurred to me and to many friends of Shairp's that he was eminently fitted to fill the post. His published criticisms had given him distinction and position as a real judge of poetry. Mr. M. Arnold, who had again been requested to come forward, stood aside in favour of his old Balliol friend, and the retirement of the present Bishop of Derry, a poet and refined critic, left the field open, and Shairp was elected. He prized the distinction greatly, and he showed in unmistakable ways his value for our friendship by invariably consulting me upon the subjects of his lectures. Many pleasant letters did I receive from him from time to time, when he was deliberating as to the subjects which he thought likely to interest his Oxford hearers. I regretted that he did not determine on some course of lectures, dealing with a particular period either of ancient or modern poetry. But he used to plead his inability to deal with classical poetry in a way satisfactory to himself, and he believed that an effort to create interest in the poets who were so dear to himself would be more fruitful. From the time of his election to the year of his death, when we met occasionally, it was clear to me that poetry and philosophy had not the same interest for him as theology.

In the autumn of 1882 I paid him a visit at his delightful summer residence, near Aberfeldy. We walked together to the grave of his brother-in-law, Bishop Douglas of Bombay, and under the trees of Castle Menzies I had one of the most solemn conversations I ever held with Shairp. The year 1882 was a very memorable one to both of us. In the spring, Hugh Pearson had followed his friend Arthur Stanley into the silent land. Shairp and these two friends and I had many delightful associations with pleasant days in Scotland, and as we stood under the trees, Shairp repeated the fine passage, at the conclusion of the *Agricola* of Tacitus, and then spoke of the effect produced upon him by the lives of Erskine, Stanley, and Pearson : ' I often differed from them, but they had one thing I longed to have more—an intense hatred of sin, and a greater love.' He then spoke of the effect pro-

duced upon him by some of the more earnest religious men
he had been meeting lately at Oxford, dwelt much upon a
sermon of Liddon's, and regretted the growing spirit of doubt,
too much fostered he thought by the diffusiveness of modern
Oxford culture.   I told him that some young men in whom
I was greatly interested had been much moved by his lectures on ' Religion and Culture,' and urged him strongly to
try and write a book which might aim at doing what Col-
ridge's *Friend* and the *Aids to Reflection* had done for
another generation.   He quite admitted his own great interest in the subject, but spoke much of advancing years
and the difficulty he felt in expressing thought, with lucidity
and power.   ' I envy,' he said, ' the ease with which Jowett
seems to write those Introductions to Plato, and read them
with a kind of despair.'   I remember being much struck
during this visit with the hold that Keble had upon his
mind.   As we drove to the station I reminded him that it
was the eve of St. Bartholomew, and told him of some pleasant historical gossip I had heard from Stanley ; but he said,
with a smile, ' I was thinking of Keble's poem ;' and he
stopped the rather jingling waggonette in which we were, to
repeat to me some well-known stanzas, illustrative of the
power of Scripture over the human heart.   No one that I
have ever known, penetrated so completely to the inner
spring of Keble's poetry as Shairp.   He delighted to dwell
upon Arnold's love for *The Christian Year*, and used to speak
with great pathos of the way in which the father of his
friend, Lord Coleridge, deplored the estrangement between
Keble and Arnold.   Something of the same kind had happened in the case of friends well known to both of us, and
he mentioned some noble traits in the character of Archbishop Tait, ' the most forgiving man,' he said, ' that I have
ever known.'   No one can feel more than I do, how crude
and imperfect these recollections must appear.   In the following year, 1883, Shairp and I met again at Megginch
Castle, and Mrs. Vaughan, the sister of Dean Stanley, was
also of the party.   At Megginch, Dean Stanley passed many
a pleasant day.   When he was there his kind host and

hostess often planned for him excursions to interesting places, and arranged that he should meet friends like Shairp and others who interested him. Shairp dwelt upon these days, in conversation with Mrs. Vaughan as he paced the green walks of the old garden, and I never heard him express himself more happily as when he described the effect of Stanley's animating presence amongst old friends, masters at Rugby in the days when he himself was a fellow-labourer there. As we went to bed at night, Shairp repeated the lines—

> Oh ! for the touch of a vanished hand,
> And the sound of a voice that is still,

and brought to my recollection what Dean Wellesley had said to me in almost the same words, used by Walter Scott at James Ballantyne's funeral, ' There will be less sunshine for you and me now that Stanley is gone.'

In the following year, 1884, we spent two days together in Perthshire. Many were the topics upon which he discoursed ; and in looking back upon that time, I distinctly remember how frequent were his allusions to the incompleteness and fragmentary nature of human interests, and how there seemed almost at that time to have come upon him the impression that his working days were drawing to a close, and that in his own words, adapted from Hallam, ' he must make haste to gather up his sheaves.' I urged him to do something in the way of editing a new edition of his *Religion and Culture*, but he said that he shrunk from touching what he felt to be full of imperfection. Newman and his influence upon English thought he dwelt much upon; and I remember well how, in speaking of old Oxford days, he described the strengthening effect which Newman's treatment of Scripture had had upon his own mind. ' To tell you the truth,' he said, ' I have always felt indifferent as to the talk about results of criticism. I got through Newman an idea of the grandeur of the Bible as a whole, and Norman Macleod and John M'Leod Campbell drove the same thought into my mind, so that it has been a rest and support to me all my life to be independent of all this talk.'

We walked together to the peaceful resting-place of
Bessie Bell and Mary Gray, and it was very shortly after
this that I received from him the letter which I now have
a painful pleasure in adding to this account—very imperfect
—of a most happy two days' visit.

'Cuil-aluinn, Aberfeldy, 22d *September* 1884.

'My dear Boyle—. . . It is one of the greatest pleasures each summer brings to meet you. And this becomes
more so as the old ties become fewer, which they are
doing more rapidly each year. I find now almost an inability to take up new acquaintanceships, not to speak of
friendships. The only exception is, when one meets young
people who are connected with the old, and who recall them
by something more than name. In these cases it is very
pleasant. How increasingly true to the heart one feels
that

I could wish my days to be
Bound each to each by natural piety.

I don't think I thanked you enough for the gift of
Fanny Kemble's little book. Besides *Absence*, there are
several more which greatly touched me — *Heart-chords*,
indeed, coming straight from and going direct to the heart.
. . . I have thought over your proposal of what I should
try to do for the Greek tragedians. It is a fine mine, and
the man who should work it as you and I should like to see
it worked would do much good. But I doubt if I am the
man. I am essentially a Teuton and a Celt, with rather
more of the latter than of the former, and find it more than
ever hard to force myself to be a Hellen. I can only write
about what I can get myself to care about warmly, and all
that, with me, lies this side the Christian era. . . .—Most
sincerely yours,   J. C. Shairp.

P.S.—I look forward to *Baxter*, whom of all the Puritans
I like best. I suppose he really was the largest, most reason-

able, and most humane. Is there any record of his ever meeting Milton, and of his opinion of that "cankered carle," as the Scotch songs have it?'

In the next year, after his brief sojourn in Italy, Principal Shairp and his wife paid a long-promised visit to Salisbury. He was far from well, but his interest in all that had occupied him was as fresh and buoyant as ever, and he enjoyed the society of my elder brother, whose friendship for him stretched over a very long period of his life. As in the previous autumn, his thoughts and conversation constantly took one direction. He was in great hopes that in the Scottish Universities there might be a greater movement, owing to the increased interest that had been called forth on the subject in Scotland, and he spoke with delight of the good work Professors Butcher and Jebb were doing in their Universities. . . .

We never met again, and the letter which now follows was almost the last I had from him. But I should not like to conclude this fragment of biography without saying how greatly I was impressed during my last intercourse with him by an extraordinary evidence of his anxious desire to do justice to friends, whose present position in politics and religious thought he had little sympathy with. It may have been the result of an internal feeling that the work day was ending, and the time of rest near.

'CUIL-ALUINN, ABERFELDY, 21st *July* 1885.

' MY DEAR BOYLE—Thank you so much for your sermon on the late Bishop. It seems to me done with very good taste, neither overdone nor underdone. I am sure his family must be pleased with it. We are so glad to have been at Salisbury and to have seen you and Mrs. Boyle in your interesting home, and to have seen, besides, the very garden that Honoria walked in. If I keep well I shall hope some day to return. I am much better and stronger now than when I was with you. We came up

here at the beginning of this month, and have enjoyed the
calm peace without dulness of this Strath. The quiet and
the good air, and the greenness, and the outlook to the
hills, all suit me and have done me good.

We go, I am sorry to say, at the end of this month to
St. Andrews, for we have let our cottage for three months.
If I could always live in as temperate a climate as this
July, and as aloof from cares and " worries," I think I
should never be ill. I have been working quietly at the
Italian subject and have yet plenty of material, if I can
only handle it aright. . . .' "

" Wherever he was known," writes Mrs. Bonamy Price,
" he must have stood out as a single figure, and was not
merged into those amongst whom he was living. Looking
back upon him, nothing strikes me more than that he was
not one of a group ; the individuality of the man was so
great. He might agree with others, and act with others,
but you felt he did not do so as belonging to a party. He
had his own views and feelings, and he acted upon these
alone. Devotedly attached as he was to Oxford, with quite
a filial love, and much as he enjoyed coming down twice a
year to deliver his lectures, he came as an independent
man—a son out in life, and no longer bound by the traditions of the family at home. I can only describe his visits
as a fresh breeze from his own mountains, sweeping across
the closer and heavier atmosphere of a plain. And yet this
was absolutely without self-assertion, or self-consciousness.
He did not mean to be different from others ; but it never
occurred to him, because he loved and admired a man, that
he should agree with him upon all points ; and yet no man
could love and admire with a more ungrudging spirit.

He was the most delightful companion in a chat by
the fireside, or a stroll on a summer evening—I had almost
said in a gossip ; for while no subject was too deep, none
was too light to be touched,—old rides at Rugby, scenery,
sunsets and storms, which we had enjoyed and braved
together, with recollections of many who have passed out

of our lives, and comparing our present and past estimate of them, all in a kindly spirit. I never knew him stern, except when he felt there was irreverence in dealing with sacred subjects. He once said to me, speaking of an occasion of this sort, ' I would have bitten my tongue out before any one should have seen the shadow of a smile ; ' and I know well the stern look which would come over his face.

With all his wide sympathies with England, and in many respects with modern thought generally, and his deep love for Oxford, which made it always a delight to him to be there, he was a Scotchman to the bottom of his heart— I will even venture to say a prejudiced one ; for he would occasionally fancy a lack of due recognition of his country's position in matters which seemed to me too indifferent to be noticed.

When I say it was a delight to him to be at Oxford, I do not mean that he was in touch with the general line of thought there. It was the Oxford of his youth which he tried to revive in talks with old friends (a breakfast with one, a walk with another, an evening with a third) ; and if he could meet two or three younger friends, and quietly compare with them present and past times, they were evenings much to be enjoyed and remembered by all who were present."

Miss Wordsworth, the Principal of Lady Margaret Hall, Oxford, writes—

" To give my recollections of the good Principal is like sketching an atmosphere rather than an outline ; and though it was an atmosphere which it was both profitable and delightful to breathe, yet it seems almost impossible to convey the effect of it to another person. I think one of my strongest feelings about him was, that he was ' so very Scotch.' By that I mean that he had in a marked degree those qualities which characterise the best Scotchmen and Scotchwomen, and which it is the glory of their literature to reflect. His tall figure, and kindly observant expression of face, his somewhat deliberate speech and self-possessed manner, his delightful smile, and the little *soupçon* of a northern accent which gave a quaintness and an air of sincerity to everything he said, left their impression at once on all who saw him. There was in him a mixture of simplicity and shrewdness, a certain self-respect and respect for others, a depth of feeling combined with manliness, a susceptibility to the imaginative side of things coupled with wholesome, everyday common sense, a natural love for what was great, good, and noble, charmingly blended with a sympathy for the lighter and more playful aspects of life. This, perhaps, came specially under my notice from the interest he took in girls and young women. He individualised them (which a great many clever men do *not!*) and seemed to have a kind of paternal affection for them and a pleasure in the little prettinesses and amusements of young-lady life, which we see a father sometimes showing in the case of his daughters.

I fear I cannot recall a single remark or conversation which would bear publication. The people who leave brilliant epigrams behind them are not always those who were most beloved by their friends, any more than fires, which are always flinging out sparks, are the pleasantest to warm oneself by ; and *his* benevolence had a steady glow—always the same—always to be counted upon, unobtrusive, but never-failing.

Others will have written of his literary attainments, and have spoken of him as a lecturer. In this last capacity he never did himself justice. His manner was not by any means equal to his matter, his glasses seemed to worry him, and his reading wanted light and shade. I doubt, too, whether critical analysis was his real *forte*. He belonged to the affirmative half of the world, a half which is not generally very well represented in Oxford. The lectures of his which struck me most were those in which he left criticism behind and gave us something positive and definite to admire, *e.g.* a lecture on Ossian,

2 A

and perhaps still more a very affecting one on James I. of Scotland. In a lecture of this kind his own real warm heart and poetical feeling came out, as well as that strong *nationality* which it is the privilege of Scotchmen to possess, and which in itself goes a long way to the making of a poet.

For my own part I could have wished that he had done more of this constructive kind. He had the power of sympathy in an unusual degree. It was this power which made his portraits, such as that of Dr. Newman, of much more than contemporary interest, and which would have come out in any narrative or biography which he might have undertaken. It was this which endeared him to so many friends, many of whom differed considerably from one another in views and opinions, but who all agreed in valuing *him*. Many have already passed away to the 'land of the leal,' whither he, as we trust, is gone. As far as human judgment goes, few could have had less of little-ness, worldliness, and self-love to leave behind them, few could have more carefully fostered those nobler qualities, both of the intellect and of the soul, which seem fittest for a better life, than he of whom these words are written. His sense of beauty was remarkably strong, and his en-thusiasm for the work of others a very characteristic trait. If I may be allowed to say so, he seemed particularly fitted for appreciating Wordsworth. The Lake District has much in common with Scotland; we find in both a certain masculine tone, a love of ideas rather than imagery, of height, depth, and breadth rather than subtlety—perhaps I ought in fairness to add a certain toughness of fibre which does not lend itself very easily to dramatic im-personation, and which is scarcely susceptible and sensitive enough to deal very much in humour of the more delicate kind—above all, a large, healthy, objective way of looking at things (one's own mind included, though this may seem paradoxical) which differs very widely from some of the poetry of the last twenty years. Perhaps he had hardly enough constitutional sympathy with the tastes of the

Oxford world of to-day to win a widely-extended hearing from younger men. One could wish this had been otherwise, for there was much he had to give which was just what they wanted to counterbalance—not to exclude—the influence of a later school. I am inclined, however, to think that it is chiefly as a writer that he has made his mark, and that as such he will long continue to influence the thinking part of the world; not by paradox, not by showiuess, not by sensationalism, not by morbid pathological introspectiveness, but by his earnestness, his thoughtfulness, his high culture and thorough mastery of his subject, and his deep love for all that is noble, pure, and good."

A resident in Oxford writes—

"I recall a walk we had together one early June evening for the purpose of hearing the nightingales then in full song. With what absorbed delight he listened to them! I remember his repeating to me, as we returned, Keats's lines to the nightingale, and his commenting on, though not sympathising with the sadness of their strain. The tendency of the true poetic instinct, he maintained, should be to raise not depress the soul."

CHAPTER XV

As this chapter includes the last decade of Shairp's life, it may be most appropriately begun by the latter part of Professor Veitch's paper on his friend.

"On a beautiful day early in September 1878, Mr. Lushington, Mr. Shairp, and I left the Loaning on the Tweed, and drove by Traquair and Newhall up the Paddy Slack to Glenlude, and then down by Mount Benger and the Gordon Arms to Yarrow. We paused at the point a little to the south of the watershed of Mount Benger Burn, memorable as the spot whence Wordsworth, in company with Hogg and William Laidlaw, first saw the Vale of Yarrow. The river opened up in its valley, in gleaming links, now seen, now lost, and overhead white fleecy clouds lay calm on the autumn blue. Proceeding up Yarrow, we left the carriage at the Kirkstead Burn, took to the moor on the right, making for St. Mary's Kirk and the wizard-priest Binram's grave. Thence we walked to Meggatdale, and paused for some time at the tomb of ' Perys of Cokburne and hys wife Marjory.' After visiting Tibbie's cottage we drove back, while the shadows were falling, in the peace of the evening.

This was a sacred Yarrow day, full of dreamy repose and soothing suggestions—the past and present happily blended. For Shairp it was a retrospect—full of memories of earlier visits; for Mr. Lushington it was a revelation —this being his first visit to the Vale. It was obvious how much and how finely the latter was impressed by the scenery and the story. Some time afterwards Shairp read to me a poem, which was suggested by this visit, entitled ' Three Friends in Yarrow, addressed to E. L. Lushington, September 1878.'[1]

. . . .

These days of Shairp's Border wanderings were not without touches of humorous incident. One evening, as I have heard him tell the story, he arrived late, wearied and seeking rest and shelter after a long day across the moors above Bellenden and Buccleuch, at a farm-house in the Rankle Burn, tenanted by a farmer of an old Border stock of the name of Grieve. He was admitted to the kitchen, and sat down. Presently the goodwife of the house came and spoke to him—a kindly woman, with some insight into the quality of even a wayfaring stranger—but evidently with constraint and hesitation as to whether he was to be housed for the night. After a little conversation she returned to the parlour, where evidently she held a colloquy with her husband on the subject of their visitor. At length, after a good deal apparently of negotiation on the part of the old lady, Shairp was allowed to remain for the night. Before he retired to rest, his considerate friend, the gudewife, came to him with a tumbler of whisky-toddy in her hand, which she proffered to him with the words, ' Ye'll be nane the waur of a cheerer after your lang day on the muirs.' The ' cheerer ' was very gratefully accepted—so he acknowledged. Next morning the secret of the old gentleman's antipathy and apparent lack of hospitality was revealed. It appeared that some months before, a stranger had called at the house under similar circumstances, had given himself out as a friend of ' the Duke's '— the farmer's landlord, the Duke of Buccleuch; had promised his help in getting certain things done on the farm— had, in fact, pledged himself to get them done; had lived well and departed, never more to be heard of—he or his pledges. Hence the virtuous indignation of the honest old

---

[1] See *Glendessary, and other Poems*, p. 201.

gentleman, and his stern resolve to have nothing in the future to do with respectable-looking 'tramps.'

There was another somewhat grotesque incident, which I remember his telling me. One evening, after a long and rugged walk across the wilds of Talla, he reached the herd's house at the foot of Talla Linns, where, as he told me, he had been often hospitably entertained by honest Walter Dalgliesh and his spouse. Thinking, as usual, to find quarters for the night there, he went to the cottage, was admitted, and cordially welcomed by the gudewife. He had had a supper of porridge and milk, had thrown his wet boots off, and was seated comfortably at the kitchen fire, thinking he was finally and restingly housed. About nine o'clock in came the gudeman, who welcomed him, but with a certain restraint. The wife was forthwith called out of the kitchen, and there was some low murmuring talk—ominous for him, Shairp somehow thought. Presently the gudeman returned to the kitchen alone—the wife could not face the matter—and with much bowing and many respectful compliments, managed to tell the guest that the room was preoccupied for that night, as two dykers had come and, according to prearrangement, were to sleep in the bed! The worthy shepherd added, 'I dinna think ye wad like to mak' a third.' Shairp woke up at this from his comfortable resting before the fire, made up his mind to emigrate, pulled on very reluctantly the wet boots, and started for the nearest resting-place, the Crook Inn, six miles away, which he reached somewhere about midnight.

Looking back over an unclouded intimacy of nearly thirty years, many days spent on the hills with my friend recur to me, touched with pleasing yet regretful memories—dear and delightful days, gone never to come again. In his prime Shairp was one of the best men for a hill walk I have known. Undaunted by distance, mist or rain, the purpose of the day, however hard, was almost invariably carried out. And certainly I have not walked with any one whose heart-sympathy with mountain and moor, the varied moods of the heavens—gleam, shadow, even storm—

the simple, free, and wild growths of the great upland solitudes, was so fine, constant, deep as his. And I doubt if
any one since Wordsworth has felt and read their kinship
with human life and feeling so well as he."

In 1879 Principal Shairp contributed a volume on
Burns to Mr. Morley's series of *English Men of Letters.*
This little book has been a good deal misunderstood. It is
not only delightfully written, but its appreciation of Burns
is deep, and as a critical study it is admirable. That Shairp
was not in sympathy with Burns, and was oblivious to some
phases of his genius, has been repeated *ad nauscam;* but he
was only out of sympathy with what in Burns was ignoble
and downward. His appreciation of the genius of the
peasant bard, of his inimitable humour, his rare insight into
character, his force, his tenderness, and matchless lyric grace,
his patriotic ardour, the width of his sympathy, his endless
vitality, and vast complex power, was as keen as was his
recoil from the excesses of passion and the earthward gravitation of Burns. That he remembers that Burns had failings,
and proceeds to point them out, is to his honour as a
moralist. If Burns himself bemoaned the fact that

Thoughtless folly laid him low,

and exhorted all his readers to remember that "self-control is wisdom's root," why should not a critic of the
bard drive the same truth home, with power and incisive force, by plainly speaking of his faults? If Burns
had something in common with *The Jolly Beggars* whom
he so exquisitely describes, and had more sympathy than
his critic with their wild and dissolute ways, it is a poor
rejoinder to say that he was more human ; say rather, less
human—for blindness to faults is not a phase of the " charity
that covers a multitude of sins." It is rather a sign of the
relaxation of moral fibre that would construe all the varying
types of action as mere phenomenal varieties of character,
produced by causes over which the agent has no control,
like the waves that rise and fall on the sea of human con-

duct. Of course there is much to be thankful for in every vindication of human instinct, against unnatural repression, or Puritanical crucifixion (which always determines a re-action the other way); and we must judge Burns leniently, remembering the man with his "passions wild and strong," and remembering the age and his surroundings, as well as the sad fact that he was himself the chief sufferer. Never-theless it is the moralist's duty to indicate the inevitable-ness of the law that man must reap as he sows, and that those laws which govern the hidden world of moral agency are as stable as that of gravitation.

It is by his *Songs* that our "Scottish son of thunder" has outdistanced every other writer—these fifty or sixty songs, that are almost as faultless in lyric form as they are perfect in natural feeling; and no one has written better of these songs than Shairp has done.

In a former chapter we have seen that on the occasion of the Burns centenary Shairp wrote to his friend, Mr. Scott, saying that there was only one man in the world to be put alongside of Burns, and that for his part, being a Scot, he preferred the Scotsman; and all throughout his later estimate it will be seen that the appreciation and the sympathy are stronger than the criticism.

The following is a sample of it:—

"Here was a man, a son of toil, looking out on the world from his cottage, on society low and high and on nature homely or beautiful, with the clearest eye, the most piercing insight, and the warmest heart; touching life at a hundred points, seeing to the core all the sterling worth, nor less the pretence and hollowness of the men he met, the humour, the drollery, the pathos, and the sorrow of human existence; and expressing what he saw, not in the stock phrases of books, but in his own vernacular, the lan-guage of his fireside, with a directness, a force, a vitality that tingled to the finger-tips, and forced the phrases of his peasant dialect into literature, and made them for ever classical. Large sympathy, generous enthusiasm, reckless abandonment, fierce indignation, melting compassion, rare flashes of moral insight, all are there. Everywhere you see the strong intellect made alive, and driven home to the mark, by the fervid heart behind it. And if the sight of the world's inequalities, and some natural repining at his own obscure lot, mingled from the beginning, as has been said, ' some bitternesses of earthly spleen and passion with the workings of his inspiration, and if these in the end ate deep into the great heart they had long tormented,' who that has not known his experience may venture too strongly to condemn him ? "[1]

What finer estimate of Burns have we than is contained in the preceding paragraph ?

To an old friend, Mr. John Boyle, he wrote after the book appeared : " It was in many ways the most difficult piece of work I have had to do. The closer I came to his life, the more unsatisfactory it became. What to say or think of the whole man is very hard to say. One thing I was sure of, that in Scotland he has been made far too much an idol of, and that to the middle and lower orders that over-admiration has done harm, coarsened their natures, and lowered their tone. Therefore I tried to speak the truth, and to be just yet charitable. I do not want to be sympathetic with the coarseness and immorality that stained his whole life, and in some degree his works. At the same time I come behind no one in admiration of his marvellous power and gifts, though I think he often misused them."

After the publication of the *Burns*, Professor Lushington wrote to his old pupil and friend from Maidstone, referring to a criticism of the book which had appeared in *The Academy*—

" It may be an open question whether a devoted admirer of Wordsworth may or may not be to some extent less likely to appreciate all of Burns as his enthusiastic admirers do. But could any sincere admirer of poetry

---

[1] *Burns*, pp. 192, 193.

(whether Burns or Wordsworth) speak of W——'s doing nothing better than writing some didactic lines against intemperance, etc., when there are the two poems ' I strive,' and ' We fail,' which are amongst the grandest testimonies to Burns's greatness—breathing such tender sympathy, and humble, loving grief for him ?   I cannot help thinking that if Burns could tell us now, he would rather have had these two poems to his memory than anything that ever Carlyle has written in praise of him. . . . And to speak of W—— W—— being incompetent to judge of a poem occasioned by the French Revolution, as if he had never felt or chanted triumphal strains upon it !"

Of the *Burns* Dr. John Brown wrote—

" It has given me as much pleasure as probably I am now capable of—most excellent, righteous in its judgment, cordial and wise.   The end is most noble and affecting. You have said the right thing and the true, as ' the poor inhabitant below' would himself say ; though his reckless, and to him (in a deep sense) unfair idolaters may say ' No.' It is most skilfully done, and the story is told to the quick. I am sure it will do good, though I feel as if it must have given you often great pain to do it.   There is so much in the wonderful and deplorable being to make one unwilling to detain the mind over his sin and misery, his greatness and his vileness.   I have nowhere seen truer or better writing on him than in the last part : but all is good. . . . I wish you had to do Wordsworth.   *There* there would be little let or hindrance, and no disgust.   What a shame printing all that trash, and worse, which Burns on his death-bed deplored he had ever written, or said, or done."

Lord Coleridge wrote : " I am delighted with Burns. I think I trace a little of the unwilling Minerva in parts of it, and certainly he is not savoury upon the whole.   But you have conveyed the impression of his terrible failings and coarsenesses ; while you have done full justice to his glorious genius, and to his great power of intellect.   This

last I had not properly estimated till I read your book.
What a vigorous, clever fellow he was, quite apart from his
undying lyrics! I think he might well have been promoted,
and he *was* badly treated. . . . You have done a good book,
old fellow, and one which will live."

Shairp's correspondence with his friends at this time was
various and interesting. To Lord Coleridge, who had just
enlarged his Devonshire home—Heath's Court, at Ottery
St. Mary—he sent some Scotch firs to be planted on a
small eminence in the grounds. Lord Coleridge wrote :
" They shall crown my little hill here, and they shall be
called ' The Principal's Grove'; and, as far as I can, my
descendants shall know of a friendship which I am proud
of, and (more than that) which I humbly thank God for."
    And there they now stand, on the wooded knoll over-
looking the railway to Ottery, an interesting memorial in a
most interesting place, of one who never saw them there
himself.

To Lord Coleridge Shairp wrote the three following letters
in 1879 and 1880 :—

"CUIL-ALUINN, ABERFELDY, 29*th July* 1879.

" How much I should like to make out the visit you have
so often proposed to your Devonshire home! ' But we are
bound by heavy laws,' so many things there are that keep
me fast to my small spot of earth. Still I do not give up
hope of making it out. Yet the time passes. To-morrow
I complete the threescore years. Clearly the autumn of
life has come, and all things wear now for me an autumnal
look. If any more years of strength are given, I would
that they were used to better purpose than the past have
been. . . .
    I am glad you, on the whole, like the *Burns*. It was
done in many parts, *invita Minerva*. The contrast between what is best and really lovable in his poetry, in the
spirit of many of his letters, and the tenor of his manhood,

was so painful to me. I have suppressed, as far as I could,
all the grosser details. . . . The Scotch prints much abuse
me for it. Prig, Prude, Pharisee, are the words they apply.
This, however, only makes me feel the more that it was
necessary that the truth should be told and not blinked.
A difficult question remains, How far, for the purpose of
Art, it is allowable or even desirable to dramatise what is
coarse and impure. Burns's *Jolly Beggars* is no doubt a
wonderful stroke of genius, showing what dramatic power
lay in him, but I dislike it for its impurity, and don't wish
to train myself to like it. Consider this question, about what
is morally allowable to the dramatic faculty—How far and
in what way it may legitimately represent the baser sides
of human nature? I don't see my way about it. When
you have time or inclination, please give me your thought
on this. . . ."

"*9th September* 1879.

". . . Lately I met two old friends of ours on the banks of
the Tay, in the Carse of Gowrie, A. P. S —— and H. P ——,
both very charming companions to spend a day or two with in
a pleasant country-house. Wonderful, is it not, to see Pearson
as he is! Stanley told me of your intention of putting up
a bust of S. T. C—— in the Abbey. He seemed much pleased
with the thought. Having got W. W—— there, I hope his
friend will be placed as near him as possible. I have not
seen Matt's Book of Selections yet, but greatly enjoyed his
essay on W —— in *Macmillan*. All he said was so true, so
penetrating, laying his finger 'there and there' with that
peculiar diagnostic power of his, yet patronising W. W——
all the while, with that sublime condescension! I greatly
enjoyed it; from one thing alone I am disposed to dissent
—the confining all his excellent things between 1798-1808.
I know as well as any one the peculiar charm of his best
things of that period—the ethereal touch that belonged to
that springtime of his genius and which never returned.
But I hold, and I think you do, that his later period, even
up to thirty or thirty-six, produced things that one would

not part with for anything, and that, though the early charm
was over, there came a mature, mellow wisdom, as of a ripe
autumn, which has a charm of its own. . . ."

" August 1880.

". . . About this time of year I begin to bethink me of
my Oxford lectures. I am just trying to put down something on what I call the prophetic character of poets, as
distinguished from their merely artistic. By this I mean
their gift of seeing some new aspects of nature, or character,
or life, not hitherto perceived, and bringing it home to
people's hearts. The sense in which they are discoverers,
and enlarge the range of thought and sentiment open to their
fellow-men. In this sense, Scott and Wordsworth were
both prophets of our time. They had truths, the one about
the past, and human history, the other about the outer world
and the deep things of man and his destiny, to communicate,
by which they benefited their kind as really, though in a
much higher way than James Watt or Arkwright or Stephen-
son. Then, perhaps, I may go on to show in another region
how imagination is fitted to be our best teacher.

I mean in religious matters or things beyond both sense
and intellect. It is quite clear that the dry intellect can do
nothing for us in that region. Hence the ruthlessness of
Dogmatics. All that can be done for us is by adumbrations
of those things which conscience and the spirit feel after.
Hence, perhaps, it was that our Lord taught by parables as
the only possible means of conveying truly to us what may
be known of the super-sensible order. But I need not
enlarge on this. *Si quid novisti . . . candidus imperti."*

To Dr. Clerk at Kilmalie he wrote the following five
letters on Highland poetry :—

" CUIL-ALUINN, ABERFELDY, 18*th August.*

" MY DEAR CLERK—I am minded, if so be, to give one
lecture, may be more, at Oxford, on Highland poetry. Not

only is it that at this season, with the heather in bloom, I cannot fix my mind on the more bookish subjects—Virgil, Sophocles, and Co.—but besides, I find that one always does best, and most interests other people, when one writes of a subject full of interest to oneself.

Now though I am growing old, and these interests are fading from me, yet I have spent so much time on them in the past, that I feel it due to the Highlands, and my own past, not to let my tenure of the Oxford Chair pass without saying some word on the Highland bards.

Ossian I don't intend to touch, but rather the more modern men, Ian Lorn, Alastir Macdonald, and above all, him whom I know and love best, my own Donach Ban, the Burns of the Highlands—Burns, but without his earthliness. . . . Remember it is not a laborious history, or antiquarian investigation of these men I intend, but a bright, interesting sketch, touching only their more picturesque points, and giving a few extracts from their very best things. . . . I feel it due to all those summer wanderings by Lochiel, Moidart, and Arisaig to make something of it. . . .

I must begin this side the Reformation, with a mere allusion to the great Ossianic background, out of which all modern song has come. Of Donach Ban's poems, besides 'Ben Doran' and the 'Farewell to the Bens,' and to 'Mary Oig,' is there any other specially characteristic of him, or specially fine ? . . .—Yours most sincerely,

J. C. SHAIRP."

Again—

" CUIL-ALUINN, 1st September 1879.

" MY DEAR CLERK— . . . As to my lectures, I am getting on with the first, of which I may send you the rough draft, if you can make allowance for it when *very rough*, as I always block out my first outline. Then I rewrite, compress, arrange, and try to polish in the second draft. I agree with you that the great Ossianic background that lies behind all Highland poetry must be noted. On the other

hand, I cannot enter into the interminable jungle of the
Ossianic controversy and M'Pherson's doings. I shall just
refer those who care for those things to my paper in *Macmillan*, June 1871. But I should like to show that, even
leaving M'Pherson out of account, there remains a great
quarry of Ossianic stuff, and to give a few fragments as
specimens. . . .

Remember it is not antiquarian discussion I wish for
my Oxford audience—they won't listen to that—but *the most
veritable and yet telling results of such investigation.* . . .—
Ever yours,   J. C. SHAIRP."

"CUIL-ALUINN, *Wednesday*, 3*d September.*

" MY DEAR CLERK—My first lecture on the general capa-
bilities of the Highlands for poetry, on the way Celtic
feeling has in modern times filtered into English poetry,
and on the Ossianic poetry with some of its characteristic
features—all this is so far roughly blocked out. . . .
But I should like a few of the most characteristic passages
to quote, three or four, part from your translation, part
from the Highland Society's Report, on some non-
M'Phersonised Ossianic poetry. A piece about a battle
that is good; also one or two pieces giving the peculiar
Ossianic wail or sadness. These are what I want for the
first lecture. For the second, on Post-Ossianic poetry, am
I to quote any of the old Bards, or ' The Owl,' or any of
these early poems ? or shall I give 'The Lament of M'Gregor
of Ross,' as translated by myself ? This must have been as
old as the Reformation.

Then of the regular bards in Mackenzie's *Beauties*,
I want *a short* characteristic piece from Mary Macleod,
translated into good prose by you.

Then ditto from Ian Lorn.

Ditto from Macdonald. These two last must both be
Jacobite pieces.

The second half of the second lecture will be all devoted to Donach Ban.

But I feel that I have material for four instead of two lectures; however, I must try to cram it all into two. . . . Mackenzie's Introduction is vague and unsatisfactory. Many thanks for Paterson. His prose is always valuable, and more or less to the point; but his verse translations are very vague, limp, and wanting in the pith and finish of which the English is capable. . . .—Yours very sincerely,

J. C. SHAIRP."

"CUIL-ALUINN, *6th September.*

"MY DEAR CLERK— . . . You will observe that I have given nearly half the lecture to the scenery, history, etc., of the Highlands, and their influence on English literature. Perhaps this may be disproportionately long. But one must pave a way between the Sassenach mind and Donach Ban, the Burns of the Gael. . . . —Ever yours very sincerely, J. C. SHAIRP."

"CUIL-ALUINN, *27th September.*

"MY DEAR CLERK—Thank you for your remarks on the lecture. You are quite right. The historical part shall be greatly shortened, and the Ossian part enlarged. . . .

My aim will be to put before an audience, who know nothing of Gaelic poetry or its spirit, some of the more salient and attractive features of it. I feel it due to the Highlands and to my long converse with them to do this in the south. . . ."

The two following letters from Dr. John Brown to Principal Shairp, are both interesting in themselves, and in their bearing on the work which Shairp was doing in the Oxford Chair :—

[Postmark, *21st September* 1880.]

"GLEN HILL, NEAR ABERDEEN.

"MY DEAR FRIEND . . . —Why set poets for ever against each other? There is one glory of the sun, and another glory of the moon, and one star differeth from another star, not only in the quantity but also in the quality of its glory. What you wrote in 1864 was felt by me to be true, and what Coleridge in his *Biographia Literaria* true also. To me Wordsworth's great defect is his want of the sense of the ludicrous, of the incongruous—of humour. I feel this more than his prosiness : but that he was a great poet, the greatest of our century, I never doubt. His is the poetry of intellect and of feeling — of humanity in the abstract chiefly; and yet what more human than *The Old Cumberland Beggar ?*

Byron when he is a poet—which very often he is not, though always eloquent — is the poet of passion, of the ' heart tumult '; but he would have been a greater poet had he had the deep feeling, the quiet, steady, human-heartedness of Wordsworth. . . .

Do you hear anything of Sellar ? Read *Don Quixote* slowly—tastingly—it is a wonderful performance for humour, and pathos too ; and in the Spanish, and to a Spaniard, must be as delicious as a ripe peach.

Do you remember what Sir H. Taylor says of Byron, in his Preface to Philip van Artewelde ?—' Byron's men and women are passions personified ; Shakespeare's are men and women impassioned.' If you have not lately read that Preface, read it ; his notions on poetry are good as far as they go—very. . . .—Ever affectionately,   J. B."

[Postmark, 1881.]

" . . . As for Chaucer, in his own line he is primary. In description he is an inspired child, finding himself in the *juventus mundi,* and getting the first crush of the grapes. It is a pity there is so much animalism here and there ; though, in a sense, of a not so unwholesome kind in him ; but it is not suited to our time. *The Wife of Bath* is worse than *The Jolly Beggars*—though full of nature and freshness. . . . *The Knight's Tale* is exquisite, ' Up rose the Sun and up rose Emily ' and *Griselda* is fine. ' She never was idle but when she slept.' I think I am quoting it wrong, but that is the sense. . . . Do you know Lowell's (the American) poems? If not, get them. He is out of sight the greatest poet our cousins have yet sent forth, both in reach of thought and feeling, and humour, and in general felicity of language, and spontaneity. Whittier comes nearest him, Longfellow is a sort of male Mrs. Hemans. But get Lowell, and study him. His *Biglow Papers* will disquiet your fine old Tory soul, but they are full of wit and wisdom and freshness of nature.

How glorious Ben Lawers will be looking from your home, especially if he has those delicate mists clinging to his shoulders, and entangling the sunlight."

Again, December 29, 1881: He (Lowell) is a true and nearly a great poet—far their greatest in depth and breadth."

Shairp's Oxford Lectures were published in 1881, under the title *Aspects of Poetry*. On receiving this volume, Cardinal Newman wrote to the author—

" BIRMINGHAM, 25*th November* 1881.

" DEAR PRINCIPAL SHAIRP—Your welcome letter and present have just come, and I thank you sincerely for both, and for the far more than kind chapter about me with which your volume concludes. But it makes me feel very much ashamed, and I do not know how to bear it, from the feeling that it is so far above what I deserve. Yet I cannot but thank God for having put it into your heart to speak so affectionately of me, however partially I can accept your critical judgments.

I wished to have talked with you in Trinity Hall more than I did, from the gratitude towards you (which I have also felt towards Lord Coleridge), for former similar kindnesses, but one cannot always speak because one wishes. And I did not do justice to myself in what I sent to you about Wordsworth. Hurrell Froude somewhat prejudiced me against him, as if he was egotistical, which he thought destructive of all true poetic genius; but no one can delight

in his odes and occasional pieces more than I do, and I
shall read what you say of him in your present volume, as
in a former, with the certainty of rising from it with a fuller
sense of his greatness as a poet.—Most truly yours,

JOHN H. CARD. NEWMAN."

No one in reading these lectures now will fail to see the
range of Shairp's knowledge of poetry, and the width of
his appreciation of it. His delight in the poetic work of
writers from whom, on other grounds, he recoiled, was not
only genuine, but it was often thrilling. I have heard him
repeat passages from the lyrics of Shelley, and the songs of
Burns, his voice tremulous with emotion, and his whole
frame moved by the utterance of them, in that self-forgetful
enthusiasm and pure appreciation which only poets feel.
And he seemed at times to dwell with special delight, to
linger over and repeat to himself, the most inspired passages
of these authors, with whom in their less exalted moods he
had little sympathy, or none at all.

On the publication of the *Aspects of Poetry*, Lord Coleridge wrote to him in November 1881—

" I am simply delighted and fascinated with it. Unless
I am quite mistaken, it will raise and help you where you
are, which at our time of life, and in the position which you
have reached, is perhaps the highest thing one can say.
Not to advance is said (and I think in youth is truly said)
to. be to go back; but in age, not to go back is really to
advance. I am specially struck with the Scott, the Shelley,
the Yarrows, and the White Doe. I think the latter has
never had its meed of praise. You have chosen the very
same passage which I chose years ago to read at Exeter, as
a specimen of Wordsworth's exquisite diction, when he chose
to lay himself out for it; and I remember saying the opening of *The White Doe* was as fine in metre as Jonson, or
Gray, or Shelley, or S. T. C ——, our four greatest metrists,
unless Herrick may claim a place amongst them."

Again, a year afterwards—

"Now then, like Iago, to be critical, Why do you speak so contemptuously of Callimachus ? In his hexameters there are some very fine passages, though he is not even at his best in them. But his elegiacs are very fine. I do not know a finer, *grander* piece of poetry than that which tells the kindness of Tiresias, in the Laværum Palladis, and the epigrams are lovely. The one on the death of a man called Heraclitus is quite perfect. Why do you give in to the German depreciation of Euripides ?—the favourite of antiquity, the favourite of almost every great man and poet from his own time till Schegel made the very wonderful discovery that he was not Sophocles, and therefore was not to be admired. Surely Ion, Medea, Alcestis, Hippolytus, have as much purity and loftiness and self-denial as any pre-Christian creations in the world. The Prometheus stands alone and inaccessible, but after that I do not think that either Sophocles or Æschylus rose to the heights of Euripides ; and think of the life of Sophocles compared with the austerity and nobleness of Euripides !"

In 1881 Shairp contributed an article to the *Princeton Review* on "The Reasonableness of Faith," a paper full of interest and beauty, but scarcely convincing to those who do not already agree with it. That "probability is the guide of life," and that in all ordinary affairs we dispense with logical facts, may be admitted, but we do not act, if we are wise, without *evidence*, and it is the evidential element that is, or ought to be, to rational men, the ground of action.

Several short papers, articles, and addresses were written by Shairp—of less permanent interest than his longer Essays and Lectures—but in all of which there are some things of more than passing value, *e.g.* his estimate of Professor Ferrier in the "Introductory Notice" which Mr. Lushington prefixed to Ferrier's *Lectures on Greek Philosophy*, his notice of another colleague—Professor Bell—in one of the lectures with which he opened the winter session of the United College, and of the Rev. Edwin Wallace, of Worcester College, Oxford

—a former pupil at St. Andrews, and the author of an important work on the philosophy of Aristotle, in a similar address in a subsequent year, his estimate of Dr. Park, St. Andrews, prefixed to a volume of his *Songs*, and his lecture on Canon Mozley, afterwards printed in *Frazer's Magazine.*

In 1867, he delivered an address at the opening of the session of the United College, in Principal Forbes's absence, on the characteristic features of the Scottish University System, as distinguished from that of England—an address well worthy of reproduction. In 1869 his address as Principal referred mainly to his predecessor in office. In 1871 he dealt chiefly with the study of History, and the importance of the subject in a University curriculum of study. In the same year he opened the winter course of lectures at the Literary Institute of Dunfermline by an address on "What books to read, and how to read them." In beginning the session of 1874 at St. Andrews, he dealt with the contrast between the physical and the moral interpretation of the Universe and Life. In 1875 he gave the history of the movement in reference to Chairs of Education in the Scottish Universities, and dealt with the work which a professor of Education might take up, and with the state of secondary education in Scotland at the time.

These addresses—and that which he gave to the School-masters' Educational Association at Edinburgh in 1878—might well be reproduced in a volume of posthumous essays.

In the year 1881, he was startled—as many others in Britain, America, and the Continent were—by the sudden death of his old-and dear friend, Arthur Stanley, the Dean of Westminster. He expressed his feelings thus in a letter to Mrs. Drummond at Megginch, where Stanley used so often to be seen and to be heard at his very best—

"ORMSARY, ARDRISHAIG, ARGYLESHIRE, 21*st July.*

" DEAR MRS. DRUMMOND—I need hardly say to you how this dreadful blow has stunned me; and yet you will allow me the relief of saying it. It was not till Monday last that we knew anything of his illness; then that startling extract from the Bishop of Manchester's sermon; then a telegraph from T. Walrond, with rather more hope; then on Tuesday morning the fatal tidings! It is all so dreadfully sudden; no loss could have come in all England that would have been so profound a sorrow to so many hearts. I do not speak of the public calamity, nor do I venture to say what he has been to you all—his relations on either side. It is as a friend, the friend of forty years, that I mourn him—the most faithful and unchanging, the most generous and noble-hearted of men; ever vivid, ever gentle, ever delightful! And what I feel, how many more are now feeling? And to every one of these his friends he had a place of his own in their hearts, which must now remain empty while they live.

To me it seems as if a darkness had fallen over all England, and that I never can return to it again with the same feelings now that he is no longer there. Even in Scotland I had visited so many of its scenes with him— scenes which he for the first time brightened into life—and now I shall not care to look on them, nor think of them again. All their interest seems gone with him. Do you remember that dim morning (Saturday, 5th March) when I last left the Deanery, and the passage from Carlyle [1] he read aloud, while I was hastening through breakfast? That passage now sounds as a presage of his own quick coming fate.

I have no doubt you were with him during these last days, and some day perhaps I may hear something of them from you. Had I been at all within reach I should have gone to the funeral. From this great distance, where we are on a long-planned visit, I could scarcely make it out. There will be enough without me, and my heart will be in the Abbey that day as much as if I were bodily present there. . . .

I think the memory of him will be a bond while they live to all who knew and loved him.—Believe me, yours very sincerely,   J. C. SHAIRP."

[1] See the *Aspects of Poetry*, Paper VII.

Two other letters to Mrs. Drummond may follow this one, though they belong to later years. The Dean of Westminster had left to the United College at St. Andrews his memorials of the East, brought with him from Egypt, Palestine, and Syria in the winter of 1852-53, when he visited these lands with Theodore Walrond and others. It is to. this that the first letter refers.

" STATION HOTEL,
" OBAN, 20th *August.*

" MY DEAR MRS. DRUMMOND—It was only last night, on our return here from wandering in Skye, that I got your letter from the Deanery, dated 10th August. The memorials of the dear Dean,[1] which you mention, will be very precious to me ; though no one will ever again make such good use of them as he did.

The collection of curiosities which he has left to the Museum at St. Andrews had better be sent addressed to me—' Care of Mr. Hodge, Janitor, the United College, St. Andrews.'

When I return thither I shall see them properly arranged and placed in the Museum, in the way which I think the Dean would have liked. In our wanderings among these western shores and islands I have seen many things which made me wish I had visited them with him ; as I know how they would have interested him, and what light he would have thrown upon them. Two things especially—the Castle of Dunvegan, in Skye, and two very old Pictish forts, as they are called, in Glenelg. These two last are on the property which will belong to Lady Francis's eldest son. I should like to interest him in their preservation, and in other things in those remote and romantic glens. . . . —Yours sincerely,

J. C. SHAIRP."

" ST. ANDREWS, FIFE,
" 17th *December* 1883.

" MY DEAR MRS. DRUMMOND— . . . Nothing I have heard for long has given such joy as Walrond's announce-

---

[1] His inkstands.

ment that he is to do the Life.[1] . . . He of all men now
living is most bound by 'natural piety' to A. P. S., and
therefore most fit to represent him to the world.   You may
trust his judgment absolutely as to what should be said or
not said, inserted or withheld.   He has asked me to do a
chapter—'Autumns in Scotland.'

I will gladly do my best; but if I do, shall need much
help from your own and your daughter's memories, and his
journals and letters when there. . . . —Believe me, yours
sincerely,   J. C. SHAIRP."

An interest, doubly melancholy, attaches to this last
letter.   Principal Shairp did not live to write, what no one
could have written better, the chapter for Stanley's Life
which he proposed to call " Autumns in Scotland," while
Mr. Walrond did not live to do more than collect materials
for the Life of the Dean.   While he was occupied with the
latter task I asked him to send me for this book some
brief memorial notice of Shairp.   He agreed to do so, and
sent me something; but, on a sudden, he too was removed,
and a most admirable life cut short in its prime.   In July
last his widow wrote : " It will perhaps interest you to
know that during his illness my husband gave me a short
sketch of his early school and college companions whose
friendship and intercourse had been of use to him ; and the
name most frequently and affectionately mentioned was that
of Principal Shairp."

In 1882 Shairp contributed two papers to *Fraser's
Magazine* on " St. Andrews, the Earliest Scottish University."
These have been republished in the posthumous volume of
Sketches in History and Poetry, edited by Professor Veitch ;
and although much had been written before about the University and its City (and possibly some things remain to be
written still), we have nothing better, and nothing half so
picturesque in its delineation, than the sketch which the
Principal has given us, in those seventy pages, into which he
has condensed the story of his University.

[1] Of Dean Stanley.

A sentence in one of these articles is referred to in some pages which Bishop Wordsworth has written of our common friend. The Bishop knew the Principal personally only during the last ten years of his life; and, although he had no official relations with him in St. Andrews, he met him frequently in the ordinary intercourse of social life. His words are significant:—

". . . In all matters that appeared to him, either as a literary man or as a man of practical energy, to require reform, he exercised an influence for good which was, I believe, universally felt and acknowledged.

He had, to a remarkable extent, the courage of his opinions. For instance, though a truly genuine and patriotic Scot, in the highest sense of the word, his partiality to his native land did not render him blind to what he considered defects in the character of his countrymen; and what he saw amiss he was too honest not to reprove. I remember what first attracted my notice and attention towards him, before I had made his personal acquaintance, was a newspaper report of a lecture delivered by him in Edinburgh—I forget the title, but I think it might be described as 'Lights and Shades in Scottish Character.' And he certainly did not spare the shades. For instance, he denounced, in very homely fashion, the far too general want of cleanliness - in the lower classes; the neglect of mothers in allowing their children to play about in the gutters of the streets, or to lie upon the pavement, in a way not to be seen in England—a fact which, I confess, had struck me when I first came into this country. But he also went deeper, and mentioned as an unlovely trait of character (a trait which required at once insight to detect and courage to expose to an audience of his fellow-countrymen) that Scotsmen, in their closeness and want of geniality, when they know of something to the praise of a friend, which it would give him pleasure to hear, do not care to tell him of it. In like manner, in an article which appeared many years after in *Fraser's Magazine* (June 1882), he gave the following

gloomy, but only too just, representation of the eventful
period in the history of this country from 1560 to 1690—
that is, from the Reformation to the Revolution : ' In this
century and a half of turbulence and disorder, when Super-
intendency, Tulchan Bishops, Melville Presbytery, Spottis-
woode Episcopacy, the Covenant, Restored Episcopacy, and
Moderate or Non-Covenanting Presbytery were jostling each
other; when the whole kingdom was full of quarrelling,
fighting, plotting, convulsions, reactions, and counter-revolu-
tions, the calm pursuit of knowledge was impossible.' In
these, and such like instances, his object, I believe, was
simply to do good ; to perform his part as an upright citizen,
as a lover of his country, which, because he loved it, he was
not only bound but anxious to endeavour to improve. He
had no taste for mere fault-finding ; no inclination to depre-
ciate ; no petty jealousies or animosities to indulge. His
pleasure would have been always to praise, and he wished
to be able always to do so with honest truth. Though a
Conservative, he was not one of those who think that what
has been, however faulty, must continue to be, merely because it is Scotch ; because, not without large admixture of
good, it lies, as it were, embedded in the history of his
native land. At the same time he admirably represented the

Justum et tenacem propositi virum,

whom nothing could have moved from what he believed to
be right.

His monograph upon Keble is well known. It has been
pronounced by competent judges to surpass every other
attempt which has been made to form a just estimate, from
a literary point of view, of that singularly good and gifted
man. The fact is, that John Campbell Shairp had much
of a lay John Keble in his own character and gifts. It
was this that led me to think that an edition of *The Christian Year*, with notes by him, in the form of a running
elucidatory comment, which, in many parts, the work greatly
needs, would have been a literary boon of the highest value,
especially for younger readers ; and I made the suggestion

to him more than once. But his modesty, I believe, more
than anything else, prevented him from undertaking it;
much in the same spirit as my uncle, the poet, once said
to me: 'I should like to have written upon Christian
subjects as Keble has done, but I have felt that it would
have been unbecoming in me as a layman to attempt
to do so.' In his series of Ecclesiastical Sonnets he had
gone as far in that direction as he could properly and safely
venture.

In regard to his ecclesiastical position, which I ought
not perhaps to leave altogether unnoticed, although Principal Shairp did not see his way to relinquish Presbyterianism, which he had imbibed with his mother's milk, and which
was deservedly endeared to him through many holy associations, yet, in his later conversations with me, he made no
secret of his dissatisfaction with it; and practically he
seemed to wish to bridge over in his own person the separation between the two communions by attending the service
of the College Church in the morning, and that of our
Episcopal Church not unfrequently in the afternoon. At the
same time, his grasp of essential principles was so firm and
strong that he could afford, better than most men, to sit
loose to ecclesiastical forms and systems in the regulation
of his own conduct, at a time when the doctrine of visible
unity has become so grievously obscured, and the practice
of it, as a rule of life for the generality of Christians, may
be said to be almost non-existent."

Professor Lewis Campbell's reminiscences of his friend
and colleague took the form of a letter to Mr. Campbell
Shairp, from which I make the following extracts. They
refer chiefly to the years of close intercourse and of common work at St. Andrews. Professor Campbell's concluding
remarks in explanation of what many misunderstood in Shairp
—viz. his reaction from Philosophy, as due to a preference
for " a synthesis however vague, to an analysis which gives
emphasis to negation "— are admirable. No one else has
put the case so well.

Mr. Campbell refers to "the severity of self-discipline with which a spirit whose chief native bent was to 'feed on thoughts that voluntary move harmonious numbers' would lay the humblest duties upon itself. The value of his work and influence as a teacher seemed, indeed, to arise partly from the unusual combination in him of educational experience with a temper the very reverse of pedantic. The observation of his fellow-students at Glasgow had awakened in him a profound sympathy for the wants and struggles of the student (especially the Highland student[1]), while Oxford and Rugby had shown him the value of a closer discipline than has often been found possible in our northern colleges. He therefore grudged no time spent over the crudest exercise, and at the end of an hour might be seen at his desk surrounded by weak Latinists receiving elementary criticisms, as if he had been the merest pedagogue. Yet a few minutes earlier he might have been heard discoursing eloquently on the essential beauties of the highest poetry, or translating Virgil in a style of noble elevation and simplicity. His influence over ingenuous youth was not, I believe, the less strong and permanent because in his endeavour to polish he sometimes cut against the grain. At least I have known instances (and there must be more than I know) in which the momentary resentment roused by some rebuke has been transformed into lifelong veneration. The very ardour of his hopes for the improvement of the higher education in Scotland made more trying to him the comparative rudeness and poverty of our actual state. And this weighed on him the more heavily because of his deep interest in the religious condition of Scotland. In the thoughtless boorishness of some rough student his mind's eye foresaw the *driech* unprofitableness of the future minister. In the prevalence of mere 'bread studies' he would lament the want of 'light.' He would sometimes complain that men left college as uncultured as they came to it. Such flaws and starts of disappointment are the inevitable lot of those who strive earnestly to actualise any

---

[1] Their lack of wholesome recreation was especially felt by him.

spiritual ideal. I rejoice to think that in this respect his spirit had found some satisfaction before the close.

One grave disappointment there was, which must not be passed over,—the failure of the College Hall. When I came to St. Andrews in 1863 things seemed to bid fair for the successful realisation of what appeared to be a felicitous enterprise. To graft something of the English tutorial system on the life of a Scottish University, to create a miniature college with a ' little *Temple* ' at the head of it, to induce parents who now sent their sons to Rugby or Winchester to avail themselves of equally good means of education nearer home,—this attempt, originating, I believe, with your father, and most energetically seconded by Principal Forbes, had much to recommend it at first sight. And it did actually provide an opportunity, for which those who enjoyed it in the years I now refer to are still most grateful. Could arrangements have been made for continuing the first warden, I think it possible (although the inherent difficulties of the task were very great) that the Hall might be even now alive and flourishing. As it was, clouds rose after a fair opening of the day, and the institution which he had reared and tended was threatened with decay. Few things in your father's life are more characteristic than the resoluteness with which he determined and the firmness with which he executed the resolve, that the College Hall should not die a lingering death. Either it should live to serve high ends, or it should be no more.

Other purposes for which he strove, the University Education of Teachers, University Extension to Dundee, the foundation of inter-University scholarships, have either been attained, or are being actively promoted by others. Perhaps of all his efforts for the good of St. Andrews, the foundation of the Guthrie Scholarship through his mediation has been the most fruitful in results.

I have just spoken of your father's resoluteness in action. There was another occasion on which this quality was shown. This was when, at the request of a majority of the College, his services were continued in the Latin Chair after he had given notice of an intention to resign it. All the circumstances are present to me now, but none more vividly than the almost solemn way in which he expressed the principle which guided him in acting at that difficult juncture, by repeating the words ' *Salus reipublicæ summa lex.*'

I have thought sometimes that for his own immediate usefulness he had too lofty a scorn of 'popularity.' Yet but for the persistent loyalty to a practical ideal which was the motive of that scorn, but for the manly perseverance with which, through rough and smooth, through evil and good report, he fought against what hindered or endangered that high aim, I do not know where our little University might be to-day. The spirit of the years I have been reviewing, of which he bore the burden and the heat, may be summed up in the words—

> For this was all thy care
> To stand approved in sight of God, though worlds
> Judged thee perverse.

.   .   .   .

There was another feature of his intellectual life that was sometimes liable to misconception. In the religious controversies which arose after his first youth his sympathies leant practically towards what may be roughly termed the ' orthodox side.' This sometimes caused surprise to those who remembered the joyous eagerness with which at Oxford he had entered on the path of speculative thought. But it would be a mistake to refer this reaction in his case to intellectual narrowness. It had a deeper source. His jealousy of the *Aufklärung* was but a result of the 'old quarrel of poetry with philosophy.' Imagination fused together past and present in an unbroken whole, which criticism seemed to threaten with dissolution. At any moment when to think clearly and to feel deeply appear as opposite terms of an antinomy, the heart of the religious poet prefers a synthesis, however vague, to an analysis which almost inevitably gives undue emphasis to negation, and thus interferes with the sense of that which is ' more deeply interfused.' In some such way I would seek to explain an attitude, which was sometimes difficult to understand, and differed at different times with changing circumstances, at - one time clinging pertinaciously to Presbyterian tradition, at another cherishing the echoes of a wider Christendom and a more distant past, but remaining constant to the main lines of ethical and religious thought which he set forth in writing on the 'Moral Dynamic' and on 'Religion and Culture.' I would add that in this and all respects his views of men and things appeared to me latterly to have been greatly softened and mellowed by the eye that had 'kept watch o'er man's mortality' and by 'the years that bring the philosophic mind.' . . ."

The way in which Principal Shairp impressed strangers, and how, with sympathetic natures, acquaintanceship soon became intimacy, and intimacy ripened into friendship, has a good illustration in the following letter from the Rev. H. D. Rawnsley, of Crosthwaite Vicarage, Keswick :—

"It was at the dinner-table of —— at St. Andrews that I first saw a man for whom a very short intercourse inspired me with affectionate reverence and regard. He looked sad, and was very silent for a time. A good story was told ; he seemed to wake from a sorrowful dream, and was a changed being. For the rest of that evening he was merriest of the merry, and I remember saying that he had the humour of Ruskin, and the fun and sallies of wit with which in old Oxford days the Slade Professor made his breakfast-table so delightful to his undergraduate friends.

Next day I called at his invitation, and before five minutes of general conversation had passed Principal Shairp was deep in reminiscences of the Lake country, and in talk about its Poetry.

What struck me was the absence of worldliness in the man ; his simplicity and straightforwardness in the expression of his real self ; his transparent candour.

. . . Here was a man, gray-headed, but with the heart of a child, who knew that the child's heart beats in every human breast, and who dared to speak openly of what that heart felt, to a younger man, whose sole claim for confidence was summed up in the fact that he was a fellow-student of Wordsworth, and a lover of and resident at the English Lakes.

I remember feeling a confidence in that serenely simple ingenuous soul as it appeared to me, and that confidence was never shaken.

A few letters passed between us, and one I well remember. A railway was threatening to invade Borrowdale, and a Slate Company was intending to destroy, in the best interests of its shareholders, not only Honister Crag, but the quiet and beauty of the shores of Derwentwater. Some of us were up in arms, and one of the fiercest bits of invective against the modern shortsight of commercial utilitarianism came to me from Principal Shairp's pen. It opened a new door into his character for me. Patriotism and poetic fervour and prophetic warning burned within his words. Prophet and poet he surely was, but first he was true patriot.

A year or two after, I chanced to be wandering down the High Street at Oxford, when, with his Scotch plaid wrapped around him, the kindly Professor of Poetry touched me on the shoulder, and bade me turn into his room at University College. He was to deliver a lecture on some aspect of Wordsworth's poetry on the morrow, and he wanted to read it over and talk about it. . . . ' I want the young men,' he said, ' to turn with all their Christian armour upon them and find wellsprings of faith and comfort in the poems of one who has marvellously helped me from my youth up until now.' Such or some such words were his. . . .

He read his lecture with great earnestness and constant pause. Sometimes I felt he was perhaps a little impatient of the views he combated, a little unable to allow

> That light divine
> In other forms and lines may shine,

and yet be light; but the humility of the Professor of Poetry struck me. He seemed to feel that he was only at the beginning, and not at the end of life and the knowable; and I came away from the earnest talk in the quiet little room in

University College, with the thought of the gracious mellow-
ness and docility of a good life and gentle thought, which
has grown upon me since the day that

> By Argyle's inland solitudes forlorn,
> God's finger touched him and he slept.

The last talk I had with him was at St. Andrews,
where, after some affectionate words about Dean Stanley
and Ruskin, and what England and Scotland owed them, he
went off into a glowing description of Highland scenery.
Told me about his father's home, and then spoke of Yarrow.
Specially did he speak of the flowers that grew upon the
Scotch braes, and the glory of being alone by a Scotch
burn. But of his own song as inspired by these sights and
sounds he never uttered a word. You could not know
from his own lips that on him too had fallen

> The light that never was on sea or land,
> The consecration and the poet's dream.

High thinker, true singer, he has gone, and we are the
poorer by his sleep ; and though nothing can bring back
the hour of happy communion with a spirit so pure, so
generous, so sincere,

> We will grieve not, rather find
> Strength in what remains behind,
> In the primal sympathy
> Which having been must ever be."

Amongst the interests of Shairp's later years in St.
Andrews mention must be made of the large amount of
philanthropic work he used to carry on—little known to his
friends and colleagues, to the students, or to the community
generally—but, though silent and unostentatious, most fruitful of good. He realised in practice as well as theory what
his great poet used to call

> That best portion of a good man's life—
> His little, nameless, unremembered acts
> Of kindness and of love.

As Dr. Rodger, the minister of the College Church, said, in

2 c

the sermon he preached on the first Sunday of the University session after his death : "If you were to go to-day into many a poor room in St. Andrews, you would be told how he had carried delicacies to the sick, and had read to the aged, and had knelt beside the dying."

Special mention should also be made of his interest in the Memorial Cottage Hospital in St. Andrews. The women's wards in this hospital were opened in 1865 by the children and friends of Lady William Douglas of Grangemuir, a relative of Mrs. Shairp. The men's wards were opened in 1880 in memory of John Adamson, M.D., and Oswald Home Bell, M.D., Professor of Medicine in St. Andrews, the physician-friend of the Principal. Shairp was president of the committee of management from the formation of the hospital. "Along with Mrs. Shairp," says Dr. Cleghorn (in his general report for 1886), "he took a most active part in founding the hospital. He was a generous contributor, and by personal kindness to the inmates ever manifested a deep interest in the welfare and prosperity of the institution." In the notice *in memoriam* in the twentieth annual report of the hospital it is said, "Than Principal Shairp the institution had no truer friend—Sunday after Sunday, during the months of the year which he spent in St. Andrews, he visited it, reading and praying with the sick inmates ; did this humbly and lovingly, and with no sense of superior knowledge or learning. He valued most highly the work which the hospital does, and used often to say how much he did so. At every critical juncture in its history, and whenever wise judgment was called for, he was both willing and able to give it."

One of the most interesting letters in reference to Principal Shairp is the following from Cardinal Newman. It was originally a private letter ; and in consenting to its publication now, the Cardinal asks me to add that nothing in it is to be taken as implying that he considers that there is any other refuge for the spirits of men than the Church to which he now belongs :—

" 7th January 1887.

" Neither my fingers nor my eyesight allow me to express in writing the debt of gratitude which I owe to the late Principal Shairp for the kindness with which he has so many times spoken of me in his publications, nor the deep sorrow with which I heard of his death. My hitherto un- fulfilled wish to comply with your request on this point has been a trouble day after day, amid my existing engage- ments, but it could not be helped. I am too old to be able to do a thing because I wish it.

But passing by my personal feelings, I lament the Principal's loss to us on a more serious account. In this day of religious indifference and unbelief, it has been long my hope and comfort to think, that a silent and secret process is going on in the hearts of many, which, though it may not reach its limit and scope in this generation or the next, is a definite work of Divine Providence, in pros- pect of a state of Religion such as the world has never yet seen; issuing not indeed in a Millennium, but in a Public Opinion strong enough for the vigorous spread and exalta- tion, and thereby the influence and prosperity of Divine Truth all over the world. The world may not in the Divine Decrees last long enough for a work so elaborate and multi- form ; so without indulging in such great conceptions, one can fancy such a return to primitive truth to be vouchsafed to particular countries which at present are divided and broken up into a hundred sects, all at war with each other.

I am too tired to go on, and I ought not to have begun what I cannot finish, especially since I have not brought home what I have been saying to the subject of Principal Shairp.   J. H. Card. Newman."

The duties of the Chancellor of a Scottish University do not bring him frequently within its precincts, but the Principal has often to correspond with him on official matters, and at St. Andrews the Chancellor and the Prin- cipals were personal friends. Reference has already been

made to Shairp's visits to Inverary, and after his death the
Duke of Argyll wrote thus—

"INVERARY, 16*th August* 1887.

"I can only say of Principal Shairp that of all the men
I have ever known with extraordinary personal charm, he
stands among the very first. It was impossible to have
any converse with him without loving him. It was indeed
a 'loyal nature and a noble mind'—most refined, most
sympathetic, most catholic, in the best sense of that much-
abused word. I felt that a light was gone out when I heard
of his death."

The Duke's eldest son, the Marquis of Lorne—who was
a student in the United College—writes—

"St. Andrews was fortunate in the men she possessed in her
University when John Campbell Shairp was a Professor there.
Honoured as were the names of Forbes, Ferrier, and Sellar, it
is doing their memory in this place no injustice to say that
a feeling akin to love attached itself especially among the
students to Shairp. His nature had in it much of what the
Americans call 'magnetic' power, the power that through
sympathy attracts and interests. There was indeed no phase
of human feeling that he could not understand. In his
kindly blue eye and open brow there was a look of gentle ab-
straction of mind. . . . For his was a soul full of poetry, and
of the love of mountain and wood and sky and sea, and
ever ready to speak of these. Nor was it only the picture
of these things which memory retained, and liked to think
of. The human interests connected with each scene, the
historic pageant contained in the past actions of the people's
life, was what he loved to contemplate. If his face ever
assumed a stern look, it was when thinking of some act of
cruelty or even of want of consideration for the lowly.
Nor was this gentleness, and delight in dwelling on
the distant, too engrossing to distract him from the work
that lay to his hand. The strong fair eyebrows gave
a sagacious look to his face—a look which told that

he was well able to take his part in present controversies, and to influence the conduct of those whom he
taught, and whose respect and affection he never failed to
win. He would turn from the pages of some book containing Scottish poetry, and illustrated by Scottish art, to
discourse with fine judgment on the politics of the day,
on the work of his profession, or on thorny theological
questions; and to praise those he admired in the arena of
action, with the same earnestness and charm with which
he had been pointing out the glories of literature and art.
None of open heart and mind were not the better of intercourse with him. He left with all a desire to have a record
such as his, as devoid of guile, and as devoted to all that is
of good report, and worthy of a Scottish gentleman."

Principal Shairp took a great interest in Lord Selborne's
election by the students as Rector of the University, and
Lord Selborne writes of him thus—

" 30 Portland Place, W.,
" 21st *March* 1887.

". . . He always attracted me, by the candour and
gentleness of his disposition, combined with a high degree
of intellectual power, chastened and tempered by reverence
and sympathy for all that was true and good, and by a very
loving spirit. He was at once a sound and discriminating,
and a very sympathetic critic—qualities which (my own
experience tells me) it is difficult to combine as he did;
for I feel that, when I am most discriminating, I am
least sympathetic; and when I am most sympathetic, least
discriminating. It was not so, however, with him."

CHAPTER XVI

THE pressure of various interests and cares, and the nervous strain which occasional worries superinduced, began to tell upon a constitution more than usually robust, five years before the close of his life. In many of his letters after 1880 there are pathetic allusions which give hint of his foresight of the end. To one he wrote of the death of a friend, and said, " The shadows are lengthening ; may we be faithful till the end comes." Meeting another old lifelong friend, he said, " A few more such meetings, and then—the kirkyard." He had left the house in which this Memoir has been written—which had been his home since 1866—in May 1880, and spent the rest of that summer in Edinburgh,. where his son was studying law. His last house in St. Andrews was in Murray Park, where many a pleasant evening was spent in the society of congenial friends, and where—as well as at Cuil-aluinn—his last literary work was done.

In 1882 he greatly enjoyed an autumn visit at Cuil-aluinn from Professor Lushington, his old teacher in the University of Glasgow ; and in the same autumn he took Dr. Butler, then Headmaster of Harrow, to Killiecrankie, and, as Dr. Butler says, " reverently showed me every stage of the battle, and the spot where Claverhouse fell." Just as another friend writes of a journey from Oban round Cruachan, when " he told us all the legends, stories, histories—one hardly knew which—he made them all so real."

Two papers in *Fraser's Magazine* on " The Earliest

Scottish University," since republished in his volume of
posthumous essays, and a sketch of his old Balliol tutor—
afterwards his colleague at Rugby and lifelong friend,
Archbishop Tait—were amongst his latest bits of work.

This last character-study which Shairp wrote has not
yet been published, but it will appear in the forthcoming
Memoir of the Archbishop. He goes back to the Edinburgh
Academy days, and traces, in his appreciative way, his own
experience of his friend in the subsequent stages of his life
—as a scholar and tutor at Oxford, as Headmaster at Rugby,
as Dean of Carlisle, and as occupant of the sees of London and
of Canterbury. It would be unfair, however, to anticipate
any of the interest of that Life, by giving extracts from
Shairp's paper here, although the Dean of Windsor, who is
writing the Memoir, has generously allowed me to do so.

An account of the last years and of the closing days of
the Principal's life has been written by Mrs. Shairp, and
from her letter I make the following extracts, in the form
in which she desires it :—

" MY DEAR PROFESSOR KNIGHT—When my husband's
friends have written their various recollections of him so
fully and freely, I must not shrink from the pain of giving
you the details of the last days.

In looking back to the last few years of his life, I feel
that the failure in bodily health and vigour began in 1880.
Then it was that the wear and strain which comes to so
many men's lives in these days, from within and from without, began to tell on him. We were all at Oxford and in
London in June of that year, and he saw Sir Andrew Clarke,
who told him that he must be careful of his health, and
give up long walks or climbing hills.

The beginning of the end dates from the first weeks of
December 1884. I remember only too well his looks on
entering his own house late in the evening of the 6th of
December, on his return from Edinburgh after attending Sir
Alexander Grant's funeral on the previous day. In his
Journal he writes : ' *Monday, 1st December.*—Startled by the

announcement of the sudden death of Sir Alexander Grant; only became ill on Monday morning at 2 A.M.—apoplexy. "Be ye also ready."' In the evening for some time wrote memoranda of A. C. Tait, for his son-in-law.

He was at this time much interested and occupied in getting subscriptions from old friends for a copy of Richmond's picture of Archbishop Tait for Balliol Hall, and this last work for one of his best and oldest friends had a happy issue in Richmond executing the copy himself. On his return journey from Edinburgh on 6th December he got a chill, but this did not prevent his going to the Holy Communion at the College Church on 7th December according to his habitual practice when in St. Andrews.

On Friday, the 30th of January, the day of Lord Reay's installation as Rector of the University, he was unable to be present officially as Principal.

When sufficiently well to leave St. Andrews for our intended visit to the Riviera, he went to Houstoun, and after a happy reposeful week—the last but one in his earliest home —we travelled to York, stayed all night at the Residence, with Canon and Mrs. Baillie. He spent an hour in the Minster with great interest. That afternoon to London; rested, then across to Paris, and by easy stages to San Remo, where we arrived on the 11th of April.

Our few weeks there proved a time of peace, repose, and blessed sunshine, though not one free from anxiety. We turned our eyes and thoughts to Florence, and found ourselves there on the 13th May. He writes in his Journal: '*Ascension Day.*—Drove straight to the Duomo. The first sight of the Duomo and Giotto's Tower, an impression never to be forgotten. A great celebration going on within; the inside not at all equal to the outside; but two things impressed me, first, some of the grand old Catholic chants sung under the dome, and next, Michael Angelo's Dead Christ behind the altar; never beheld anything in marble like it.'

And again he writes: '16*th May.*—A lovely morning. At eleven drove out and up to the Via de Colli to the " Place

Michael Angelo," looking over Florence, perhaps the finest
view I have ever seen. Florence at our feet flowed through
by Arno in full flood, Fiesole Hill beyond and to the right
and east, the Apennine ranges white with snow, westward
high hills, running down from the Apennines to the Western
Sea—all fresh and green in the spring sunshine.' To him
our fortnight was one of daily and intense interest. And at
San Marco : ' 18*th May.*—Spent nearly two hours there most
delightedly, looking at the exquisite Fra Angelicos, and at
the cell and relics of Savonarola.'

Left Florence on the 27th of May, and travelled by
way of Bologna and Milan to Varesi. We left beautiful
Varesi 5th of June on our way homewards. 'Drove for
nearly three hours a delightful route or road through the hills
to Luino ; passed Madonna della Monte, with its many
chapels on the crag. Then through glens walled from the
sun and shaded with beautiful Spanish chestnuts, walnuts,
and acacias in white flower. . . .' And we hastened on
by the St. Gothard and its wonderful railway—after a night
at Luino, and a passing glimpse of Lago Maggiore—to
Lucerne, 6th June, leaving on the 8th by Basle and Amiens.
A beautiful cathedral certainly, but an ungenial air ! The
first plunge back into gray skies and chilliness from sunshine and light airs.

' We crossed the silver streak,' he writes, ' and travelled
gladsomely through Kent with Mr. and Mrs. Stirling of
Kippendavie, reaching London on the 10th of June.' On
Friday the 19th, till 22d, we ran down to Salisbury to visit
his old friend the Dean and Mrs. Boyle. Back to Edinburgh, and on the 26th the last visit (how little we know
when last things are to come !) to his dear old home Houstoun ; six days there ; then Cuil-aluinn, 2d July, the last
home-coming. ' Arrived at Cuil-aluinn about seven o'clock.
Evening very fine, the outlook to Ben Lawers calm and
soothingly beautiful.'

' *Sunday* 12*th.*—Refreshed my memory of Keble's poem
for the 6th Sunday after Trinity.'

' 21*st.*—Warm weather begun. Such views of Schiehallion, eastward to Ben-y-Gloe, and the Athol hills from Lochnacraig. Tea by the loch.'

'*Sunday, 26th.*—I read J. H. N.'s wonderful sermon, "The greatness and littleness of human life." '

'*28th July.*—Another warm day. At 6 P.M. drove down to call at Edradynate. Delightful evening and pleasant east wind—the first pleasant east I ever knew; lights along the braes so lovely made us more than ever regret our leaving.'

'*30th July, Thursday.*—My sixty-sixth birthday. Makes one serious to think of—only a few more there can be even at longest. Have written numberless letters to-day. . . . And so have passed like a dream our four quiet pleasant weeks here, and so will all life be when it comes to an end.'

We then went to St. Andrews.

'*Sunday, 9th August.*—Wet morning at home. Read the services and J. H. N. on "The thought of God the stay of the soul." In the evening George M'Donald preached at the College Church a very earnest impressive sermon to a crowded audience, "If ye know these things, happy are ye if ye do them." ' And I remember that next day he called on us. They had of late met at Bordighera.

At St. Andrews one day the east wind struck him in the College Green. A few days after there came quite unexpectedly an invitation to Ormsary from our young friend, Farquhar Campbell. On Tuesday, 1st September, his Journal entry is as follows : 'Warm sun, but cold east wind, from which I hope to find a refuge at Ormsary.' We reached Ormsary 3d of September in the afternoon, travelling from Greenock by steamer to Ardrishaig, and driving thence to Ormsary—a long but beautiful drive. Shortly before leaving St. Andrews he had repeated his favourite lines—

> And stepping westward seemed to be
> A kind of heavenly destiny ;

and there was relief to us all in the feeling that we had left the east far behind us. The weather, so bad when we started, brightened on our way from Greenock. Ever since his first visit to Ormsary in the autumn of 1881, and the friendship then formed with the late Mrs. Campbell, he had loved the place.

The following is from his Journal of 1884 :—

'ORMSARY, 23*d August* 1884.—After breakfast Campbell,[1] Maitland, and I went to the hill.   I walked with them as far as Loch-na-Torrin ; about twelve o'clock saw Eilan More, over Knapp,—so lovely.   Lunched near the loch, then left the shooters to go on, and returned.   From the heights again, such views over Knapp and Eilan More and Jura—Eilan More looking so pale and visionary, such deep blue and lilac colouring, and then the sun-gleams breaking out of a shadowy sky, and travelling over the sea to light up the shores of Islay.'

'29*th August* 1884.—A fine fresh breeze.   Farquhar, Emily Campbell, Mr. and Mrs. M——, and I left in the yacht at a quarter to one o'clock ; cast anchor in Keills Loch at half-past two.   For full an hour and a half Farquhar, Emily, and I explored the famous cross, and the old roofless chapel with its sculptured gravestones.   Then to the ridge above— such a view !   The cross and the old chapel in all the " imploring beauty of decay," below it the blue slip of Loch Eilan Dana—in such variety of colours ; then across Loch Swein to grand old Castle Swein in its woods on the farther shore.   I know no view that for variety of feeling it calls up can equal it.   Started again at five o'clock, got briskly out of the loch, then a dead calm, and we lay for full an hour opposite Carraignan Dainibh ; a brief breeze took us through the strait between Eilan More and Coreilan ; much and heavy rain returning and going—such lights over Jura and the islands ; dark rain-clouds, so purple-black yet dashed with white sunshine.   Ashore at Ormsary 8.30 P.M.'

Returning to 1885 and September—

' I shall not attempt long expeditions this time,' he said, ' but just take the near walks.'

On the 5th he went out down to the shore and sat

[1] His son.

there, and next day (Sunday) was by the shore with his son, while the family went to church. He had felt faint before luncheon, and when his friends returned from church he talked with interest for awhile about Highland matters and crofters with the minister of the parish. He felt ill again while talking, and a sudden pain came on in his left side, and he went to his room. The boat was sent across the loch to Ellary where Dr. Jefferson of Leamington was on a visit—regular medical aid being distant at Ardrishaig. Everything that care and forethought could do was done by the loving household at Ormsary, and by Mrs. Tarratt of Ellary.

On the 10th Dr. Grainger Stewart came, in consequence of Dr. Jefferson's wish for more advice, and his visit did not bring much comfort, but confirmed the fear that lung and heart were much affected. He said to Dr. Grainger Stewart, ' I have wished to be acquainted with you e'er this, but it is now in the end of the day.'

Then followed a week of alternating hopes and fears, much sleeplessness and some painful suffering. That suffering was borne with unmurmuring patience. ' Tell him I have been wonderfully supported,' was his message to his brother-in-law. His last day on earth was Thursday, the 17th September. That morning his pulse was very low. It was a beautiful autumn afternoon, and a wonderful sunset time—the lights across the loch and away to Jura. He woke up and said, ' Get the Prayer-Book quickly and read me the Collect, Epistle, and Gospel for Sunday.' Our friend, Miss M—— C——, fetched the book and opened it at the 22d Sunday after Trinity, and was turning the page to the right place, when he put his hand hurriedly on the page before her and said, ' Read these quickly.' So she did not wait to find the Collect for the 15th Sunday, but read as desired. · When she came to the words in the Epistle, ' And this I pray,' etc., he folded his hands together, and repeated the words after her, but in such a low voice that it seemed only a movement of his mouth. At the end of the Epistle M—— asked if he was tired—' No ; please go on ;' so she read the Gospel ; then with shut eyes he said some words, impossible

to catch except *one* word, ' support '—that she caught clearly,
and then a beautiful smile. He now asked for the blind
to be drawn up. He sat up in bed, and said, 'My eyes are
dim, but I shall see light clearer soon.' The blind was
then drawn down again, as the window was so near his bed
—it remained down till I came in from breathing the air.
On my telling him of the lovely evening, and again raising
the blind that he might see what I had been looking at
from that side of the house, he gazed from his bed towards
it and said, ' I know it all.' Then, as before, he spoke in
a quick and hurried way, ' Get me *The Christian Year;* read
the one for the 16th Sunday after Trinity.' It was read
close beside him by the fading evening light, from the first
lines 'Wish not, dear friends, my pain away' down to the last.
How terribly true it felt ; but had we known it was our last
evening, could we have got through it at all ? Rather later
his son and I each took a hand, and had a little chat with
him, to cheer him as we thought, and to try to cheer ourselves ! poor selves and blind ! His strength seemed to
revive during the evening, and he spoke in a clear tone.
After ten o'clock came our usual evening prayer, and it was
ended with the words, ' Lighten our darkness, we beseech
Thee, O Lord.' So often had that been his concluding
prayer in his own evening worship with his family. At
11 P.M. he said, ' Let not the faintest whisper be heard,'
that he might get to sleep, but he did not. About one
o'clock he was asked to turn on his side, which he did, and
quietly lay on it—no symptom alarmed any one, when
suddenly came two loud startling breathings. They were
his last. It was syncope of the heart. . . . We left
Ormsary on Monday 21st, taking him with us to Houstoun.
He was carried to the room where he was born. . . . God's
will be ours, now and for ever. He was with us to uphold
us.—Believe me, yours very sincerely, ELIZA SHAIRP."

One who was at Ormsary wrote thus to a friend at Oxford—
"I remember his saying on his arrival, 'This air is balm
to me.' Ill as we all thought him, I do not think he was

apprehensive on his own account.   He was happy and contented with everything around him.   I remember how easily and with what geniality he joined in the talk of those assembled round the dinner-table in the evenings; they were chiefly young people.   I recall how, without losing anything of its brightness, the conversation seemed to take a higher tone.   Unconsciously, I think we all brought him of our best.   Indeed, who could be with him without being, or at least wishing to be, better than we were !

A visit he had made in the spring of that year to Florence had been a source of great pleasure to him, and he often spoke of it.   'If you have never visited Florence,' he said to one of our party, 'do so by all means.   It is an education to any one who is awake.'   On those last days I cannot do more than touch.   For himself, he was to the end just what we had always known him, and there seemed a fitness that when that end came it should be 'in the dear hopeful west.'"

The funeral was from the old House of Houstoun to the family vault within the Parish Church, on a day of still autumn sunshine.

"Last Thursday," said Dr. Rodger in his funeral sermon, " I followed his mortal remains to their last resting-place at his ancestral home.   It was a bright autumn day, and the sunshine which fell on harvest-fields and tinted woods spoke not of the darkness of the tomb, but of the light beyond."

It is a quaint old church, and in the family vault there is a marble tablet in the west wall to this effect—

> " In this Aisle
> beneath the stone which
> bears his name
> lies
> JOHN CAMPBELL SHAIRP,
> third son of Norman Shairp
> and E. Binning Campbell his wife,
> Born at Houstoun, 30th July 1819,
> Died at Ormsary, Argyll, 18th Sept. 1885.
> This tablet is placed here
> by his three sisters
> in loving remembrance."

The inscription on the stone over the grave is to the following effect :—

"In Christ shall all be made alive."

"In most loving Remembrance of
JOHN CAMPBELL SHAIRP, LL.D.,
16 years Principal of the United
College, St. Andrews, and 8
years Professor of Poetry
in the University of Oxford,
this stone is placed by his
widow and their son."

"One family we dwell in Him."

On the east wall of the aisle there are tablets in memory of the Principal's grandfather, Thomas Shairp, of his brother Norman, who was in the navy, and of his three sisters, Anabella, Mary, and Christian.

On the south wall there is a tablet in memory of his father and of his mother; and for the north wall there is one to Sir Stephen Shairp.

The following stanza closes one of Shairp's poems called *The Blue Bells :*—

In your old haunts, O happy blue bells!
Ye, when we are gone, shall wave,   .
And as living we have loved you,
Dead, one service would we crave,
Come, and in the west winds swinging,
Prank the sward that folds our grave.

And there last season they were to be seen, gathered by loving hands, and placed in reverent and affectionate memory over the spot where he reposes.

The following letter in reference to the Oxford Chair of Poetry was dictated at Ormsary on the night of Sunday, the 12th September 1885 :—

"ORMSARY, ARDRISHAIG.

"MY DEAR VICE-CHANCELLOR—I have now held the Professorship of Poetry at Oxford for eight years, and if things had so suited had hoped to have continued to hold it to the end, but during the last year I have received warnings which seem to show me it is time to demit.

Last winter, owing to severe bronchial affection, I was not able to fulfil my duties to the University at Lent or Easter term. I shall never forget the kindness with which, acting on behalf of the University, you made this easy for me. I had hoped to have returned to my duties in October with renewed strength, but I have lately been made to feel that this is not to be reckoned upon.

I therefore thought it right, both to the University and myself, to place in your hands my resignation of a position which has been to me a source of continual gratification, and I hope not wholly without profit to some of the younger members of the University."

In December of the same year a proposal was brought before the College of which he had been Principal, to raise a fund to erect some memorial of his connection with it. The following circular was issued to friends throughout the country :—

" *Memorial to John Campbell Shairp.*

" DEAR SIR—It has occurred to some friends of the late Principal Shairp, that a memorial of his long and intimate connection with the University of St. Andrews, and especially with the United College, might be most appropriately placed within the chapel of Saint Salvator's College, where he habitually worshipped.

The stained-glass windows in that chapel have been placed there in memory of Dr. Chalmers, Principal John Hunter, and other distinguished men associated with the University of St. Andrews, while the canopies of the Professors' Stalls were erected as a memorial of Principal James D. Forbes, by his own bequest. One window still remains undecorated, and Principal Shairp frequently expressed his desire to have the blank supplied.

On this ground, and because of the deep interest which he took in the College services, and in the religious life of the students, it is now proposed that a Memorial Window should be placed in the Chapel, with an inscription to perpetuate his memory, and that at the same time, should sufficient funds be available, a portrait of him by some good artist should be put in the Hall of the College. A committee of the United College has been appointed to take the necessary steps for carrying this proposal into effect."

One hundred and seventy-nine persons responded to this appeal, and the sum of more than £460 was raised.

After much consultation the Committee selected a design for the memorial window, by Mr. Henry Holiday, A.R.A. It was executed by Messrs. James Powell and Son, of Whitefriars Glass Works, London, and placed in the College Church in December 1886.

The following is Professor Campbell's description of the window: " The subject of the design is taken from the words of Scripture in 2 Peter i. 5-7 : ' Add to your faith, virtue ; and to virtue, knowledge ; and to knowledge, brotherly kindness ; and to brotherly kindness, charity.'

In the central light Faith is represented threading a dark wood. She treads on brambles which break into bloom beneath her feet. Her head is slightly depressed as in meek submission. In the compartment under her is a group of smaller figures,—Stephen before the Sanhedrim. He is looking upwards, at the moment when they ' saw his face as it had been the face of an angel ' (Acts vi. 15).

To the left of Faith, and to the spectator's right, stands Knowledge or Contemplation. She holds a book, but is looking off from it, as if feeding upon thoughts that have a distant range. Under her is St. Paul on Mars Hill, making known the unknown God (Acts xvii.). The locality (Athens) is shown by the Greek sculptures represented. The Stoic, the Epicurean, Dionysius the Areopagite, and the woman named Damaris, are all finely indicated.

To the spectator's left, and to the right of Faith, is

Virtue,—a strong martial figure, like a Christian Pallas, recalling the lines—

> Self-reverence, self-knowledge, self-control,
> .   .   .   to live by law,
> Acting the law we live by without fear,
> And because right is right, to follow right
> Were wisdom in the scorn of consequence.

In the space under Virtue is Brotherly Kindness, in the person of the Good Samaritan. The story is well told—the perspective being so arranged that the retreating figures of the Priest and Levite, intent on their pious preoccupations, are visible along the winding pathway.

In an upper space, under the crown of the arch, is Charity with children at her knees.

The remaining interspaces are filled with decorative foliage, and Gothic canopies surmounted by angels.

Under the principal figures are the words—

VIRTUS.   .   FIDES.   .   SCIENTIA.

Sufficient room has been reserved at the foot for the inscription, which runs as follows:—commencing from the centre—

JOANNI CAMPBELL SHAIRP :
QUI HUIC COLLEGIO PRÆFUIT : MDCCCLXVIII–MDCCCLXXXV.

Great care has been spent on the selection and arrangement of the colours, and the whole effect is rich, yet simple and dignified."

The portrait was kindly undertaken by the late Mr. Robert Herdman, R.S.A., who painted it from memory, with the help of photographs and the suggestions of friends.[1] The following is his own account of it :—

" St. Bernard's, Bruntsfield Crescent,
" Edinburgh, 12*th October* 1886.

" . . . I have wished to represent the Principal mainly in repose, but to suggest the activity of his nature by turning

---

[1] This portrait, which is partly taken from the last photograph by Mr. Marshall Wane, has been recently engraved.

the head a little aside—as though something of interest drew his attention. The expression of countenance which I most sought for, was kindly steadfastness of purpose, and the ideality which seemed to dwell visibly in the eyes and expressive brow ; and I have endeavoured, in the general effect and composition, to suggest the deep rich well-balanced nature of the man.

The three books point to where his special sympathies lay, in literature and thought ; while the robe, hood, and cap sufficiently indicate his academic position. The column behind him may point to classic culture, whilst more obviously the bit of distant open-air nature, floating cloud and misty hilltop, disclose themselves as in peculiar affinity with the poetic side of his character.

All this may look fanciful, and I do not expect, or indeed wish, that it should be apparent to the ordinary spectator ; but it has been under the impulse to express such things that I have worked. If those who knew and valued the man, should find that he is sympathetically recalled to them by the portrait, I may be well satisfied."

In another letter Mr. Herdman says, " I did it mainly because of my strong and early affection for St. Andrews, and the old College, where I passed my youthful days."

This portrait now hangs in the Hall of the United College. On the frame are inscribed the words,

" JOHN CAMPBELL SHAIRP, LL.D.,
Principal of the United College
of St. Salvator and St. Leonard
from 1868 to 1885.
Born 1819 ; died 1885."

Steps were taken to ascertain whether a tablet to his memory should be put up in Rugby Chapel, and it was thought that Mr. Walrond might write an inscription. The proposal was not carried out, but this was simply because it might be supposed that the promoters of it were thinking more of Rugby than of him. They therefore united in the realisation of the other memorials. A window has been recently placed in the Balliol Library—which in his undergraduate days was the College Hall—to commemorate his relation to Oxford. Virgil, Wordsworth, and Scott are the figures represented in that window.

From the numerous letters written to Mrs. Shairp after her husband's death the following extracts may be given.

Professor Lushington, now Lord Rector of the University of Glasgow, wrote—

"LLYADINDUR, NEWBRIDGE-ON-WYE,
"RADNORSHIRE, 25*th* *September* 1885.

" It was a startling shock of pain to me to see the notice of so dear and honoured a friend's removal. From my first year at Glasgow College, where his richly poetical nature first attracted and impressed me, whatever I have seen of him has always strengthened my regard and admiration. I never knew a better or more lovable man, nor a more affectionate and warm-hearted friend. Inspired with the truest and noblest feelings, he was also in a rare degree gifted with a winning frankness and simplicity, which made his expression of them touchingly graceful and beautiful. Sincerity and genuine goodness were manifest in every word and look and tone of his voice. . . . I feel I ought to be grateful for the blessing of having known intimately one whose character was so pure and lofty, so worthy of all esteem and love ; and I will hope that the lasting influence of that intimacy may be helpful and strengthening to me, as it ought to be."

Again, at a later date—

" Whenever we met, I found the same kindly courtesy, joined to earnest sincerity, and a generous tolerance towards dissimilar views ; the same vivid interest in all matters of high import ; freshness and richness of thought, sustained by quick insight, and recognition of whatever was beautiful and true ; the most genial and warm sympathy with all aspects of good, which made his conversations always delightful and inspiring. Whoever saw much of him must have felt his own better nature strengthened, and the more intimately he came to know him the stronger this influence would grow."

The Master of Trinity College, Cambridge, wrote—

"MARSHAM, 24th September 1885.

"The sad news has reached us here, and struck sadness into my heart. There are very few men of whom I have seen so little whom I loved and honoured so much as the noble-hearted Principal. In his looks and in his character there was a Christian chivalry, as well as a genius, which made him one of the purifying and elevating powers of our day. How many young spirits has he turned to lofty thought and feeling ! . . ."

The Master of Balliol wrote from Oxford, 19th September 1885—

"He was a noble-minded and generous man, whom we all loved and respected. It is about forty-five years since I first made his acquaintance, when he came up to Balliol, as Snell Exhibitioner, full of life and joy and happiness, taking a great interest in the place, and in the persons whom he met there. I see him now swinging in a chair, and talking merrily to a knot of undergraduates whom he had gathered round him one summer's evening. I received a great deal of affection and kindness from him, for which I am grateful. . . ."

Mr. Patrick Cumin wrote—

"16 CHESTER SQUARE, 6th October 1885.

"It is now more than forty years since I first knew him, and during all that time I never met a more truly good man, or one who commanded more affection or respect. I never was in his company without feeling a kind of moral elevation, and a desire to be more like him. I cannot help thinking that by this kind of influence he did more good to his generation than it is easy to estimate. . . ."

Rev. Dr. Whyte, Edinburgh, wrote from Strachur, Argyleshire—

". . . We never met without plunging immediately into the world of books, and many were the delightful talks we had. We had many favourite authors in common, and I often thought of the Principal, as I read them. He was an altogether unique man in his combination of learning and culture, refinement and Christian faith. . . ."

His old Rugby friend, Mrs. Bradley, the wife of the Dean of Westminster, wrote—

"*15th October* 1885.

". . . There was always a special tenderness and reverence in our talk of him, and the expression used frequently to arise : 'What a fresh, wholesome, mountain breeze his presence is ! Like nobody else's.' We were so sorry when the vortex of London seemed to deprive us of the enjoyment of seeing him in the old familiar way. . . . Ever since I was a girl I have felt how delightful, and how wholesome, and how loving a friend he was to my husband ; how the singlemindedness, loftiness of ideal, and poetic truthfulness of his nature was an element in our Rugby life, distinctly purifying and elevating. I can recall now his face and voice as he used to stand with his back against the chimneypiece in our Rugby dining-room, whilst we were taking an early breakfast ; walking in from first lesson, so full of some subject that he hardly ever remembered to look round or say good-morning, but would break at once into the middle of whatever occupied his thoughts, as if he had been with these thoughts all along, and must needs take up the thread, and march along there and then. How we used to say, 'Who is there but himself, who could pour out things new and old, of heaven and earth, metaphysics and poetry, as fresh as a mountain stream, after first lesson on a winter morning, and before breakfast ?' These are things we never forget, and that go to enrich one's life. How we did miss all things when he left Rugby! And yet, in after days, one always learned more and more of his lovableness and unique largeness of soul. I used so often, in old days, to think of him, when we were reciting Shelley's ' Lark.' . . ."

Mr. Edward Scott, Rugby, wrote—

"16*th August.*

"I well remember how he used to find fault, though always very gently, with those people who were not content to ' be themselves.' *He* was *himself* to the last, in his intercourse with myself, and with others."

Again—

"I feel the debt which I owe to his friendship to be greater than that laid upon me by any other person. And, what is more, it seemed to me that my obligation increased with every visit, and that it drew within its circle those who are nearest to me as well as myself. In years long past, my mother, and more recently my wife and my children, regarded him with affection, which was based on different grounds from mine, but was not less real, or seemed to arise more naturally."

CHAPTER XVII

THE following paper was written for this Memoir by one of his oldest friends, Lord Coleridge, and one of the " Balliol scholars " celebrated in Shairp's poem :—

"HEATH'S COURT, OTTERY ST. MARY,
"*December* 1887.

" With copious eulogy in prose or rhyme
Graven on the tomb we struggle against Time,
Alas ! how feebly ! but our feelings rise
And still we struggle when a good man dies.

These well-known lines describe in a general way the feeling which oppressed me when I learnt that you desired me to tell you what I could recollect of John Campbell Shairp, especially of his undergraduate days, that what I wrote might be embodied in a book to keep alive his memory if it may be, and tell at least to this generation something of the remarkable man whom we have lost. How difficult, how all but impossible it is to go back nearly fifty years, and give colour and reality to scenes which have faded and become indistinct in the misty distance, and to breathe life into characters who, seen even ' by the habitual light of memory,' are now but the shadows of a confused dream ! I have no contemporary journals or memoranda of any kind to refer to ; I know how lapse of years impairs accuracy, what tricks it plays with recollection and belief ; how assertions as to fact are often made in perfectly good faith, but with absolutely no foundation ; how present feelings and judgments are confounded with the past, so that a narration of events is not so much a narration of what the events actually were, as a record of the impression they make upon us now, and an account of what we wish to believe they were then. There are those living who, if they care to read the following lines, may probably be able to convict me of error and mistake ; and, making at once the confession that they are very likely to be right, I will do my best to recall that time.

A term or two his senior in University standing, I well remember the coming of John Campbell Shairp amongst us at Balliol. You will no doubt have recorded that he was one of that distinguished line of Glasgow Exhibitioners to whom Balliol owes so much of its reputation—a line to which, to mention no others, Lockhart and Christie and Sir William Hamilton and Tait (the Archbishop) and Inglis (the Lord President) belonged. He talked Scotch—at least what seemed so to us Englishmen. He rejoiced in waistcoats of a rainbow brilliancy, which dazzled all our eyes ; he rode well and enthusiastically, pulled up a horse dead-beat in a ploughed field, and leaped a ladder which two men were carrying across High Street, because it obstructed his course up that academic stadium to Quarterman's (I think it was) Stables.

To some of us this sort of thing was just at first startling and even, perhaps, unpleasing. But it soon appeared how much of goodness, of cordial kindness, of high feeling, of true modesty, underlay his slightly rollicking exterior. The unruffled good temper with which he bore a rude remark from one of us as to the silence becoming in a freshman, not only made the utterer ashamed of himself, but laid the foundation of a lifelong friendship. And as he came to be known so was he by us all more and more respected and beloved. We joked about 'old Shairp,' his waistcoats, his enthusiasms, his recitations becoming all but inarticulate from his emotion, his straining to make us feel if we could not comprehend the indefinite (one of us, I remember, christened him the Great Aorist).

We joked, I say, but our jokes had no bitterness in them, nothing but kindliness and good humour on both sides; they drew us closer together and were the subject of many a pleasant recollection in after years. But there was much more than this even at that time in our friend. The intellectual and religious interests prevalent in the place were such as to arouse and satisfy his best powers and instincts — the influences such as were peculiarly fit to mould, strengthen, purify, exalt such a character as his. A few months only before he came to Oxford Wordsworth had received in the theatre an enthusiastic welcome, a cordial, reverent homage which I at least have never seen equalled, and an honour which, although it has no doubt been often given before and since to men unworthy of it, is yet the highest which the University can bestow. Frederick Robertson has recorded that the cheers in the theatre, and the acknowledgment of them by their object, seemed to him out of keeping with the austere simplicity of the poet-sage, and the lofty and unworldly character of his writings. Most of us did not think so then, and on reflection it seems to me that we were right. Wordsworth was at that time at the very height of the fame which he ever achieved in his lifetime; he had got away even from the echoes of Lord Jeffrey's shallow and silly mockery; his renown was fulfilled; and to many of us he was an object of worship, and of an honour 'on this idolatry' which, if it was but the due of him it was paid to, ennobled also those who paid it—

> We who had loved him so, followed him, honoured him,
> Lived in his mild and magnificent eye,
> Learned his great language, caught his clear accents,
> Made him our pattern to live and to die.

But we had small patience then (I will own that I have none now) for the 'critical deductions,' the patronage, the measured praise, the superior censure of men as incapable of seeing his greatness as a blind man of seeing colours, and who were hopelessly unaware that they were the contem-

poraries of one who had changed English poetry, drawn new
tones (how sweet and how deep!) from 'the still sad music
of humanity,' and invested alike the humblest and the
sublimest forms of Nature with fresh splendour and undying beauty.

Looking back to those days and to the Shairp of
that time, it seems strange, but it is most certainly true,
that he, afterwards one of the most powerful, the most
enthusiastic, and withal the most reflective and philosophical of the admirers of Wordsworth, was then but a
half-hearted though respectful student of the great poet.
Remembering what I have heard of the literary storms
which he raised by his book on Burns and his lectures
upon Shelley, it is also strange, but it is also most certainly
true, that in 1840-42 he placed Burns and Shelley upon a
higher level than Wordsworth. He thought they had more
of the divine afflatus, more spontaneity, more 'go' (forgive
the slang), and while he respected and admired Wordsworth,
he revelled in, perhaps he was intoxicated by, the magnificent passion and energy of Burns, and the exquisite
diction, the lovely melody, the magic beauty of Shelley's
verses. Again and again in endless but delightful disputes
did we wage war on one another's views, never convincing
one another at the time, but perhaps each leading the other
to a truer and higher appreciation of his friend's favourites.

There was a society called the Decade in those days
(a Balliol scout, long since gone to his rest, persisted in
embodying the external world's judgment on it by always
calling it the Decayed) which I think did a good deal for
the mental education of those of us who belonged to it—
those of us, at least, who came from public schools where we
were taught to construe, to say by heart, to write verses and
Greek and Latin prose, but where our minds were allowed
to lie fallow and to grow on unclouded by thought in
an atmosphere of severe and healthy unintelligence. Who
has the books of the Decade I do not know, and I cannot
pretend from memory to give a list of its members. But
amongst them Shairp found when he joined it Sir Benjamin

Brodie (the second Baronet), Deans Church and Lake and
Stanley, Bishop Temple, the present Master of Balliol,
Arthur Clough, Matthew Arnold, James Riddell, John
Seymour, I think Lord Lingon, Constantine Prichard,
Theodore Walrond, Canon Butler, and a number more
whose names have faded from a memory decaying, or perhaps, like the club, decayed.   We met in one another's
rooms.   We discussed all things human and divine—we
thought we stripped things to the very bone—we believed
we dragged recondite truths into the light of common day
and subjected them to the scrutiny of what we were pleased
to call our minds.   We fought to the very stumps of our
intellects, and I believe that many of us—I can speak for
one—would gladly admit that many a fruitful seed of knowledge, of taste, of cultivation, was sown on those pleasant
if somewhat pugnacious evenings.   I believe they did
Shairp great good.   They pressed upon him the knowledge
that Scotland was not the world, that Scottish Presbyterianism was not the only form of Christianity which
could fill and sustain the heart and mind of reasonable
men, that other hills besides the Highlands were robed in
the gold and purple of gorse and heather, that other lakes
as clear reflected skies as blue,—that there were worlds of
religious of poetical of philosophical thought, to which he
had been a stranger, but which lay open to his intelligent
and genial inquiry.   At this time he was intensely—he was,
to say the truth, excessively Scottish, and, if one may dare
speak of Scotland as a province, he was provincial.   To the
end of his life he remained intensely Scottish ; but though
prejudices, especially political prejudices, grew upon him, he
could never after his Oxford days be truly described as
narrow-minded.   On few men did Oxford ever exert so distinct and so beneficent an influence.   He lived on intimate
terms with the ablest, but, what was more, with the best
men in the University ; bright days, happy evenings,
hard work, half-jesting but half-serious discussions with
them day after day opened his mind, enlarged his sympathies, kindled his affections, ripened his whole nature.

It was a simple, noble nature, which assimilated all that was good in its surroundings, and from which all that was harsh, illbred, impure, quietly fell away. To the end of his days he generously recognised what Balliol and Oxford had done for him. In more than one letter he has said in terms that he found in his High Church friends something which, though he did not intellectually agree with it, was strangely and specially attractive to his moral nature. I have no gift for reproducing those young men as they were when Shairp lived in their company; but if I had, I should shrink from attempting either to rival or to supplement those beautiful and loving sketches of some of them which Shairp himself made in verses as well known as anything he ever wrote, and destined, I believe, to be as long remembered. That poem shows how he felt towards them; it suggests quite truly how they must have felt towards him— what mutual benefits he and they both gave and took. . . .

But no notice of Shairp—no notice of any Oxford man of that period who took life seriously and gave himself the trouble to think—can omit that great penetrating influence, that waking up of the soul, that revelation of hopes, desires, motives, duties not of this world, not ending here, even if they had here their beginning, which came to us week by week from the pulpit of St. Mary's, and day by day from the writings and the silent presence amongst us of that great man who still survives at Birmingham in venerable age, but with undimmed mental eye and unabated force of genius, a Roman cardinal in title, but the light and guide of multitudes of grateful hearts outside his own communion and beyond the limits of these small islands. No man has described better than Shairp that wonderful preaching, no one has done fuller justice than Shairp to the prose-poetry of Cardinal Newman. I can recollect the beginnings; I followed the gradual, half-reluctant, and doubtful, yet at last hearty and most generous growth of his admiration. Cardinal Newman's was at that time the only really religious teaching to which undergraduates were subject. A lecture on the Thirty-Nine Articles and a terminal address

before the terminal Communion were supposed to supply
them abundantly with any religious guiding they might
need. The tutors, many of them, were not only good men,
but I believe very good men; they only followed the traditions of the place. But the authorities, as in the case of
Wesley so in the case of Newman, altogether objected to
any one else doing what they did not do themselves. In
the rougher days of Wesley they encouraged the pelting of
him, as he went to church, with mud and pebbles. In our
day other means were used: four tutors protested, six
doctors suspended, Hebdomadal Boards censured, deans of
colleges changed the Sunday dinner-hour, so as to make the
hearing of Newman's sermon and a dinner in Hall incom-
patible transactions. This seemed then—it seems now—
miserably small. It failed, of course; such proceedings
always fail. The influence so fought with naturally widened
and strengthened. There was imparted to an attendance at
St. Mary's that slight flavour of insubordination which
rendered such attendance attractive to many, to some at
any rate, who might otherwise have stayed away. In 1839
the afternoon congregation at St. Mary's was, for a small
Oxford parish, undoubtedly large—probably two or three
times the whole population of the parish; but by 1842 it
had become as remarkable a congregation as I should think
was ever gathered together to hear regularly a single
preacher. There was scarcely a man of note in the
University, old or young, to whatever school of thought
he might belong, who did not, during the last two or three
years of Newman's incumbency, habitually attend the service and listen to the sermons. One Dean certainly, who
had changed the time of his College dinner to prevent
others going, constantly went himself; and the outward
interest in the teaching was but one symptom of the deep
and abiding influence which Cardinal Newman exercised
then, and exercises now, over the thoughts and lives of
many men who perhaps never saw him, who certainly never
heard him. Of this Shairp was a very striking instance.
He came under the wand of the enchanter, and never threw

off, or wished to throw off, the spell; to the end of his days there was no one with whose writings he was more familiar; no one who exerted a more poetical influence over his thoughts, his feelings, his whole nature. I do not mean that he ever became in doctrine what is commonly called a High Churchman; Newman taught principles of life and action rather than dogmas, though no doubt he himself drew his principles from what he believed to be dogmatic truths; and so it has happened in a hundred instances, of which Shairp is one, that men who have been unable to follow the Cardinal to his dogmatic conclusions have been penetrated and animated by his religious principles, and have lived their lives and striven to do their duty because of those principles which he was God's instrument to teach them. His loyalty to Cardinal Newman ended only with his life; what kindled it in him and in others I cannot describe without danger of seeming to exaggerate. How it was appreciated I hope the world will learn from your book in the Cardinal's own words.

Whether it was under this influence I know not, but he entertained for a while the thought of taking orders in the Church of England. Several letters passed between us on the subject, but there were obstacles, not necessary to detail, which he was on the whole disinclined to encounter, and, fortunately I think, the project came to nothing. After we left Oxford, although our intercourse by letter was frequent and unbroken, we met, with one or two exceptions, in London only, where Shairp was never quite at home nor at his best, though he enjoyed some of its diversions, especially what he called 'fooling' in Hyde Park. For a time, possibly under Rugby influences, his political opinions were so Liberal as to be what I should call Radical, and they were expressed with characteristic force and vehemence. He soon deflected from what I should call the true faith, but there was nothing bitter in his politics; he could not dislike a Radical if he was a good fellow and behaved like a gentleman; and though I must say that latterly it seemed to me his Toryism became somewhat blind and extreme, yet there were plenty of other topics to discuss on paper or in talk, and I believe that such differences never interposed the lightest cloud between his affections and the objects of it, whatever might be their opinions.

Twice I met him out of London, and I think twice only—once in Edinburgh, once in Iona,—both memorable occasions to me, both places the associations of which drew out many of the most interesting points in Shairp's own character. Holyrood, with its memories of Queen Mary, and Rizzio, and Darnley, and John Knox ; the Castle, the Grass-market, the Parliament House, Arthur's Seat, St. Giles's, the Flodden walls—these things and many others Shairp, with abundant knowledge and keen enthusiasm, displayed to a friend's intelligence, which was at least sufficiently alert to comprehend what he was told, and to see the beauties and feel the interests of Walter Scott's 'own romantic town' when pointed out to him by such a guide. We had, I remember, a most lovely day ; and the view from the top of Arthur's Seat, with him to explain its various points, was something to remember for one's life. Our meeting at Iona was to me more interesting still. We spent the best part of two days there ; we saw as thoroughly as we could that venerable spot ; the collection of ruins, beautiful and strik-ing indeed, grouped together on the side looking towards Mull, consecrated by a thousand memories and associations of profound and tender interest to the Christian, the his-torian, the man of letters ; we wandered all over the little island, and rowed round it in a four-oar, stopping to gather pebbles on St. Columba's beach, and to watch the seals play-ing in the little inlets of bright water between the jagged granite reefs, thrust out into the Atlantic like the jaws of some vast animal, along which, though the day was absol-utely still, the sea rose and fell without a break, with slow sighs of restless and resistless power, suggestive of what the reefs must be in time of wind and storm. All this we enjoyed together. But Shairp was anxious, to an extent which I could not follow, to fix exactly all the spots of St. Columba's landing, his progress across the island, and

where precisely he had placed his rude buildings, every
trace of which it was certain had long since been obliter-
ated by the ruins of the pointed architecture which now
remain. The area containing all the buildings is not, I
suppose, much larger than twice Lincoln's Inn Fields; and
when you stand on the top of the granite boulder, some 100
feet above the sea, and said to be the highest spot in Iona,
you no doubt *must* look upon every inch of ground on
which St. Columba built, and probably stand on the spot
from which he often preached, and from which, it is said,
he last looked upon the settlement which he had founded.
But whether a particular building stood a hundred feet this
way or a hundred feet that; which of two or three little
rills, which find their way into the sea at short distance
from each other, flowed by Columba's hut,—questions such
as these, which seem of very small importance, excited
all the energies of Shairp's investigating powers; and he
was manifestly disappointed that I failed to appreciate the
cogent arguments which a spit of sand or a pool in a rill
afforded in these grave controversies. The evening we
passed in company with a delightful young Scottish clergyman, a school inspector, who maintained, greatly to Shairp's
discomposure, the wisdom and the value of teaching English
in all the Highland schools, and discouraging Gaelic. He
showed how it weighted the young boys and girls in the
race of life to speak and think in a tongue unintelligible to
the great mass of their fellow-countrymen. Shairp grew
eloquent on the duty of keeping up the ancient, noble,
imaginative, poetical language—the language of their ancestors, which had, he said, so marked an effect on the
characters of those who spoke it. The young clergyman, I
remember, very much surprised me by meeting this sort of
argument by the statement that at least in the Islands and
in many parts of the Western Highlands the Gaelic was *not*
old; that it was as much an exotic as English would be
now; that it was, in fact, but about 150 years old, before
which time the people of those parts had all spoken Norse.
I do not know whether the statement was as new to Shairp

as it was to me, still less do I know if it was historically
correct, though I have no reason to doubt it; but I remember being amused to see that for the time at least it silenced
Shairp, and appeared to have much more weight with him
than the practical considerations which had been urged upon
him with so much force.

We went back from Oban to the Trosachs by the Highland Railway, and he made our journey delightful by many
a reminiscence of the Bruce and the Breadalbane Campbells
as we passed this spot or that, never ceasing all the while
to protest against the railway altogether, chiefly because a
very tender passage of his life had been spent at or near
Tyndrum, and that then he had seen eagles and other wild
and noble creatures and sights of Nature which the railway
had banished. We parted (I think) at Stirling, and except
for one or two short visits in London — the last one
when his health was manifestly failing—I never saw him
more.

But he was a man whom no one he honoured with his
friendship could possibly forget. His letters, which, though
not frequent, were yet constant and always full of thought
and striking language; his books, his poetry,—these things
kept alive in his friends' hearts their absent and beloved
companion. Above, however, and beyond all this, was the
character of the man, the man himself; more poetical than
his poetry, more affectionate than his letters; fuller of charm,
weightier in influence, than even his best and ablest writings. Others must estimate his poetry and his criticism,
for me there abides, and will abide while I live and have
my mind, the image of the man himself—his outward
aspect: 'his solemn yet sparkling eyes, his open and
thoughtful forehead, a head of virginal floridness, which
might be distinguished even among gray hairs, and the
traces of meditation and labour,' which Marzoni attributes
to Cardinal Fedingo in the *Prosseni Sposi*—he himself as
simple as a child, open to every tender and generous impulse, high-minded and pure-thoughted, yet full of harmless
fun and playful humour, a steadfast friend, whose life was a

charm to us, and whose death was 'like a disenchantment.'

Sir Charles Dalrymple of Newhailes, Musselburgh,—who said, shortly after Shairp's death, that it was " a great loss to all best causes in Scotland, and far beyond it too,"—writes—

" We had many meetings in London about the different University Bills. . . . The last time we had communication on the subject of a University Bill was in the summer of 1885 (not long before his death), when I happened to be a Lord of the Treasury, and responsible for the moment for Scotch business in Parliament. Principal Shairp greatly lamented the delay in passing a University Bill, and felt sure that, with the appointment of a strong and wise Commission, the difficulties which arose on various grounds would speedily pass away. He often talked to me about Scotch ecclesiastical matters, deploring the movement against the Established Church. I remember his saying : ' We have much to regret at present ; but I am convinced that if the Established Church was gone, we should have an end of that " sweet reasonableness " which, with all our defects, we still have. There would be a regular war of sects, that would make life intolerable. For my own part, I should probably seek peace by attending the Episcopalian service, which I have been familiar with ever since my Oxford days, and I should at least know where I was ; but for most people in Scotland there would be no such escape.' One day I remember, in the lobby of the House of Commons, he was deploring the style of much of our Scotch preaching, and said, ' The effect on me of some of the sermons that I hear in the North and in the South, except perhaps in Edinburgh, is just like buckets of cold water poured down my back.' . . . The freshness and purity of his ideas were always apparent, and he seemed to combine in a high degree the chastened and mature thought of later life with the simplicity and freshness of a much earlier age."

The following reminiscences are by Mrs. Inge of Worcester College, Oxford :—

". . . Our first acquaintance with him was derived from his little essay on Keble in 1866. When all hearts were full of the divine and minstrel who had just been withdrawn from us, and all were trying to utter something not unworthy of him, this witness from 'over the Border,' written, as we were told, by a young Presbyterian, a friend of Dean Stanley's and of Archbishop Tait, came upon us with a strange and sweet surprise. It seemed like an echo of some of the best and noblest teaching of the great 'movement,' and to prove how, apart from controversy, the influence of that movement had prevailed to ennoble, purify, and sanctify minds, that from circumstances were outside the sphere of its direct operation. More than this, the enthusiastic affection for Oxford, the discriminating appreciation of what was best in the Oxford of his own day, which characterised this little brochure, gave it a singular charm, something of the delight which men feel when what they know and love dearly themselves receives a graceful tribute from a disinterested outsider. This delight was hardly diminished by the discovery that the writer had so given his heart to Oxford as to be almost more truly filial in his affection than most of her English-born sons, and that in sympathy of the best kind he was so truly one with English churchmen that it was difficult to remember that any fence existed between his field and ours. His position in this respect is not easy to define, nor perhaps to consider absolutely satisfactory as final; but I think he lived, as much as any man could, in the spirit of Bishop Ken's prayer, to which I am almost sure I once heard him refer : 'O my God, amidst the deplorable divisions of Thy Church, let me never widen its breaches, but give me Catholic charity to all that are baptized in Thy Name, and Catholic communion with all Christians in desire.'

Our first direct intercourse with him was in 1874. His papers on 'The Three Yarrows' and on 'The White Doe of

Rylstone,' which appeared in *Good Words,* were lent to us during my father's last illness, and afforded him very great pleasure. I came into the room just as my mother was finishing the last of these papers, reading aloud. My father's eyes were glistening, and his whole frame thrilled with the delight it gave him. ' I wish I could tell that man how much I thank him !' he said. ' Why shouldn't you ? ' I replied; and accordingly I wrote for him, and sent the letter with a copy of my father's own little poem on Sir Walter Scott. In answer, I received the following reply, which reached me on the very day of my father's death :—

'CUIL-ALUINN,
'ABERFELDY, 2d *July* 1874.

' DEAR MADAM—I cannot tell you with how great plea-sure I received your letter, and read the poem and essay of Archdeacon Churton, which you so kindly sent me. The poem, so mellow with thoughtful beauty, expresses exactly many of my own feelings about Scott. And the essay well vindicates the real friendship that existed between the two great men. I have always felt somewhat indignant at the insertion of that chance remark in Wordsworth's *Life* (vol. ii. p. 444), doing, as I think it does, more injustice and wrong to Wordsworth than to Scott.

As time goes on, and no other poets, at all equal to these great men, arise, the world, I think, must learn to know better how great were the gifts given it in them. Thank you for telling me that Archdeacon Churton likes the things I have written about them. To know that anything of mine could have given recreation to one so honoured and revered as he is, is more than I could have hoped for. Will you say to him how highly I appreciate his good opinion, which might well stimulate me to do anything more I could in the way of interpreting these men to the world ? Often I have had misgivings whether the time given to this might not have been better spent. But from Scott and Words-worth I have from childhood drunk in so much of what was healthful and delightful, that I wished to tell the younger generation what I had found in these poets, and what, I feared, they were neglecting for less wholesome fare. It may, perhaps, interest the Archdeacon to know that I have just edited the Journal of Miss Wordsworth's Scottish Tour, 1803, entire. Had I yet received any copies from the publishers I should have liked to have forwarded one with this letter to the Archdeacon. But they have not arrived yet. — Again thanking you for your most kind letter, I remain, yours sincerely,   J. C. SHAIRP.'

.   .   .   .

When the small volume of my father's poetical remains appeared in 1875, Principal Shairp, at our request, kindly wrote a notice of the book for the *Guardian*, and several letters passed between us and him on this subject. But it was not until our coming to live in Oxford that we had the opportunity, so long desired, of making personal acquaintance with him. In November 1881 his professorial lecture brought him to Oxford, and for the first time he was our guest. I do not think that we found him in any way different from our expectations: his own pen had portrayed him with entire truth; only the charm of his actual presence filled up the outline with life and warmth. What struck us especially was the sense as of 'a finer air' which he brought with him, in which it seemed that all that was true and pure and lovely and of good report in those with whom he conversed came fearlessly forth, elicited by his quick and generous sympathy; and all that was mean, worldly, or self-ish, or, quite as much, all that was flippant or irreverent, instinctively slunk away.

He was much pleased to meet his Oxford friends, especially Archdeacon Palmer, whom he loved for the sake of his most dear friend, James Riddell, as well as for himself. Many old reminiscences rose up between them, and some stories of the old master of Balliol were told with much humour and enjoyment. The story of his admonishing a hunting undergraduate that 'if he wanted to hunt, he might hunt all the Long Vacation!' which was told 'nameless,' brought Principal Shairp to confession. 'I *should* know that story, for I was the undergraduate!'—'Then, Shairp, you must give us the true version.'—'I had *not* been hunting, as it happened, but I had met with some men who had, and I was riding home with them rather late in the afternoon, very near Magdalen Bridge, the master saw us, and I capped him. In the evening he sent for me, and said, "Mr. Shairp, I am sorry to see you have taken to the idle amusement of hunting. If you wish to hunt, you can hunt all the Long Vacation, all over the Highlands of Scotland!"'

The question was raised whether the master knew and meant the joke, or whether he said it in good faith; but Principal Shairp said he was convinced he knew what he was saying. And then he said how the master used to seem to know nothing, and really knew everything.

Another day he met Miss Wordsworth, and was greatly interested about Lady Margaret Hall. We had much talk about the higher education of women, which was an uppermost subject among us just then. I do not think he was so much opposed to innovations as I was then. Only I remember his saying, 'Miss Wordsworth was not brought up at a ladies' college;' and 'the real, highest education is to be brought up under the shadow of a great mind and heart as she was.'

. . . .

He was in St. Mary's when Dean Church preached the University sermon, June 1882, and was deeply impressed by it; it led him to speak of Newman's preaching, and how unlike it was to all modern preaching. Dean Church, he thought, was the only man who even could *remind* him of Newman. Afterwards he wrote, 'I have got the sermon, . . . interesting as all he does is. But there is in it a tone of sadness—I don't say greater sadness than experience warrants; only, as life gets on, one feels more than ever the need of what will hearten and strengthen one.'

He was greatly pleased with Mrs. ——'s saying that she

divided the world into 'people that kindled, and people that didn't! . . .'

He was with us on Sunday, and we had much deeply interesting talk of a graver sort.   We were but beginners at Oxford, and the new statutes were still quite new, and were filling the air with anxious forebodings.   We spoke to him of the article in *The Church Quarterly* for April of this year, 1881, 'Recent Fortunes of the Church in Oxford.' . . . To this conversation he alludes in the following letter, which I received soon after he left us :—

'UNIVERSITY, ST. ANDREWS, N.B.,
'*December* 7, 1881.

'DEAR MRS. INGE—Only last night I reached home after my wanderings, and I now sit down to tell you how plea-sant is my retrospect. . . . Somehow it put me more in mind of the old Oxford that I knew than most of my recent visits there have done.   I feel quite sure that a good work lies before the Provost and you to do within your college and beyond it; and I trust you may be given strength and guidance to do it.   Amid many changes which older Oxon-ians must regret, and perhaps dread, much may be done to strengthen the things which remain.   This will not, I think, be done by minimising the good that still exists.   This was rather the tendency of ——'s paper last spring in *The Church Quarterly*, in which, though it is "an owre true tale," I seemed to see a tendency to over-despondency, and to ignore good work and good men in Oxford because they do not altogether follow his own way.   But perhaps I have said too much.   What more there may be to say, I may, perhaps, another day, have an opportunity of saying to the Provost by word of mouth.'

The following February he came to us again.   On both these visits he allowed me to lay hands on the MS. of his lectures, and to read them to my mother, who greatly enjoyed them. . . . Mother remarked upon some passages in the Lecture

on the Poets of the Seventeenth Century, and ventured to
observe that Henry Vaughan was worth more space than had
been allotted to him. This led to our talking over the *Silex Scin-
tillans* afterwards, and he seemed much pleased to have been
reminded of the little volume. The next year, in May 1883,
he devoted an entire lecture to ' Henry Vaughan, the Silurist';
and this was perhaps one of the most characteristic of his
later lectures. It closes with a beautiful passage, suggested
by the *Retreat* of Vaughan, and the very remarkable resemblance between that poem and Wordsworth's *Intimations of Immortality.* Principal Shairp, however, seizes
upon the one thought—and this the best—which Vaughan
has, and Wordsworth has not. It is this : that ' hereafter,
in the perfected Christian manhood, the child's heart will
reappear—*Of such is the Kingdom of Heaven.* It is a beautiful, and I trust, a true faith, that a day is coming when
the soul shall put off the incrustations it has gathered here,
when we shall regain all that we have lost, and combine the
matured wisdom of the man with all that is lovely in the
child. And so our life is rounded both ways by a childhood,
—the imperfect childhood we pass through here ; the perfect childhood which shall be hereafter.' Some who heard
the lecture will remember how, with the strong emotion
which this thought stirred in him, his voice sank lower and
lower, to a solemnised impassioned whisper, as was always
the case with him when deeply moved, so that the last
words were hardly audible ; then he closed his MS., took off
his glasses, and looked up with cordial pleasure to welcome
the greetings of his friends. One felt that for that soul
there must be very little ' incrustation ' to put off !

But there is another side of his character which ought
not to be omitted. To an optimist in the best sense, as he
was, the pain of giving pain was acute indeed ; and one felt
that anything like severity from him had tenfold force from
the very keenness of the pain it cost him. This struck me
first when he was speaking of his little volume on Robert
Burns. He told me with evident emotion that what he

had felt bound to say in that book had wounded his countrymen, and almost estranged some whom he heartily
loved; 'but,' he said, 'I felt that the idolatry of Scotchmen
for Burns must not be allowed to warp the moral sense; it
was needful to make strong protest against the fatal doctrine
that men of genius hold a charter of exemption from the
obligations of the divine law.'

.   .   .   .

His lecture on Friendship, as exhibited in ancient and
modern poetry, beginning with David and Jonathan, and
ending, I think, with Coleridge's noble lines on hearing
Wordsworth's *Prelude,* were full of delightful bits. It was a
subject of genuine heartfelt experience to himself, and his
beautiful words about Oxford-born friendships were the
natural and unexaggerated description of that which he has
enshrined in verse, not more poetic than his prose—his own
Balliol friendships.

Altogether, his memory is one of those precious things
which, as years go on, one only learns to prize more and
more dearly; and in days of discouragement and gloom
the remembrance of having even for a little while had the
privilege of such a friendship brings a quickening ray of
sunshine to revive drooping faith and hope and love.

> O, if within me hope should e'er decline,
>   The lamp of faith, lost friend! too faintly burn,
> Then may that heaven-revealing smile of thine,
>   The bright assurance, visibly return:
> And let my spirit in that power divine
>   Rejoice, as thro' that power it ceas'd to mourn. "

APPENDIX I

THE following is an extract from a very characteristic paper on *Undergraduate Life at Oxford*. It was written at Rugby, when Shairp evidently intended to write at much greater length on the subject of Oxford :—

"There are few who do not look back on their first years at Oxford as among the happiest and most important of their lives. They were dear while present, but we knew not then how they were colouring all our after-existence. They are dearer to memory, and every year as we recede from them they grow in beauty and dimensions.

What makes those years so fair and ideal in remembrance? Why do they stand out so singly prominent from the long level of the past? What so endeared them to us? the peculiar time of life, or the sanctities of the place, or the friends who were then our daily companions? Whatever be the reason, no one who has himself been an undergraduate can look on another just entering college life without feeling for him a more than common interest. He has left behind the thoughtlessness of boyhood, but not yet lost its freshness. You feel that the soft light of morning is still upon him—that his horizon is not yet shut in; the large uncertainties, the boundless possibilities, are on his side. He knows not himself, and none know, what he may grow to—how life may shape itself for him.

But pass over three or four years, and he who was a freshman will be leaving college for the world. What was promise must be now ripening to performance, or withering to disappointment. What was fluid and unfixed must be setting into solid character, or have evaporated to leave him more hard and shallow-hearted than he came. This result the natural lapse of time would have produced, quite apart from the university. The question then may fitly be asked, What does Oxford do for undergraduates that three years elsewhere would not have done ? with what peculiar influences are they there compassed ? how do these influences act on different natures ? what colour do they give to their mental training, views, feelings, habits, their entire character ?

That Oxford does lay its hand on most men in some very real way—gently it may be but all the more strongly for its gentleness—all acknowledge, both those who themselves have undergone this discipline, and those who from without have watched its results on others. You will hear it said on all hands, in praise or in blame, There is no mistaking an Oxford man, meet him where you will. The impress is stamped deep, showing itself not mainly in scholarship, nor in logical power, nor in metaphysical, nor in historical—not in one nor in all of these, nor in anything which schools or lecture-rooms can teach—but in the constant transpiration of a common character, that breathes through all their thoughts, words, actions.

To understand the agencies that are at work, we must remember how widely the English Universities differ in most things from those of Scotland, Germany, indeed of all other nations— and further, how the peculiarities of the English system are concentrated at Oxford. Two points stand specially prominent, (1) the striking fact that Oxford education is accessible only to the wealthier part of the nation ; (2) the predominance of Collegiate over University life. Whatever the cause may be, it cannot be denied that Oxford now educates the rich, not the poor. It is the inheritance not of the nation, but only of the upper section of the nation. Many rejoice in this, rejoice to see the flower of England's youth breathing an air of calmness and of beauty, undisturbed by the world's vulgarities. To others, not insensible to these things, the thought cannot but occur—Is that refinement worth preserving which can be secured only by a selfish exclusiveness ? To them it seems that those Universities in other countries which throw wide their gates to all comers gain in justice and generosity what they lose in refinement. There it is no uncommon thing for poor students to travel more than a hundred miles on foot yearly from secluded homes to the University, to maintain themselves by labouring in their leisure hours at the humblest employments, and to return in summer and win their livelihood by teaching in distant schools, or labouring with their hands in the fields, or teaching the children of a few shepherd families in some district remote from the parish school. Facts could be told of privations still greater than those, undergone cheerfully for the sake of education—of youths who, for years ill lodged and poorly fed, worked their way through Universities, which afterwards had reason to honour their names. In making this contrast, it is not forgotten that even in our day there have been remarkable cases of men living in Oxford on a third part of what a moderate undergraduate usually spends, but these, so few in comparison, hardly affect the general reckoning. Certainly they make nothing against the statement that Oxford is the University of the rich. They do not remove from her institutions the reproach (for such it is) that they turn a cold side to the poorer men, and bid them go elsewhere, for this is no place for them. A change in this long-cherished exclusiveness might, no doubt, be difficult and intricate, might sweep away many things hitherto most cherished by Oxonians. It certainly would make Oxford something very different from what any now living have seen it. So much is at once conceded ; still it is worth considering whether the change would really destroy anything truly valuable—whether even the rich men themselves might not gain by it in moral culture ; and, even if they gained nothing, the present exclusiveness can hardly defend itself on grounds of justice.

The second point of contrast between the two English and all other Universities is, that while the former maintain a strictly collegiate mode of life, in the others this is wholly unknown. This feature, so familiar to university men, may need explanation for strangers. In the existence of a University nothing more is essential than a body of men endowed by charter with the right of granting degrees to students in certain arts and sciences. This is seen in Dublin University, where an undergraduate, after entering his name on the college books, may live in any part of the world, provided only, when his terms are over, he appear again to pass his examination and take his degree. German and Scotch Universities have generally superadded to this a body of Professors, attendance on whose lectures is made necessary for a degree. The Professors' lecture-room then becomes the centre of university life and interests. Each student must be present at one or more of these, for an hour a day, and when this is over he may reside where, and live how he pleases. Unless he break into open outrage the University does not intermeddle with him, nor hold itself responsible for his conduct. So that a man may pass through many years of such lectures, and not be known except by name to any professor he attends, nor even if he so pleased to a single fellow-student. But the two English Universities have generally professed a larger aim than this—to train not the intellect only, but in some sort

the whole man, as far as this can be done by any outward institution. And this has been attempted by dividing all the members
of the University into separate Colleges, whither men resort, not
merely to attend lectures once a day, but for three years together
—to make them, as it were, their second home.[1]   Before a youth
joins the University he must first have been entered at some College
with which henceforth lie his most real daily relations ; those with
the University are more remote.   When he comes into residence,
the head of his College assigns him rooms within the walled and
gated building, hands him over as a pupil to one of the tutors,
and henceforth the college in general and his tutor in particular
charge themselves with some care of his conduct. . . .

That the collegiate system makes in the main for good, that it
is not well that youths just escaped from school should wander
wholly at will, that college rules and life, if here and there a ' sweet
restraint,' allow of a still more blessed range, they will be the
first to grant who themselves have undergone that discipline.
They will need no argument to justify collegiate life.   None, but
the remembrance of those with whom for three years within the
same college walls they enjoyed an endearing intercourse, hardly
possible but under the shelter of a collegiate home.   Any one
who looks back on his undergraduate years, and asks himself
what it was that then most laid hold of his character, will find that
besides the direct influences, such as college lectures, college discipline, reading for the Schools, and other things compulsory, he
breathed an air of influences sidelong and indirect.   The former
do not fall to be treated here, but are reserved for a chapter by
themselves.   The latter, though more subtle and indefinite, and
therefore more difficult to describe, are perhaps not less strong
to mould men than the other more obvious ones.   By indirect
influences is meant whatever by its nature cannot be reduced to
rule and system, whatever is left to each man's will to do or
not to do, to feel or not to feel.   Such is the feeling, so strong
in Oxford, that flows in upon him at all hours from the old
beauty of the place.   Such too the tone, hardly less peculiar,
of tastes and manners, which he gathers insensibly from the men
about him, whether known or unknown, from the society of the
many friendly ones, the intimacy of the favourite few, from the
reading the place encourages, from the necessary work, from the

---

[1] Many of these Colleges are several centuries old, and although they have
undergone many changes, they are still the nearest representatives of the religious houses of the middle ages, part of whose revenues are still preserved
in these foundations. There are some twenty such in Oxford.

power that lies in great names, Oxford's peculiar inheritance.
These, acting silently and unceasingly, sink down to the very
depths, and make the man—if anything from without can.

Of course the same set of influences do not tell on all.
The disposition and circumstances of the individual must determine which are to be for him the telling ones. And such are
the varieties of men as almost to foil any attempt to describe
them, at once generally and discriminately. For, sort and divide
men into classes as you will, the real character of each still
escapes your classification, and clings to the individual. It is easy
to divide the whole body of men, by the help of set phrases, into
reading, and rowing, and riding men; but the same difficulty meets
you here as in the attempt to divide the whole mind into separate faculties. When your analysis has done its best, the mind's
real secret remains unspoken. It were pitiable to imagine that
human beings really contain no more than these classifications
concede to them, that even the commonest man's nature can be
exhausted by current phrases like these. Though it seems a
mere truism, yet it is well to bear full in mind that these divisions are insufficient; that given the set a man belongs to, and the
outward appearance he wears, we have got but little, that there
is something more behind all these things. If we remember this,
outward facts and appearances will not be taken at more than
they are worth, but used only as guide-posts to fix and steady
the eye, in its survey of Oxford undergraduates and Oxford
influences.

Let us go back in thought to the opening of the academical
year, and think of the various characters that are gathered under
one chapel roof, on that first Sunday morning after a long vacation. The College, say, is not a close one, confined by local
restrictions; for its elements, freely gathered from many quarters,
are happily intermingled. Each of the Public Schools has there
its representatives, Etonians, Wickamysts, Harrowians, Salopians,
Rugbeans—each coloured somewhat in manner and character
according to the school from which they have come—all agreeing
in that independent and self-reliant bearing, which is thought to
be the peculiar product of public schools; agreeing too in a
classical training, and general habit of mind, more or less shaped
to meet university requirements. Others there are trained at
private schools, with less manner it may be and less scholarship,
but more information perhaps than most public schools furnish.
And then there are a few from no school at all, but educated in
their own home—or abroad—or anyhow. Their scholarship is
often miserable, their attainments all neglected; much lost, some-

thing too they may have gained.   Again, these are at all different
stages of their undergraduateship.   Some who have nearly
finished, some midway the journey, some who have but begun.
The first having returned from some long vacation retirement, where
they have been labouring all summer for their approaching great
go, are now—with their work done or undone—waiting within the
shadow of the Schools.   The second, by this time familiar with
college life, are beginning to look on it more gravely.   Their
early terms have slid by, in that too dreamful and delicious
leisure, which for so many hangs like a golden cloud over the
gateways of Oxford—too indolent, too delightful, but to some
not wholly profitless.   Especially if boyhood has been spent at
a hard-working school, fretted and fevered there as some have
been by examinations and emulations without end.   Here is a
cooling pause between that fever-heat and the world's—time to
wake and know that there are other things than those—an interval for freer breathing and calmer growth than may ever again
be allowed them; but now their day is westering, the degree
draws on, and they have come up resolved to break clear of that
leisure dream, and gird themselves in earnest to the work.
Lastly, there are the freshmen—some now entering on that life
to which at school they have long looked forward; others, with
few friends here, opening their eyes on this large scene where
friends are meeting, they strangers and solitary.   Such are they
who meet in one chapel the first Sunday morning of term, differing in their past lives, to differ still more in their future, differing in disposition, natural powers, attainments, circumstances; in
the one thing only agreeing, viz. that they have come to spend
three years—among the best in their lives—within the same
College walls.

Leaving the others, we shall fix our eye on the freshman
and follow him through the long line of experiences now opening
on him.   A reading-man let him be, not a mere plodder either,
but one of keen and clear intellect, and a heart free to enjoy all
things true and beautiful.   Setting aside college lectures and
discipline, what are those oblique but powerful influences which
will come to such an one?

First in order, and almost in importance, are those which
belong to the freshman's term.   The first glimpse of Oxford
city, and the first view of Oxford life, in both how much depends
on the avenue by which you approach them!   How different the
first term there to him who comes from a public school, and to
the one educated at home, or in other private way!   To the one
it is but a step more in the gradual ladder of his life; to the

other a transition as between two worlds. The one finds himself welcomed at once by a host of acquaintances, cheered perhaps by old school friendships renewed; and if college life imposes some few restraints and etiquettes, the restraints are freedom compared with school discipline; as for the etiquettes, he has put up with the like before, and now takes them as things of course. The other, a stranger amongst strangers, with few introductions, knowing scarcely any one, has to pass through that ordeal which there awaits every unknown freshman.

As in no place is the intercourse of friends more free and warm, so in none is the stranger received with such chilling stiffness if he be unknown, and have nothing peculiar in manner and appearance to recommend him. At the usual hour when others go out to ride or walk or row together, he strolls alone in the fall of the year among the fading college gardens, or by the riverside where the grey walls and autumnal decay breathe a feeling not alien to his own. 'All things here,' it seems, 'go on as they have done from immemorial time. Along these old avenues the leaves come out, and then they fall. Within these colleges the generations of men arrive one after another, and then depart. For centuries the great tide has flowed through them, and it will flow on for centuries to come. They pass, the old buildings remain; the old bells chime on, till they too pass, and all be forgotten. Here is nothing new, nothing fresh and buoyant; all free impulse and individuality weighed down under a load of customs and routine, that holds of an unknown antiquity.' Such perhaps are his feelings in his lonely walk; and in the winter evening when, after hall, he passes through the quadrangle to his own solitary room, and sees all others adjourning to wine with this or that friend or acquaintance, perhaps for the time he feels strange and out of place as in a crowded wilderness. Or if asked to wine by some senior man, bearing in mind that a freshman is 'an animal to be seen, not heard,' he acquiesces in this condition of undergraduate society; and after sitting one whole hour speechless, listening to miscellaneous talk of boat-races and doings on the river, or feats in the hunting-field, or with the drag, or to anecdotes of scholars and examiners, or of college tutors and undergraduates, of all of which he has no knowledge and less interest, he returns again to the solitude of his own armchair. All this, however, is considerably relieved if a large band of freshmen happen to come into residence at the same time. They can then herd together, can walk or wine together, and go to each other's rooms without any stiffness. And if the number be large and like-minded, they continue to pass their first term happily, with less help from the rest of the college. And yet through some ordeal all freshmen must pass—longest and severest to those who do not come from a public school, and yet not wholly to be escaped even by these. Indeed to one who has been the eldest boy of a boarding-house, or captain of the school, bearing there perhaps authority beyond his years, looked up to by all under him, the change is often felt to be trying enough. But on the whole, though elders do sometimes presume on their college standing, and bear themselves too coldly and distantly to new-comers, and although on some this has fallen too severely, even cruelly, yet this quarantine to which freshmen are put is not without obvious use. Where such multitudes meet there must be many gradations of intimacy, and in large Colleges it is impossible that each man should know every other. Here there is the rampart by which college society hedges itself against forward intruders, preventing any from forcing themselves on other's acquaintance, and enabling men to know something of each other before becoming too intimate.

But a few months gone—the freshman's probation over—and then there succeeds one of the most delightful seasons that ever comes to us in 'this changeful being.' What other, after men have left their homes, can compare with that one, the springtime of friendship — the dawn of intimacies which next to home ones have made us what we are ? Rightly to speak of that time, and the new feelings it awakened, one would have to go back, and in thought live over how many hours of delight. They say that the remembrance of sorrows shared together is the surest foundation on which friendship can build ; but this does not make summer friends of those whose first meeting was beneath a cloudless sky. Naturally a man's earliest companions are some of his own year whom he sees at lecture, by whom is his place in chapel and hall, and whose rooms are perhaps in his own staircase. Through these he gets to know others of older standing, and these again open to him new acquaintances, and every day shows him some new side of the University world ; till by the end of his first year he may have cast his eye over all his own College and taken his line in it, besides knowing something of out-college men, and the ways of the University in general, and its various kinds of undergraduates. Still, whatever may have been a man's after-experience, his first impressions shared with his first friends outlast the others. Most Oxonians who have not been at Eton will remember well the day when, with some others of their own

standing, they first ventured on the river in a skiff to Iffley, or
tried their hand in an eight-oar, or on a summer afternoon skiffed
up the river to Godstone or the Charwel to Islip. They can
well remember the excitement of their first rides into the
neighbourhood, and their first 'hack' across country. For an
Oxford hack has something peculiar in it, although the hacks
are like other hacks (only better jumpers), and the falls they get
like falls elsewhere, and the countrymen raise the hue and cry
after the fence-breakers as elsewhere — only somewhat more
fiercely from much provocation.

Of all seasons of the year two are specially endeared by
such memories — the first young spring days, and the long
golden afternoons in that first happy idle summer term. Perhaps some one of a band of friends has got over an examination, or other toilsome work; a weight of care is thrown aside,
and the others go out with him, to make a day of it in the
open air. They ride to Blenheim, or as far as the Wychwood
Forest, with its beech-fringed glades, and endless wood rides;
or they walk through the fields till they have gained some of
the heights that stand about Oxford, whence the eye has free
range, and can see on the horizon that the spring is flowing in
on the south-west wind, and the earth far and near awakening from its long dream. In that group there might not be
more than two or three years' difference of age, yet much difference
of character. There might be there the fair face untouched by
pain or sorrow, the clear voice and merry laugh, that come from
one who might well rejoice in the birthday of the year, for in
his heart it seemed always spring. Another less graceful, but
more ardent and powerful, strong in body, strong in mind, of
large heart for all things, and in intellect straightforward, truth-
loving, and eager to grasp it. Another more thoughtful than his
years, yet whose thinking so blended with warm and earnest
feeling, you know not which was stronger—though young, both
nature and experience had made him dwell on the sober
side of life, so that to him, even spring could not be wholly
glad. These (others might be added) so different in temper and
circumstances walked together that day as friends; and if friends
it found them, it left them not less so.

There are few more unclouded hours than that in which
the young undergraduate looks for the first time on the river, in
the glory of the boat-races. Afterwards this, like other things,
may turn insipid enough, but it is otherwise when it is new.
With one or two others he walks slowly down the green
meadows of the riverside, or dropping down the stream

leisurely in a skiff, stations himself under the willows to have a good view of the finish. The sinking sun looks back from the Cumnor Heights, and the waters in the setting light flow calm and golden. One by one the racing-boats, with their various liveries, pass down to the starting-place—shooting beneath the toughest arms each college can furnish, and guided by the steadiest eye. No need to speak of the race itself, with the crowd of undergraduates thronging, shouting, holloaing from the banks—boats bumped and bumping, this one swooping upon its fellow, that sinking back in distress, and then the rounds of cheers from the barges to crown the whole. And when all is over, and the men troop home to their colleges, and meet in hall for supper, or by twos and threes in each other's rooms, what genial flow, and calm joy !

Or perhaps, on some such evening, you were not disposed for the crowd on the river, but with some like-minded one you turned aside, to see the sun go down from Shotover, to walk in Bagley Wood with its nightingales, or to wander along the range of fields that from over Ferry Hinxey look down on the 'fair city, seated among groves, and green meadows, and calm streams.' There, as you walked apart, the shouts from the river came up to you. Many voices blended into one, but they did not disturb, only deepened the stillness. And as day wore into twilight, you became attuned to the quiet, and more freely than at other times your inmost feelings found themselves words. And as you returned home each felt himself touched, and soothed, and drawn more closely to the other. And year by year, as you recede from it, that evening has a tenderer remembrance—all the tenderer if some who walked with you then will not walk with you any more. Of course these are not common walks—they did not come every day or every week. Indeed after a time, perhaps, they hardly come at all, and walks at Oxford as elsewhere become constitutionals. But they did, and they do occur, when life there is still new ; and their remembrance blends with whatever is beautiful in the place, and dear in its early friendships."

"It is an old subject the antiquity of Oxford, and its beauty of situation—yet an ever new and active influence in the life of each succeeding generation. Not to speak of natures keenly sensitive to beauty, or deeply interested in local histories, who must always be few, it cannot be without effect even on the mass of men that their place of education lies undisturbed by the world's vulgarities, and encompassed on all sides by calmness, beauty, and venerableness. In a place in which at all hours, turn where you will, the eye rests on these things, something perhaps may by degrees pass from the eye to the heart even of the least susceptible. If any one doubts this, let him think what the difference would have been had there grown up around the University, and overshadowed it, a Birmingham or a Manchester.

In the late revival of Gothic architecture, which from Oxford overspread the country, it has been seen how much the re-kindled imagination may draw from this storehouse of beautiful forms. This revival, and other things connected with it, may appear to some a pure evil, to others a very mixed good. But without expressing any opinion of its worth, it may be cited as a proof how this beauty lays hold on the minds of men. And although, because the same causes can never again concur, a like revival need never be looked for, yet the calmness and the majesty that is there will not cease, through all changes of opinion, to speak to the imagination and the heart. And indeed it would not be a small gain if this action were confined to these —the parts of our nature to which it more immediately appeals. For there is much in men not to be called out by scholastic training, and starved often for lack of nutriment, under intellectual discipline, or in the routine of life. Over these suscep-

---

1 The following paper, found in a detached form amongst Principal Shairp's MSS., is also evidently part of the projected work, so often referred to by him, on University Life in Oxford.

tibilities the presence of old buildings and august institutions has a kindly influence, drawing forth and sheltering whatever is true and healthful, rebuking what is flimsy and superficial. Here each individual must feel his littleness in the presence as it were of so many of the great of old. The proudest and most ambitious soon learns that the University can confer much honour on him, and from him can receive little. And the busiest image of self must sometimes shrink abashed before presences which, while generation after generation passes, seem to combine their human interest with the permanence of the elements.

But this influence does not stop with the feelings which are 'the parents of our thoughts,' but it extends to thoughts themselves. These colleges, with their large charities, their chapels, halls, libraries, cloisters, gardens, represent the past in its most unselfish side, and make men realise it in thought more vividly than books can do. They witness visibly that there were in past ages men not wholly absorbed in themselves and their own times, but with hearts large enough to think of those who should come after them. A truth which, though none deny, all may bear to be reminded of. For hence some have given a greater largeness of view, a truer insight into history and the powers with which it is bearing on us, and a juster appreciation of our own place between a long past and a coming future. But some will say this so-called regard for antiquity is but another name for that Conservatism which is stagnation, and of which Oxford has long been the chosen nursery. Without going into this question now, it is at once admitted that both the home prejudices and University training of undergraduates combine to this result. But the Conservatism there engendered is something wider and more generous than that selfishness which, comfortable in itself, is deaf to the needs or claims of others ; and the Liberalism which grows there is a deeper and truer and humaner spirit than that which seeks to make good its own ground by belying or misinterpreting the past. Thus far of the intimacy of friends, and the local interest of Oxford, which— though in general felt more intensely by the quieter sort of men—are in a measure common to all undergraduates.

It is now time to fix attention more exclusively on the life of the reading-men—the class which of all others must be most fully noticed here, since they, entering more thoroughly into the work and spirit of the University, bear with them through life its most lasting impress, and are to be regarded as its truest representatives. Of the details of their studies little need here be

said, and that little only in a general way, since this whole subject will be discussed in another part of this book.[1]   The indirect
but very powerful influences which will fall to be described are
such as these—general reading, debating societies, subjects of
public interest, favourite authors, tutor friends, university pulpit,
men of influential character.   But to describe these things in
succession might, unless guarded against, easily produce, not a
true impression, but a caricature.   It might seem as if the whole
life of the studious were absorbed in one unnatural excitement;
so that one who had himself known it would be ready to say,
'How untrue all this is! how unlike the easy, natural life we used
to lead there!' while a stranger would be apt to pity those who
are doomed to live in so restless and unhealthy an atmosphere.

But such a false impression may be avoided, if it be remembered that the facts here thrown together within a few pages are
spread over three or four years' space, that they are but a few
prominent features standing out from the wide background of
everyday life, that this everyday life is made up of many uneventful items, not to be described, but to be borne in mind
throughout—of hours of work, and hours of relaxation, daily
walks, frequent boatings, occasional rides, parties to Newnham,
parties to Godstow, breakfast parties, large wines, and best
of all, when two or three friends were met, those sweet and
quiet talks which closed in the evening.   These fill up a much
larger space in time, though one narrower in description, than the
things here dwelt on.   In themselves they may appear trivial,
yet (whether for good or evil) they are by no means unimportant
in the whole sum of agencies.   It would serve no purpose to describe such ordinary matters even if it could be done, only it
will be well to keep them steadily in mind.   Let us take one of
the higher order of studious men, one of good intelligence, ready
sympathy, and heart open to impressions from without, and let
us follow him through the objects and interests with which he
will come in contact.   Till his residence at college begins, say
in his nineteenth year, his mental training has been confined to
acquisition, that is, to mastering the language and the thoughts
of others, and imitating their style.   And although in all study,
both in the University and afterwards, this process cannot be
dispensed with, yet if it is ever to issue in anything beyond
itself, there must now advance, side by side with it, that other
process of thinking in some measure and judging for oneself.
A multitude of new outside agencies are at work—new studies,
wider general reading, new scenes, new acquaintances, the

---

[1] The aim and extent of his intended work may be gathered from this.

conflux of character from many quarters, differing in nature and in education,—new pleasures, and with them new trials,—these all bear upon men from without, and make them feel the need of some inward standard by which to judge of what comes before them, to reduce to harmony what seems so complex and confused. And from within, too, like tendencies are at work.

To all the keener-minded a time comes which is as the wakening up of thought, when the mind that hitherto has rested satisfied on the surface of things begins to discover that there is something more behind. To some it comes slowly, to some suddenly —roused, it may be, by some new book or new acquaintance—to almost all it comes, if ever, during their University residence. A few perhaps, either being by nature prematurely thoughtful, or from contact with some stirring mind, or having been reared under a too forcing system, may have been urged across this threshold before their time. But with most men this transition, if it occurs at all, is reserved, and rightly, for their first years at college. Such a change comes of itself as the natural effect of time. But when once it has occurred naturally, systems of education may do much either to encourage or repress it. It is possible to take no account of such a state, not to seek to use it nor direct it, but simply to starve it. By keeping the whole attention fixed on outward studies, and things quite aloof from real human interests, it is easy to sharpen the attainments, to give shape and energy to the lower faculties, and to fit a youth for being active and successful in a profession; but these processes, having in them nothing to ennoble, often leave the whole man strangely uncultivated. Whatever be the faults of Oxford education, they do not lie in this direction. There is much in it which falls in with whatever thoughtfulness early manhood brings; much which may call it forth when latent, and deepen it if begun. Not to speak of what may seem so shadowy as that historical succession of character, which some declare to have clung to Oxford through centuries of change, there can be no doubt that the fact spoken of has some connection, whether of effect or merely of coexistence with the historical studies, and a much greater with the ethical ones, which have long been native there. Of these last the practical results are perhaps such as these.

They fill up that wide gap which lies between the more external studies and a man's real interests ; they tend to make men more thoughtful, more unworldly, more deep and stable in their feelings. That the gap here spoken of does actually exist is clear. For the tendency of many studies is to produce this isolation. Scholarship, for instance, and Mathematics taken

alone are in this like handicrafts.   That they absorb a man in
themselves—confine him to one limited field in which he may
labour long enough, without once looking over the hedge to see
how it fares with his neighbour in the next field.   Ethics on the
other hand approach to the nature of that architectonic science,
which the ancients thought should give to all other sciences their
due place and gradation.   And though Oxford ethics are much
humbler in their pretensions, yet the study of Aristotle can
hardly fail to suggest some principles, seen from which, as from a
centre, the various knowledges and the facts of life fall into their
true relative position.   No doubt the so-called Oxford science
would show but poorly side by side with the wide philosophic
courses of foreign Universities.   But though of narrow range
and unscientific method, it has tempered speculation with a
soberer feeling and a warmer humanity, and has discouraged
that 'impudent knowingness' often so offensive in young philosophers.   The questions common in lecture-rooms and the schools
about the first grounds of duty, the governing powers of human
nature, the standard of right action, the relations of interest and
duty, the building up of character by formation of habits, are
not altogether idle speculations, but when they fall on minds
ready to receive them, gradually pass inwards and take a permanent place in their thoughts.   The Greek terms in which
these questions are clothed may at first sound as foreign as an
algebraical notation ; but as they express unchanging facts of
human nature, reflection translates them into inward experience ;
what men feel in themselves and observe in others becomes their
living commentary.   And although on these subjects any undergraduate's thoughts will be but meagre, and such as in after
years he will not be likely to look back on too complacently,
still they are the first movements of an impulse which will
perhaps be permanent.

   But philosophical abstractions, however sound and judicious,
are apt to fall chillingly on the character.   Many humanising
elements were at work in Oxford to counteract this, none stronger
than the presence of a theology which, whatever be its faults, has
not of late years been wanting in religious intensity.   To teachers
it added force and warmth to feel how directly the truths with
which they were dealing bore on other still higher subjects, and
to pupils it raised other feelings than mere curiosity when they
knew that men but a few years older than themselves were sacrificing much in the endeavour to act out these principles in their
lives.   Connected perhaps with the habit of mind so engendered
was the absence of worldliness, at least in its grosser forms,

which still is very general among studious men in Oxford.   Here more than elsewhere emulation was so tempered that it lost nearly all its evil.   Of course those who were reading for honours were anxious to gain them, but the life of the place was not absorbed in this struggle.   It was amusing to observe how soon the ardour of some young aspirant, who had come up athirst for college honours, would cool down in this atmosphere, where the esteem of contemporaries did not rise and fall with the class list, but where the worthiest looked in their friends for something that makes no show in examinations.   Of the better sort of studious men it may be said in general, that in looking forward to their future life the common idols of the market had but small hold on their affections.   Indeed one of the evils of Oxford perhaps is, that these idols in many cases entirely disappear, and leave nothing sufficiently definite of a higher kind to fill their place.   This may be adverted to afterwards.   At present it is to our purpose to remark that Oxford does somehow make men feel that money-making and getting on are not the worthiest aims ; and few inherit its better spirit without unlearning these grosser forms of idol-worship.   It is not pretended that they had no idols, that they had reached that state in which a man, for duty's sake, is content to toil in obscurity, and not to be known in his generation.   Blended with some wholly selfish feelings there floated before the minds of many some image of elevated character, combined with intellectual cultivation, which was not to be measured by worldly success, by legal distinctions, or church dignities, but which to attain were in itself reward enough without the adjuncts of applause.   In different natures these two elements were variously combined ; in some the side of religious duty was paramount, in others the notion of cultivation ; but in none perhaps was either element altogether absent."

THE following is the report which appeared in a local newspaper of a Lecture which Principal Shairp gave to the University Club in Dundee, of which he was elected President :—

"Principal Shairp said there was perhaps nothing which more marked the mental character of the century to which we belonged than the growth and expansion of what was called the historical spirit in every region of thought. By this he meant that men had everywhere woke up to the appreciation of a fact which had indeed been always as real to them as it was now, but which had come home to them as a practical conviction with a force it had never done before. It was this—that we men of the present hour were not only the heirs but the products of all the ages— that the thoughts and feelings within us, as much as the outward framework of our lives, were an inheritance from the past—that of all the mental and moral furniture which makes us what we are, by far the larger portion had come down to us from a remote antiquity—that if we would know ourselves and understand our generation we must bear ever in mind that great atmosphere of history which encompassed us, and in which, often all unconsciously, we live and move. This sense of the historical continuity of the race, and of the power with which the past centuries press upon us, seemed to have made itself felt during the present century with such a quickened consciousness that it might almost be taken for a newly-discovered truth. The tendency was seen in the new aspect literature, with the opening of this century, put on. Since that day its effects in every department of popular literature had been visible enough, and he knew not if the force of the movement had yet spent itself. In abstract studies the same tendency was at work. Last century metaphysicians, little regarding the history of thought, made their own individual consciousness the Bible of philosophy, out of which they span with perfect confidence rounded *a priori* systems, that embraced, as they believed, all projects, thought, and things.

So changed was all this to-day that a man would be thought
either crazed or an ignoramus who should venture on such an
individualistic experiment in philosophy. Our most prominent
teachers had abandoned the attempt at rounded systems, and
had almost reduced philosophical teaching, both in thought and
morals, to a history of the continuous movement of thought from
the earliest Greek schools to the present time. In the natural
sciences the tendency might be seen displaying itself in the most
exaggerated form. There the historical spirit, breaking away
into the prehistoric ages, piercing to the utmost confines of
space and time, brought back thence a fairy tale of the doings of
the first monad whence all things had come, and pretended to
describe the earliest gyrations of the atoms out of which the
universe had been evolved. In its pretended revelations regarding man it dwarfed all history and made our oldest chronicles
seem comparatively as recent as yesterday's newspaper. . . . He
then noticed the changes that had taken place in the styles of
architecture. Next, in the highest region of all—in religion—we
saw everywhere, though in diverse forms, the sense of unity, deeper
than all diversities, which underlies the true branches of the
Christian Church—the vision of the one catholic and apostolic
communion so filling and penetrating the hearts of men that
discords and divisions must die down before it, and in its presence mere sectarianisms could not much longer live. Their
education could not but share in this historic impulse. As to
the substance of what was taught both in universities and in
schools it would be interesting to show how much this had been
already affected by the sense of historic continuity, and how much
more remained yet to be done, especially in Scotland, to give
the historic spirit its full scope ; but from that aspect of the
subject he must turn aside. Last century the Universities in
England had fallen into such a torpor that public interest in
them, though it never died out, became in all save their own
teachers and beneficiaries very languid. At the beginning of
this century, however, public favour began to return to Oxford
and Cambridge, and now they not only were doing their work as
they had never done it since the Reformation, but were also
taking the lead in organising middle-class school education and
coming forward to meet those intellectual wants which the great
centres of industry increasingly felt, and which Mechanics' Insti-
tutes had proved powerless to satisfy. As centres of thought
they also powerfully influenced the intellectual, social, and religious life of the whole nation. He would not say one word in
disparagement of the modern foundations. There was a wide

field of usefulness for them; but it was the more mediæval Universities which had lived down through so many centuries and were alive at every pore to the influences of the present, which most penetrated the world with their influence. The great era of the first foundation of Universities in Europe was the twelfth century, when the Universities of Paris, of Bologna, of Salerno, and of Oxford were established— the University of Cambridge seeming to date from the thirteenth century. He took the University of Paris as the model of our own Universities, gave a short history of it, and then gave an explanation (1) of the meaning of the name University; (2) of Faculties; (3) of the origin of academical degrees in Paris; and (4) the rise and nature of Colleges. In speaking of graduation, he remarked that it was by it a University reproduced itself, and sent forth to the world persons accredited by their stamp and seal as having made a certain definite progress in learning. It was a momentous, not to say a sacred, trust; for society looked to the University, not only to train its youth, but to send forth none with its stamp upon them but those who were really possessed of some solid attainment. It was the culmination in the crown of a University course—the flower, or rather the fruit, into which a University course should ripen. As the flower could not exist without the stem and root, so neither could a University in the proper sense exist by mere graduation. Reduce a University to a mere Examining Board, as some clever men had of late proposed, and they destroyed that which was its real life and soul. He stated that a University and a College were often spoken and thought of as one and the same. Many persons thought that a University was a school of universal knowledge. This was an entire mistake. The term University came from the Roman jurists, and meant a corporation or society combined for some specific purpose recognised by law. In its modern use University has been defined as the whole members of an incorporated body of persons, teaching and learning one or more departments of knowledge, and empowered to confer degrees in one or more Faculties. On the other hand, a College is a corporation entirely distinct from and independent of the University, endowed for the purpose of maintaining a certain number of graduates and scholars within its walls, living according to laws and usages laid down by its founder. In fact, Colleges were intended as places of residence for students, instead of their living in lodgings in a University town. He called attention to the founding of the Universities of St. Andrews (1411), Aberdeen (1494), and Glasgow (1452), the first

two being modelled on the pattern of that of Paris, and the
latter on that of Bologna. At St. Andrews, after the foundation
of the Colleges—the first being St. Salvator's in 1458—nearly
all the students resided within their walls. After the Revolution residence out of college became more common, and, with
some fluctuation, continued to increase till early in this century
when residence within college entirely ceased. , It had ceased
not from any conviction that such residence was undesirable, but
wholly from the decay of the college rooms and the want of
funds to maintain them. In the two ancient Universities of
England, Colleges had all but absorbed the University, and had
monopolised most of its functions. In Scotland the opposite
process had taken place—Colleges had all but disappeared, and
the Universities were all in all. In the English Universities,
Colleges had taken on themselves the instruction of their students
in arts, and the Faculty of Arts had all but disappeared. If the
invigorating and inspiring influence that comes from the teaching
of able professors speaking to the combined students of the
University had been lost, much had been gained from the more
careful superintendence and closer and more accurate tutorial
teaching, stricter discipline, and the influence which was exercised
by good tutors in well-ordered colleges. One function the English
Universities had retained—that of public examination for degrees.
These examinations were carefully conducted and rigorously
impartial, and were carried on in that thorough and perfect
manner which was only acquired by the experience and tradition
of ages. In Scotland the stress was on professorial teaching.
The teaching was still in the hands of the University, and the
students felt the stimulating influence of professors' lectures. If
only with this were combined a higher standard of attainment in
average students when they entered the University, their influence
would be much more powerful. From want of this preliminary
training the Universities greatly suffered. The blame was not,
however, with the Universities, but from want of good schools in
sufficient number, and the unwillingness or inability of parents to
keep their children long enough at school. He believed that
with the materials at their disposal, and the state of preparation
with which most students went to college, the Universities could
hardly do more than they were at present doing. Would the
day ever dawn in Scotland when the average student would
come to the University at as ripe an age and as well prepared
as they now were when they entered the best Colleges of Oxford
and Cambridge? As for the mode of living of the students,
lodging where and how they would in the town, he did not think

anything could be said except it was the cheapest and roughest way in which they could rub through. That great social evils did not arise out of it he could only attribute to two things : (1) the great good sense of Scotch students, which kept most of them from falling into the license that might be expected from so uncared for a mode of living; and (2) the fact that most of them had no more money in their pockets than enabled them to pay their way. Were a body of students all in easy or affluent circumstances to be collected together he did not believe that the mode of living now practised in our Scottish Universities could last a single year. He considered the present social arrangements for students in all the Scotch Universities very far from what one would wish to see. It was to be justified only by the great poverty of the country out of which it arose. Now that Scotland could no longer be called a poor country, some better mode of housing and superintending the students should be attempted. If he were asked what he considered the ideal of University life for students he should answer : One in which the public action and teaching of the University was in full play, combined with a social life of the students in colleges where they were cared for, counselled, disciplined, and in some measure influenced by wise, considerate, and friendly tutors. All the chief and important work of teaching should be done by the University Professors. In their lecture-rooms the students of all the Colleges or Halls should meet, and from them receive that stimulus and personal impulse which come from the living voice of a really learned and enthusiastic teacher, and which is the intellectual life of a University. In the colleges should be carried on only such subordinate teaching as would enable the students to profit by professors' prelections. The college, by its usages and modes of living and regular hours, would supply that sense of discipline which youth in and even beyond their teens still need ; while the friendly advice, influence, and example of a tutor, not perhaps more than ten years older than the student, would bring to his side that timely aid which often prevented a fall, and which did so much to build up the character. He could not omit to mention as a further advantage that good colleges used to require that regularity of worship and religious observance which, though enforced as a college rule, was often found to be no bondage but perfect freedom, but which when left entirely to young men's free will was so apt to be neglected. He regretted to have to say ' used to require,' as though it were a thing of the past, for in many Colleges of Oxford, under the new liberal *régime*, the old observance of morning and evening chapel had all but disappeared. This he could not look on but with regret. If colleges ceased to be leavened by habitual worship they lost their finest influence and must quickly deteriorate. He alluded to the cessation in St. Andrews University of an attempt to establish the college system, but stated that it was caused not by the feeling that it was not doing good but from want of funds. Having called attention to the absence in our Universities of form, ceremonial, and academic usage, he concluded by remarking that he rejoiced in the formation of the Dundee University Club. It might do much for the Universities on the one hand and for the public welfare of all this part of Scotland on the other. He believed that its members would show by their own lives, characters, and influence that a University training was no vain thing, but a solid advantage to a man in after life. Then, the members might diffuse a truer understanding and appreciation of what the Universities were. Especially they might disabuse the public mind of the prevalent fallacy that to a young man intended for trade or business a University training was useless. Whatever they felt that they had brought from their University —a wider intelligence, mental refinement, and higher aims and views of the meaning of life —whatever advantages of mind and character they had got from their University training, let them communicate them to those around who were less favoured than themselves. He trusted that the Club would long live, and grow to be a centre from which benign influences would largely emanate."

INDEX

ABERDEEN, Earl of—reminiscences, 198.
Adams, Professor, 190.
Addresses to boys at Rugby on Sunday evenings, 159.
Albert, death of Prince, 206.
Analytic method in morals, 244-250.
Annamoe, visit to seven churches, 117.
Apostolical succession, 292.
Argyll, estimate by Duke of, 388.
Aristotle—ethics, 94.
Arnold, Charles, 130, 138.
Arnold, Dr., influence at Rugby, 37; appointment to Professorship of Modern History at Oxford, 37; influence of, upon the intellectual and religious life of Shairp, 37, 130.
Arnold, Matthew, death (footnote) 32; 40, 137, 207; essay on St. Paul, 215; testimony in favour of Shairp as candidate for Chair of Moral Philosophy at Glasgow, 239; letter from, as to his poem of *Thyrsis*, and Clough, 244; letter from Dr. John Brown as to *Tristram and Iseult*, 266; letter from, as to Professorship of Poetry at Oxford, 330.
Arnold, Thomas, estimate of Shairp's character, 106.
Aspects of Poetry, 370; letter from Cardinal Newman as to, 370; letter from Lord Coleridge as to, 371.

Balliol Scholars—a poem, 32, 58, 408.
Bannockburn—poem on, 12.
Battersby, Canon, a member of reading-party at Grasmere, 63.
Bayne, Thomas, notice, in memoriam, by, 195.
Bell, Mr., tutor at Houstoun, 4.
Bell, Professor Oswald — notice of, 372.

Ben Alder and Prince Charlie, 104; Ben Alder and Ben Nevis, a September walk between, 254; letter to Dr. Clerk in reference to, 257.
Benson, Archbishop, master at Rugby, 98; reminiscences, 130; testimony in favour of Shairp as candidate for Chair of Moral Philosophy at Glasgow, 240.
Billings's *Scottish Castles*, 132.
Biography, advice as to writing a, 227.
Blackett of Merton, 50; a friend of Congreve, 111.
Blue Bells, The—a poem, 399.
Bonspiel—a song, 126.
Books, what to read, and how to read them—an address, 373.
Border country, appreciation of, 260, 263; speech on the Literature of the Borders, 323.
Borrowdale, a visit to, 65, 112.
Bothie of Clough, 110, 113, 144.
Boyle, John, 43; letter to, 307; letter to, as to volume on Burns, 361.
Boyle, Very Rev. G. D., Dean of Salisbury—reminiscences, 56, 151, 206, 345; visit to, 393.
Bradley, Very Rev. G. G., Dean of Westminster—master at Rugby, 98; companions at Rugby, 101, 130; reminiscences, 137; reminiscence of Shairp's visit to Oxford as Professor of Poetry, 333.
Bradley, Mrs., letter from, as to death of Shairp, 406.
Braes of Yarrow—a poem, 19.
Brewster, Sir David, 189, 272.
Bridges, J. H., 146.
Brown, Dr. John, of Edinburgh, letter from, 193; letters from, as to Mr.

2 G

Erskine of Linlathen, 222 ; friendship of Shairp for, 223 ; letter from, as to Mr. Erskine's published letters, 224 ; letters from, as to *The Bush aboon Traquair*, 232 ; letter from, as to *Kilmahoe, and other Poems*, 231 ; testimony in favour of Shairp as a candidate for Chair of Moral Philosophy at Glasgow, 242 ; excursion with, 264 ; letter from, as to *Moral Motive Power*, 265 ; letter from, as to Matthew Arnold's poem on *Tristram and Iseult*, 266 ; letter from, as to *Culture and Religion*, 285; letters to, 304 ; letters from, as to Wordsworth's *Journal of Tour in Scotland*, 314 ; letter from, as to *Burns*, 362 ; letters from, as to work of Oxford Chair, 368 ; letter from, as to Chaucer, 369.

Burns Centenary, 200 ; lecture on Burns, 336 ; volume on Burns, 359 ; criticism evoked by volume, 361, 411, 425.

Bush aboon Traquair, 17, 224.

Butler, Rev. Arthur T., of Oriel College, Oxford—reminiscences, 134 ; of professorship of poetry, 335.

Butler, Rev. Dr., Master of Trinity College, Cambridge ; visit to Killiecrankie, 390 ; letter from, on death of Shairp, 405.

CAMPBELL, Dr. M'Leod, influence of, 43 ; his work on *The Nature of the Atonement*, 178 ; *Thoughts on Revelation*, 207 ; letter to, sending copy of *Culture and Religion*, 304.

Campbell, Professor Lewis, St. Andrews —reminiscences, 380 ; note on memorial window in College Church, St. Andrews, 401.

Campbell, Rev. Donald, letter to, on receiving copy of his father's *Reminiscences and Reflections*, 304.

Cardwell, the late Lord, 33.

Carlyle—his influence on Shairp, 38, 156 ; *Miscellanies* : essay on Edward Irving, 38 ; earliest estimate of, 44 ; *Life of Sterling*, 156 ; rectorial address in Edinburgh, 281.

Catholicity, his, 288.

Celtic scholarship, 299.

Character studies of his friends—
Dr. M'Leod Campbell, 305.
Arthur Clough, 53, 73.
Bishop Cotton, 119.
Thomas Erskine of Linlathen, 216.

Professor Ferrier, 372.
Principal Forbes, 310.
John Macintosh, 21.
Dr. Norman Macleod, 23.
Dr. Park, 373.
Bishop Patteson, 91.
Archbishop Tait, 391.

Charles XII., prize poem on, 39 ; acknowledged by King of Sweden, 39, 51 ; synopsis of, 52.

Charlie, interest in haunts of Prince, 104, 145 ; letter to Rev. Dr. Clerk as to Prince's wanderings, 128.

Charm, the, of his conversation, 339.

Chaucer—letter to Dr. John Brown on, 369.

Child's grave at Rugby—letter to Edward Scott as to his, 182.

Church of England—thoughts of taking orders in, 31, 42, 77, 82, 415.

Churton, Archdeacon, 421 ; notice of poetical remains for the *Guardian*, 422.

Classics, appreciation of the, 188.

Clerk, Rev. Dr. of Kilmalie—fellow-student, 13 ; letter to, as to Prince Charlie's wanderings, 128 ; letter to, as to a September walk, 257 ; letter to, as to walk from Kilmalie to Rannoch, 258 ; letter to, as to walk over moor of Rannoch, 260 ; close intercourse and correspondence, 298 ; letter to, on Ossianic poetry, 299 ; 329 ; letter to, on Rev. Mr. Clark Aberfeldy, 307 ; five letters to, on Highland poetry, 365.

Clough, Arthur H., as poet and thinker, 33 ; reading - party at Grasmere, 33, 40 ; Dean Bradley's reminiscences of, 49 ; Shairp's reminiscences of, 53, 73 ; fellow of Oriel, 54 ; reading - party in Wales, 55 ; at Grasmere, 63 ; in Scotland, 87 ; elegiac poem on, 88 ; *The Bothie*, 106 ; instance of warmheartedness, 113 ; death of, 205 ; letter from Matthew Arnold as to, 244.

Coleridge, influence of, 14, 208 ; conversation on, at dinner at Clough's, 50 ; article on, in *North British Review*, 194, 227, 228 ; written at Luib Inn, 238 ; service to philosophy, 245.

Coleridge, Hartley, 33, 71, 73.

Coleridge, Lord, 32 ; dinner at Clough's, 50 ; elected fellow of Exeter College, 65 ; letter from, as to Shairp's article on Keble, 266 ; another, 267 ; letter from, as to *Burns*, 362 ; letters to, 363 ; letter from, on *Aspects of Poetry*, 371 ; another, 372 ; paper in memoriam, 408.

Coleridge, Sara, letter to Dr. John Brown on '*Memoirs and Letters*' of, 303.

College Hall, St. Andrews, 100, 189 ; Principal Forbes's interest in, 273, 381.

College Hospital, St. Andrews—Shairp's interest in, 386.

Columba, St., paper in *Good Words* on, 194 ; visit to Iona, 416.

Combe Abbey, visit to, 115.

Congreve, Richard, dinner at Clough's, 50 ; Blackett, a friend of, 111.

Cordery, John, 146.

Cotterill, C. C., of Fettes College, reminiscences by, 278.

Cotton, Bishop—estimate of, 119 ; close friendship between, 138, 207.

Cry from Craig-Ellachie—letter from Dr. John Brown as to, 235 ; recitation of, 264.

Cuckoo, The—authorship of, 312 ; letter from Sir William Stirling Maxwell on, 312 ; letter from John Bright, on, 313.

Cuil-aluinn built, 306 ; letter to Dr. Clerk on meaning of name, 306.

Culture and Religion, 195, 284 ; remarks of Dr. John Brown on, 285 ; of Cardinal Newman, 286.

Cumin, Patrick, Secretary, Education Office, 34 ; letter from, on death of Shairp, 405.

Curling, 122, 125.

DALRYMPLE, Sir Charles, reminiscences of, 419.

Dalwhinnie, 104.

Davey, Sir Horace—pupil at Rugby, 98, 123, 146 ; reminiscences of, 142 ; 252.

" Decade, The," 139, 411.

Derry, Bishop of, in Oxford Chair of Poetry, 331.

Donach Ban's Songs, 258, 367.

Douglas, Henry, Bishop of Bombay, fellow-student, 13, 34 ; letter to, on first visit to Oxford, 43 ; one of a reading-party at Grasmere, 63 ; influence upon Shairp, 207 ; drowning of son of, 310.

Douglas, Col. Hugh M., Shairp's brother-in-law, death of, 205.

Douglas, house of, 204.

Dream of Glen Sallach, 4, 6.

Drumnadrochit, [110 ; background of Clough's *Bothie*, 110.

Dundee High School, interest in, 320.

Dundee University Club, formation of, 319 ; extracts from address to members, 437.

Ecce Homo, appreciation of, 291.

Edinburgh Academy, speech at jubilee dinner of, 316.

Education, Scottish Chairs of — an address, 373.

English school system, appreciation of, 100.

" Enterkin, The," of Dr. John Brown, 264.

Ericht, Loch, visit to, 104 ; lines on, 104 ; Thomas Arnold's account of visit, 104.

Erskine of Linlathen, influence of, 43, 203, 207, 208 ; letter from, on death of Shairp's mother, 175 ; letters to, 176, 177 ; visits to, 205 ; reminiscences of, 207 ; letter from, as to the Fatherhood of God, 210, 214 ; letter from, as to internal evidences of Christianity, 211 ; letter from, as to Renan's *Life of Christ*, 211 ; letter from, as to ordination vows and Sir William Stirling Maxwell's rectorial address, 212 ; letter from, as to Professor Flint's candidature for Chair of Moral Philosophy at St. Andrews, 213 ; letter to, as to Matthew Arnold's papers on St. Paul, 215 ; character-study and estimate of, 216 ; in memoriam, notice of, in *Scotsman*, 222 ; letters of Dr. John Brown as to illness and death, 222 ; letters from, as to Shairp's candidature for Chair of Moral Philosophy at Glasgow, 240.

Essays and Reviews, opinion of, 201.

Ethics, Shairp as a contributor to, 228.

Evans, Canon, master at Rugby, 130, 138.

Evans, Charles, master at Rugby, 130, 138.

FARRAR, Prof., of Durham, pulpit reference by, 341.

Ferrier, Prof., 190, 272 ; estimate of, 372.

Ferrier, Mrs., 191.

Fichte, study of, 111.

Fishwife's Advice to her Bairn, 237.

Flint, Rev. Prof., letter from Mr.

Erskine of Linlathen as to candidature of, for Moral Philosophy Chair at St. Andrews, 213.

. Flodden, visit to, 84.

Forbes, Principal, 189 ; death of, 192, 270; historical account of University and of his connection with and interest in it, 270-275 ; joint-editor of *Life* of, 310 ; estimate of, 310 ; address on, 373.

Forrester, Rev. Mr., of Boarhills and Port Elizabeth—respect for, 295.

Freeman, Prof., 36, 40.

Frenchman, story of, 107.

Friendship, 200, 426.

Froude, J. A., 40 ; article on Spinoza by, 151.

Gillon, Mrs., of Wallhouse, 126.

Gladstone, Dr. John Brown on, 226.

Glen Almain, 155.

Glen Desseray, 235.

God, and our moral consciousness, 93.

Golf, regret at not having learned to play, 101.

Good Lord James, The, 204.

Good Words, historical papers in, 194.

Gosling, John Frederick, 155.

Goulburn, Dr. (Dean of Norwich), . master at Rugby, 98, 131 ; estimate of Shairp, 162 ; letter from, as to Oxford Chair of Poetry, 331.

Grant, Sir Alexander, 33, 41, 151, 191 ; testimonial in favour of Shairp as a candidate for Chair of Moral Philosophy in Glasgow, 240 ; death and funeral of, 391.

Grasmere, reading-party at, 63 ; lines on, 76.

Greens—owners of Pavement End, 63, 68.

Gruim—reminiscence of his deerhound, 136.

Guthrie Scholarship founded through his influence, 381.

Helvellyn crossed, 66 ; Scott's and Wordsworth's poems on, 66.

Herdman, Robert, R.S.A., description of portrait of Shairp in Hall of United College, St. Andrews, by, 402.

Herstane of Broadlaw, The, 261, 263.

Highton, H., master at Rugby, 130, 138.

History, address on the study of, and the importance of the subject in a university curriculum, 373.

Hodgson, Shadworth, 146 ; reminiscences, 153 ; letter to, 156 ; another letter, 158 ; series of letters referring to philosophical aspects of experience, 244-252.

Hogg, James, referred to in *Braes of Yarrow*, 20.

Houstoun acquired by Shairps, 1 ; description of, from *Kilmahoe*, 3.

Hunter, Dr., of St. Andrews, 272.

Hunting, his amusement at Rugby, 101 ; appreciation of, 102 ; story of, 136, 147.

Hymn of Pan, by Shelley, 155.

Influence of Dr. Arnold, 37, 130.
  Carlyle, 38, 156.
  Coleridge, 14, 208.
  Bishop Douglas, 207.
  Thomas Erskine, 208.
  Glasgow teaching, 18.
  Cardinal Newman, 36, 203, 413.
  Sir Walter Scott, 16, 204.
  Dean Stanley, 208.
  Tractarian movement, 202.
  Wordsworth, 11, 204, 208, 226.
Influence of Shairp, 136, 296, 418.
  On Earl of Aberdeen, 198.
  Thomas Bayne, 195.
  Shadworth Hodgson, 153.
  Godfrey Lushington, 160.
  An Oxford tutor, 198.
  Henry Rhoades, 165.
  Students, 194, 277, 297.
Inge, Mrs.—reminiscences, 420 ; letter to, 421 ; another letter to, 424.

Irvine, Dr., of Pitlochry, 278.

Jacobite Memoirs, 128.

Jacobite sympathy, 127.

Jenkyns, Dr., 32.

Jex-Blake, Dr.—pupil of Shairp's at Rugby, 98 ; reminiscences, 146.

Jowett, Prof., 33, 115, 152 ; letter from, on death of Shairp, 405.

Keble, essay on, 37, 56 ; extracts from essay as to Newman, 58, 60 ; letter from Dean Stanley as to essay, 61 ; appreciation of *Christian Year*, 62 ; article on, in *North British Review*, 194, 227, 228 ; letter from Lord Coleridge as to article on, 266 ; another letter, 267.

Kennedy, George, master at Rugby, 138.

Kentigern, St., paper on, in *Good Words*, 194.

Kilmahoe, description of Houstoun

House in, 3 ; picture of his mother, 174, 191 ; published, 194, 230 ; letter from Theodore Walrond as to, 233 ; letter from Shadworth Hodgson as to, 233 ; letter to, as to, 234 ; press notices of, 234.
Kitchener, Mr., of Newcastle—pupil of Shairp at Rugby, 98 ; reminiscences, 166.

LAKE, author of article in *Quarterly* on Stanley's *Life of Arnold*, 85.
Langdale Pikes, 65.
Lawley, 66, 67.
Lawrence, author of *Guy Livingstone*, 111.
Lingen, Lord, estimate by, 167.
Lockhart, J. G., met, 16, 77, 88.
Lockhart, Walter Scott, enters Balliol, 77.
Lorne, Marquis of, a student at St. Andrews, 388 ; reminiscences, 388.
Low, Dr. Richard, of Dundee High School, regard for, 320.
Lushington, Prof., influence of inaugural lecture, 14 ; letter from, as to *Burns*, 361 ; visit from, 390 ; letters from, on hearing of Shairp's death, 404.
Lushington, Godfrey—pupil at Rugby, 98, 146 ; reminiscences of, 160 ; visit to Yarrow and Dumfries with Dean Stanley and Shairp, 182.
Lushington, Vernon—pupil at Rugby, 98 ; letter from, as to article on Wordsworth, 228.

MACAULAY, opinion of, 226.
M'Donald, George, preaches in College Church, St. Andrews, 394.
M'Intosh, Adam, John, and Donald, gamekeepers in Corrour, 259.
Macintosh, John, *The Earnest Student*, 13 ; estimate of, 21 ; Life of, 28, letter from, 30 ; visit at Oxford, 65.
Macleod, Dr. Norman, makes acquaintance of, 13 ; estimate of, 23 ; letter to Dr. Clerk on death of, 28 ; visits Shairp at Houstoun, 83 ; Shairp visits at Dalkeith, 107, 126 ; visit of, to St. Andrews, 301 ; asked to write Life of, 302 ; lines on, 302 ; letter to Dr. Donald Macleod on, 303.
Macleod, Mrs. (Norman's mother), letter to Dr. Clerk on her death, 28.

MANNING, Cardinal, sermon by, 46.
Manor Water—a poem, 261.
Margaret, St.—a paper in *Good Words*, 194.

Marriott, 65, 66, 67.
Martial spirit, 141.
Maudesly's *Mental Pathology*, 251.
Maxwell, rectorial address at Glasgow by Sir William Stirling, 212.
Merivale, Herman, article in *Edinburgh Review* on Goethe festival, 152.
Methven Castle, visit to, 209.
Mill's *Political Economy*, 120.
Milton-Lockhart, visit to, 87.
Minchmoor, 225.
Moral Motive Power, article on, in *North British Review*, 194, 227, 248 ; letter from Dr. John Brown as to, 265.
Morven, Manse of, visit to, 145, 152.
Mozley, Canon, lecture on, 373.
Murray - Gartshore, Mrs., 107, 111 ; verses to, after visit, 107.
Mythology and Natural Religion, 94.

NATURAL Religion and Mythology, 94.
Nature, love of, the master passion of his life, 16, 41.
Newdigate prize at Oxford, 337.
Newman, Cardinal, influence of and admiration for, 36, 203, 413 ; extract from *Balliol Scholars*, 58 ; extract from essay on Keble, 58 ; letter from, as to essay on Keble, 61 ; sermons, 124, 132 ; influence of, in Tractarian days, 209 ; letter from, on *Culture and Religion*, 286 ; letter from, on *The Poetic Interpretation of Nature*, 323 ; letter from, on *Aspects of Poetry*, 370 ; estimate by, 387.
" Newman's Law," 250.
Ninian, St., a paper in *Good Words*, 194.
North British Review, series of articles in, 194.
Northcote, Sir Stafford, 33.

ORIEL Fellowship, 41.
Ormsary, visit to, 394.
Ossian, article in *Macmillan's Magazine* on, 301.
Ossianic poetry, letters to Dr. Clerk on, 299, 300.
Oxford, first visit to, 43.

PALGRAVE, F. T., 33 ; editor of *Glen Desseray*, 235 ; letter from, as to Oxford Chair of Poetry, 330.
Palmer, Archdeacon, 33 ; reminiscences, 163, 422.
Patterdale, 66.
Patteson, Bishop Coleridge, makes

acquaintance of, 90 ; estimate of, 91.
Pattison, M., 40.
Paul, St., Matthew Arnold's papers on, 215.
Pavement End, 63.
Peel Club—one of founders, 15 ; its influence, 14.
Philosophical aspects of experience, 244.
Philosophy—its sphere, 251.
Physical and Moral Interpretation of the Universe and Life—an address on the contrast between, 373.
Plato's knowledge of God, 94 ; dialogues, 151.
Poetic Interpretation of Nature, lectures on, 321 ; letter from Cardinal Newman on, 323.
Poetical feeling and its utterance in poetry, 92.
Poetry coexistent with the outward world and the human spirit, 92 ; province of poetry, subject of lecture at Oxford, 331 ; knowledge and appreciation of, 371.
Poets · of the seventeenth century, lecture on, 425.
Poste, Edward, visits Germany with, 119.
Price, Bonamy, master at Rugby, 98 ; discussions with, at Rugby, 99 ; "a remarkable man," 101 ; 138.
Price, Mrs. Bonamy, a cousin of Macaulay's, 101 ; her reminiscences, 351.
Prichard, C. E.—visit to Norman Macleod, 29 ; estimate of Seymour by, 73 ; 151.
Pyper, Prof., St. Andrews, 187 ; death of, 192.

Rab and his Friends, 223.
Rannoch Moor, 259.
Rawnsley, Rev. H. D., of Crosthwaite—reminiscences, 383.
Reading-man's life at Oxford, 35.
Reay, Lord, Lord-Rector of St. Andrews University, 392.
Reformation, The, a scramble for selfishness, 115.
Religious life—an address, 307.
Retrospect, or Days from out the Shadows, 6 ; extract from, referring to student days in Glasgow, 29.
Rhoades, Henry—pupil at Rugby, 98, 148 ; reminiscences, 165.
Rhoades, James—pupil at Rugby, 98.
Riddell, James, 422.

Robertson, Rev. James, of Whittinghame—reminiscences, 287.
Rodger, Rev. Dr. Matthew, minister of College Church, St. Andrews — Funeral Sermon by,'385, 398.
Rugby, visit to Dr. Tait at, 85 ; appointed one of the masters, 98 ; Professor Sellar's account of life at, 99 ; Shairp's own account, 100', proposed memorial in Rugby Chapel; 403.
Run, The, a lyric on hunting, 102.

St. Andrew's Day at Oxford, 40, 44.
St. Andrews, delight in, 191 ; historical account of University, 270 ; the earliest Scottish University, 376, 390.
Sanders, T. C., 33.
Sandford, Sir Francis, 34.
"School Time," from *Retrospect*, 11.
Scotland, love for, 130, 132, 135, 140, 142, 154.
Scott, Archdeacon, reminiscences, 111, 116.
Scott, Dean, of Rochester, letter from, as to Chair of Poetry at Oxford, 331.
Scott, Edward, pupil at Rugby, 98 ; reminiscence of tour in Highlands, 106 ; letter to, 129, 148 ; reminiscences, 148 ; letter to, as to son's grave at Rugby, 182 ; letters to, 199 ; letters from, on death of Shairp, 407.
Scott, Sir Walter, influence of, 16, 204 ; referred to, in *Braes of Yarrow*, 20 ; disparagement of, resented, 39 ; poem on Helvellyn, 66 ; as a novelist and writer, 209 ; Scott, and Border life and habits, 325.
Scottish Song, projected series of papers on, 201.
Selborne, Lord, estimate by, 389.
Sellar, Prof., account of early years by, 8 ; life at Glasgow University, 14 ; at Oxford, 32 ; at Rugby, 99 ; account of removal to St. Andrews, and earlier years there, 187 ; concluding part of reminiscences, 342.
Seymour, death of, 46 ; dinner at Clough's, 50 ; letter to, 70.
Shairp, Miss B., letters to, 14, 44, 63, 67.
Shairp, Campbell, allusions to childhood of, 205 ; matriculation at Oxford, 331.
Shairp, Miss Grace, letters to, 45, 65, 84, 115.

Shairp, Sir John, 1.
Shairp, Mrs. (his mother), name, 1 ; picture in *Kilmahoe*, 3, 174 ; death, 174 ; letter from Mr. Erskine of Linlatheu on her death, 175.
Shairp, Major Norman, 1 ; character, 2 ; letter to, as to curacy and chance of fellowship, 77 ; letter to, as to class and prospects, 81 ; letter to, as to fellowship at Oriel, 86 ; letter to, descriptive of Duke of Wellington's funeral, 168 ; *Kilmahoe*, dedicated to, 230.
Shairp, Mrs., letter to, descriptive of Wells of Dee, 252 ; account of last illness by, 391.
Shairp, Principal—birth, 1 ; ancestors, 1 ; early education, 4 ; visit to Argyle-shire, 4 ; sent to Edinburgh Academy, 7 ; came under influence of Words-worth's poetry, 7 ; account of early years by Prof. Sellar, 8 ; love of home, 9 ; hunting and curling his only pastimes, 10 ; Wordsworth's influence, 11 ; entered Glasgow Uni-versity, 13 ; friendships, 13 ; pro-fessors, 13 ; discussions on Coleridge, Wordsworth, Sir Thomas Brown, and Jeremy Taylor in Bath Street, 13 ; Peel Club, 14 ; election of Lord Rector, 14 ; prize essay, 15 ; politi-cal enthusiasm, 15 ; love of nature, 16 ; appointed a Snell Exhibitioner, 17, 31 ; class honours, 18 ; enters Balliol College, Oxford, 31 ; visits London, 31 ; thinks of taking orders in the Church of England, 31 ; as a letter-writer, 31 ; popularity at Ox-ford, 34 ; love of hunting, 34 ; a reading - man, 34 ; difficulty with Latin prose, 35 ; love of poetry, 39 ; wins Newdigate prize for English poem, 39 ; takes B.A. and placed in second class, 40 ; a conservative in politics and religion, 42 ; in-tended visit to Germany, 43 ; long-lived dream of becoming a sheep-farmer, 44 ; "Schools," 45 ; dinner at Clough's, 50 ; reading-party in Wales, 55 ; reading-party at Gras-mere, 63 ; thinks of fellowship at All Souls, 77 ; visits Honstoun, 79 ; returns to Oxford, 80 ; visits Houstoun, 83 ; visits Berwickshire, Flodden, Newcastle, and Rugby, 84 ; candidate for fellowship at Oriel, 86 ; autumn in Scotland, 87 ; Coleridge Patteson, 90 ; fruit of Oxford training, 91 ; appointed one of the masters of Rugby, 98, 119 ; succeeds to boarding - house, 99 ; as a talker, 99 ; *The Run*, 102 ; walking excursion in Highlands, 108 ; study of Fichte, 111 ; thinks of visit-ing Germany, 115 ; visit to Combe Abbey, 115 ; visit to Ireland, 116 ; visits Germany, 119 ; extracts from diary, 123 ; *z he Bonspiel*, 126 ; dis-like of school life, 135, 140 ; influ-ence at Rugby, 136 ; difficulty as to reading Litany in school, 139 ; classi-cal tutor in house of Rev. R., B. Mayor, 142 ; Sunday evening ad-dresses to boys, 159 ; candidate for Chair of Moral Philosophy in Edinburgh, 171, 239 ; marriage, 174 ; death of his mother, 174 ; death of son, 141, 177 ; lines on death of child, 179 ; at Tibbie Shiels's, 180 ; taught Professor Lushington's class in Glasgow University, 183 ; assistant to Professor Pyper of St. Andrews, 187, 191 ; personal interest in students, 189 ; appointed Professor of Humanity at St. Andrews, 192 ; appointed Principal of the United College, St. Andrews, 192, 269 ; articles in *Good Words* and *North British Review*, 194 ; *Kilmahoe, and other Poems* published, 194, 229 ; summer holidays, 205 ; death of Colonel Hugh Douglas, 205 ; a critic and delineator of character, 228 ; candidate for Moral Philosophy Chair in Glasgow, 238 ; result, 246 ; interest in and sympathy with students, 269 ; President of Educa-tional Institute of Scotland, 276 ; built Cuil-aluinn, 306 ; fatal accident to nephew at Moness Falls, 310 ; edits Dorothy Wordsworth's Journal of the Tour in Scotland, 314 ; speech at jubilee dinner of Edin-burgh Academy, 316 ; University extension scheme, 319 ; appointed Professor of Poetry at Oxford, 330 ; Latin oration at Oxford, 338 ; visit to Salisbury, 350 ; incidents in Border wanderings, 357 ; volume on Burns, 359 ; *Aspects of Poetry* published, 370 ; account of last illness by Mrs. Shairp, 391 ; visit to Hous-toun, York, and the Riviera, 392 ; visit to Ormsary, 394 ; death, 396 ; funeral, 398 ; memorial tablet and tombstone, 398 ; resignation of

Professorship of Poetry, 399 ; proposed memorial, 400 ; memorial window in College Church, St. Andrews, 401 ; portrait in Hall of United College, St. Andrews, 402 ; memorial window in Balliol Library, Oxford, 404,

Shelley, lecture on, 336, 411.

Shiels's, Tibbie, cottage, meeting of Professor Veitch and Shairp at, 180.

Sinton, Rev. Thomas—reminiscences, 276.

Sketches in History and Poetry—a posthumous volume, 376.

Smith, Prof. H. S., 33.

Smith, Rev. John, minister of Ecclesmachan, 124, 223.

Song of the South Countree, 260.

Sophocles and Shakespeare, essay on, 15.

Spalding, Prof., 190.

Stanley, Dean, 33 ; affection for, 131 ; letter from, as to Duke of Wellington's funeral, 170 ; visit to Yarrow and Dumfries, 182 ; delight in Scottish history and admiration for Sir Walter Scott, 208 ; influence of, 208 ; death of, 373 ; letter from Shairp to Mrs. Drummond of Megginch on death of, 373 ; legacy to United College, 375 ; Shairp's letters to Mrs. Drummond, 375.

Stanley, Lady Augusta, her regard for Mr. Erskine of Linlathen, 207.

Studies in Poetry and Philosophy, 194, 227 ; letters from Bishop Patteson as to, 267, 268.

Sweetheart Abbey, 264.

Systems of Philosophy, 95.

TAIT, Archbishop, invites Shairp to become a master at Rugby, 98, 99 ; his influence secures for Shairp the Chair of Humanity at St. Andrews, 183 ; estimate of, 391 ; Richmond's portrait of, 392.

Talker, Shairp as a, 202.

Temple, Bishop, of London, 32 ; testimonies in Shairp's favour as a candidate for Chair of Moral Philosophy at Glasgow, 239.

Tennyson, 38, 139.

Theology—in perfect accord with neither the High Church doctrine nor Broad Church theology, 41 ; discussion with Bonamy Price at Rugby, 99.

Thompson, E. M.—keeper of MSS. in British Museum—pupil at Rugby, 98.

Three Friends in Yarrow, 1.

Threave Castle, 204.

Thyrsis, by Matthew Arnold, 244.

"Toper-na-fuosich," 105.

Torphichen, 125, 126.

Tractarian experiences, 132 ; influence upon Shairp, 202, 207 ; the movement, 228, 382, 412.

Tulloch, Principal, 190, 213 ; his opinion of Shairp, 298.

UNDERGRADUATE life at Oxford, 55 ; extract from paper on, 427.

Universities, Wants of the Scottish, and some of the Remedies—a pamphlet, 183 ; extracts from, 183.

University Club in Dundee, lecture to, 443.

University life in Oxford, paper on, 437.

University System, characteristic features of Scottish as distinguished from English—an address, 373.

Uses of the Study of Latin Literature—subject of inaugural lecture as Professor of Humanity, 192.

VAUGHAN—lecture on, Henry, 425.

Veitch, Prof., of Glasgow University—reminiscences, 180 ; bond of sympathy between, and Shairp, 190 ; appointed Professor of Logic at St. Andrews, 202 ; reminiscences of years at St. Andrews, 202 ; excursion to Braemar Highlands, 252 ; reminiscences of Border wanderings, 263 ; conclusion of reminiscences, 356.

Virgil, lecture on, 283.

WALLACE, Rev. Edwin, notice of, 373.

Walrond, Theodore, death of (footnote) 32 ; 33 ; 138 ; love of tennis, 41 ; master at Rugby, 98 ; resigned mastership, 99 ; death of, and letter from widow, 376.

Ward, 132.

Wellington, Duke of, 46 ; description of funeral of, 168 ; letter from Dean Stanley as to funeral of, 170.

Wells of Dee, description of, 253.

"White Doe of Rylstone, The," 421.

Whyte, Rev. Dr., of Edinburgh, letter from, as to Shairp's death, 406

Wilderness, The, lines on, 104.

Williams, Archdeacon, Rector of Edinburgh Academy, 9.

Wilson, Prof. (Christopher North), contrasted with, 17.

Wordsworth, influence of, 11, 204, 226 ; sees at garden gate, 33, 76 ; religion of, 47 ; poem on Helvellyn, 66 ; delighted to quote, 155 ; article on, in *North British Review*, 194, 227 ; his estimate of, 227 ; letter from Vernon Lushington as to article on, 228 ; as an interpreter of, 282.

Wordsworth, Bishop, of St. Andrews—reminiscences, 377.

Wordsworth, Dorothy, Journal of the Tour in Scotland, 314 ; letters from Dr. John Brown as to, 314.

Wordsworth, Miss — reminiscences, 352 ; meeting with, 423.

Wythburn Church, 67.

YARROW, lines on visit to, 179 ; visit to, with his sisters, 181.

Yarrows, The Three, 420.

THE END

Printed by R. & R. CLARK, *Edinburgh.*

ALBEMARLE STREET, *October* 1888.

MR. MURRAY'S
LIST OF FORTHCOMING WORKS

Notes of Conversations with the Duke of Wellington,
1831-1851. By PHILIP HENRY Fifth EARL STANHOPE. Crown 8vo.

Daniel O'Connell, the Liberator: His Letters and Correspondence. Edited, with Notices of his LIFE and TIMES, by WILLIAM
J. FITZPATRICK, F.S.A. Portrait. 2 vols. 8vo.

The Viking Age: The Early History, Manners, and Customs
of the Ancestors of the English-speaking Nations, illustrated from
the Antiquities discovered in Mounds, Cairns, and Bogs, as well as from
the Ancient Sagas and Eddas. By PAUL B. DU CHAILLU, Author of
"The Land of the Midnight Sun," etc. With 1200 Illustrations. 2 vols.
8vo.

International Law. Being the WHEWELL LECTURES, delivered
before the University of Cambridge in 1887. By the late Sir H. SUMNER
MAINE. 8vo. 7s. 6d.

Three Counsels of the Divine Master for the Conduct of
the Spiritual Life. By E. MEYRICK GOULBURN, D.D., Dean of Norwich. 2 vols. Crown 8vo.

Lives of Twelve Good Men. By JOHN W. BURGON, B.D., late
Dean of Chichester. 2 vols. Crown 8vo. 24s.

I. Martin Joseph Routh.
II. Hugh James Rose.
III. Charles Marriott.
IV. Edward Hawkins.
V. Samuel Wilberforce.
VI. Richard Lynch Cotton.
VII. Richard Greswell.
VIII. Henry Octavius Coxe.
IX. Henry Longueville Mansel.
X. William Jacobson.
XI. Charles Page Eden.
XII. Charles Longuet Higgins.

Three Generations of English Women: or, Memoirs of
Mrs. John Taylor, Mrs. Sarah Austin, and Lady Duff Gordon.
By Mrs. JANET ROSS. Portraits. 2 vols. Crown 8vo.

Life of Sir William Siemens, F.R.S., Civil Engineer. By
WILLIAM POLE, F.R.S., Hon. Secretary of the Institute of Civil
Engineers. Portrait and Illustrations. 8vo.

The Scientific Papers of the Late Sir William Siemens,
F.R.S. Illustrations. 3 vols. 8vo.

[*Continued.*

Buddhism in its Connection with Brahminism and Hinduism, and in its Contrast with Christianity. Being the DUFF LECTURES for 1888. By Sir MONIER WILLIAMS, K.C.I.E., D.C.L. 8vo.

The Infallibility of the Church. A Course of Divinity Lectures. By GEORGE SALMON, D.D., Provost of Trinity College, Dublin. 8vo. 12s.

A Broken Stirrup-Leather. By CHARLES GRANVILLE, Author of "Sir Hector's Watch." Post 8vo. 2s. 6d.

The Railways of England. By W. M. ACWORTH, M.A. Crown 8vo.

North Western.	Great Western.
Midland.	Great Eastern.
Great Northern.	Brighton and South Coast.
Manchester, Sheffield, and Lincoln.	Chatham and Dover.
North Eastern.	South Eastern.
South Western.	Infant Railroads.

The Career of Major George Broadfoot, C.B., in Afghanistan and the Punjab. Compiled from his Papers and those of Lords ELLENBOROUGH and HARDINGE. By Major WILLIAM BROADFOOT, R.E. Portrait and Maps. 8vo.

Stephen Hislop: Pioneer Missionary and Naturalist in Central India. 1844-1863. By GEORGE SMITH, LL.D., Author of "Life of William Carey," etc. Portrait and Illustrations. 8vo.

The Invisible Powers of Nature. Some ELEMENTARY LESSONS in PHYSICAL SCIENCE for BEGINNERS. By E. M. CAILLARD. Post 8vo.

The Voyage of the Marchesa to New Guinea. With Notices of FORMOSA and the ISLANDS of the MALAY ARCHIPELAGO. By H. GUILLEMARD, F.R.G.S. *Cheaper Edition.* Maps and Illustrations. Medium 8vo.

Major Lawrence, F.L.S. A Novel. By the Hon. EMILY LAWLESS, Author of "Hurrish." *Cheaper Edition.* Post 8vo.

Kirkes' Handbook of Physiology. *New and Revised Edition, chiefly rewritten.* By W. MORRANT BAKER, F.R.C.S., and V. DORMER HARRIS, M.D. With 500 Illustrations. Crown 8vo. 14s. (*Ready.*)

A History of Greece from the Earliest Period to the Time of Alexander the Great. By GEORGE GROTE. *New Edition.* Portrait, Map, and Plans. 10 vols. Post 8vo. 50s. (*Ready.*)

*** *This Edition is printed from the last Library Edition, which contained the Author's final revision, and is now the only Edition in circulation. The volumes may be had separately.*